Dominica

Other Places Travel Guides
Dominica

Anna McCanse

Published by
OTHER PLACES PUBLISHING

First edition
Published May 2011

Dominica
Other Places Travel Guide
Written by: Anna McCanse
Cover designed by: Carla Zetina-Yglesias
Published by:
Other Places Publishing
www.otherplacespublishing.com

ISBN 978-0-9822619-7-2

The Authors

Anna McCanse

After teaching for several years in California, Anna decided to take her skills on the road and joined the Peace Corps where she served in Dominica from 2006-2008 as an Education Volunteer. When she wasn't working at her village's primary school, she could be found swimming beneath waterfalls, jumping into rivers, hiking up mountains, learning to play steel-pan drums, playing with the kids in her village and reading lots and lots of books. She was overjoyed to have the opportunity to travel back to Dominica to write this guide and share her favorite places with everyone. She's also happy that she can stop assaulting innocent bystanders with her stories of Dominica and can now just say "hey, go buy the book!"

Zak Klein (Contributing Writer)

Zak originally discovered Dominica nine years ago after a friend's suggestion that he and the island might be perfect for each other. He relocated to a tiny village on Dominica's quiet east coast to settle a small hillside plot with a hand-built shack. His friend was correct. Zak embraced the local rhythms of waking, walking, working and bathing accented with notes of laughter and fresh harvest from the soil and the sea.

Since that original adventure, Zak has worked several years as an instructor for wilderness expeditions across North America for Outward Bound and the National Outdoor Leadership School. Currently, he continues the mission of helping people explore the outdoors in San Francisco with Bay Area Wilderness Training. After several visits back to Dominica and continued exploration, Zak is grateful to share his local knowledge and outdoor expertise to explore the Nature Island's trails with readers.

Contents

Background 25

The Basics 53

Roseau 103

Roseau Valley 126

West Coast 139

Portsmouth & Picard 155

Acknowledgments

First and foremost, thanks goes to Christopher Beale for giving us this opportunity and for his consistent guidance throughout this process. A special thanks to Jerome Nelson and Emily Rice for their help and generosity both on the road and off. A huge thanks to the Peace Corps Volunteers whose help was completely invaluable. I simply could not have written this without your contributions and advice: Veronica Bagnole, J.R. Lujan, Amanda Shannahan, Ella Rychlewski, Cathy Lin, Alicia Dodds, Michelle Garavaglia, Nika Helmer, Jasmine Landry, Emily Hendrick, Allegra Asplundh-Smith, Brendan Bacon, Hillary Teed, Tymothy McGuire, Judy Joyce, Lesley Yen, Kathryn Fenneman, Andrea Felix, Elise Law, Rhiannan Price, Nicole Stroot, Jennifer Helton, Jenni Stanford, Beth Hanson, Becky Williams, and Michael Farrell (an honorary PCV).

Also thanks to all of those in Dominica who were incredibly helpful and supportive: Cyrilla Alexis and Isaline Carter at Discover Dominica, Patrick Henderson, Pamela O'Callaghan, Billy and Samantha Lawrence, Delbert Benjamin, and the Burton Family.

Of course, many contributed to this guide and I would like to thank Lennox Honychurch and Shane Gero at Dalhousie University for their expertise and knowledge.

I have to thank my parents, Rick and Becky, and Kathryn Znameroski and Lindsay Wood for your help, support, and stellar editing skills.

- Anna McCanse

Anna, your work ethic and perseverance are truly inspiring. I offer my deepest thanks for teaming with me to celebrate and reveal Dominica's richness.

Matt, your contributions on island and back home are beyond calculation. Your

---

A Brief Disclaimer

Every effort has been made to make this guide as precise as possible. Each review is based on our own experiences and opinions. However, you may discover that prices have gone up, popular restaurants and hotels have closed, good places have taken a turn for the worse, new restaurants and hotels have opened and other places have greatly improved by the time you visit. So go with your instincts and if there is a restaurant or hotel that looks great and isn't listed in this book then by all means, check it out.

This book is best viewed as a jumping off point. We'll get you there, give you advice and guidance but hope that once you're there, you will engage with the people and culture and decide how you want your vacation to play out. If you find there are inconsistencies between information and the guide or just want to let us know about an amazing new place, please do write and let us know so that our next edition can be that much more useful. Thanks and happy trails!

expertise, sweat, friendship and ingenuity were critical. Thanks for being there for it all.

Jahvis, it's so far beyond words. Yet, I'll try one...*Bushiwi*.

To the entire Baron family: Ten years later, your generosity still surprises me. Each time I return, it feels more and more like home. You are the heart of my community, my lifeline in Dominica. From shelter and healing to meals and wheels, you made our frequent and sprinting explorations possible. Gratitude coming strong!

Eric, your passion for the monumental task of linking the island with a world-class footpath and your consultation to inform our product was critical. Additional thanks the entire staff at the Waitukubuli National Trail office as well as the Lands and Surveys division.

To PCVs Judy Joyce and Michelle Nicole among others: your knowledge, energy and generosity were a joyful necessity for us, and a great gift from the USA to the communities you serve.

Finally, to someone who least expects and most deserves it. Jared, my utmost gratitude for the seed you planted. Your words on an ordinary day led me to the extraordinary island. When I speak of your generosity and the events that followed, friends say that you were instrumental in my fate. Thank you. Yes, the place is perfect for this person.

- Zak Klein

Motherly Advice

Throughout the book you will find boxes with advice from my very own mother, Rebecca McCanse. She was the first person to introduce me to Dominica, which she randomly discovered in a magazine article and hearing that she could go on an island vacation, close to home, that still maintained a sense of culture and rugged beauty, she planned her trip there and brought along my father and some friends. They fell in love with the island and have been back several times since. It was pure luck that I ended up in Dominica as a Peace Corps Volunteer (volunteers don't get a say in where they will be doing their service) and as I was getting ready to pack my bags and head to the island, she gave me some worthwhile advice. This advice served me well as I pass it along to my readers, I hope it will be as useful to you as it was to me.

Highlights

SWIM BENEATH A WATERFALL

Dominica has spectacular waterfalls. Some can be accessed very easily, while others require a a bit more effort to locate. Regardless of how you get there, it is a truly unforgettable experience to swim in the cool clear water amid lush verdant rainforest, surrounded by timeless beauty.

TRY A LOCAL JUICE OR BUSH RUM

Juice is the favored drink of the island and you'll find it everywhere. The fruit is generally picked in the morning and is turned straight into juice as it has been done for generations. Bush rum is made from locally produced rum, using sugar cane grown on the island, and then flavored with local fruits, spices, barks, and herbs. Whether you drink it straight up or as a rum punch, you'll be pleasantly surprised at how good it is.

EXPLORE AN UNDERWATER VOLCANIC CALDERA

Head to the Sourfrière/Scotts Head Marine Reserve to dive or snorkel around this unique geological formation. What used to be a volcano millions of years ago, is now a fascinating and pristine marine ecosystem with underwater gases that seep through the ocean floor to create warm bubbles, sheer cliffs that drop to 1,000 feet below, and a diverse array of marine life everywhere you look. There's a good chance you'll find yourself swimming with sea turtles if you stick around long enough.

SWIM IN A RIVER

Dominica may lack white sand beaches, but it more than makes up for that with its 365 rivers. The water is some of the cleanest and clearest you will ever encounter and swimming in the peaceful rainforest surrounded by fruit trees, tropical birds, and every shade of green you can imagine is not a bad way to spend an afternoon.

VISIT THE CARIB MODEL VILLAGE (KALINAGO BARANA AUTE)

Get a taste of Caribbean history by taking a stroll through the Caribbean's only piece of reserved land for the remaining indigenous population, the Kalinago (also known as Caribs). The model village was set up to educate the public about their traditional way of life and makes for a fascinating tour. Buy conventional handmade baskets or crafts and enjoy a wonderful Creole lunch while you're here.

RELAX IN A NATURAL HOT SPRING

There's no better way to unwind after a hard day of playing on an island than relaxing in a natural hot sulphur spring. Head to Wotten Waven any evening to soak in the therapeutic waters beneath the bright starry sky and let all of your worries melt away.

HIKE TO THE BOILING LAKE

Although not for the faint of heart, hiking this will get you serious traveler bonus points. Is it difficult? Yes. Is it worth it? Absolutely. You'll be blown away around every turn from the parrots and vistas, to the Valley of Desolation and milky white river pools. This is a journey not to be missed.

Quick Reference

Official Name: Commonwealth of Dominica

Official Language: English, French Creole

Location: West Indies between French islands Martinique to the south and Guadeloupe to the north; 15°N and 61°W

Country Size: Approx 29 miles long and 16 miles wide

Total Area: 289.5 sq miles

Capital: Roseau

Airport: Melville Hall (DOM), Canefield (DCF)

Climate: Humid, tropical; Avg 80°F; Dry season: Jan-June, Rainy season: Aug-Oct; Peak hurricane season: late Aug/early Sept

Annual Rainfall: 50" (west coast) 300" (interior)

Terrain: Steep, rugged, volcanic, rainforested

Highest Point: 4,747' (Morne Diablotin)

Population: 70,000 (2001 census)

Economy: Agriculture and tourism-based

Ethnic Groups: Black 87%, mixed 9%, Amerindian (Carib) 3%, White 1%

Government: Parliamentary Democracy

Prime Minister: Roosevelt Skerrit

Flag: Green background with a cross of yellow, black and white stripes. Red circle in the center with 10 yellow and green stars around the perimeter and a sisserou parrot in the middle.

GDP (gross domestic product): US$357 Million

Per capita: US$4,883 (2008 estimate)

Currency: Eastern Caribbean Dollar (XCD)

Religion: Mainly Roman Catholic

Life expectancy: 77 years (2002 estimate)

Business Hours: Varies but generally most businesses open around 8am with lunch from about 1pm-2pm and close at 4:30pm or 5pm. Saturdays many businesses are open in the morning and close around 1pm or 2pm. It is rare for a restaurant or business to be open on Sundays.

Metric System: Measurements based on traditional metric system

International telephone code: + 1 767

Time zone: GMT -4 hours

Rate of Exchange:

1 USD = EC$2.70 (fixed)

1 EUR = EC$3.50

1 GBP = EC$4.20

Electricity supply: 220/240 volts, Type G plug

National Bird: Sisserou parrot (Amazona imperialis)

National Flower: Bwa kwaib (Sabinea carinalis)

Public Holidays (2011):

Jan 1-2: New Year

Feb: Carnival (takes place the Monday and Tuesday before Ash Wednesday)

Apr 22: Good Friday

Apr 25: Easter Monday

May 2: Bank Holiday

Jun 13: Whit Monday

Aug 1: August Monday

Nov 3: Independence Day

Nov 4: Community Service Day

Dec 25: Christmas

Dec 26: Boxing Day

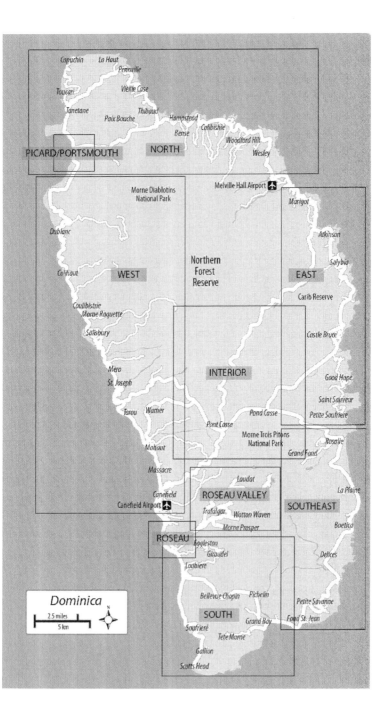

Introduction

They don't make places like Dominica anymore, at least not in the Caribbean. With its unspoiled, pristine rainforest-shrouded peaks, it has been said that the island is the only place in the Caribbean that Christopher Columbus would still recognize. Dominica is the newest island to be formed in the Caribbean, rising up out of the sea a mere 26 million years ago. All rough and tumble in character, it's the little brother of all of the islands. Dominica's relative youth accounts for its rugged and mountainous character, not having had the 100+ million years to be worn down by wind and water into gentler hills and valleys. And this is what makes Dominica so visually stunning. Its majestic peaks blanketed in clouds and covered in brilliant greenery leap from the sea to provide a vividly scenic backdrop to a very relaxed way of life. Flying in over Dominica, it's easy to picture yourself descending into a virtual Jurassic Park, where the coasts are wild and the island still harbors secret places.

Known as "The Nature Island," Dominica plays host to eco-enthusiasts who enjoy being in nature and are looking for more than a manicured resort vacation. The island will charm your socks off with its friendly and outgoing people, and tempt you to quit your job and retire to the rainforest after a visit to one of its many beautiful rivers or waterfalls. Although the tourism industry is just starting to gain some momentum, it's doing so in an environmentally friendly and sustainable way. The Dominican government has been recognized internationally for its efforts to preserve the island's unique ecology and culture while simultaneously making it accessible to tourists — no easy task. It was the first country in the world to receive the Benchmarking designation from the prestigious eco-tourism organization Green Globe 21 and has won a host of other prestigious awards and recognitions:

- Rated as the 2nd most "pure island" in the world by Islands Magazine.
- Included in Travel & Leisure as one of the most compelling destinations to visit in their 100 Greatest Trips.
- Island Magazine included Dominica in its 2007 Blue List for being a leader in responsible tourism and ensuring an environmentally and culturally sound island for future generations.
- Dubbed the most sustainable island in the Caribbean and one of the ten most sustainable islands in the world by the venerable National Geographic Center for Sustainable Destinations.

Emerging from a turbulent history of attacks, pirating, colonization, slavery, and a struggle for independence, Dominica offers a unique and intriguing cultural blend. The fusion of French, British, indigenous, and African traditions means that you can sit down for an afternoon cup of tea while listening to local reggae music and hear folks telling jokes in the French Patois dialect.

Dominica is home to the only remaining territory of Kalinago (or Carib) people in the world. The Carib Territory is in many ways similar to most typical villages in Dominica, but a visit to the Kalinago Barana Aute, or "The Model Village," will give you a glimpse as to how Arawak and Kalinago people lived in harmony with the land before the island was colonized.

When visiting Dominica, leave your Type A tendencies at home. It's hard to find a nation with a more easy going approach to life and this island lifestyle will compel its visitors to unwind as well. Spending an afternoon swimming beneath waterfalls, floating in the clear blue sea, or snorkeling along pristine reefs with sea turtles, you can lose yourself in this rare paradise. The activities in Dominica are endless. As long as you are up for an adventure, the island is your eco-playground.

Itineraries

Although Dominica is often marketed for adventure-seekers, the activities you can find on the island are as diverse as its visitors. Here are a few to get you started.

DAY TRIPPERS

Dominica has recently doubled the number of cruise ship passengers coming to the island and if you are one of the lucky ones, here are a few ideas for how to spend your time wisely if you don't want to take a packaged tour and would like to avoid the crowds. For all tours, I recommend grabbing a fresh fruit smoothie made with local produce from "J.B. Juice" stand in Roseau before heading out and ending your day at "The Ruins" in Roseau, where you can try the homemade island bush rum and buy some to take home with you.

When you get off of the cruise ship, you can hire any of the taxis waiting outside for a private tour. Before you jump into a taxi be sure the driver is a trained and licensed guide (they should be willing to show you their ID issued by the tourism authority with their picture on it). Here are two that are popular and are consistently praised for their excellent service:

Ken's Hinterland Adventure Tours *Tel: 767-448-4850, www.kenshinterlandtours.com*

Pepper's Tours *Tel: 767-440-4321, 767-245-1234, 767-616-4321; askpepper@pepperscottage.com; www.sweetdominica.com*

Option 1

A good option if you don't want to venture too far is to head up to Roseau Valley and hike to **Middleham Falls**. It's one of the less crowded waterfalls in this area and easy to get to in an afternoon. Afterwards, have your guide take you to **Papillote** for lunch, where you also have the option of taking a garden tour or sitting in the hot pools for a small additional fee.

Option 2

If you want to venture a little further to see more of Dominica's dramatic landscape, head to **Sari Sari Falls** (pg 260) which is only a 40 minute hike out and is well worth the effort. Afterwards have lunch at the **River Rock Café**, a relatively new French-inspired restaurant situated next to a gorgeous river where you can relax in hammocks with a cup of coffee before heading back to Roseau.

Option 3

For those who want something less athletic and more cultural, have your guide drive you to the other side of the island where you will get a feel for rural village life. Be sure to check out the Carib Model Village called "**Kalinago Barana Auté**" where you can take a tour and learn about the way the Amerindians lived before Columbus's arrival. There is a restaurant on site where Rose, the cook, will make you an incredible Creole style lunch served with delicious fresh juice or rum punch. There are also women who make traditional Carib crafts, as they have for centuries, on site and sell their handmade baskets, woodcarvings, and calabash bowls for the best price you'll get on the island.

Option 4

If you like a little beach with your island vacation, head up north to **Calibishie** and go to one of the beaches in the area – **Batibou** and **Hampstead** are great options. Have lunch in the village and then hike around the **Red Rocks** area at Pt. Baptiste. For the more adventurous, go to the village of Bense and hike down the short path, cross the river, and walk upstream a short ways to **Chaudiere Pool** where you'll find a small waterfall and deep basin to swim in. Jumping off of the surrounding cliffs into the pool is a popular way to spend an afternoon here.

THREE DAYS

Three days in Dominica will give you just enough of a taste to make you wish you were staying longer. A good idea is to find accommodation someplace central in the Roseau or Roseau Valley area. Spend one day at a waterfall – **Trafalgar** and **Middleham** are good choices – followed by a trip to some hot pools like **Screw's Spa**, **Tia's**, **Ti Kwen Glo Cho** or **Pappillote**. On day two, if you're up for it, try the **Boiling Lake Hike** or, for an easier trek, hike to **Glassé Point** or **Sari Sari Falls** on the east coast. Relax a bit on the third day with some snorkeling in the southwest at **Champagne, Sourfrieré,** or **Scotts Head.** Stick around for some of the island's best fish at the **Fish Pot** in Pt. Michel at sundown.

ONE WEEK

This is just the right amount of time to make you fall in love with Dominica and see a good portion of the island. For the first half of the week, stay in or near Roseau Valley. Start by hiking to a waterfall like **Trafalgar** or **Middleham,** and then spend that evening at the **hot springs** in Wotten Waven. The next day consider challenging yourself by hiking the **Boiling Lake** or, if the Boiling Lake isn't on your agenda, take a swim at **Titou Gorge,** ride the **Aerial Tram** or hike around **Freshwater Lake.** On the third day snorkel around the southwest at either **Soufrière, Scotts Head**, or **Champagne.** On day four, travel to **Kalinago Barana Auté (Carib Model Village by the Sea)** for a cultural and historical lesson about the island. Grab lunch there then

hike over **Horseback Ridge** to swim at **Basen Majo** on the Pagua River. Take the next day to relax on a beach in Calibishie such as **Hampstead** or **Batibou** then have lunch in the village before hiking down to **Chaudiere Pool** from the village of Bense.
On your last day, go to **Portsmouth** to visit **Cabrits/Ft. Shirley** then take a ride on the **Indian River** or a scenic drive through the northern peninsula. If your flight is in the afternoon, spend the morning hiking down to **Sandy Bay Beach** in Marigot and grab lunch at **Pagua Bay Restaurant** before you head out.

> Staying in the north around Calibishie, in the interior, or on the east coast will allow you to get around faster and provide an easier trip to the airport.

TWO WEEKS

This is the perfect amount of time to really see a good portion of the island. It makes sense to start in the north and there are plenty of accommodation options in **Calibishie**. Recuperate from the long journey by relaxing on the beach at **Woodford Hill, Batibou** or **Hampstead**. Have lunch in the village then head down to **Chaudiere Pool** from Bense for a short hike and refreshing swim. Spend a day in the northern peninsula by driving up the scenic route, picnicking at **Capuchin Point** then taking a **hike to Penville**. You may also want to go **horseback riding** with one of the outfitters in between Borne and Portsmouth to get a different perspective on the area. Spend a day in Portsmouth and take a boat ride up the **Indian River** and check out **Cabrits/Ft. Shirley**. Call up the folks at Wave Dancer to arrange a boat trip to the **Secret Beach** that lies between Dublanc and Picard. This also puts you in a good spot to explore the Carib Territory. Be sure to go to the **Carib Model Village by the Sea (Kalinago Barana Auté)** and plan to spend a few hours there. While you're in the area, hike up **Horseback Ridge** then down to the **Pagua River** for a swim at **Basen Majo**. Or drive down the coast a bit and hike to **L'Escalier Tete Chien**.

You may want to spend a few days in the **Roseau Valley** so that you can explore the capital and experience some hikes and waterfalls in that beautiful area. Hike to a waterfall – **Middleham** and **Trafalgar** are close by – and spend the evening enjoying the hot springs in **Wotten Waven**. If you came to Dominica to hike or get in shape then this is your chance to do the **Boiling Lake Hike**. Be sure to get plenty of rest the night before and plan to spend all day hiking. If that's more exertion than you want on your Caribbean vacation, then take a tour on the **Aerial Tram** instead. Round out your day with a swim in **Titou Gorge**, which is just up the road. The next day you'll probably want to relax so head to Roseau to go **whale watching**, visit the **farmers market**, or stroll through the **Botanical Gardens.** Before you leave the Roseau area, spend one day in the southwest to dive or snorkel around **Champagne, Scotts Head,** or **Soufrière.**

> Before you leave, spend one day on a **community tour**. It's a great way to get to know the people, the island, and the culture all while supporting their local economy.

For the final portion of your trip, stay in the southeast region where there is a plethora of hikes, waterfalls, and beaches to keep you occupied for days. You may wish to drive there from Grand Bay and head north – over a sort of scary road with some amazing views – and past the bay leaf fields and factories in Petite Savanne.

While you're in this region, be sure to spend a day hiking to **Sari Sari Falls** or **Victoria Falls**, both of which are lovely hikes. Walk the trail to **Glassé Point** and spend an afternoon at **River Rock Café** where you can fuel up with lunch and coffee, relax in a hammock, and swim in the river on their property. Spend a morning in the **Rosalie River** or **Beach,** and then **hike north to Petite Soufrière**. You can walk up the road (a very hilly road) to the tiny picturesque village **San Sauveur** and rest at the **Rasta Bar** before heading back. And while you are there, and if you are somewhat brave, you must hike to **Wavine Cyrique**. Spend a day on the beach or under a waterfall then hike back up and rinse off in **Trois Basen**. If you have an early flight out, it makes sense to spend your last night in Marigot or back in Calibishie.

FAMILY FRIENDLY

If your trip to Dominica is a whole family affair and you have a variety of abilities and interests to accommodate, here are a few activities that everyone will enjoy.

Whale Watching This will run you around US$50 per person but is worth it for the once in a lifetime chance to see whales in their natural environment. pg 97

Indian River Sit back and enjoy a river like you've never seen before as your guide paddles you down this peaceful waterway while you look for iguanas, land crabs, and beautiful flowers along the bank. pg 156

Red Rocks Hike An easy and beautiful hike for all ability levels with stunning views of the sea and surrounding Calibishie area. Kids can look for the hidden caves while parents sit back and enjoy the scenery. pg 169

Market Day Visit this centuries-old farmers market by the riverbank in Roseau on a Saturday morning to get a true cultural experience while you pick up some fresh local produce. pg 110

Douglas Bay/Toucari Bay Beach These gentle beaches on the west coast are great for picnics and relaxed afternoons by the sea without the crowds and allow for some swimming and snorkeling as well. pg 174

Emerald Pool An easy walk down a well maintained path takes you to one of Dominica's most stunning waterfalls. Swim below the falls if you want a cool and refreshing dip. pg 231

The Cabrits and Ft. Shirley Get a taste for the fascinating history of the Caribbean and some exercise at the same time while you check out the grounds and striking views of the surrounding area. pg 158

Carib Model Village By The Sea (Kalinago Barana Auté) Learn how the original occupants of the island lived before Columbus arrived. Be sure to also buy some original Carib crafts and enjoy a stellar lunch. pg 193

Trafalgar Falls Although crowded when a cruise ship is in port, this is a nice spot that everyone will enjoy. You can view the waterfalls from a convenient platform, sit in some natural hot pools, and – for the more adventurous – climb over the rocks to swim at the base of the falls. pg 131

Papillote Hot Springs and Garden Tour Not only is this a good place to have lunch, it also offers hot pools, massages, an on-site waterfall, and a wonderful garden tour with a very nice souvenir shop to boot. pg 133

Champagne Reef Snorkeling Located between Pt. Michel and Soufrière, you can rent snorkel gear, swim amongst warm geothermic bubbles, check out a reef where sea turtles and schools of colorful fish are a common sight, or just sun bathe with a mean rum punch in hand. If a cruise ship is in town, come in the early morning or late afternoon to avoid the crowds. pg 222

Rainforest Aerial Tram Ride through the tree tops of the rainforest on a small gondola as you discover the unique plants and animals that inhabit this rainforest ecosystem. pg 95

Visit the *Pirates of the Caribbean* filming locations The second and third installments of Walt Disney's Hollywood blockbuster *Pirates of the Caribbean* were filmed in Dominica, providing fans the opportunity to visit the actual filming locations. In some areas, like Indian River (pg 156), evidence of the movie set still remains.

RAINY DAY

Although it does rain almost daily in Dominica, it's always in short bursts and then the sun returns in full force. Occasionally a tropical storm rolls in and the rain doesn't let up all day. Thankfully there are not many of these in Dominica but just in case you find yourself on the island as a storm is coming through, here are few ways to remain occupied until it passes.

Dominica Museum Learn about the fascinating and tumultuous history of the island to give the rest of your trip more depth and insight. Pg 110

Wotten Waven Hot Springs Sometimes the best time to sit in a warm pool on an already hot island is when it's chilly and rainy. pg 133

Try some bush rum at **The Ruins** in Roseau. pg 115

Diving and Snorkeling You're going to be wet anyway so you might as well be underwater. Obviously you won't want to go out if the sea is really rough so check with your dive operator to make sure it's safe.

Grab a drink at **Veranda View** in Calibishie and enjoy the picture perfect scenery. pg 177

Go to **Old Mill Cultural Center** in Canefield to learn about how they used to make sugar cane into rum during the early days of colonization, then head to the **Macoucherie Rum Distillery** just up the road on the West coast to see how rum is made today. pg 144

Have a leisurely lunch at **Jungle Bay Resort** and enjoy the peaceful surroundings. If planned in advance, you can also schedule a massage or facial while you're there. pg 212

Take a **yoga class** with Rainbow Yoga, Rainforest Shangri-la or Jungle Bay Resort. pg 100

Flash Floods
One thing you don't want to do when it's raining is go to a river or waterfall. Dominican rivers are known for their flash floods when it's raining hard and people have been swept away in the recent past.

LAZY DAYS

Need a day to recover from the Boiling Lake Hike or just want to put your feet up and relax? Here are a few activities that don't require much energy but still allow you to enjoy some of what Dominica has to offer.

Visit a Beach Hampstead/Batibou Beach (pg 170) in the north and Purple Turtle (pg 156) or Coconut Beach (pg 149) in the West are all good options for those looking for the classic Caribbean vacation activity.

Indian River Boat Tour If you need a day to let someone else do the work for you, hire a guide at the entrance to Indian River and sit back while they school you on Dominica's flora and fauna. pg 156

Wotten Waven/Soufrière/Papillote Hot Springs Natural hot springs are abundant in Dominica and the locals believe they have healing properties for the skin and muscles. "Relax de bones," as Domincans say, in one of the many hot pools for a very small fee that is completely worth every penny. pp 133, 223

Whale Watching If you want a day off from the strenuous activities but don't want to miss out on anything mind-blowing, then take a whale watching tour to see these magnificent creatures in their natural environment. You'll likely also encounter pods of friendly dolphins along the way. pg 97

River Tubing Make arrangements with Wacky Rollers (Pg 149) who will take you down the Layou River and while you sit back and enjoy the view. Refreshments and rum punch provided at the end of the journey.

Antrim Sculpture Garden For those interested in art, this is a place worth exploring. Internationally recognized artist, Roger Burnett, and his wife, Denise, have created a beautiful sculpture garden behind their house that is open to tourists. Be sure to make arrangments with them for lunch afterwards. pg 150

Horseback Riding Call up Rainforest Riding or Brandy Manor Equestrian Center to arrange a peaceful ride through the rainforest, on the beach, or even to Cabrits National Park. pg 97

Scenic Drive up the Northern Road Follow the road through the northern peninsula to see a cold bubbling sulphur pool in the crater of a volcano, some sweeping views of Marie Galant and Les Saints, and get a feel for small village life in this very rural area. pg 175

Rainforest Aerial Tram Ride through the tree tops of the rainforest on a small gondola as you discover the unique plants and animals that inhabit this island rainforest ecosystem. pg 95

HIKER'S PARADISE

Hopefully you packed your hiking shoes because this island has more amazing hikes than you probably have time for. Here are some favorites.

Waitukubuli National Trail A newly developed trail that goes from North to South, zigzagging across the island to hit many of Dominica's best spots for exploring. Do it all in one go or just a section or two. pg 243

Boiling Lake The mother of all hikes in the Caribbean, this isn't your grandma's afternoon stroll. A rigorous climb up, followed by a steep descent into the "Valley of Desolation," around some hot rivers, and a few more ups and downs will get you to the world's second largest boiling sulphuric lake deep in the rainforest. Totally worth the pain your legs will be in the next day. pg 252

Sari Sari Falls A magical spot in what feels like the middle of the rainforest is actually only a reasonable and fun hike away. pg 260

Middleham Falls A beautiful 300 foot waterfall that, if you want to mix it up a bit, can be accessed by two different trails. Check out the stinky bat cave while you're there. pg 255

Victoria Falls This waterfall is a bit harder to reach, but is worth it when you do. The hike can be intense if the river is high and a guide is recommended to help you navigate the many river crossings required to get there. pg 264

Highest Peaks: Morne Trois, Morne Anglais and Morne Diablotin Although Dominica's highest peak is only 4700 ft, the ascent begins from sea level with muddy trails requiring some agility and climbing to reach the top, making these destinations challenging for novice hikers. For many, the journey is better than the destination and you are bound to encounter some interesting flora and fauna on your way up. pp 258, 262

Wavine Cyrique This is a hike that will take you to one of the most secluded and awe-inspiring beaches on the island. After a climb straight down a cliff via a series of root systems that make up a natural ladder, you will end up on a black sand beach with a waterfall shooting right over the edge of the cliff. The trek is simply beautiful. pg 297

Canyoning Tired of getting sweaty while you hike? Well here's the perfect solution: hike through pristine rivers and rappel through waterfalls with Extreme Dominica – they are focused on taking you on safe and exhilarating adventure while you discover some of Dominica's hidden gems. pg 95

A GEOLOGICAL WATER PARK

Water activities in Dominica are endless with 365 rivers, a lake that boils, a reef that bubbles and rivers with naturally occurring hot pools. You like it fresh? Go to Freshwater Lake or take a swim in a deep clear river pool. You like it hot? Go to one of the many hot pools for a soak. You like a little "something else" with your water? Go to a mineral pool or bathe in the sulphuric White River. No matter what your preference, you'll be sure to find it here.

Snorkeling or Scuba Diving at Soufrière / Scotts Head Marine Reserve There is no better way to explore the water than to go beneath it and swim alongside its inhabitants. Most of the dive outfitters offer "discover" scuba courses if you aren't certified and just want to check it out. pg 226

Swim in the Sea Mero (pg 144), Purple Turtle (pg 156), Toucari Bay (pg 173), and Douglas Bay (pg 174) beaches are all great for swimming and you won't have to worry about the unpredictable ocean currents here. Great for kids too and a few also offer snorkeling options.

Titou Gorge *Ti-tou* means "little throat" in Creole and swimming through this small crevasse between two tall rock faces you can understand where they came up with the name. You'll encounter a small waterfall at the end and a hot water spring at the beginning to really round out this aquatic experience. pg 130

Hot Springs Head to Wotten Waven (pg 131) or Soufrière (pg 222) for a relaxing bath in Dominica's completely natural hot water pools. It's a perfect evening activity after a hard day of hiking.

River Tubing Call up Wacky Rollers (pg 149) to arrange a trip down the Layou. They'll stop at one of the Layou's deep pools for a quick swim and offer refreshments and a dangerously good rum punch at the end of your journey.

Chaudiere Pool Hike down a short path from the village of Bense and cross a river to get to this hidden jewel. A picture-perfect deep-water pool with a small waterfall is great for a relaxing swim and the more adventurous can jump off the surrounding cliffs into the water. pg 170

Glassy Pool (Glassé Point) This is another interesting geological site at the end of a relatively easy hike with breath-taking views along the way. Sit in the warm deep pools carved into the rock from the ocean's waves and stick around for a picnic while you enjoy the sweeping views of the sea. pg 206

Waterfall Hikes Any hike that ends in a swim beneath a beautiful waterfall has got to be a good one. Here are a few of my favorites: Victoria Falls (Pg 264), Sari Sari (Pg 260), Trafalgar (Pg 131), and Middleham Falls (Pg 255).

Layou River Hot Pool As if swimming in this crystal clear and gorgeous river wasn't enough, Mother Nature went and deposited a hot water spring along the bank where locals have built up rocks to contain it, creating a natural hot tub. pg 231

Basen Majo on the Pagua River In the land of deep river pools, this one is king and it is easily accessed from the road to Concord or a hike over Horseback Ridge from the Carib Territory. It's beautiful and secluded from the road, with a giant rock for adrenaline junkies who want to climb up and jump off and can be a great spot to hang out with locals who come to do their laundry or take a swim. pg 189

Indian River Just when you thought you'd seen all that Dominica's rivers had to offer, along comes the Indian River, which is not like any other spot on the island. Fringed with elegant mangrove trees and full of wildlife and beautiful flowers, you can relax while your guide paddles you upstream and points out all of the interesting stuff. A quick stop at the end for some refreshments and a walk around and then you'll be paddled back to the mouth of the river where you started. pg 156

Kayaking Calibishie Cove (pg 176) in the north and Nature Island Dive or A.L. Dive (pg 226) in the south offer kayaking tours and rentals.

Canyoning If you can't decide between a hike or a swim, this is the ideal option. You'll hike along and through rivers and rappel down waterfalls, giving you the best of both worlds. pg 95

NATURAL WONDERS

When your plane descends over Dominica it may feel as if you are entering the set of Jurassic Park, a place full of wonder and excitement around every corner. Although you probably won't run into any dinosaurs here, you will find some extraordinary natural features that will likely blow your mind.

Titou Gorge A unique swimming hole that formed by a split in the rock after flowing lava cooled and contracted during a volcanic explosion thousands of years ago. Swim through a deep ravine to a small waterfall at the end. Hot water springs in the large pool at the beginning will warm you up after your swim in the cool water. pg 130

Boiling Lake and the Valley of Desolation If you are interested in geology, volcanic activity, or just mind-blowing hikes, this is a must see. With a "Valley of Desolation," steaming fumaroles, bubbling rock, hot sulphur pools, great views of the entire island, and the world's second largest boiling lake, there won't be a dull moment. pg 130

Wotten Waven Hot Springs Go to any of the hot pools in Wotten Waven to experience naturally warmed water that is said to have fantastic healing properties. pg 133

Scotts Head Caldera Snorkel or scuba dive at the Scotts Head peninsula and you'll swim above a 1,000 foot drop that acts as the rim of a prehistoric volcanic crater. pg 226

Champagne Reef Swim amongst warm geothermal bubbles that come from underwater volcanic vents. This reef is named "champagne" because it feels like you are swimming in a glass of bubbly while you explore the reef. pg 222

Glassy Pools Hike through farmland and rainforest until you reach an old volcanic flow, jutting out into the ocean, known as Glassy Pools or Glassé Point. Waves crash around on all sides and have formed perfectly circular pools that warm in the sun. It's a nice place for a picnic, too. pg 206

Whale Watching One of nature's most amazing creatures can be viewed fairly easily off the shores of Dominica. Because of the extreme drop in depth just off the coast of the island, many whale families and dolphins make their homes in this region. pg 97

Cold Sulphur Pools Located off the northern scenic route, it is only a short 10 minute hike to see this unique geological feature. Depending on the time of year, you're likely to see either many small pools or a bigger lake of cold bubbling water that smells strongly of sulphur. pg 175

Leatherback Sea Turtles These big guys (many weigh 1,500 lbs) make their way onto the shores of the north and east coast from June to September to lay eggs. Go on a moonlit night to watch this prehistoric ritual in action. pp 176, 202

HISTORY AND CULTURE BUFF

If you travel internationally because you are fascinated by the way other cultures operate and like to dig into the history and lifestyle of the people there, here a few things you can do to get a better understanding of Dominica.

Dominica Museum An excellent place to begin understanding the history and culture of the island. You'll find old photographs, tools, maps and artifacts dating back to when the Amerindian tribes inhabited the Caribbean islands. pg 110

Cabrits National Park and Ft. Shirley A recently restored fort and garrison from the 18th century with a great visitor center that explains the geology and history of the area. pg 158

Old Mill Cultural Center A former mill that once produced rum made from sugar cane and processed limes to make Rose's Lime Juice. Get a tour of the mill or check out some of the local artwork in the gallery. Cultural events are frequently held here in the evenings as well. pg 144

Carib Model Village Experience life as it was before Columbus's arrival. The model village features traditional wood and thatched buildings, handmade canoes, ancient song and dance and time-honored crafts for sale. This is an excellent way to spend an afternoon. pg 193

Roseau Walking Tour Pick up a brochure from Dominica's historical society to take a self-guided tour of Roseau and get the inside scoop on many of the colonial style buildings in the capital and why they were built. pg 105

Saturday Farmers Market This Saturday tradition has been going on for centuries, exactly as it is today. Get a lesson in culture as you walk the aisles of food stacked in traditional West African style and listen to the vendors speaking Creole while you try some of Dominica's traditional foods. pg 110

Jacko Steps The site of a former maroon (escaped slave) encampment run by a chief named "Jacko." These steps were carved into the side of a mountain to provide easier access in and out of the camps. Today, it's an interesting and historical hiking trail for all to enjoy. pg 234

Community Tours This new initiative run by Discover Dominica is an innovative idea to connect tourists to the local people and community while hightlighting some of Dominica's popular attractions. Take a tour of a farm or Creole garden to get a feel for how Dominicans live off the land today. (Community tours can be found in the Sights section of each regional chapter.)

Independence Day and Creole Music Festival This festival takes place in late October and provides a plethora of cultural activities from traditional song and dance competitions to the world's largest Creole music gathering, usually featuring local artists as well as big names in the Caribbean music scene such as Wyclef Jean and Shaggy. pg 79

Carnival A true time-honored cultural tradition that usually happens in February. Check out the Calypso shows and Carnival Queen contests leading up to Carnival. "Jump up" in the streets during early morning J'ouvert, watch the colorful parade, and take part in Vaval – a late night burning of the sprit of Carnival in the Carib Territory. pg 79

Ride the Bus If you want to truly feel the pulse of this island, try riding the local bus. Many times you'll be drawn into conversations with locals or can participate in spontaneous sing-a-longs that are common occurrences during the rides.

Dance like a Local Go to Jungle Bay (pg 212) for dinner on a Friday night and try your hand at some traditional dances such as the Bele and Quadrille while a Jing Ping band keeps the beat.

HEALTH AND WELLNESS VACATION

If you came to Dominica to rejuvenate and relax, these places cater to that and do a great job of it:

Jungle Bay Offers yoga retreats, Spa and Adventure Packages, and Fitness Boot Camp all in a luxurious and healthy environment. pg 212

Rainforest Shangri-la This geothermal area provides ample mineral rich mud for mud baths, wraps, and facials. Guests can take part in any of these complimentary activities: Tai Chi, Watsu, Qi Gong, herbal medicine, early morning hikes, and natural hot or cold water stone baths. Organic nutritious meals provided in an eco-friendly relaxing environment. pg 134

Screw's Spa Natural hot mineral water pools said to have healing properties and spring freshwater pools interspersed throughout the property in the rainforest. Do-it-yourself mud wraps are also available here. pg 133

Papillote Wilderness Retreat Spa with four hot mineral pools throughout the property, massage therapies including physiotherapy, reflexology, and aqua massage available. pg 133

Picard Beach Wellness Eco-Cottages Located right on the beach, this eco-lodge offers yoga and massage on site for guests. pg 163

Exotica Cottages Exotica prides themselves on being one of the most relaxing places on the island and will take care of you as much or as little as you like. It's a good place to just get away from it all. pg 229

Background

FIRST INHABITANTS

Dominica's first known inhabitants arrived in dugout canoes from the Orinoco River region of South America from as far back as 3000 BC. They lived a nomadic lifestyle, going from island to island hunting and fishing with the use of roughly hewn stone tools and conch shells. Sometime around 200 AD, the Arawak-speaking people from the same region took up permanent residence here. They were peaceful fishermen, hunters and farmers who settled in fertile river valleys. Being more artistic than the previous inhabitants, the Arawak left paintings and depictions near their dwellings. Using a system of slash and burn agriculture, they planted tobacco, which was used ritually, maize, beans, sweet potatoes, pineapples, peppers, cassava, and guava, which was also used medicinally. Although the Arawak language has essentially died out, several words are still in existence today: *canoe, guava, barbeque, manatee, hurricane,* and *tobacco,* which was actually their word for pipe.

The Arawak's way of life was disrupted around 1200 AD when the aggressive Kalinago people arrived from South America and eventually began to take over the islands of the Caribbean. They gave Dominica the name *Wai'tukubuli* meaning "tall is her body" in reference to the mountainous character of the island. The Kalinago were sophisticated builders and made their homes out of straw and wood. They were also expert cotton spinners and weavers, and were described by visitors as handsome, graceful people with long black hair and a light brown complexion. The Kalinago dominated the Caribbean islands and their presence was feared by the

---

Motherly Advice

Choosing Dominica as a travel destination is natural... literally.

After reading an article about Dominica in a travel magazine many years ago, it was immediately on my "must see" list. It was described as being one of the few remaining Caribbean islands that have not been significantly impacted by tourism, and we found that to be true. On our first trip, before our daughter lived there, we discovered an incredibly beautiful country and friendly people. We were immersed in their culture and, while we were treated politely, there was not the sense that the Dominicans were molding their behavior to please us as tourists.

European explorers who claimed that they were cannibalistic. This theory of cannibalism is unfounded, however, and many historians believe it was made up as an excuse to dominate the Kalinago and take over their land. Regardless, they called these people Carib, the word used for cannibals, and it stuck. Their reputation was so far reaching that the Spanish named the entire region after them – the Caribbean.

EUROPEAN ARRIVAL

On the 3rd of November 1493, Columbus's ships sighted the island and since it happened to be a Sunday, they gave the island the name *Dominica*, meaning Sunday Island. They landed at Prince Rupert Bay near modern day Portsmouth and documented seeing Carib settlements there. This bay would become an important stopping point for many ships that would make use of the fresh river water, hot springs, timber and firewood, and trading opportunities with the Kalinago. Everyone from Spanish treasure ships to famous pirates would stock up here before their outbound trip. However, because of the extreme terrain, lack of gold prospects, and a fierce resistance by the Caribs, the Spanish had little interest in colonizing the island. For the next 250 years, the Caribs retained their peaceful existence in Dominica. As it would turn out, Dominica would remain the last regional stronghold of the Caribs. Those from other islands fled to Dominica to escape the brutal colonization of their homelands.

Carib Canoes

In ancient Kalingao life, canoes held extreme importance and their relationship with the sea was evident in all facets of life from fishing and hunting to trading, and inter-island migration and travel. All of the canoes were dugout style and some were known to hold as many as 40 people. They were masters of the canoe but today, only a handful of canoe builders remain.

The process starts in the forest and will take up to three months. Canoe-makers choose a large, tall gommier tree and around the time when there is a new moon (it is not visible), they will cut the tree. According to tradition, trees cut during this time can be on the ground for an entire year without being eaten by pests. The tree is transported to the village and then, using fire, a chain-saw and hand axe (traditionally, sharp volcanic rock would have been used), they begin to hollow out the tree. Once the tree starts to take the shape of a canoe, large stones are heated in a fire and placed in the interior of the canoe. Water is poured over them to create steam and then the sides are pushed out using propped tree branches, helping to expand the width of the interior. After the preferred shape is attained, the canoe can be cooled down and the maker can use the axe once more to trim outsides, making sure it is balanced. Extra boards are added to the exterior and sealed with the gommier sap. Ornate additions are hand carved from white cedar and attached and sealed. The boats are then varnished or brightly painted to the buyers liking.

If you venture up the road from Salybia to Horseback Ridge (see pg 188) you may find Napoleon "Beto" Sanford building canoes behind the Carib Council office. He is especially busy before Dive Fest in July, when he's getting boats ready to sell for the annual Carib Canoe Race.

BRITISH AND FRENCH CONTROL

Eventually, France claimed Dominica and in 1642 they sent their first French missionaries to the island with the intention of Christianizing the Caribs. The Kalinago intensely defied colonization and in 1686 a neutrality agreement declaring Dominica a Kalinago territory was put in place. But the French lumbermen and farmers still managed to sneak in from the surrounding islands of Martinique and Guadeloupe. These immigrants established relationships with the Kalinago and were able to set up small estates and errect stone houses. The British retaliated, claiming a breach on the neutrality agreement and took over Dominica in 1761. Once the British gained legal control a few years later, they opened the doors for development. Estates were expanded, slaves were brought in, a legal system was put into place, and towns and fortifications began to come to life. During the period of British control, the French maintained a strong presence because of the sizable population of French farmers still on island.

At this point the population of Kalinago had been almost completely wiped out due to the years of fighting coupled with the influx of disease from the Europeans, and the widespread destruction of their settlements. By the mid-1700s, there were only around 400 Kalinago left in existence.

Because the British were preoccupied with the American War of Independence from 1778 to 1783, the French managed to wrest control of the island during this time. It would be short-lived as the Treaty of Versailles turned Dominica over to the British once more. This tug of war continued for many years and in 1805 the French gave it one last shot as the Napoleonic forces managed to take over and set fire to Roseau. The British were outnumbered and the French were able to hold members of the legislature hostage, loot Roseau of its valuables and slaves and left with a sizeable ransom before sailing back to their colonies. This was the final attempt of the French and from then on, Dominica remained in British hands.

SLAVERY

As in other slave-holding nations, plantations across the Caribbean were worked by large numbers of African slaves. In fact, at one point, the Caribbean islands held more slaves than all of the Americas. But Dominica is a rugged island, full of hiding places and many of the slaves fled the plantations and set up camps in the interior mountains and valleys, using the harsh terrain as a base from which to launch attacks on the plantations and their owners. The British called these renegade slaves Maroons.

Although the movement to abolish slavery in Britain was gaining momentum, a war was launched against the Maroons to quell their rebellious activity – nearly 600 had been killed or captured by 1814. Slavery was outlawed in 1833 and today, around 95% of Dominica's population is of African descent.

POST-SLAVERY

By 1838, after the end of slavery, hurricanes and a raging coffee disease had destroyed the economic infrastructure of the island. The estates ceased to be profitable and the British estate owners began to abandon their plantations, selling them off to the free mulattos who were arriving in force from the surrounding French islands. During this time new villages emerged and a new society was forming from inde-

Background

pendent farmers who, for the first time, were accountable to no one. The feeling of independence became pervasive.

When the legislative assembly was established in 1763, it represented only the white population. After slavery was abolished, Britain's Brown Privilege Bill granted political and social rights to free nonwhites and in 1838 Dominica became the first and only British Caribbean colony to have a Black majority legislature in the 19th century.

In 1865, feeling threatened, the wealthy English class lobbied for more direct British control and the colonial office replaced the elected assembly with one that was half elected and half appointed. In 1871, Dominica joined the Leeward Island Federation and the power of the African descended population eventually deteriorated.

> Following WWII, Dominica endured another economic depression and it wasn't until 1950, when bananas or "green gold," became the primary crop that things picked back up.

CHANGING TIMES

At the turn of the century, Dominica saw vast improvements to its economy due to the introduction of cocoa and lime production. This economic uptick can also be attributed to the start of a progressive infrastructure development program created by the first Crown Colony administrator, Hesketh Bell. During his six-year reign at the turn of the century, Bell can be credited with connecting and modernizing the island via road and bridge construction, telephone lines, the introduction of electricity, a new jetty in the Roseau harbour, and obtaining funding from American philanthropist Andrew Carnegie to build Dominica's first library. In 1903, Bell granted the Kalinago, who had been forced to live a shadowy existence in the rainforest for over 150 years, a 3,700 acre (1,500 hectare) piece of land in the northeast side of the island, which is now the Carib Territory. It remains the only Carib reserve (see pg 188) in the Caribbean and today has a population of over 3,000.

> **Crown Colony Admin**
> When the government in London has some legislative control over its British Colony, which is usually administered by an appointed governor or other official.

INDEPENDENCE

On November 3, 1978, 485 years to the date after it was sighted by Columbus, Dominica achieved its independence from Britain and became what it is today: an independent republic within the British Commonwealth. Unfortunately, nothing came easy for this new nation. Not even a year after Dominica gained independence, the government had already been forced out by popular unrest and the banana industry, which the fragile economy depended upon, began to falter. Already one of the poorest nations in the Caribbean, Dominica was struck by one of the most devastating storms it had ever seen, Hurricane David. And to top it off, in "stranger than fiction" style, a coup was organized by a small group of heavily armed American leftist mercenaries who hoped to take advantage of the devastation and political unrest by making millions off of an attempt to put the former prime minister,

> A wonderful book, *Bayou of Pigs* by Stewart Bell, was recently written that narrates the events of the coup.

Patrick John, back into power. Their plot was ill conceived and poorly planned. In the end, it failed miserably. Patrick John was tried twice for his involvement in the coup and was eventually sentenced to 12 years in prison. Eugenia Charles, who had been in power during the coup, remained in place as the Caribbean's first female prime minster for the next 15 years.

DOMINICA IN THE PRESENT

Dominica today is a wonderful mélange of all of the historical influences that have made their impressions on the island. Built on a foundation of Kalinago and African traditions, and structured with a logical British framework that has been touched with French passions and customs, the result is an intriguing amalgamation known as West Indian Creole culture. This unique culture is evident in everything, including the governmental structure, cuisine, language, dress, traditions, and beliefs. Driving through the island, you'll find Kalinago, French and English village names, Roman Catholic churches and remnants of broken down mills that peek through the greenery. Banana farms dot the hillsides, a testimony to its former economic mainstay, and more and more indications of the burgeoning tourism industry can be found sneaking into the dramatic scenery, providing a glimpse into Dominica's future.

Hurricane David: August 29, 1979

No one likes a hurricane. They're loud, wet, messy and sling mud everywhere. But when they completely destroy a new struggling island nation, it's a downright brutal affair.

Hurricane David emerged off the west coast of Africa. As the tropical heat warmed the ocean waters and as the winds picked up, the storm blew north, and then west. The radio broadcast warned that a storm was coming but it was predicted to hit Barbados until suddenly David changed course and was headed straight for Dominica. The islanders were taken by surprise and were entirely unprepared. They mused that "God must be from Barbados" and had to trust that the tall mountains would protect them. Then at 9am, David arrived.

For six straight hours 175 mph winds ravaged the island, sending buildings and trees spinning through the skies, tearing up roads, bridges, and power lines and destroying the water supply. The fragile banana trees, the source of Dominica's income, collapsed in unison by strong gusts of wind. In the Botanical Gardens a large Baobab tree flattened a yellow school bus (it still remains there today as a small piece of evidence of the destruction that occurred that morning).

When the storm finally passed, nearly seventy-five percent of the population was homeless, 37 people were killed and 5,000 injured. Luckily, assistance came swiftly and The Royal Navy sent a boat immediately through the choppy seas to bring essential services and medical care to the island. The UK, US, France, Canada, and surrounding nations chipped in their support and aid in those first months. Even with the political divide among the population, the people came together to assist each other and start the long arduous process of rebuilding their nation. Today, you will still hear the adults talk about Hurricane David and how it affected them.

Historical Timeline

3000 BC The first people, Arawakan-speaking people called the Igneri, came from the Orinoco River in South America to settle on Dominica.

1000 AD The Kalinago (Carib) people journeyed by canoe from South America through the island chain and became the dominant group. They named the island *Wai'tukubuli*, which translates to "tall is her body."

1493 Christopher Columbus comes to the island on a Sunday and uncreatively gives it the name *Dominica*, meaning "Sunday Island."

1518 The first ship of African slaves was brought to the Americas, opening the door for tens of millions of Africans to be brought to the islands for the next three and a half centuries.

1627 The King of England gives the Earl of Carlisle rights over the Lesser Antilles islands, including Dominica. The steep forested terrain was more that they were willing to tackle, however, and the island was left alone for some time.

1635 France claims Dominica and French missionaries begin to arrive on the island.

1686 France and England sign a treaty giving the island neutrality and handing it over to the Kalinago.

1730 Kalinago are defeated and the population falls to only around 400.

1763 The Treaty of Paris, which ended the Seven Years' War, was signed and gave the British possession of Dominica. France challenges this until 1805. Estates begin to be established and slaves are brought to Dominica to work them.

1768 Britain establishes a Legislative Assembly in Dominica, and is the only white population on the island.

1776 Small piece of land in the northeast set aside for Caribs by the British.

1778 The French regain control of Dominica.

1783 Dominica is returned to Britain by the Treaty of Versailles.

1784 Maroon revolt reaches a climax and an assembly is formed to deal with it.

1831 Full political and social rights are given to free non-whites.

1833 Coffee constitutes a third of Dominica's exports.

1834 Slavery is abolished.

1838 Dominica forms a black-controlled legislature, the first and only one of its kind in the British West Indies.

1865 Britain changes the assembly to consist of one-half elected and one-half appointed members.

Historical Timeline

1898 Crown colony rule is established in Dominica.

1903 Official establishment of the Carib Territory.

1945 Universal adult suffrage introduced in Dominica and everyone over the age of 21 is allowed to vote.

1960 Britain grants Dominica self-government and a legislative council and chief minister are put in place.

1978 Dominica gains its independence with Patrick John as the prime minister.

1979 Hurricane David devastates the island.

1980 Dame Eugenia Charles replaces Patrick John as prime minister, making her the first female prime minister in the Caribbean. Another hurricane hits Dominica.

1981 Two coup attempts fail. Patrick John tried and acquitted.

1983 Dominica participates in the US invasion of Grenada

1985 Patrick John retried and is found guilty. He is sentenced to 12 years in prison.

1995 Edison James becomes elected prime minister. Eugenia Charles retires after 27 years in politics.

1999 Hurricane Lenny blows through, causing extensive damage.

2000 January- Rosie Douglas becomes prime minister in a close election. October- Douglas dies and is succeeded by Pierre Charles.

2001 Dominica suffers a financial crisis. Help from the International Monetary Fund is requested.

2004 Pierre Charles dies in office at age 46. Roosevelt Skerrit named the new prime minister. Dominica establishes diplomatic ties with China. Earthquake damages buildings in the north.

2005 *Pirates of the Caribbean 1 & 2* are filmed in Dominica, providing an economic boost. Skerrit wins the general election.

2007 Dominica strengthens ties with Venezuela. Hurricane Dean sweeps through Dominica, killing 99% of the banana crops, putting more stress on the island's economy.

2008 Carib chief Charles Williams tries to pass a legislative law that Kalinago (Carib) people can only marry each other for self-preservation.

2009 Skerrit wins another election but is challenged by the opposing party, stating election fraud.

Economy

Dominica's economy has never been particularly strong and is widely considered to be the most challenging of all of the Eastern Caribbean islands. Income and exports are heavily based on resources from its rich and fertile land. Throughout history, the agricultural focus has shifted from coffee, sugarcane, limes and vanilla to cocoa, coconut products and **bananas**, the last of which is still the agricultural mainstay of the island. From 1950 to 1992, Dominica had several decades of relative prosperity through banana cultivation. Under a contract between the British government and the fruit company Geest, bananas in the Caribbean were guaranteed a market in Britain. Dominica became dependent on this trade relationship for its economic survival and over the years banana production became the main source of employment and earnings for over a third of the population. In 1992, upon passage of the free trade agreement, Dominican banana prices were pitted against those of larger, more developed countries in Latin America, some of which had farms that were larger than the entire island of Dominica.

Economy at a Glance

GDP: US$364 million

Main Exports: bananas, soap, bay oil, vegetables, grapefruit, oranges

Main Imports: manufactured goods, machinery, food, chemicals

Main Trade Partners: United States, United Kingdom, Netherlands, Canada, and Eastern Caribbean nations

Since the free trade agreement, many farmers have abandoned their professions as it is no longer as profitable. Those who have stayed in the industry have had to be innovative and cater to a niche market in order to stay in business. They have done this through utilizing organic fair trade farming methods with help from The Fairtrade Foundation. Still, the banana industry is a vulnerable one and hurricanes can quickly wipe out the entire banana crop on the island. Farmers have worked to diversify their agricultural products to safeguard their earnings and many grow a mix of tropical fruits, spices, vegetables, coffee, and cut flowers.

In response to the dwindling banana and agricultural industry, Dominica has recently begun placing an emphasis on developing its **tourism** sector. Because the island's coasts are not lined with the characteristic white sand beaches that are the siren song of other Caribbean islands, tourism has been slow to develop. Using Costa Rica as its model, Dominica is working to put its gorgeous mountains, rainforests, waterfalls, hot springs and top-notch diving spots to work as it markets itself as an attractive eco-tourism destination. Over the past several years, eco-friendly hotels and businesses have been popping up. Local community tours that highlight the culture and natural features of individual villages have also just started to gain momentum. Cruise ship tourism has been on the increase but the revenue generated by the hundreds of thousands of day-trippers that file off of the ships each day pales in comparison to the revenue from stay-over tourists, of which there is still under 100,000 per year. Most locals will tell you that they don't want their island to become the developed and over-done typical Caribbean destination with chain hotels and golf courses (residents joke that the balls would just roll down the mountains). Dominicians would prefer to keep the development low-key and catered to those who come to hike, dive, and enjoy being in nature.

Dominica is said to have a "**barrel economy**" because of the large shipment of 55 gallon barrels that roll in every week, sent by the diaspora of Dominicans who moved overseas and continue to support their families still living on the island. Many are critical of this type of assistance because they say it hinders the economy from having any incentive to grow and create its own manufactured goods. Many people get their clothes, shoes, school supplies, electronics and even food from these barrels, which are cheap to send down from New York or Florida, where most Dominicans reside when they move to the U.S.

> There are many registered fishermen in Dominica, yet most use **fishing** as supplemental income and either farm or hold other jobs as well. Fish is caught and sold in the villages directly to consumers or sold to restaurants and hotels.

The **cottage industry** is still relatively healthy in Dominica and people make and sell everything from bush rum, hot sauce and jam to handmade soaps, crafts, packaged spices, and leather sandals. This type of production is the livelihood of many families on the island and is an important economical facet of communities. As you look for souvenirs to bring home as mementos and gifts, consider forgoing the "made in China" goods found at many souvenir shops for the handmade and locally grown items that can be found throughout the island.

Dominica is the recipient of **foreign aid** from several countries but it always seems to come at a price. Many more developed countries such as China, Taiwan, and Venezuela take advantage of Dominica's small size and lack of economic opportunity by offering money for small projects – playing fields, boardwalks, fisheries complex, and sports stadium – in exchange for their votes at international conventions. Or, in Venezuela's case, to build an oil refinery on the shores of Dominica. The government has been at odds with trying to maintain their reputation and dignity as the "Nature Island" and wanting to provide for their citizens. Recently Dominica made the decision to vote against Japan, a long-time funder of projects in Dominica, at the International Whaling Convention, dropping its support for the practice of commercial whaling. Greenpeace and conservationists applauded this effort and hope that Dominica continues to honor its commitment to maintain its precious environment.

Lifestyle

Dominicans generally live in either a one-story concrete block home, which keeps the house cool and protects against hurricanes, or small wooden homes, which are generally very small and better suited in the case of an earthquake. Roofs are either made from tin sheet metal or concrete. Homes are always furnished with care and attention, regardless of how poor a family may be and even if a homeowner only owns a small patch of dirt in front of their house, it will be swept clean almost daily as cleanliness is highly valued. The majority of newer concrete homes have running water and electricity and nearly all have indoor bathrooms. In the very rural areas where poverty is more widespread, people rely heavily on the rivers and fresh water springs for their bathing, clothes washing, and daily water supply. The rivers in these areas are often a busy place in the mornings as children are being scrubbed down to get them ready for school, clothes are being washed so that the kids have clean uniforms for the following day and in general the atmosphere is lively and amiable.

Unfortunately, indoor plumbing is lacking and pit latrines are the norm for many in these more rural areas.

The porch is an essential item of most homes as many people will spend their evenings outside where there is a cool breeze and a chance to exchange gossip with their neighbors. You'll find that anyone with electricity has a radio that is almost always on, as it is the main source of news and entertainment. If it can be afforded, television is a staple in many homes as well. Despite modern influences, family and community are still very important in Dominica and often the home becomes a meeting place for large gatherings of extended family and friends who share meals on weekends and holidays.

Most Dominicans work hard during the week either doing physical labor outside in the hot sun or if they are fortunate enough, in an office in Roseau. Add to that the task of hand washing clothes, towels, and sheets for an entire family, taking care of children and elderly relatives, working in their gardens, making every meal from scratch and keeping a house clean and you've got a nation full of busy people. But Dominicans don't let these tasks take a toll on them. Stress isn't welcome on this laid-back island and people know when it's time to relax. People are never too busy to stop for a chat or to exchange pleasantries.

Education

Primary school is free and compulsory in Dominica and just recently, in 2005, secondary school became universal as well. Before 2005, students had to test in to secondary school and those who didn't, were not able to attend. The formal school system was introduced by the Roman Catholic missionaries in the 1800s and was eventually handed over to the government to administer. However, until roads were built in the 1960s, only children who lived close to Roseau or a regional school could attend. Even today, with only a handful of secondary schools on the island, attendance rates are very sporadic in rural areas where there may not be a public bus, and many children have to hitchhike to school and can only make it if they are able to get a ride. The schools in Dominica have a distinct lack of books and resources and until recently, many school teachers had no formal training. Despite this struggle, the literacy rate in Dominica is high among youth and education is highly valued. However with the rise in education, there has been a correlating drop in the amount of youth interested in farming and agricultural work, which is cause for concern for many Dominicans.

The Dominica State College, which opened in 2002 and is located in Roseau, is the sole tertiary educational institution on island for Dominicans. They offer programs in agriculture, business, tourism, education, engineering, and health sciences. The government and other organizations hand out scholarships to study abroad for promising students and those who receive them generally attend the University of the West Indies, which is located in Trinidad, Barbados, and Jamaica, or they can receive scholarships to go to school in Cuba, Venezuela, the U.S., Canada, or the U.K. There is some controversy around this practice of sending the best and the brightest away, as many feel is it s a "brain drain" on the population since most who study abroad don't come back to live in Dominica after they attain their degree.

There are two overseas medical universities on the island: Ross University and All Saints University. Both are for-profit schools that offer degrees in medicine and are attended by mainly Americans. Both schools provide a very small amount of scholarships for Dominicans to attend.

Government & Politics

Dominica has a parliamentary democracy headed by an elected prime minister and president both of whom make up the executive branch. The prime minister is the head of parliament, which consists of a 32-member House of Assembly. Of those seats, 21 members are elected from single-seat constituencies and nine senators are appointed. Elections are held every five years.

There are 10 administrative parishes in Dominica and the Carib territory has its own chief and Carib council whose interests are represented by the Ministry of Carib Affairs in the government. There are elected village councils in 41 areas with a council chairperson as the head of each and they take care of village services, utilities and any local issues that may arise.

Dominica's main political parties are the Dominica Labour Party (DLP), which is currently in power and is considered to be left of center. They came into power in 2000 and are the considerable majority in the assembly. The only current opposition is the United Workers Party (UWP), a centralist political party, which was in power previously but now only holds three seats in the assembly.

> Roosevelt Skerrit is the current prime minister and was placed in power in 2004, after the death of Pierre Charles. Born in 1972, he is currently the youngest prime minister in the world and was reelected in 2009.

Population

The last census in 2005 placed the population of Dominica around 70,000. Dominica's population is actually on the decline, however, because many people immigrate to more developed countries if they get the chance, with a large number ending up in the British and U.S. Virgin Islands, Canada, the United States, and Britain. In fact, there are actually more Dominicans living outside of Dominica than in the country itself.

Language

ENGLISH (OR SOME VERSION OF IT)

So you wanted to travel in a country where you can speak the language and won't have to deal with misunderstandings and frustrating communication mishaps? You then get off the plane only to realize that "English" is a subjective term and that the fact that you have a shared language doesn't necessarily mean that you'll be in the clear when it comes to effective communication with the locals. Don't feel bad if you spend half of every conversation saying "huh?" (If it makes you feel better, they often won't understand you either.) The English that has evolved in Dominica is a mix of old British with some French influences and a *very* casual grammatical structure. Dominicans who are involved in the tourism industry will likely communicate with you very clearly and you should have no problem speaking with them. But once you get out in the rural areas and speak with people who don't usually encounter tourists, communication starts to break down.

Note that Dominicans don't usually pronounce the "th" sound and will replace it with a "d" or an "f." They will also frequently add "oui" (sounds like wee) or "nah" to the ends of their sentences as a yes or no, respectively. You'll also find that people can have an entire conversation using only the words "ok" and "alright." It's acceptable to say "ok" in nearly every situation, many times in multiples "ok, ok, ok, ok, ok." You will hear everyone being called "boy" as well, whether it be their friend, their child, their grandmother, or you.

DOMINICAN CREOLE

Many languages that were created in the last few centuries of human history and are spoken by only a handful of people are heading towards extinction. Dominican Creole, however, is thriving, a stark contrast to the days of British rule when it was forbidden to be spoken in schools and during official business. From special Creole radio programs, The World Creole Music Festival, to everyday gossip between friends, you'll find that all are performed best in Creole. The language itself, similar to Haitan and St. Lucian Creole, stems from the days of slavery. As slaves from Africa were brought to the island, their native dialects were suppressed and they had to quickly learn to communicate with their French, and later their British, slaveholders. Gradually, as a result, the language of Creole (or Kweyol) emerged, mixing French, English, and African vocabularies with an efficient grammatical structure and a melodious cadence. It has been an almost exclusively oral language until just recently when a small dictionary was made to document the language. In some villages, such as Grand Bay, Creole is the predominant language and you'll find people effortlessly switching between Creole and English throughout a conversation. Although English is the language used for business and in schools, Creole has a prevalent and important place in Dominican society.

Dominican-ism *Formal English*

How far you reaching? *How far are you going?*

You ok? or You alright? *How are you?*

I der oui, I safe, I propa, ok, alright, irie *I'm fine, thanks*

Boy de sun coming hot *It's hot today*

Free dollars *Three dollars*

Wha you sayin now boy *how are you?*

Go so *or* I going so *go there or I'm going there*

Ahwah *no way*

De rain going to fall *It's going to rain*

How you find de nature isle? *What do you think of Dominica?*

Have a lime *or* free up *hang out*

Come awhile *Come here for a second*

Jah *God*

Just now *Can mean any amount of time from now until a year from now*

Culture

PEOPLE

The people of Dominica are fiercely strong in their beliefs yet maintain a gentle spirit and old-world affability, evident in their warm greetings on rural roads and their forthrightness when it comes to sharing their opinions.

Dominicans share a powerful sense of national pride and it is important to them that you enjoy your stay. You can expect to be asked on more than one occasion how you are enjoying "The Nature Isle" and as you spend time traversing the island, you'll see that their friendliness is not just a show for tourists. Outside of the capital you'll find that greeting everyone you pass is a way of life. Just a simple "good day" will conjure up affectionate smiles and a welcoming demeanor among even the most austere appearing Dominicans.

Stress and hurriedness are looked down upon in Dominica and you won't find people rushing about in a state of anxiety like you might in the "developed world." This is not because they don't have anything to worry about. They are a long-suffering people who work hard and don't expect wealth or great rewards in return, but appreciate what they have: family, religion, and the land that gives them so much. Because Dominicans believe in living a stress-free life, you will hear a lot of laughter coming from their homes but you may also encounter loud debates and spirited disputes. To an outsider it may sound like a fight is about to break out, however it nearly always ends in a good joke and a lot of laughter. You will notice that even though the lifestyle of Dominicans feels very relaxed and liaise-faire it is intertwined with a lot of British formalities, especially when dealing with government officials or offices.

Dominicans are a religious bunch and with over 80% of the population in attendance at the Roman Catholic churches on Sundays. The people adhere (or attempt to adhere) to those conservative, traditional values. They rely on religion to make sense of their lives and struggles, and their faith gives them hope and a strong sense of purpose in life. Religion seeps into every nook and cranny of the daily lives of Dominicans and Sundays are a sacred day in which stores don't open and buses don't run so that everyone can spend the day in church and with family. When making plans with Dominicans you'll often hear them end with "I'll see you there, God willing."

Despite their hardships, Dominica was recently rated the fourth happiest country in the world according to the Happy Planet Index. The lack of wars and violence, an incredibly low crime rate, a strong sense of purpose through their religion, a beautiful environment, strong family ties, and healthy

Creole Phrases

How are you? *Sa ka fet*

I'm fine *Mwen la*

Good day *Bon jou*

Good afternoon *Bon apwe midi*

Good evening *Bon swa*

Please *Su ple*

Thank you *Mesi*

I want a Kubuli *Mon vley yon Kubuli*

What's your name? *Sa ki non'w*

My name is... *Non mwen sé...*

How much? *Kouma pou sa?*

Background

food and water give way to a long and happy life expectancy.

Ethnicity Breakdown

According to the 2001 census, 87 percent of Dominica's population are descendants of enslaved Africans, brought over in the 1700s by colonial planters from France and England. Roughly three percent, or around 3,500 people, are indigenous Kalinago (or Carib). Dominica is the only country in the world with a reservation for the indigenous population of the Caribbean islands. About nine percent of the population has a mixed heritage and less than one percent of the population is white.

MYTHS AND TABOOS

As West African cultures that the slaves brought with them collided with the French Creole culture of the West Indies, myths and superstitions became intertwined. This resulted in some very strong beliefs about magic and spirits that to outsiders may sound absurd or impossible, but to those who have spent their lives on the island, they are very much alive and real. The stories change from village to village but here is a general idea of what you're dealing with, spirit-wise, in Dominica.

The **soukouyan** is a female witch that can leave her skin and fly through the sky as a fireball, attacking people by taking their blood in their sleep. There are several ways to tell if someone is a soukouyan, one of which is to place a cross made from grass on the steps of a church when the soukouyon is inside. It will be impossible for her to leave the church if the cross is there. If you suspect someone is a soukouyon you must never call them out on it or they will surely attack you next. To avoid being taken by the soukouyon, you can carry garlic with you to act as a repellant. Also avoid leaving hair or nail clippings around as they can be taken and used to place a curse on you.

Jumbies are evil spirits that live in the forest and will attack those that stay in the forest after dark. You'll know they're coming by their terrible smell but they can be repelled rather easily by cursing them or their mother. To protect yourself from the jumbies, wear your shirt backwards, place soil on your head, or take off your shoes and point them backwards while sitting on them. Those who are left-handed are automatically protected.

The **lajablesse** is similar in that it is an evil creature that lives in the forest but this spirit sometimes has animal hooves and will steal people and take them into the forest for days until they go mad. The **loogawoo** can turn themselves into animals, or part animals, to trick people. They won't pass you on their left, which is how you can identify them. When a loogawoo dies, it rains all day.

An **obeah**, a modern day shaman or herbalist, can be called upon to treat mysterious ailments, remove curses, or cast spells when needed and can treat those who are afflicted by the above mentioned spirits.

SPORTS

Go to any village playing field in the evenings or on the weekends and you'll see one of three sports being played: soccer (or football to non-Americans), cricket (thanks to the British colonizers), or rounders (a woman's game that is a hybrid of baseball, dodge ball, and cricket). Volleyball and basketball are popular as well but not many villages have the facilities to play.

The new Windsor Park Stadium, opened in Roseau in 2007 with funding from China, can hold up to 12,000 people, making it a viable venue for international sporting events. Admission is reasonable and watching a game makes for a nice evening out in Roseau.

Dominica has a national football team that unfortunately doesn't do well in competition, nor does the Windward Islands Cricket Team, in which Dominica has representation. But that by no means diminishes Dominica's spirit to continue playing. You'll find that little boys can construct a cricket game out of anything, using sticks for wickets and fruit for balls. Cricket is played in the middle of the road if necessary and pick-up games are played almost daily in most villages.

ARTS

Music

Ride in a local bus long enough and you'll get a feel for the popular musical culture of the island. Reggae, bouyon, and calypso are all staples as well as other pan-Caribbean styles such as *soca*, an upbeat dance rhythm that mixes synthesizers, strong percussion, and the melody of Calypso. *Zouk*, a funk and salsa blend with African rhythms, is also popular. For generations, music has been a fundamental component of Caribbean culture and Dominica has produced its share of talented musicians. Michele Henderson, Ophelia Marie, The Swinging Stars, Nasio Fontaine, and Midnight Groovers have all gained international recognition and have cds available for purchase at music stores in Roseau.

Bouyon music, which to the untrained ear can sound like high-speed techno

---

Rastafarians in Dominica

The first Rastafarians to appear in Dominica came sometime in the early 1970s, having been influenced by the growing movement in Jamaica and the music of Bob Marley. This was a turbulent period for Dominica as it was the end of British rule and people were just beginning to be exposed to the Black Power movement happening in the United States. Young people found meaning in the Rastafarian movement, which believed Haile Selassie, a former Ethiopian leader and descendant of King Solomon, was the Jesus incarnate. The followers moved deep into the forested interior and lived solely off the land, ascribing to an all-natural lifestyle. Their diet, called Ital, is almost entirely vegan, organic, and without salt or processed ingredients. Most grow their hair into dreadlocks in accordance with verses of the Old Testament (Leviticus 21:5) and use cannabis (marijuana), which is seen as a sacrament and is used to clean the body and soul; bringing one to a higher level of consciousness and thereby closer to Jah (God).

During this time, some "Dreads," as they were called, adopted a militant ideology and committed acts of violence against the white colonizers. This conflict erupted in a controversial law being passed called the "Dread Act" which gave police the power to arrest anyone associated with the Dread Society and the license to shoot on sight those who were part of the Rastafarian movement. After untold human rights violations, the act was condemned for good in 1982. Over time, the Rastafarians have been more widely accepted in Dominican culture. To this day many Rastas live in the forested hills of Dominica, living off of the land.

music accompanied by whistles and loud repetitive singing, is a Dominican phenomenon and a favorite genre among Dominica's youth. Popular Bouyon bands like
WCK and Triple Kay combine traditional Dominican styles of music such as
cadencelypso, jing ping, zouk, soca, and traditional drumming, with modern
instruments and fresh beats. Dominicans listening often can't help but rise into
joyful spirited excitement, marching in place to the beats wherever they may be – on
the street, in their homes, or at a shop. Don't miss a chance to "jump up" at a concert,
festival, or street party with the locals when a bouyon band comes to town.

Originating in Trinidad, most Caribbean islands celebrate their freedom of
speech through **calypso** music, expressing opinions about politics, currents events,
and daily life. Every year around Carnival time, Dominica names a calypso king for
the calypso song of the year. With such titles as "Real Pirates of the Caribbean,"
"Gallon Bottle Model," and "Man Eating Everything" it's worth listening to the
humorous lyrical interpretations calypsonians have of corruption in the government
and Caribbean lifestyle, among other issues.

Popular Jamaican **riddim** tracks always find their way down to Dominica.
Riddims consist of a basic drum pattern and bass line, while various singers add
their own voices, lyrics and main melody. During public activities and events, you
may hear local musicians trying their own skills with popular riddims. You'll know
you're listening to a riddim when it sounds like the same track playing over and over
and over again.

Many of these current musical trends find their roots in traditional **folk** music,
which originated in the days of slavery. Slaves would fashion instruments out of any
available materials and songs were created for every occasion from work to festivals
to dance rhythms. Many of these instruments are still in use today, played in
traditional *jing-ping* bands and during street jump-ups. You'll find the *la peau cabrit*,
a goat skin drum, as the staple instrument that keeps the beat and is often accompanied by the rhythmic *shak-shak*, a tin rattle or scraper, a long horn called the
boumboum, and the occasional accordion, triangle or tambourine accompaniment.

A great time to hear local music at it's best is during Independence season in late
October and early November when traditional bands compete and musical events,
culminating in the annual three-day **World Creole Music Festival**, are in abundance. For dates and information go to www.wcmfdominica.com.

Dance

Dominica's traditional dance is a direct reflection of the mélange of cultures that
have historically influenced the islands customs. The *bélé*, one of the oldest Creole
dances in existence, has its roots in African fertility dance. It's an energetic exchange
between a male and female dancer engaging in a courtship ritual with a single drum
that keeps the beat and is the focus of the stage. The dancers leap, bounce and parade
wildly to the rhythm as the lead vocalist calls out in French Creole and a choir
responds, resulting in an utterly captivating performance.

The **quadrille** is a popular dance that you'll find in national competitions during
Independence season. It is a spin off of a very formal French square dance and is
composed of four couples who rotate positions and if performed to completion, can
end up being incredibly long. A traditional jing ping band keeps the beat as the
poised dancers display refined sophistication and grace. The **lancer** is the British

version of the quadrille and the *mazook*, also called Heel and Toe, is the Caribbean evolution of polka and is common during competition time as well.

Contemporary Art

There are many talented contemporary artists living and working in Dominica today that use the beautiful scenery and the local people and culture as their muse. **Earl Etienne** is probably the most well-known and distinguished Domi-

For a list of art galleries in Roseau, see page 118.

nican-born artist on the island. His work incorporates bright landscapes with unique scenes from daily life that really encapsulate the culture of the island. His work can be seen at the Art Asylum Gallery in Jimmit (Tel: 767 449-2484) and online at http://avirtualdominica.com/earletienne.

Ellingworth Moses is another of Dominica's favorite artists. Born in the southeastern village of Petite Savanne, he studied under Etienne but has developed his own unique style of vivid textural landscapes. His gallery is located at 27 King George V Street in Roseau (Tel: 767 440-4396).

There are several European artists that have settled in Dominica and find their inspiration in Dominica's landscape and people. **Marie Frederick** is a French-born artist who lives and works in the village of Borne. You can see her and her husband's work at **Indigo Gallery**, a breathtakingly beautiful tree house and that showcases her bright expressive island-inspired paintings. Displayed alongside them are her husband's, a gentleman named Clem, unique sculptural pieces created out of local materials. You can see her work online at http://indigo.wetpaint.com, or call 767-445-3486 to arrange a time to stop by the gallery.

Yoriko Kondo hails from Japan and her fresh perspectives on Dominica's land and people have resulted in an East meets West Indies series of paintings depicting landscapes, unique architecture and even a Kubuli beer series. Her paintings are very captivating with an ethereal quality that captures the essence of the island. She can be contacted at 767-445-6912 to arrange a viewing.

Swedish artist, **Annika Wide**, specializes in photo-realism of island scenery. She lives and works in the northern village of Savanne Paille and can be contacted at 767-445-3787.

Louis Desire, a Haitan born wood sculptor, has a studio and classroom at the Old Mill Cultural Center in Canefield where he displays his beautiful figurative sculptures. Desire uses white cedar and mahogany to create expressive pieces and functional items. You can reach him at 767-245-4574.

Orlando Cuffy studied under Desire and his hardwood sculptures are very much a reflection of Desire's style. He sometimes uses a very unique wood called blue mahaut that is found in the Dominican rainforest and is a lovely blue-green and yellow color, which makes for a distinctive one-of-a-kind piece. Cuffy can be contacted at 767-425-5866.

Internationally acclaimed artist and sculptor, **Roger Burnett**, left his home in England in 1974 to travel and work around the Caribbean. He eventually set up shop in Dominica. His paintings, books, and realistic figurative bronze sculpture can be seen at the Antrim Sculptural Gardens (pg 150).

LITERATURE

Dominica's best-known and loved literary figure is **Jean Rhys**, author of the 1966 novel "*Wide Sargasso Sea*," which was the winner of several literary awards. The novel, which was inspired by her childhood in Dominica, is meant to be a prequel to Charlotte Bronte's 1847 novel, *Jane Eyre*. The theme of the novel draws on her experiences feeling neither part of the white European society nor the black creole society. Born in Roseau in 1890, she was the daughter of Welsh doctor and a Creole Scottish mother. Rhys lived in Roseau and on Grand Bay's Geneva Estate until the age of 16, when she was sent to school in England where she lived the remainder of her life. She is also the author of the lesser known "*Tales of the Wide Caribbean*," a collection of short stories inspired by her life in Dominica. It was published in 1985, six years after her death.

Phyllis Shand Allfrey (1907-1986), author of "*The Orchid House*" was deeply involved in Dominica her entire life. Born in Roseau, she was sent abroad to the United States and later to England to attend school. Her novel is somewhat autobiographical in that it tells the story of three daughters of a white family that had fallen from wealth and led a penniless life as told by through the eyes of their black nurse,

---

Centenarians: Life after age 100

Looking for the fountain of youth? Well Dominica may just be the place to find it. When getting to know Dominicans, their age is always surprising. People who appear to be not a day older than 29 are actually 50, and 80 year olds easily pass for someone half their age. Dominican's life expectancy is nearly 15 years longer than that of the United States, not to mention they have one of the highest concentrations of people living past age 100 in the world.

So what is their secret? It's attributed to lifestyle. Growing up in Dominica, before there was any type of real development, people worked hard, walked over steep mountains to get anywhere they needed to go, ate fresh and organic fruits and vegetables, drank clean water, and lived a stress-free life infused with a sense of purpose from their families and religious background. These are all keys to longevity according to Dan Buettner, researcher and author of the book "*Blue Zones*" in which he researches other places in the world like Dominica.

In 2003, Dominica held claim to the oldest living person on earth, Elizabeth "Ma Pampo" Israel who died at the age of 128. Unfortunately, because she was the daughter of slaves there was no official record of her birth and therefore was not accepted by the Guinness Book of World Records. I recently spoke to a centenarian living in Grand Bay who was 104 years old. When asked what her secret was she claimed "family, a bit of rum each day, and a healthy dose of gossip." Ma Pampo on the other hand, attributed it to bush tea and lots of dumplings.

Scientists, however, have speculated that Dominica may not keep this distinction for long. As more processed imported food is introduced and people prefer to take a bus rather than walk, some of the essential factors in the longevity equation have been removed. As a result, many Dominicans may be relegated to those ranks of those of us expected to live, well only an average life

Lally. It is viewed as a classic of Caribbean literature and was made into a movie in England in 1991. She returned to Dominica in 1954 and founded Dominica's first political party the Dominica Labour Party in 1955. She was passionate about grassroots activism and went on to be made a member of the parliament of the Federation of the West Indies, taught at the Wesley High School, became editor of the Dominica Herald and the Dominica Star newspapers and later founded the Dominica Freedom Party in 1968.

Although she was born in Antigua, **Jamaica Kincaid**'s "*Autobiography of My Mother*" takes place in Dominica and is a story about the life of a young woman of Carib, African, and Scottish origin. The book touches on the themes of mothers and daughters, sexuality and power, and the legacy of colonialism in places like Dominica.

"*Rain on a Tin Roof*," written by Dominican-born **Gabriel J. Christian** is a delightful collection of short stories about his childhood in the village of Goodwill. His stories paint a colorful picture of life on the islands that touch on themes of family, rural life, superstition, island politics, romance and exile. He also co-authored "*In Search of Eden*" with **Irving Andre**, a collection of essays about the history of Dominica.

Finally, one can't talk about Dominican literature without mentioning **Lennox Honychurch**, Dominica's own historian, artist, conservationist, writer and poet who has chronicled Dominica's history in fascinating detail in "*The Dominica Story: A History of the Island.*" Born in Portsmouth in 1952, he received his Doctorate of Anthropology at Oxford and has dedicated his life to Dominica's heritage. You'll find his artwork in many of his murals around the island, his conservation work at Ft. Shirley in the Cabrits National Park and at The Dominica Museum, at which he is the curator. He is a staff tutor at the University of the West Indies, served as a member of the House of Assembly, and has published a long list of books about the island, its history, people, culture, and even its cuisine, most of which can be found at local bookstores in Dominica.

A Cutlass Carrying Culture

The term "cutlass" often conjures up images of no-good pirates brandishing a length of shiny steel as long as a sword in order to threaten their enemy. In Dominica, however, the term cutlass refers to an inventive and valuable tool, which others may refer to as a machete. Seeing men and women walking around with a cutlass is an everyday occurrence in Dominica as these tools are needed for tasks as far ranging as tending garden and clearing brush, to opening coconuts or killing pesky centipedes. Most households have at least one cutlass, if not more, and most are adept at using them. Unsuspecting tourists can be caught off guard when they jump into the back of a truck to hitch a ride only to be surrounded by ten cutlass-carrying men. But after a friendly greeting, one will find that these peaceful farmers have no intention of using their cutlass for anything other than chopping bananas off the tree or digging up provisions.

TRADITIONAL DRESS

Around Independence time, you will notice an explosion of colorful madras fabric, the traditional pattern, everywhere you look. This bright, multicolored checked fabric originated in India and became popular when the French and British merchant ships began trading madras in the 18th century and eventually it made its way to the Caribbean. When slaves gained their freedom, the women began emulating the European styles of dress and the white floor length skirts with a madras apron, and white ruffled blouse became the norm and eventually the traditional dress for women. The head wrap is an essential part of the outfit and the elaborate way in which it was wrapped was an indicator to signify if a woman was single, engaged, married, or looking. The men traditionally wear black pants, a white shirt and a red sash and occasionally a madras tie or vest.

ARCHITECTURE

Dominica is one of the only islands in the Caribbean to maintain much of its original tropical colonial architecture that now serve as a reminder of Dominica's history. Because Dominica hasn't seen the intense development of most islands in the Caribbean, the historic buildings have remained much they same as they were originally, without being dolled up for tourists. While European colonizers may have enjoyed traveling, they wanted to bring the comforts and familiarity of home with them. French and British designs were recreated using local materials and adding the necessary flourishes that would increase airflow and withstand the heat, humidity, and storms, creating a Creole architecture that became a distinctive feature of that time period.

Walking through Roseau, one can see the influence of the British and French in the wooden homes with large verandas and intricate fretwork, having withstood hurricanes and fire. The city's history is on display in a very authentic way.

As you walk through Roseau take note of the buildings that offer a glimpse into the past. They can be spotted by these distinguishing features:

Wooden Structures Original buildings were made with local hardwood that could hold up against high winds and termites. Some of the strongest are braced together with wooden pegs and mortise and tenon joints.

Verandahs Many verandahs in Roseau are placed on the second story level, as they provided a nice breeze, protection from the sun, and a great spot for people watching.

Jalousie Windows Jalousies are slats built into windows and doors that are usually moveable and allow residents to control the amount of light and air that come in. Many modern buildings in Dominica still use this feature.

Fretwork These intricate designs built into walls and railings are a beautiful touch and also a key feature that provided privacy and enhanced airflow simultaneously.

Hurricane Shutters With the frequency of storms and hurricanes and lack of a sophisticated forecasting system it was important to be able to batten down the house quickly. These sturdy shutters offered strong protection against flying debris and strong winds.

Dormers A dormer is a structural element that protrudes out of a sloping roof and looks a bit like a "mini roof" sitting on top of a building. These provided ventilation and a way for the warm air that would rise to escape.

Hipped Roof Many of the old roofs in Dominica are built at an angle to deflect the force of strong winds. And even sturdier are the half-hipped roofs which only angle down half-way and are joined to the wall.

Eventually this delicate style was replaced with concrete, which is much stronger and more likely to withstand a hurricane. Today, heavy looking concrete block is the most common type of building you'll encounter in any new development.

Geography

Dominica covers almost 290 square miles, which makes it a little smaller than New York City but a little bigger than Chicago. The Nature Isle is home to nine potentially active volcanoes, giving it the distinction of having the highest concentration of volcanoes in the world. It lies between two tectonic plates that collided about 26 million years ago, squeezing up a little piece of land that we now know as Dominica. These plates are still active and whenever they decide to get frisky, Dominica is subjected to earthquakes, which are usually small and insignificant although not always.

> Dominica was named *Waitukubuli* by its original inhabitants, which translates to "tall is her body" and gives name to the mountainous peaks that distinguishes Dominica as the most rugged island in the Lesser Antilles.

The volcanoes in Dominica are not only fun to climb and provide fantastic scenery, but they also add an interesting dimension to the activities available to tourists. Because the hot molten rock underneath needs to release its heat and steam in order to remain underground, you'll find the world's second largest boiling lake in the interior, hot and cold sulphur springs, geothermal bubbles in the waters off the west coast, a sunken caldera just off of the southwest coast and steaming fumaroles in the Valley of Desolation.

These tall mountains are densely covered with rainforest, which is the main type of vegetation on the island, followed by dry scrub woodland that can be found at lower elevations, especially on the west coast. Dominica loves to boast that is has 365 rivers, one for every day of the year. Although many of these should technically be called creeks, the larger ones are some of the most beautiful you'll find in the world and are extremely clean and clear.

Dominica isn't outlined in white sand as many Caribbean islands love to boast. Rather, much of its coastline is comprised of sheer cliffs that drop straight into the sea. The beaches it does have range from black volcanic sand to rough rocks and pebbles to light golden sand. And as storms come and go, beaches can be transformed from one to the other rather quickly. The best area for swimming is in the calm and placid Caribbean Sea on the west coast as the Atlantic can have strong undercurrents and rough waves.

Hurricanes are always a threat to this small-unprotected island but since the last big one blew through in 1979, Dominica has been fortunate to only have had small tropical storms and low level hurricanes, which haven't left much damage. Hurricane season runs through the late summer and early fall and when visiting during this time, you'll want to stay abreast of the news to be sure you are prepared for storms and rough seas should they occur.

ENVIRONMENTAL ISSUES

Dominicans love their native land and hold a deep respect for all that it provides. However, the knowledge for how to keep it pristine is severely lacking and environmental awareness campaigns are still in their infancy. Littering is currently the main environmental issue in Dominica. Throughout history, as people lived solely off the land with little to no imported goods, it was common practice to throw refuse onto the ground to decompose with no ill effects on their environment as most of that refuse was comprised of fruit and vegetable waste. Yet as Dominica has become more developed and people turn to soda and candy over local produce, the resulting litter is subtly damaging their precious rivers and coastlines.

There has been no education around the negative effects of this kind of littering, as most people assume it will just be washed into the sea and "go away" and many are simply not aware that it could be bad for the land and water they rely upon. Within the past few years there has been a noticeable push to raise awareness about the effects of littering and a few signs have been posted to bring attention to the issue. That said, there is still a serious lack of waste management and many people have to resort to burning their trash.

Venezuela has recently pressured Dominica into developing an oil refinery in exchange for financial assistance. Although the deal was never signed, they did agree to place on the island a holdinging tank for oil, which is now situated on the west coast. As Dominica strives to keep its image as the "Nature Island" it has struggled with the complex issue of developing its economy while keeping the island in its natural state.

Parks and Protected Areas

Located within its 290 square miles, Dominica holds claim to three national parks and several natural protected areas, with two-thirds of the island still covered in original rainforest. The Morne Trois Piton National Park was the first UNESCO World Heritage Site to be established in the Caribbean. Within its borders are multiple waterfalls, peaks, rivers, freshwater lakes, hot springs, fumaroles, and the world's second largest boiling lake. Other national parks include the Cabrits National Park, which is home to an 18th century garrison, and Morne Diablotin National Park, that houses Dominica's highest peak. Both of these are located in the north. The Central Forest Reserve covers over 1,000 acres and the Northern Forest Reserve covers over 13,500 acres and includes the Syndicate Parrot Reserve, which makes up 200 of those acres.

Another important protected area is the Soufrière/Scotts Head Marine Reserve located just off of the southwest coast. This is a hot spot for divers and snorkelers who wish to engage with some of the islands precious marine life.

The parks and forest reserves are well maintained by an enthusiastic group of conservationists at the **Dominica Forestry and Wildlife Division**. They are responsible for the regulatory measures of the parks and reserves and also provide books, pamphlets, and educational materials for those interested in learning more about the flora and fauna of the island. They can be found on Bath Road just north of the Botanical Gardens or can be reached at Tel: 767-266 3817 or forestry@cwdom.dm. Their website is www.avirtualdominica.com/forestry.

Wildlife

Dominica's rainforests are rich with an astounding variety of flowers, trees, lizards, birds, and butterflies. But as is typical of many small isolated islands, the number of mammals is relatively small. Many of Dominica's wildlife species came from South America and the floodwaters of the Orinoco River via strong winds and ocean currents. Others were carried by birds or placed there by man either unintentionally or, as is the case with many of the fruit trees, with the aim to cultivate and harvest. From whale watching off the coast to parrot watching on the Syndicate Trail or visiting a local farm on a community tour, the opportunities that exist to witness and interact with some of Dominica's most treasured residents is abundant.

BIRDS

There are around 170 species of birds on Dominica with the rulers of the forest being the parrots. There are two species of parrots that are endemic to Dominica: the Sisserou (*Amazona Imperialis*) and the Jacko (*Amazona arausiaca*). The **Sisserou** is the national bird and can be found in the center of Dominica's flag. It is also highly endangered and harder to sight as it is very secretive and prefers to live at higher elevations, usually over 3,000 ft. The **Jacko** is more able to tolerate human activity and although it prefers the northern rainforest region, its territory is spreading and has even been sighted all the way down by the sea. Both types of parrots have suffered a decline in population due to hurricanes damaging their habitats as well as hunting and poaching by humans. Education, monitoring, habitat protection and public awareness have brought them back to some extent. Since both are protected species, heavy fines are in place for any person that is caught with one. Breeding season, from February to August, is the best time to spot them as they are much more active and willing to come down to lower elevations. You can see both species in captivity at the Parrot Sanctuary in the Botanical Gardens in Roseau.

Also in abundance are **hummingbirds**, which can be seen darting from flower to flower, glowing with greens, blues, and purples. Nature's authority figure, David Attenborough, came to Dominica to highlight one of the island's endemic hummingbirds, the Purple Throated Carib, for the BBC's "Life" series.

Magnificent **freshwater** and **coastal birds** are in abundance in Dominica as well. The incredible red-necked frigate bird can be found frequenting the inland rivers along with the handsome kingfisher, elegant heron, and the striking white egret. If you head to the seashores you'll easily sight pelicans, seahawks, cormorants, boobies, storm-petrels, sand pipers and tropicbirds. When you are inland listen for the mournful song of the mountain whistler and keep an eye out for the hawks, doves, tremblers, warblers, bananaquits and bullfinch.

Background

Saving the Whales

Dominica has long been considered the "whale watching capital of the Caribbean" because its deep waters just off shore allow for whales to be seen year round. But the country recently found itself in the middle of an international dispute over the practice of commercial whaling. Japan has been pushing for years to legalize commercial whaling and has offered aid to small developing countries if they agree to vote along with them at the International Whaling Commission (IWC) annual meetings. For years Dominica was a staunch ally of Japan and, in return, Japan funded small projects like the building of a fisheries complex. But in 2008, Dominica announced that it would no longer support the whale killing by the Japanese government at the IWC. So far, Dominica is the only country in the Eastern Caribbean that does not back Japan as it strives to put its long-term future ahead of the short-term benefits of foreign assisted projects. You can learn more about this issue from the award winning documentary film, "The Cove."

Spotlight on Whales by Shane Gero

About one third of the world's whales, dolphins and porpoises are found in the Wider Caribbean. With the exception of the humpback whale, which migrates between feeding off North America in the summers and the Caribbean during breeding season (February through April), most of the commonly sighted species can be found year-round in the waters off Dominica. Such species include the pan-tropical spotted dolphin, the bottlenose dolphin, and short-finned pilot whale. But you never know when you might spot one of the rare or endangered species, like the pygmy killer whale or the Cuvier's beaked whale. What makes Dominica unique is the opportunity to observe the largest of all the toothed whales, and star of Herman Melville's Moby Dick, the sperm whale. Typically an animal which lives far from shore in waters over 1,000 meters deep, the shape of the volcanic islands in the Caribbean and the basin on the west coast of Dominica allows for the proper living conditions for sperm whales easily within the reaches of a day trip.

The sperm whale is truly an animal of extremes. They are the longest and deepest divers of marine animals, the most sexually dimorphic (males can be one and a half times longer and twice as heavy as females reaching 18 meters and 60 metric tons), they have the most powerful natural sonar system, and they have the longest intestine and the largest brain on the planet! They also have a complex social life in which the females and their young live together in small family units that stay in tropical waters year-round. The mature males, however, live alone and can be found all the way up to the pack ice at both the north and south poles.

A research group from Dalhousie University in Canada, led by Shane Gero, has been working off Dominica since 2005 and has identified over 20 different families in the area, with an average of seven animals in a family. Adult females share the responsibility of caring for the young in the family by babysitting each others' calves while mothers make dives over 1,200 meters in search of squid. Sperm whales eat almost exclusively squid which they find using the sonar system located in their nose. (In fact, sperm whales can remove as much squid from the ocean in a year as all of the human fisheries worldwide combined.) Although a given family may only be around the island for a few weeks, sperm whales can be found off of Dominica year-round.

The Caribbean population is small (estimated around 225 animals) and isolated from other sperm whales found in the Gulf of Mexico and the rest of the North Atlantic.

From a conservation standpoint, the Caribbean is still an area of concern. Major whaling nations have political influence over the small island nations in terms of international conventions on whaling. Certain islands have begun to ratify international conservation treaties, but Dominica is lagging behind its neighbours in that regard. In Dominica, the whales have no formal legislative protection and the whale watching industry is, at the time of publication, still unregulated. Some whaling continues in the Caribbean region on the order of tens of animals a year, but it is mainly small dolphins and primarily for food.

Whale Research with Shane

"Shane, we have whales!" It's early. 5:15am. But we've been following them all night and even though I just got to bed at 4am after my two hour night watch, I'm out of bed. Most of the crew is still asleep. I put the kettle on and head up on deck. Hal, my supervisor who was the first to track wild sperm whales over 30 years ago, asks, "Who is it?" It's "Pinchy" and her calf, "Tweak." She is a good mom. "Tweak" is her second calf since we started the study in 2005. When Pinchy dives, she lifts her tail flukes into the air and we take a picture to identify her by the marks on the trailing edge. For most animals, you'd need to wait to see the flukes to know who they are, but I have spent so much time with this family, hundreds of hours, that I can just tell who they are when they are milling about at the surface. When Pinchy disappears, we move the boat up and check for anything she might have left behind in the calm spot of water, known as the "flukeprint." We are looking for skin to use for genetics or fecal matter, which will tell us what she has been eating. We record her as she descends into the darkness of the deep. At first, there is no sign of her, but three minutes after she dives she calls; perhaps to Tweak to say "I'll be right back" or to another member of the unit to ask them to babysit Tweak while she is down. Then the echolocation starts. She is making loud clicks with the most powerful natural sonar system on the planet, at first to find the bottom for navigation then to search for squid. Tweak stays at the surface. He is still too young to dive deeply to feed like her mother. Eventually, he makes a shallow dive without lifting his tail. He'll be gone for about 20 minutes, so there is time for tea and breakfast.

Over the last seven years it has been a privilege to live among the sperm whales in Dominica. Spending my days watching and learning from these animals and passing the nights on the sailboat tracking the families by listening to their echolocation clicks in order to be with them in the morning. It has really been the first time that anyone has come to know these leviathans from the deep as individuals with personalities, as brothers and sisters or as mothers and babysitters, and as a community of families each with their own ways of doing things, their own dialects, their own cultures. Sperm whales are a lot like us and their family lives are much like our own, but we still known very little about these enormous creatures. In fact, there is really no place on the planet that we know less about than the deep ocean. We have put a man on the moon and a robot on mars, but the part of the ocean in which the sperm whales have made their home is still mostly a mystery and Pinchy and Tweak are a small part of unlocking this enigma. Actually, we named Tweak's cousin just that, Enigma.

MAMMALS

There are only two noteworthy furry four-legged creatures that live in Dominica's rainforest: the agouti and the manicou. The **agouti** looks rather like a large guinea pig with long legs, brown fur and little pink ears. It is an herbivore, living underground, and uses its speed to its advantage when running from predators.

The **manicou** is a type of opossum that only comes out at night. It lives in a tree and is almost completely blind during the day.

You'll likely never see one, but there are **wild pigs** that run around the interior of the rainforest. These were popular game for the escaped slaves who set up camps deep in the bush.

There are 12 species of bats in Dominica and you'll see many of them swooping down around rivers at dawn and dusk, helping us out by eating the pesky flies and mosquitoes.

REPTILES AND AMPHIBIANS

Regardless of where you stay in Dominica, you'll no doubt be welcomed by the intrusion of **lizards**. Some are cute and fun to watch, like the zandoli, which is endemic to Dominica and has a brightly colored throat fan that males will sometimes display. Others, like the white geckos (locally called *mabouyas* which is the Carib name for evil spirits) are less appealing and can often be heard making a deep cackling sound. Larger lizards will likely keep their distance, such as the ground lizard, called the *abóló*, which can be identified by its blue spots, and the elusive **iguanas**, which roam along many parts of the island but can most certainly be found along the Indian River.

There are a few species of **snakes** on Dominica however none are poisonous. The one that strikes fear in most people is the boa constrictor (locally called the *tete chien*), which can be anywhere from four to ten feet long. These snakes are actually harmless and nothing for humans to worry about.

There are many types of frogs in Dominica that range from tiny colorful tree frogs to the large and endangered endemic **mountain chicken**, also known as the *crapaud*, which is in fact a very large edible frog that has no relation to a chicken. A fungus infected the mountain chicken population and killed nearly 70% of the frogs between 2002 and 2004. Measures are currently being taken to revive the population. At this time it is illegal to hunt these frogs so if you see them on a menu, please do your part and refrain from ordering them.

MARINE LIFE

With an abundance of hard and soft **coral**, good water visibility, and relatively large populations of rare and unusual marine life, Dominica has become a favorite spot in the Caribbean for divers. In many dive locations you'll encounter hawksbill and green **sea turtles**, eels, parrotfish, squid, angelfish, flying gurnards, trumpet fish, and puffers. If you are really lucky you'll see the mysterious frogfish, seahorse, stingray, octopus, lobster, or a nursery shark.

If you are in the right spot at the right time you may even hear the clicking sounds of **dolphins** or hums of **whales** in nearby waters.

FLORA

With over 1,000 species of flowering plants, 74 species of orchids, and 200 species of ferns, it's clear that Dominica's rainforest is thriving. For being such a small island, there is quite a wide array of **microclimates**. From the heights of the mountains that drip with moss in the windy cloud covered elfin woodland, through the fertile rainforest, to the swamps, grasslands, and dry scrub covered coasts, each habitat has its own unique plants, wildlife and special features.

Where you find people, you'll find **fruit trees** and it is fun to learn and discover where your food comes from while exploring the island. In one garden or patch of land you can typcially find enough fruit to supply an entire grocery store. Depending on the season you'll likely encounter trees full of mangos, guavas, oranges, grapefruits, lemons, limes, cherries, passion fruit, papaya, star fruit, avocado, and lesser-known fruits like the sweetsop, soursop, custard apple and tamarind. You may also see nut and spice trees like the cashew, almond, coffee, cocoa, cinnamon, and nutmeg trees as well as the rare vanilla vines. A great place to discover the many plants, flowers and herbs of the island and their traditional uses is Papillote Gardens (pg 133) in Trafalgar where you can take a guided or self-guided tour of their extensive gardens.

Background

Recommended Reading

HISTORY

The Dominica Story, Lennox Honychurch (1995)

A Short History of the West Indies, J.P. Parry, Philip Sherlock & Anthony Maingot (1987)

NATURE

A Guide to Geology, Climate and Habitats, Peter G.H. Evans & Arlington James (1997)

A Guide to Dive Sites and Marine Life, Peter G.H. Evans (1997)

A Guide to Nature Sites, Peter G.H. Evans (1997)

Dominica's Birds, Arlington James, Stephen Durand, and Bertrand Jno. Baptiste (2005)

Birds of the Eastern Caribbean, Peter Evans (1990)

LITERATURE

Wide Sargasso Sea, Jean Rhys (1966)

Bayou of Pigs, Stewart Bell (2008)

The Orchid House, Phillis Shand Allfrey (1996)

Rain on a Tin Roof, Gabriel Christian (1999)

The Island Man Sings His Song, Giftus John (2001)

Unburnable, Marie-Elena John (2006)

Tales of the Wide Caribbean, Jean Rhys (1985)

Mesyé Kwik! Kwak, Giftus John (2005)

A Caribbean Life, Phillis Shand Allfrey (1996)

LANGUAGE

Dominica's Diksyonne, English-Creole, Marcel Fonatine (1991)

WEBSITES

www.discoverdominica.com

www.avirtuatldominica.com

www.newsdominica.com

www.visit-dominica.com

The Basics

When to Go

Dominica has warm tropical weather year-round. Although it's going to be hot regardless of when you visit, if you come between December and April there is generally a cool breeze from the trade winds that brings the temperatures down in the evenings and makes the weather a bit more comfortable. This is also considered the dry season although short bouts of rain will occur. Visiting during the dry season can make hiking less challenging because trails will be dry (no mud), especially in the interior. Because of these conditions, this also coincides with tourist season when the number of cruise ship tourists goes way up making popular sites more crowded and hotel prices and car rentals more expensive.

Coming in the summer months means more rain and humidity (although generally the rain comes in short bursts and then the sun is immediately out again) and slightly warmer temperatures, but less tourists to contend with. This also corresponds with hurricane season, which runs from late August to October.

If you are interested in cultural festivals, you may want to visit the last week of October or first week of November for Independence celebrations and the World Creole Music Festival. You'll get to experience a lot of Dominica's traditional music, dance, and cultural traditions during this time. Another entertaining season is around Carnival when there are parades, calypso and princess shows, and street "jump-ups" when the island is one big party. This begins in January, gearing up the entire time for the days before Ash Wednesday. Both of these are busy seasons so book tickets, accommodations, and car rentals well in advance.

Information Once On-Island

Once on-island, visit the tourism office (*Tel: 767-448-5840; tourism@discoverdominica.com*) on the bay front of Roseau beneath the Dominica Museum to get the most up-to-date information and advice. Maps can be picked up here and at the Melville Hall Airport when you arrive. There is a Food and Drink publication that reviews many of the restaurants on the islands and provides recipes for some of Dominica's favorite dishes. There is also an excellent publication called **100+ Things to do in Dominica** that is available in many hotels and at the tourism office in Roseau.

CLIMATE

The average temperature in Dominica is 80 degrees Fahrenheit (27°C). You can expect a lot of sunshine with frequent but generally short bouts of rain showers. The heat and rain do result in humid days, but a breeze from the trade winds will help make the temperature more comfortable. The coasts are typically warmer than the inland areas and evenings spent in the villages that sit in the center of the island can actually get to be quite cool. Don't bother packing a sweatshirt or coat, a light jacket or long sleeve shirt is all you will need to stay warm.

July to November is considered the wet season and it is also the time that tropical storms, depressions and hurricanes may occur (hurricane season peaks in late August and early September). If it is especially rainy, flash floods can and do happen. Under very rainy conditions, you should be advised to stay away from rivers and waterfalls until they've had a chance to return to normal levels. Hiking in the rainy season is a bit more challenging because the trails turn to mud.

	F*		C*		RAIN FALL	
	AVG DAILY		AVG DAILY		AVG MNTHLY	
	MAX	MIN	MAX	MIN	IN	MM
JAN	82	71	28	22	6.5	159
FEB	82	71	28	22	4.4	107
MAR	83	71	28	22	5.5	135
APR	84	73	29	23	5	122
MAY	85	75	30	24	9	220
JUN	86	76	31	25	6.6	162
JUL	86	76	30	25	7.4	181
AUG	87	76	30	24	10	243
SEPT	87	75	30	24	12	298
OCT	84	74	29	23	14	334
NOV	85	73	29	23	15	240
DEC	83	72	28	22	10	215

Getting There

BY AIR

By far the fastest way to get to Dominica is by air, but it isn't always the easiest. Because of the mountainous nature of the island there is no place to put a large runway capable of handling a passenger jet. Therefore only small inter-island planes can land on Dominica, which forces visitors to transfer flights on another island prior to arrival. There are three airlines that fly to Dominica: **American Eagle**, **LIAT**, and **Win Air** and nearly every flight will enter and leave from **Melville Hall Airport (DOM)** in the northeast. Canefield Airport, in the southwest, is too small for most planes. Flying American Eagle Airlines is the most reliable and generally the cheapest over LIAT and Win Air. LIAT flights tend to be unreliable and frustrating and Win Air, which only recently started limited service to Dominica, is slightly better but like most things Caribbean, isn't always on time. The major hubs to fly through are Antigua (ANU) and Puerto Rico (SJU). You can, however, catch LIAT and Win Air flights from many islands including St. Lucia (SLU), Barbados (BGI), and St. Thomas (STT). At the time of writing, night landings into Dominica were just being introduced which is great for the overseas traveler. Without night landings, most visitors had to overnight in Puerto Rico as the flights got in too late in the evening to land in Dominica. Theoretically, visitors can now get to Dominica with only one day of travel.

Flights from the US
Flying on American Airlines is the easiest option since you will only have to purchase a one ticket for the entire trip. Continental, Delta, Jet Blue, United, US Airways, Air Canada, Air Jamaica, and Air Tran all offer flights to the Caribbean where you can then catch another flight into Dominica. Your easiest connection points will be Puerto Rico or Antigua.

Flights from the UK and Europe
British Airways and Virgin Atlantic will take you into Antigua and it is possible to get a same day flight into Dominica from there on a different airline. Air France also flies to Martinique or Guadeloupe where you can take a ferry into Dominica. This often requires an overnight on those islands, sometimes two nights depending on the regularity of the ferry schedule.

Flights from Australia
A good place to start looking for flights is www.airfaresflights.com. It will connect you to other websites that offer deals from Australia to Dominica. Expect for it to take at least 24 hours to reach Dominica with connections in New York or Miami and again in San Juan, Puerto Rico.

Airline Operators

American Airlines and American Eagle *Tel: 1-800-433-7300; www.aa.com*

LIAT *Tel: 1-888-844-5428; www.liatairline.com, reservations@liatairline.com*

Win Air *Tel: 1-866-466-0410 (USA/Canada), 599-545-4237 (all other countries); www.fly-winair.com, reservations@fly-winair.com*

Charter Flights
The only charter airline that lands in Canefield Airport at the moment is **SVG Air** (Tel: 1-800-624-1843; info@svgair.com, www.svgair.com). You can schedule the time you want to be picked up and dropped off from Barbados, St. Lucia, Grenada, Martinique, Trinidad and Tobago, St. Vincent or Antigua. Flights are over US$1,200 but planes can fit at least five passengers, which actually makes the price somewhat reasonable.

BY SEA

You can reach Dominica's closest neighbors by taking **L'Express des Isles**, a high speed ferry that has direct service to Guadeloupe and Martinique and connecting service to St. Lucia, Marie Galante, and Les Saintes. The ferry comes and goes from the ferry dock on Roseau's bay front on Wednesdays, Fridays, and Sundays, although the schedule changes at certain times throughout the year. You may also find that if there is a cruise ship occupying the ferry dock, you will have to leave from (or come into) the port at Woodbridge Bay, a half mile north of Roseau. If that's the case there will likely be plenty of taxis around to take you to Roseau. (Or, alternatively, you can easily catch a west coast bus.) The waters can be rough at times between islands so if you are prone to seasickness, it's a good idea to bring motion sickness medicine with you. This is also available at Jolly's Pharmacy in Roseau. Ask for it at the pharmacy counter.

It is around US$85/one-way from Dominica to Martinique or Guadeloupe with a departure tax of EC$30. There is a 10 percent discount for those under 26 and over 60 years of age. The ferry generally doesn't travel onwards from either of these islands until the next day so plan to spend the night in Guadaloupe or Martinique before heading to St. Lucia, Marie Galante, or Les Saintes. For more information, go to www.express-des-iles.com. To book tickets, call Whitchurch Travel Agency in Dominica (Tel: 767-448-2181; hhvwhitchurch@cwdom.dm, www.whitchurch.com).

Sailing/Yachting

Yachts traveling to Dominica should clear one of the three ports of entry: Portsmouth in the northwest, Anse-de-Mai in the northeast, and Roseau, the port of entry, in the southwest.

Three copies of the crew and passenger list must be provided at customs and a nominal environment fee must be paid in order to sail around Dominica. New measures have been created in order to make sailing and yachting in Dominica as easy as possible. This means that as long as you are not changing crew members, you may check in and out at the same time for a two week period.

There is no marina, but the most popular spots for anchoring yachts are in Prince Rupert Bay, Mero, and at Castle Comfort. Sailors should receive clearance from customs and immigration before anchoring. The Soufriere/Scotts Head Marine Reserve is a protected area that is off limits to sailors. See page 120 for services in Roseau and page 159 for Portsmouth services.

Dominica Port Authority *Roseau; VHF channel 16; 767-448-4431; domport@cwdom.dm.*

Cruise Ships

Cruises to Dominica have recently increased in number and there are several popular lines that visit Dominica on a regular basis: Princess Cruises, Norwegian Lines, Holland America, Clipper Cruises, Cunard Lines, Royal Caribbean, Silver Sea, Celebrity Cruises, Regent Seven Seas, and P&O Cruise Lines. Most come into port at around 9am and leave by 5pm. Nearly all Caribbean cruises depart from Miami, Ft. Lauderdale, Tampa or San Juan, Puerto Rico and last anywhere from three days to two weeks.

Departure Tax

When leaving Dominica you will need to pay an exit tax of EC$59 (US$22) at the time of check in for your flight. You can only pay in cash so be sure to have money on you before you reach the airport.

Entry Requirements

ENTRY AND VISAS

Visitors must possess a valid passport upon arrival into Dominica and be able to show a return or onward ticket. Canadian citizens need only show a document of proof of citizenship with an official photo. French nationals can stay for up to two weeks with a valid ID card. No visa is required for visitors from the following countries who intend to stay less than 21 days: Argentina, Belgium, Costa Rica, Denmark, France, Germany, Greece, Ireland, Israel, Italy, Japan, Luxembourg, Malta, Mexico, Netherlands, Norway, Portugal, South Korea, Spain, Sweden, Taiwan, United Kingdom, United States, and Venezuela. Visitors who will remain in Dominica for less than 24 hours (including cruise-ship passengers) do not require a visa to enter.

> For current information on visa requirements and to download a visa application visit: www.dominica.dm

Customs

You will be required to fill out a customs declaration and may be asked to open your luggage for customs officials, which is fairly common and nothing to be overly concerned about. Items you must declare include plants (including cut flowers), fresh produce, meat, pharmaceuticals, commercial merchandise, and currency over US$10,000.

Baggage Allowance

Since there is a real concern of overloading the small planes that service Dominica, the airlines are quite strict about baggage allowance. If you adhere to the following guidelines, you'll have a much easier time at the airport.

When traveling on American (American Eagle) the total weight baggage allowance per passenger cannot exceed 70 lbs plus one carry-on bag that cannot exceed 40 lbs. If one bag is over 50lbs there will be a charge of US$25.

When flying LIAT or Win Air the baggage allowance is even more restricted. You can bring one piece of luggage for free that weighs less than 50 lbs and an extra bag will cost you US$60. You can bring one small carry-on that must weigh less than 15 lbs (less than 6 lbs on Win Air). If it goes over the allotted size or weight, you will be required to check it and pay US$60.

Pets

If you wish to bring your pet into Dominica, you must obtain an Import Permit and contact the Immigration Department (Tel: 767-448-2222) to verify requirements and procedures.

Packing List

What you bring with you will be determined in large part by how you plan to travel. If you are staying at one of the nicer hotels that cater to all a guest's needs, then you can probably do without some of these things and won't have to worry about scaling down your luggage as much. If you are taking public transportation, it will serve you well to not carry more than what you can fit on your lap (like a large backpack and small day pack). Although many essentials can be bought in Roseau, there are a few items that are difficult to find so remember to plan ahead and pack thoughtfully.

For all Travelers

- ✓ Sunscreen
- ✓ Bug spray
- ✓ Water bottle
- ✓ Flip-flops
- ✓ Sturdy sandals with good traction (Tevas or Chacos work best)
- ✓ Day pack
- ✓ Umbrella
- ✓ Hat
- ✓ Sunglasses that absorb UV rays
- ✓ Poncho (small and lightweight are key)
- ✓ Modest clothing (skimpy outfits won't be appreciated in Roseau and will only bring unwanted attention at best).
- ✓ One set of dressier clothes for dinner out or if you plan to really integrate and attend a church service. Knee-length skirt or dress with short sleeves, not spaghetti straps, is appropriate for women. Long pants and button up shirt for men.
- ✓ Long pants (one pair, lightweight)
- ✓ Long sleeved shirt (just one)
- ✓ Camera with extra battery or charger
- ✓ Contact lens solution, which is very difficult to find here, and a back-up pair of glasses.
- ✓ Copy of passport, airline tickets, visa, and travelers check numbers (packed separately)
- ✓ Driver's License (if you plan to rent a car)
- ✓ Tampons or sanitary napkins (these can be expensive and hard to find)
- ✓ First Aid Kit (with Pepto, ibuprofen, motion sickness tablets, band-aids, aloe vera, calamine lotion, tweezers, moleskin, and Neosporin)
- ✓ Universal outlet converter (check with your hotel, they may have one you can use)
- ✓ Underwater or waterproof camera

For the Adventurer

✓ Flashlight or headlamp

✓ Snorkel and mask (if you have one); fins if you have room

✓ Small towel that you can carry with you on hikes (micro-fiber towels are lightweight, compact, and dry quickly)

✓ Leatherman

✓ Toilet paper

✓ Hand sanitizer

✓ Zip-lock plastic bags to keep things dry

✓ Clothesline or cord to hang wet things

✓ Decent tent with a ground sheet

✓ Duct tape

✓ Energy bars or snacks for hiking (double bag these in closed zip-locks to keep bugs out)

✓ Universal sink plug if you want to wash your own clothes

> **For Divers**
> Scuba certification card and dive log and if you bring your own gear, a light 3mm wetsuit is sufficient.

Health & Safety

IMMUNIZATIONS

There are no required immunizations for Dominica. However, the government requires travelers arriving from countries where yellow fever is present to show proof of yellow fever vaccination. It is recommended that you have all of your regular immunizations up to date, including: measles, mumps, rubella and tetnus, diptheria, polio. Although it's not required, the CDC recommends getting vaccinated for Hepititus A and B and Typhoid, especially if you are traveling extensively over a long period of time.

Water

The water in Dominica is safe to drink straight from the tap unless there has been a major storm, which can sometimes put dirt and debris into the water source. If that is the case, wait a day or two and then turn on your water until it runs clear. If there is any doubt, bottled water is widely available from any village shop.

STAYING HEALTHY

Visitors to Dominica are not likely to suffer from any real health problems during their stay. One of the biggest health issues tourists will face is from the **sun and heat**, which can sneak up on you quickly in the tropical climate. If you will be in the sun a lot, be sure to have a wide-brim hat and wear lots of sunscreen. Stay in the shade as much as possible and always stay hydrated with plenty of water. If you start to feel weak, dizzy, and have a headache you should get out of the sun and hydrate yourself as soon as you can, as it may lead to full on heat exhaustion. If you will be snorkeling for a long length of time it's a good idea to wear a t-shirt so that your back doesn't get scorched. You can buy sunscreen and aloe vera gel at Jolly's Pharmacy in Roseau.

Dengue Fever
Although it is rare, dengue fever does occur on occasion. It is transmitted through mosquito bites and can be very unpleasant, but isn't fatal. Symptoms are a high fever, intense headache, muscle and joint pain and eye pain. It's easily treatable so seek medical attention right away if you feel like you may have it. The best method of prevention is to wear insect repellant with DEET, especially around dusk and dawn when mosquitoes are out in force. Sleep under a mosquito net at night or with a fan, which acts as a good deterrent.

Insect Bites
Insect bites will happen. There are plenty of little creatures all around in this rainforest environment and many of them bite. Yet none are poisonous and won't cause any real harm. One that is worth paying extra attention to avoiding is the centipede. These long gnarly creatures can bite from both ends and it is incredibly painful. They aren't particularly common but if you see one, don't get too close.

Heat Rash
If you aren't accustomed to hot and humid weather you may find your skin breaking out in a slight rash. This is likely the result of the heat and humidity and can be remedied with a cold shower, air conditioning, and aloe vera gel. Take it easy for a day or so to let your body get used to the new climate.

Medical Packing Checklist

Although you can find many of these things in Dominica, it's wise to bring them with you just in case the island happens to have run out and it will save you a lengthy trip to Roseau to buy them if you are staying in any other part of the island.

- Your regular medications (plus a copy of the prescription)
- Diarrhea medication
- Insect repellant
- Sun screen with SPF 30 or higher
- Aloe vera gel
- Motion sickness relief medicine
- Pain reliever (aspirin, ibuprofen, acetaminophen)
- Band-aids
- Triple antibiotic cream
- Antibacterial hand gel
- Anti-itch cream
- Moleskin for blisters
- Elastic bandange wrap for sprains
- Extra pair of contacts or glasses
- Emergency contact numbers of family or physician at home
- Epi-pen if you're prone to severe allergies

Animal Bites

There are lots of stray dogs on the island and they aren't always nice to humans. So even if you are a dog-lover, do not under any circumstances try to pet them or you may find yourself with a dog bite. Luckily there is supposedly no rabies on the island so your biggest concern if you do get bit, is to keep the wound clean and free of infection.

Traveler's Diarrhea

Although it's uncommon, it can happen. Rest, drink fluids and take some over the counter medicine until you get back on your feet. If it's getting worse rather than better, go to a clinic to get some antibiotics and give yourself plenty of time to recover.

Motion Sickness

This is a common complaint from visitors who aren't used to the windy roads, fast driving, and heat. Bring some non-drowsy Dramamine or its equivalent. If you didn't think to pack any, you can buy some at the pharmacy counter at Jolly's in Roseau.

Leptospirosis

This very rare type of bacterial infection is found around contaminated fresh water that gets into a cut or open wound. Symptoms include a high fever with severe chills for a day or two. It then goes away and comes back several days later with more intensity. Seek medical attention if you have these symptoms so any necessary antibiotics can be administered.

HIV/AIDS

Like anywhere in the world, Dominica has its share of HIV/AIDS cases, making it extremely foolish to engage in unsafe sex while you are visiting the island. While condoms are available at some shops, they have likely been sitting out for a long time so it's advisable to bring and use your own. If you do have unprotected sex, visit a health clinic within 24 to 72 hours to receive post-exposure prophylaxis.

Basics

Traditional Medicine

In Dominica, Western and traditional medical practices are at a crossroads. Dominicans come from a long history of using their natural environment to treat common ailments and this belief still plays a prominent role in providing baseline medical treatment, especially when the Western medical infrastructure on the island is plagued with inadequacies. Traditional medicine is so ingrained in the culture that natural remedies are sold alongside Western packaged medicine in the pharmacies and are often local's first line of treatment. Common remedies include a variety of "bush tea" concoctions made from indigenous herbs, plants, and bark, which are used for anything from insomnia and colds to diarrhea and headaches. Sulphur cream is a popular treatment for any and all skin issues – acne, rashes, eczema, and bug bites, to name a few. Castor seeds grow on the island and many people roast them and then extract the oil which is used to relieve a wide range of ailments, the most popular being constipation and gastro-intestinal issues.

Getting Medical Care

The only major hospital on the island is Princess Margaret (Tel: 767-266-2000), which is located just north of Roseau in Goodwill and handles any serious emergencies. It's not very well equipped but does a decent job with what they have. Many of the doctors – who are really very good – were trained in Cuba and are doing a required year of service before they can practice medicine in their own country.

Most villages have small health centers that are staffed by nurses and nurse practitioners and can take care of less-serious ailments. The larger regional health clinics can be found in Grand Bay (Tel: 767-446-3706), Marigot (Tel: 767-445-7091), and Portsmouth (Tel: 767-445-5237).

Insurance

Visitors who need health care while in Dominica are required to pay before they are treated, so it's wise to make sure your health insurance is in order before you travel. You can buy travel insurance, which is always a good idea, that includes medical coverage along with lost baggage, evacuation, and theft. Note that in the event of a medical emergency you'll need to file a police report in order to make an insurance claim. Also, be sure to keep any receipts if you do seek treatment, as you'll need those to be reimbursed by your insurance company. There are a lot of good travel insurance companies out there so shop around if you don't immediately come across one you like.

DANGERS, CRIME AND ANNOYANCES

Overall, Dominica is an incredibly safe place to visit and many Dominicans are of the belief that developed countries, specifically the US, are very dangerous places that are riddled with crime and danger based on what they see on the news (if that gives you some perspective). There are, however, a few things to be aware of to make sure your visit is a safe and enjoyable one.

In the Wild

Other than one type of tree that is quite rare, there are no poisonous plants, animals, or snakes anywhere on Dominica. The tree to avoid is called a **Manchineel tree** and they grow along the shoreline. There are very few of them in Dominica and the ones that do exist are well marked with warning signs and locals are quick to point them out to tourists. There is one on the beach at Scotts Head with a sign below it. Do not touch these trees, eat their fruit, or stand under them when it is raining, as the sap that covers the tree is toxic to humans.

Embassies

United States (based in Barbados)
Tel: 246-436-4950

United Kingdom
Tel: 767-448-7655

Canada (based in Barbados)
Tel: 246-429-3550

France
Tel: 767-448-0508

Norway
Tel: 767-449-8300

Netherlands
Tel: 767-448-3841

Sweden
Tel: 767-448-2181

Hiking is the main activity for many tourists who visit Dominica and as with hiking anywhere in the world, there are certain precautions that must be taken to stay safe, most of which are common sense. Don't hike off of the established trail. Even the most competent hikers who are familiar with the land and have a GPS in hand have gotten lost and have needed to be rescued. The terrain in Dominica is very rugged and you can get yourself into a sticky and dangerous situation very quickly. If you find that you accidentally wander off the trail, and can't get back to it, the best advice is to find a river and follow it down stream where it will eventually lead to a coast. From there, you should be able to find a village. And of course you'll want to plan your excursions so that you're finished hiking by nightfall, which is around 6pm.

Swimming in the sea is another popular attraction in Dominica and is also really quite safe. There are no dangerous sharks lurking around and aside from sea urchins and jellyfish, there are no harmful sea creatures. **Sea urchins** usually live on rocks, coral and the sea floor and are circular in shape with long black spines. If you step on one it is pretty painful and you may end up with the broken tip of a spine embedded in your foot. The best way to relieve the pain is to soak the area in white vinegar for as long as possible and it's likely that the spine will dissolve. Wash with anti-bacterial soap and water and cover with a bandage and antibiotic ointment. Another effective treatment is to get a soft wax from the pharmacy, heat it up and cover the area with the wax and a bandage and leave overnight. The spine should be gone in the morning.

Jellyfish stings can also be painful, especially by the larger ones, and the best treatment to ease the sting is a good soak in white vinegar. If you can see any of the tentacles in your skin, remove them with tweezers but avoid touching them so as not to get stung again.

As mentioned elsewhere in this guide, swimming in the Atlantic side of the island is risky due to strong **currents** and **undertows** and visitors must exercise caution in those waters. A good way to tell if it is safe to swim is by asking locals, they know which waters are safe and which are not. Stay in shallow waters and take note of what's going on in the water. If the waves start to get bigger and more aggressive, don't linger.

Waterfalls are one of Dominica's most precious attractions and getting to them usually means a hike, many times along and through a river. If you are planning to hike to one of them, take note of the weather beforehand. A large storm with lots of rain that lasts for several hours can (and does) cause **flash floods** in rivers and

---

Advice from Mom
Better to be safe than sorry

I consulted our various travel companions from the three trips we made to the island, and everyone concurred that they always felt safe. That being said, we stayed in villages rather than Roseau, always locked our doors at night and when we left, and kept our car doors locked. Common sense safety precautions are always wise. The only thing I (and others) found scary was the driving conditions. The roads are treacherous and you must have a skilled and confident driver. (Fortunately, we did.) As for health, no one ever got sick even though we ate and drank whatever we wanted.

"Won't forget it" moment: Seeing so many men walking along the road carrying big cutlasses (machetes). It was a little disconcerting at first, but there was no need for alarm. The cutlass is an essential tool used by everyone for everyday tasks from farming to opening coconuts to clearing brush while hiking.

people have been swept away in the past. If you are unsure about whether or not it is safe, inquire with your host or a local guide to get their opinion.

Dominicans and **dogs** don't have a great relationship. In fact, in many cases they hate each other. The dogs bite, bark and growl to scare people. So people defend themselves by throwing rocks at the dogs in order to not be bit. It's a vicious cycle that you'll likely notice in your travels. If you are walking down a road and a dog starts to act aggressively towards you, the best thing you can do is to look down and away. Dogs see this as an act of submission where as if you looked them in the eye, they take that as aggression. This usually does the trick. However if you feel like you need some other recourse, sometimes the act of picking up a rock is enough or pretending to throw one will scare the dog off and you won't feel too much like an animal abuser. Also, if you yell "MOSH!" at them, this will get them to run. ("Mache" is the Creole word for "walk" and is what the dogs are accustomed to hearing from locals.)

Personal Safety

Dominicans are very attentive to keeping visitors safe and happy. Many locals will go out of their way to intervene if they find someone is treating tourists badly or subjecting them to harassment. When traveling in Dominica, follow the same precautions that you would anywhere: don't flash you wealth with expensive jewelry or electronics, don't carry large wads of cash, keep your wallet and personal items in a front pocket, dress conservatively, and don't get involved in conflicts. If you are driving a rental car, put valuables in the trunk and never leave items unattended at the beach. Walking around Roseau late at night can be risky as that is when most muggings happen. Before getting into a "taxi" be sure to check that there is an "H" on the license plate before jumping in. Petty theft does occur but it's still rather rare. You can report the theft to the police and because the island is small and anonymity is impossible, there is a chance you may get your things back. It may, however, take longer than you'd like it to.

Transportation

Although **driving** in Dominica feels like a free for all and riding in a bus can seem like a terrifying roller coaster ride at times, there are surprisingly few serious road accidents in Dominica. If you are the one driving, go slow, use your horn around corners, and don't be shy about pulling over when other drivers are being pushy. For most, you'll get used to driving on the left side of the road rather quickly and with a passenger to tell you when you're getting too close to the middle, you'll be fine.

If you choose to **hitchhike,** you'll generally be engaged in chit-chat and people are very friendly and happy to give you a ride. But getting into a stranger's car can, of course, carry some risk. The safest ride you can get is in the back of a pick-up truck. If you are a woman, don't hitchhike alone if you can help it. And no one should hitchhike at night – you may end up riding with a drunk driver and could easily get yourself into a bad situation.

DRUGS

Marijuana is illegal and also very prevalent in Dominica, especially among the youth and Rasta populations. You may even encounter people smoking it right in front of you or as they are walking down the road, as the law is not enforced all that much.

That doesn't mean that tourists should take this opportunity to start a drug habit since as a tourist you stand out and there is the possibility of getting caught and locked up. Men are frequently approached and asked if they would like to buy some. If you choose to, remember that you're on a very small, gossipy island and your transaction is not only between you and the dealer, but also between everyone else in the vicinity and all of their friends and family, one of whom may be a police official.

Travelers with Special Needs

CHILDREN

There is no reason why you couldn't bring your young one to Dominica as there are no major safety risks to be worried about. However, there aren't any specific "kid-oriented" activities in Dominica and getting to most sites requires some hiking and physical activity. Older kids who are into the outdoors will have a great time here and will enjoy snorkeling, horseback riding, and the less strenuous hikes.

Most baby necessities are readily available at the supermarket and pharmacies. However you should bring enough special food or formula with you to last the entire trip, as the stores are known for running out of things.

SOLO TRAVELERS

If you travel through Dominica by yourself, you'll likely get a good mix of solitude and socializing, depending mainly on where you stay. Dominicans are very friendly and won't pass up the opportunity to make conversation, especially if you are by yourself. Unfortunately there aren't hostels or other tourist meccas to meet other travelers. So if that is your intention, stay somewhere that offers family-style dinners, such as Cocoa Cottages or sign up on www.couchsurfing.com to meet, and possibly stay with, someone locally (see page 82 for more on couchsurfing.com).

Alternatively, if you came here for some alone time you can find that as well. Stay in one of the rural guesthouses and you'll have plenty of time to reflect and relax.

One drawback to traveling alone is not having anyone to share the cost with, thereby making your trip more expensive. Women traveling alone will likely have to deal with more unwanted advances than what is typical.

TRAVELERS WITH DISABILITIES

Dominica is not the easiest country to navigate with a disability, especially for those that are in wheelchairs and have a hard time with mobility. There are only a few sidewalks, and those that do exist have holes and are frequently blocked in places. There are only one or two elevators on the entire island so finding ground level accommodation could be tricky as well. However it isn't impossible and if you rent a car or hire a driver, you'll be able to get around just fine.

Mobility International USA (www.miusa.org) offers advice for disabled travelers on mobility issues, runs exchange programs, and publishes some useful materials for travelers. Also **Ready, Willing, Enable** (www.rwenable.org), offers volunteer opportunities for those who would like to come to Dominica to help run camps for persons with disabilities.

WOMEN TRAVELERS

Women traveling in a group or with a male companion will likely not have any special problems traveling in Dominica. Solo women, however, will likely experience an uncomfortable amount of attention at times from men who tend to come on rather strong in their pursuits. Yet this is usually more irritating than threatening and if you can inject some humor into it, it will diffuse rather quickly. Men will hiss and call-out to women, both Dominican and otherwise, as a national pastime and sometimes ignoring them only makes them try harder. Many times they just want to know they got your attention so a quick "ok" is all it takes to call them off.

> Attacks are very rare but don't let your guard down just because you're in paradise.

To minimize potential problems, dress conservatively, don't go to isolated areas alone, don't get into a car or run off into the rainforest with someone you don't know, don't wear your swim suit around the village or capital, don't go out to bars or parties alone, and trust your instincts. Even the slightest friendliness, including eye contact, can be interpreted as interest. A firm "no" should get your message across if you are the recipient of unwanted attention and if you feel like it's taking a turn for the worse, make a lot of noise and head for a crowd. And if you can have a sense of humor about it, it won't ruin your good time.

Getting Around

Getting around Dominica is probably one of the most frustrating aspects of visiting this island. With the hard to navigate and dangerous roads, high cost of renting a car, and unreliable bus service it can feel like a real "adventure" to get from one side of the island to the other. If you're not on a time crunch and don't mind doing a lot of waiting, then **buses** are the cheapest way to get around, plus you get the added bonus of having a great cultural experience. Fares aren't more than EC$11.

Hiring a **taxi** is another option but costs can add up fast, becoming extremely expensive if you are traveling around a lot. Renting a **car** is ideal if you have a driver who is brave and confident enough to take on the challenges of Dominican roads and it will afford you a lot more mobility. Rentals usually cost around US$40-$50 per day. There are **scooters** that can be rented by the cruise ship dock in Roseau but in my opinion, it's not a safe option to say the least.

> **Hitchhiking** is a very common and accepted way to get around while getting to know the locals.

In order to drive in Dominica you must purchase a temporary international license (EC$30, valid for one-month), which can be purchased at the car rental companies or at the airport. All you need is a license from your country of origin.

Gay Travelers in Dominica - *Anonymous Author*

Dominica's intoxicating landscape is a wistful daydream-come-true for two travelers in love. But what if those two travelers are of the same sex? Caribbean islands with British heritage are generally very conservative and even antagonistic towards gays and lesbians. Consensual sex between adult men in Dominica is still criminalized. Docking rights for gay cruise ships are repeatedly denied. Dancehall reggae songs by artists like Bounty Killa and Buju Banton espousing violence against gays are blared by bus drivers and in village rum shops. It is extremely rare to find a Dominican who openly identifies as gay.

Despite this hostility towards gays, Dominicans aren't out on a witchhunt. Locals won't think anything of two men (or women) traveling together. When I had dinners at a restaurant in the capital or beers at a beach-side bar with a gentlemen-caller, I never perceived an instance of scrutiny or inhospitality (at least not for seeming gay). Locals won't confront someone about their homosexuality unless they're engaging in public, affectionate acts or openly discussing being gay. On the island, discretion is the order of the day. Dominica definitely is not the place to reenact a same-sex version of the Burt Lancaster/ Deborah Kerr beach make-out scene from *Here to Eternity*. So a rule of thumb for enjoying your "vay-kay" with your partner: in public, go nuts with platonic male-bonding. In private, do as you please as two passionate, veritable partners-in-crime.

Gay Night Life

Religiosity of island culture + diminished anonymity of a small population – a viable gay community = zero gay scene. On Dominica, there are private parties held by tightly-associated groups of gay and gay-friendly individuals. Getting invited to one as a passing traveler is not very likely unless you're being hosted by a gay local or ex-patriot. And don't expect anything from the island capital. One of my favorite things to do when visiting a capital city for the first time is to hop into a cab and bellow at the driver, "To your gay district, my good man! And don't spare the accelerator." This won't get you anywhere in Roseau.

Final Thoughts

If you're looking for the next gay vacation hot spot, Dominica is not the place. U.S. territories and islands of French/Dutch heritage are more progressive and welcoming of gay vacationers. But I would encourage you not to dismiss visiting Dominica. Having to go into the closet during a vacation you've paid for is a hard pill for liberated gays to swallow. After all, why shouldn't we have the privilege to openly share our tropical vacation with our partner as a romantic bonding experience the way our straight counterparts do? But that's part of the allure of visiting a rugged place like Dominica. It separates the gay tourists from gay travelers. An adventurous traveler, gay or straight, is willing to veer off the beaten path of fashionable shopping districts and manicured beach resorts. They suspend any inflated sense of entitlement for the time being, and diplomatically defer to local social mores expected of guests. It's easy to feel morally conflicted about supporting a homophobic tourism industry. But you don't have to let that stop you from falling in love with Dominica.

Basics

CAR RENTAL

Renting a car will cost you at least US$40 a day and can go upwards of US$100 per day depending on the type of car you rent. If you have a choice, it is very wise to rent a 4WD vehicle as the roads can be very rough and steep in places. You can sometimes get a deal when renting something longer than a few days and prices are a bit cheaper in the off-season, but not by much. Keep in mind that if you come during high season, at Christmas, Carnival, or Independence season you have to reserve a car with a rental agency well in advance or there will not be any cars left when you arrive. (Buses don't run during national holidays so renting a car may be the best option during these times of year.) Mileage is unlimited for rentals but you will have to pay for your own gas, which is expensive, around EC$100 to fill up a car. There is an insurance fee that is optional and generally costs around US$8-$15 per day. It can sometimes be waived with a credit card (check with credit card company before leaving home). Some also require a credit card to use for a US$1,125-$2,500 deposit.

Driving in Dominica: A Visitor's Perspective

If you enjoy interesting and challenging driving, you might really like driving in Dominica. Or it could freak you out.

As a rule, the roads are in poor to fair condition. They are very windy and can be ridiculously steep. Often there is a sharp drop-off on the downhill side and/or a deep narrow gutter on the uphill side (no shoulder). If you drop a tire, bad things happen. Did I mention that the roads are narrow, full of potholes, and there are frequently people, dogs, and livestock walking on them? Despite all this, I really enjoyed driving on the island and it afforded us a lot of freedom of movement.

Due to British influence, Dominicans drive on the left. This can be confusing at first. It helps to have passengers scream "left! Left!! LEFT!!!" when you pull into the wrong lane. However, laughing every time you turn on the wipers instead of the turn signal is not especially helpful. (I was surprised how many times I did this!)

Courtesy Car rental agency at Melville Hall airport was very helpful. Their vehicles were clean and in good condition. After our first trip, I rented only 4WD vehicles because of the wet steep roads (seriously steep!). Make sure you know how to use the engine and transmission to slow down the vehicle on long down grades. The only time I was frightened driving the island was when I badly overheated the brakes on the long grade between Grand Bay and Delices.

Native drivers honk often, both as a greeting and as they approach blind curves, of which there are many. They expect you to do the same.

Remember that driving in Dominica is not a race, although it sometimes feels like one. Drive slowly and cautiously and pull over to let people pass. Dominican drivers will pull right up to your rear bumper and honk if they wish to pass, so there is no ambiguity here.

People standing in bus stops will sometimes yell their destination as you pass, hoping for a ride. Use your discretion in picking them up. The advantage of doing so is that they can help a lot with directions. Navigation is challenging, so don't hesitate to ask the locals. They always gave us reliable directions.

A word about distances. Although two villages may be less than 20 miles apart, it will probably take at least an hour to drive between them.

Drivers must be at least 21 and some companies have a minimum age of 25 with at least two years of driving experience. Many offer free pick-up and drop off and some also rent child car seats and cell phones.

Be sure to check that you have proper tread on the tires and that you have a spare tire and a working jack before you sign for the car. Getting a flat tire is pretty common. Also check that the lights, horn and turn signals work properly.

There are not that many gas stations on the island and even fewer that stay open late so it's important to check your gas tank before you head out on an adventure. The gas station in Marigot stays open until 7pm and usually one of the gas stations in Canefield is open in the evening as well.

During normal business hours, gas stations are available in Anse Du Mai, Calibishie, Canefield, Castle Bruce, Coulibistrie, Delices, Jimmit, Marigot, Newtown, Picard, Portsmouth, Pottersville, Roseau, Riviere Cyrique, St. Joseph, and Wesley.

Car Rental Companies

Accessories Plus Vehicle Rental *Goodwill; Tel: 954-905-9638 (USA), Tel: 767-440-6073; acprentals@gmail.com , www.accarentals.com*

Courtesy Car Rental *Goodwill & Melville Hall; Tel: 767-448-7763 (Goodwill), 767-235-7763 (cell), 767-445-7677 (Melville Hall); courtesyrental@cwdom.dm, www.dominicacarrentals.com*

Budget Rent A Car *Canefield & Melville Hall; Tel: 767-449-2080 (Canefield), 767-445-7687 (Melville Hall), 767-449-1908;*

Quality Rent A Car *Roseau; Tel: 767-275-8899 (cell), 767-448-6215; aqualityrentacar@hotmail.com*

Road Runner Car Rental, *Roseau; Tel: 767-235-2952 (cell), 767-276-3804; roadrunnerrental@cwdom.dm, www.roadrunnercarrental.com*

Valley Rent A Car *Roseau & Portsmouth; Tel: 767-448-3233 (Roseau), 767-445-5252 (Portsmouth), valley@cwdom.dm, www.valleydominica.com*

Garraway Rent A Car *Roseau, Tel: 767-448-2891; Garraway@cwdom.dm; www.avirtualdominica.com/garrawaycarrental*

Bonus Car Rental *Roseau; Tel: 767-448-2650; cphillip@cwdom.dm*

Discount Car Rental *Melville Hall; Tel: 767-445-8291, discountrental@cwdom.dm*

Economy Car Rental *Roseau; Tel: 767-449-9559*

Island Car Rental *Roseau & Marigot; www.islandcar.dm; Tel: 767-445-8789 (Marigot), 767-255-6844 (Roseau), 767-255-6867 (cell); resevations@islandcar.dm*

Silver Lining Car Rental *Portsmouth; Tel: 767-445-3802; silverlining@cwdom.dm, www.silverliningrental.com*

JX Rent A Car *Picard; Tel: 767-445-3498*

Lindo Park Car Rental *Goodwill; www.lindoparkrental.com; Tel: 767-448-2599, 767-275-3410 (cell); info@lindoparkrental.com*

TAXIS

Dominican taxis look exactly like the 16 passenger buses and have an "H" or "HA" on the license plate. The government licenses taxi drivers and they should have their credentials prominently displayed. You'll find taxis lined up outside of the airport as you get off of your plane and at the cruise ship docks when a ship is in port. The taxis are unmetered and there are set fares from the government so it is rarely possible to negotiate a deal. When arriving at Melville Hall airport, it is very difficult to catch a public bus so if you aren't renting a car, it's worth it to pay for a taxi to take you to your accommodation that first time. Drivers accept EC and US currency. If you have problems or questions call the **Dominica Taxi Association** (Tel: 767-235-8648) or **Dominica Tourism Division** (Tel: 767-448-2045). A few reliable taxi companies include:

> **Typical Taxi Rates:**
>
> Melville Hall to Roseau:
> EC$65 (US$26)
>
> Melville Hall to Soufrière:
> EC$85 (US$34)
>
> Melville Hall to Calibishie:
> EC$30 (US$12)

> **Mally's Taxi and Tours** *Roseau; Tel: 767-448-3114, 767-235-2105*

> **Island Tours & Taxi Service** *Roseau; Tel: 767-440-0944*

> **A1 Taxi Services** *Portsmouth; Tel: 767-445-4154*

> **Faithful Taxi Services** *Roseau; Tel: 767-277-1126, 767-612-4497; faithfultaxi@gmail.com*

> **Ducky Tours & Taxi Service** *Roseau; Tel: 767-265-7246, 767-265-7484*

BUS

Anyone who is interested in having a true Dominican experience should hop on a bus once for a generally uncomfortable, yet cultural-ly rich excursion. A ride in these brightly colored buses is a great place to hear local gossip, listen to some popular Caribbean music (sometimes with an all-passenger sing-a-long), interact with delightfully curious children, listen to the melodious cadence of Creole, and get to know some locals who will likely delight in telling you about their island.

The buses are large 16 passenger vans with the driver's name or a slogan pasted to the front window such as "Let Dem Talk" or "Jah Run Tings." Buses are privately owned but fares are set by the government and are quite inexpensive ranging from EC$1.75 to EC$11. Schedules are less predictable and often drivers generally won't leave until the bus is full.

> **Sample Bus Fares from Roseau**
> (see regional chapters for more fares)
>
> Carib Territory EC$11
>
> Calibishie EC$11
>
> Canefield EC$2.50
>
> Delices EC$11
>
> Grand Bay EC$5
>
> Laudat EC$4
>
> Marigot EC$11
>
> Portsmouth EC$9
>
> Soufrière EC$4
>
> Trafalgar EC$3.50 (EC$5.00 to the Falls)

The main bus hub is Roseau (see map in Roseau chapter) and a smaller one in Portsmouth that serves the north. You can also flag buses down from the side of the road and they will stop if they aren't full. Most start running around 6am and stop around 5pm on weekdays and earlier on Saturdays. Almost no buses run on Sundays. Getting to Portsmouth, Soufrière, and Grand Bay via bus is usually quick and easy.

Buses run frequently all day and sometimes as late as 6pm. Getting to the east and southeast is much more difficult. Buses leave for those areas around noon from Roseau and again between 4 and 5pm.

It's a good idea to check with drivers before that to see when you should be at the bus stop so that you don't get left behind. Many villages only have one or two buses and they fill up fast. Note that if you get a bus to the east or southeast, you won't be able to get back to Roseau that same day by bus. You'll need to make arrangements to stay the night in that area and come back the next morning or afternoon.

Buses to Roseau Valley are fairly frequent, except to Laudat, which only has one bus and therefore only runs a few times a day.

If you are going to the northern villages you can get a bus to Portsmouth and then find a connecting bus once you get there. These run fairly regularly. Always be sure to ask your driver where they are going to be sure you don't jump into the wrong bus, as many park in the same area.

HITCHHIKING

Hitchhiking is a perfectly acceptable way to get around Dominica as most people don't have cars and buses aren't reliable, especially in remote areas. Dominicans who own cars, and especially those with trucks, are accustomed to giving rides and will gladly pick you up if they are able to. Flagging down a hitch is just like flagging down a bus: stick your arm straight out and wave your hand up and down (please don't stick up your thumb, you'll only confuse people). Ask the driver how far they are going and if it works for you, jump in. When you are in the back of a truck and want to be let down, tap the top of the cab to signal that you are stopping. You do not need to offer money for the ride, normally the drivers don't expect it but every once in awhile they'll ask and then it would be appropriate to hand over EC$5 or so to help pay for gas. If you are a woman traveling alone, hitchhiking becomes more risky. Be picky about who you take rides from and try to get a truck as opposed to getting into someone's car. And no one should hitch at night unless it's absolutely necessary. This is when drunk drivers are out in force and the roads are too dangerous to risk it. Also, if you are renting a car, it's acceptable to pick up passengers and they will definitely ask, and is a great way to get to know people. Use your judgment as to who you pick up.

ORGANIZED TOURS

If you want to see the island and don't want to drive or spend a large portion of your day waiting for a bus, jumping on board a tour isn't a bad idea if you don't mind hanging out with other tourists. You can find tour guides at the cruise ship docks when a boat is in port or can arrange a tour with your accommodation (or though Fort Young Hotel). The tour guides are trained and licensed through the Ministry of Tourism and have thorough knowledge of the history and flora and fauna of the island, not to mention a local's perspective. Most tours will take you to points of interest, waterfalls, beaches, view points, and on easy to challenging hikes. Most will take up a good portion of the day. They range in price from US$65-$90, depending on the activity.

Bus Etiquette

There is a certain etiquette when riding the bus. While it is not a big deal if you don't follow these customs, you'll just appear more seasoned if you do.

If you are flagging down a bus from the side of the road, the recognized signal is sticking your arm straight out and waving your hand up and down. This also works when hitching a ride. Sticking your thumb up will only confuse people.

Some buses have what's called a chauffer, which is a hired person who is positioned by the back door and helps to organize passengers and their belongings. They may direct you as to where you should sit and will often take your things and place them in an empty space if you are carrying luggage or a lot of bags.

When entering the bus it's appropriate to greet the other passengers with a "good day." They'll be impressed at your politeness. If the bus is full, you may be forced to squeeze into spots you never imagined you could fit and will possibly have bags or children piled on your lap.

The seats on the end of the row fold down on most buses to accommodate a few extra passengers, but this means that when someone at the back of the bus wants to exit, all passengers on the end row must get up to let them out so be prepared to do some frequent shuffling.

If you aren't sure where you need to get off, tell the driver where you are going and they will let you know when it's your stop. Other passengers are helpful with this as well. When you reach your destination, say "stopping" loud enough for the driver to hear but without damaging anyone's eardrums.

You pay after you exit the bus. If you are unsure of the fare, don't hesitate to ask the passengers or driver. It's very unlikely that you'd be quoted unfairly.

A few things to note:

- If you are going a far distance, especially through the interior of the island, and are prone to motion sickness, you may want to take some motion sickness medicine. If you neglected to bring your own, you can purchase some from Jolly's pharmacy in Roseau.
- Don't slam the bus door! Nothing angers a driver faster than having their door slammed. Close the door gently but firmly.
- Buses leave out of Roseau from designated spots, which are generally not marked. To find your stop, see the map (pg 107) in the Roseau chapter.
- Designated buses have an H, HA, or HB on the license plate.
- If a bus passes you when are waiting for a ride, don't take it personally. They may be privately hired, full, only going a short distance, or may not be taking passengers at the moment.
- Complaints should be directed to the Dominica Taxi Association (Tel: 767-235-8648) or the Dominica Division of Tourism (Tel: 767-448-2045). Try to get the license plate number before you call if possible.
- When coming into Roseau, you will most likely be let out at that bus's regular stop. You can ask to be let out at a different spot but may have to pay an extra dollar. Bear in mind that drivers may only go a certain distance and you'll have to either pay more to go further or walk the rest of the way.

Recommended Tour Agencies

KHATTS Tours *Tel: 767-448-4850; info@khatts.com, www.khattstours.com*

Wacky Rollers *Tel: 767-440-4386; wackyrollers@yahoo.com, www.wackyrollers.com*

Off the Beaten Trail Adventures *Tel: 767-275-1317; adquatics@yahoo.com*

Cool Breeze Tours *Tel: 767-245-1776, 767-265-3760; coolbreezetours@yahoo.com*

Pepper's Tours *Tel: 767-440-4321, 767-245-1234, 767-616-4321; askpepper@pepperscottage.com, www.sweetdominica.com*

Bumpiing Tours *Tel: 767-265-9128, 767-315-0493, www.bumpiingtours.com*

Jungle Trekking and Adventure Safaris *Tel: 845-367-4264 (U.S.); 767-440-5827, 767-275-5827 (Dominca); jtas@cwdom.dm, www.experiencescaribbean.com*

Money, Costs & Banks

Basics

BUDGET

Like nearly every island in the Caribbean, Dominica isn't a "cheap" place to visit. However if you plan it right and can do without some luxuries, you can make your visit quite affordable. The accommodation you choose will have the biggest impact on the cost of your trip. High-end accommodation will cost you upwards of US$225 per night for a double room. You can, however, find a moderately priced but still decent place for around US$75-$100. If you really want to cut corners there are some guesthouses for as little as US$30-40 for a double room.

Renting a car is another expense at around US$50 per day. Traveling by bus is very cheap (while hitchhiking is free) and efficient when planned in advance.

Meals will run you about US$10-$20 for a full meal. Some visitors prefer to stay in a guesthouse with self-catering facilities cutting their costs significantly by buying their food from local fisherman, vegetable stands, and roadside markets. So with those money-saving strategies in mind and by splitting costs with a travel companion, you can safely bet on spending about US$40 per day per person.

CURRENCY

Dominica uses the Eastern Caribbean Dollar (EC$ or XCD) which is also the official currency in Anguilla, Antigua and Barbuda, Grenada, Monserrat, St. Lucia, St. Kitts and Nevis, and St. Vincent and the Grenadines. The exchange rate is EC$2.67 to US$1 and is tied to the U.S. dollar, varying only by a few cents since its adoption in 1979. Eeastern Caribbean cash comes in denominations of EC$100, EC$50, EC$20, EC$10 and EC$5. Coins come in EC$1, as well as 50, 25, 10, 5 and 1 cent.

In hotels and touristy restaurants, you'll find prices quoted in EC and US dollars and most places are willing to accept either currency. Change is almost always provided in EC dollars.

ATMs are the easiest way to get money and can be found at the main banks in Roseau, at the National Bank of Dominica in Portsmouth, and at both of the airports. They only dispense EC dollars and many banks charge a hefty fee at the ATM – in addition to the fee your bank may charge.

Traveler's checks can be exchanged in the main banks and at some larger hotels. **Credit cards** can be used at the larger hotels, the nicer restaurants, and big grocery stores. Always ask beforehand to be sure as sometimes the machines are down unexpectedly. No business will accept American Express.

BANKS

The majority of banks are found in Roseau and Portsmouth. Hours are Mon-Thur 8am-2pm and Friday 8am-4pm. Banks usually offer the best exchange rate.

Roseau Banks

First Caribbean International Bank *Old Street, Tel: 767-448-2571; M-Th 8am-3pm, Fri 8am-5pm ATM*

Royal Bank of Canada *Dame Eugenia Charles Blvd, Tel: 767-448-2771; M-Th 8am-2pm, Fri 8am-4pm ATM*

Scotiabank International *Hillsborough St, Tel: 67-448-5800; M-Th 8am-2pm, Fri 8am-4pm ATM*

National Bank of Dominica (Head Office) *Hillsborough Street; Tel: 767-255-2300; Hours: M-Th 8am-2pm, Fri 8am-4pm. ATM; (Roseau Branch) Independent Street; Tel: 767-255-2624; M-Th 8am-2pm, Fri 8am-4pm. ATM*

Portsmouth Banks

First Caribbean International *Bank Granby St; 767-445-5271; M-Th 8am-2pm, Fri 8am-5pm ATM*

National Bank of Dominica *Bay St; 767-445-5430; M-Th 8am-2pm, Fri 8am-4pm ATM.*

Canefield Banks

National Bank of Dominica *Imperial Rd; 767-449-2140; M-Th 9am-4pm, Fri 9am-5pm*

WIRING MONEY

You can transfer money from Western Union locations in Roseau, and at some village credit unions. Moneygrams are also available in Roseau.

Western Union Locations

Roseau *Whitchurch, Old Street*

Portsmouth *Whitchurch, Michael Douglas Blvd*

Grand Bay *Credit Union, L'Allay*

La Plaine *Credit Union*

Castle Bruce *Credit Union*

Marigot *Credit Union*

Calibishie *A&A Low Cost Center*

Moneygram Locations

Roseau *Cambio Man on Cork St; Going Places Travel on Old St*

Goodwill *Bull's Eye Pharmacy, Federation Drive*

Canefield *Breezee's Mart*

Picard *G&A Enterprises*

Portsmouth *M&R Trading, Granby St.*

Calibishie *Business Links Limited*

TAXES AND GRATUITIES

Hotels in Dominica will often add an extra 10% service charge and 8% government tax to the rate, which can quickly bring your bill up at an alarming rate. Be sure to check with your accommodation before booking to see if that tax is included in the quoted rates. Some restaurants, especially the ones that cater to tourists, may add an additional service charge to the bill as well.

Tipping isn't the norm in Dominica and most wait staff and bar staff will not expect a tip (which may explain why the service isn't always top-notch). If you feel like you get especially good service, it is fine to leave a tip as a way of saying "thanks." It is expected that you tip luggage porters at the airport (EC$0.50 per bag), tour guides, and cab drivers a modest amount. If you are taking the bus and the driver goes out of his way to drop you somewhere or helps you carry your bags, it's nice to tip them an extra couple of dollars as well.

Keeping in Touch

The **telephone** system in Dominica is reliable and easy, albeit expensive, to keep in touch with friends and family at home. Pay phones are scattered throughout Roseau – and the rest of the island –and take EC coins, credit cards or prepaid phone cards through *Lime* (sometimes called *Cable and Wireless*). You can purchase pre-paid calling cards at nearly any shop or pharmacy in any village.

You can rent a **cell phone** from many car rental companies or hotels, which is easier and much cheaper than using pay phones or a hotel phone. You can purchase a cell phone for around EC$100 from the *Digicel* or *Lime* store directly. These will take pre-paid cards as well so be sure to ask what kind of phone you have if you rent so that you'll know what kind of card to buy. Calling local numbers is nearly as expensive as calling internationally so ask the retailer or renter what kind of deals are going on so that you don't end up spending a fortune. Calls within the same network are much cheaper than across networks (Digicel to Digicel calls are cheaper than Digicel to Lime or Lime to Digicel). A Digicel number will start with a 61, Lime numbers start with a 2 or 3, and land lines start with 44 at the beginning of their seven digit phone number.

INTERNATIONAL CALLS

To call Dominica from overseas, use your country's international access code followed by area code 767 and the seven-digit phone number. For instance, to call Dominica from the States, simply dial 1-767-number.

International Access Codes

U.S., Canada, and the Caribbean: 1 + area code + number

UK 011+44+number	Ireland 011+353+number
Australia 011+61+number	Netherlands 011+53+number
France 011+53+number	New Zealand 011+64+number
Germany 011+53+number	Norway 011+53+number
	Spain 011+53+number

MAIL

The mail system in Dominica is pretty reliable, but mail sent from the island will take *at least* two weeks to reach any overseas location. A letter to the U.S. and Europe will cost about EC$1. The main post office is in Roseau located on the westernmost end of Dame Eugenia Charles Blvd and is open from 8am-4pm, Mon-Fri.

Faxing can be done through the business center at the larger hotels (Ft. Young, Garraway, Sutton Place) in Roseau. There will be a fee plus the cost of the call.

If a package was mailed to you it must be picked up in the post office and opened in front of a customs official. You will need to show then an official photo ID and they will sort through the items in the package to determine how much you have to pay in customs. This isn't highly regulated and for electronics and luxury items you can pay as much as 60% of the value of the item.

Shipping Services

If you want to mail a package home in a timely manner, consider using a FedEx, UPS, or DHL services which are quick and very reliable, although rather expensive.

DHL *Whitchurch Travel Agency on Hanover and Kennedy St, Roseau Tel: 767-448-5887; Hours M-F 8am-4pm; Sat 8am-1pm*

FedEx *Cork and Old St, Roseau Tel: 767-448-0992, 767-448-0993; Hours M-F 8am-4pm*

UPS *LIAT Ltd, 64 King George V St, Roseau Tel: 767-448-3185; Hours M-F 8am-4pm*

INTERNET

Dominica has fast and reliable internet access and many hotels offer DSL or wireless internet services to guests. There are also a growing number of internet cafés where you can either rent a computer or access wireless.

Roseau Internet Access

Ruins (Wireless) *Across from the Old Market, Roseau; Hours: M-Sat 8am-late, Open Sunday if a cruise ship is in port.*

Computer and Trading Solutions Internet Center Offers copy service, scanning and faxing. *Independence Street, Roseau; Hours: M-F 8:30am-6pm, Sat 10am-7pm Cost: $3.50EC/30 min.*

Zenith Internet Café *Hanover Street, Roseau; Hours: M-F 8:30am-5:30pm, Sat 9am-5pm; Cost: $3 EC/30 min.*

Cyberland *Great George and Cork Street, Roseau; Tel: 767-440-2650; Hours: M-F 8:30am- 6pm, Sat 10am-5pm; Cost: $3EC/30 min.*

Roseau Public Library (Wireless) *Victoria St, Roseau; Tel: 767-266-3341 Hours: M-F 9am-5pm, Sat 9am-12pm.*

Rituals Coffee House (Wireless) *Dame Eugenia Charles Blvd, Roseau; Tel: 767-440-2233/440-2633; Hours: M-F 7am-7pm, Sat 10:30am-7pm, Sun 10:30am-4pm; Cost: US$3/hr.*

Cocorico *Dame Eugenia Charles Blvd, Roseau; Tel: 767-449-8686; Hours: M-F 8:30am-4pm, Sat 8:30am-2pm; Cost: EC$5/30min.*

Top Shottaz Internet Café Two computers available for use. *Dame Eugenia Charles Blvd, Roseau; Hours: 10am-very late; Cost: EC$3.50/30 min.*

Portsmouth Internet Access

Alpha-2-Omega *Bay Street, Portsmouth; Tel: 767-445-3370; Hours: 9am-10pm Mon- Sat; Cost: $3/30 min.*

The Tomato (Wireless) *Picard; Tel: 767-445-3334; www.thetomatocafe.com; M-Th 9am-9pm, F-Sa 9am-10m closed Sun; Cost: free for customers.*

Bar De Champ (Wireless) *Picard; Tel: 767-445-4452, 767-275-3660; Cost: free for customers and guests.*

Business Training Center *Bay Street, Portsmouth; Tel: 767-445-3480; Hours: M-Sa 8am-5pm; Cost: EC$2.50/30 min.*

MEDIA

The main source of information for everything in Dominica, including news and events, is on the radio. In particular **DBS Radio** which can be found on 88.1FM. Two other popular stations are **Kairi FM** on 88.7FM, 93.1FM, and 107.9FM and **Q95FM** on you guessed it, 95FM. Most of the stations broadcast some type of religious programming but if you are looking for all religion all the time, check out **Voice of Life** on 102.1FM and 106.1FM.

Dominica's newspapers provide information about entertainment news as well as interesting cultural insights and make for a fun read. The three national newspapers are *The Times*, *The Sun*, and *The Chronicle* and *The Tip!* magazine is good for entertainment news.

There are two cable television stations that broadcast U.S. television shows and news stations, as well as some local programming.

Shopping

Dominica is not a very enticing destination for the avid shopper. Recently though there has been an increase in the number of duty free shops and you'll be able to find a good selection of crafts easily on island. Most shops are open from 8am-5pm, Mon-Fri and from 8am-1pm on Saturdays. All of the **duty free shops** are located in Roseau (see page 117) and offer everything from liquor, leather goods, t-shirts, sunglasses, watches, and jewelry to cigars and special foods. Keep in mind that just because things are labeled "duty free" they aren't necessarily that much cheaper than what you'll find at home. So be sure you are getting a deal since you may have to pay customs on it when you enter back into your home country.

> For information on supermarkets and purchasing food, see page 90.

Crafts and Souvenirs

Locally made products are probably going to be the best option for buying a quality souvenir from Dominica. The best crafts for the best prices are located in the Carib Territory and are sold on the side of the road at stands, small shops and there is always an excellent selection at Kalinago Bara Auté (pg 193). You'll find handmade baskets woven out of local reeds or banana leaves, carved calabash bowls, masks made out of wood or local fern trees, jewelry made from seeds and shells, and items made from bamboo.

There are also some great options to purchase locally made souvenirs in Roseau. In Whitchurch Supermarket there is a special section of local products that includes hot sauce, jams and jellies made from local fruits, bay rum (a natural aftershave),

Coal Pot soap, cocoa sticks (used to make hot chocolate), local spices, tamarind balls and candies made from coconut and sugar called "tablet." They also sell gift baskets that have small packets of spices and small jars of jam.

The Old Market in Roseau is the place to find things that were made in China but have the name "Dominica" imprinted on them somewhere. This is where you'll find t-shirts, beach wraps, bags, key chains, magnets, coffee mugs, and shot glasses. There is also a stand with jewelry, purses, and small locally made drums.

Across from the Old Market is the Ruins Café, which is an excellent place to get handmade bush rum in hand-painted bottles and lots of local spices.

If you want to pick up some local artwork, there is a great gallery around the corner from Cocorico Café on Kennedy Ave and Long Lane and another really outstanding and prominent artist Ellingsworth Moses works out of a gallery that is located in the back of Mangé Domnik on King George V Street in Roseau.

Recommended Souvenirs
Handmade Carib baskets
Carved fern tree mask
Sorrel jelly (hibiscus)
Handmade jewelry
Calabash bowl
Local spices
Local rum in hand-painted bottles
Coal Pot soap

Holidays & Festivals

Dominica's main events every year are Carnival and Independence Season, which includes the World Creole Music Festival. These events attract a lot of tourists and you'll find that there will be a plethora of exciting events and cultural performances. With that also comes a higher price for air fare, accommodation, and car rental. Also note that for all public holidays, most businesses will be closed and buses will not be running.

PUBLIC HOLIDAYS AND EVENTS

January New Years holiday include January 1-2 (public holidays). Most Dominicans go to church for New Years Eve (maybe to repent for all of the partying that goes on during Christmas).

February/March Carnival always takes place the Monday and Tuesday before Ash Wednesday (so in 2011 it will actually be March 7-8, in 2012 it will be February 20-21). Both days and Ash Wednesday are public holidays.

April Good Friday and Easter Monday are public holidays.

May Labour Day is a public holiday and takes place the first Monday of May. Some years a Flower Show is held during this month in Giraudel and DOMFESTA, which promotes the arts in Dominica, takes place as well. In Grand Bay the Feast of St. Isadore will take place in May and is a celebration of the harvest. It involves a church service, villagers dressed in traditional madras wear and cultural dances and events.

June Whit Monday (always the day after Pentecost) is a public holiday. Feast of St. Peter takes place at the very end of June or early July and involves a church service and the blessing of fishing boats in villages where this is the main source of income. San Sauveur has a nice festival during this time.

July Dive Fest takes place for one week in July and is a great time to try diving for the first time or take part in competitions for the more experienced diver. Typical events include a Carib canoe race, a wine and cheese sunset cruise, underwater scavenger hunts, photography contests, and quiz show nights. It's always a fun, family friendly event. You can find the dates and more information online at http://dominicawatersports.com/divefest.cfm

August August Monday, a public holiday, takes place the first Monday of August.

September Carib Week generally takes place in September and celebrates the cultural traditions of the indigenous people of the Caribbean. Call the Carib council office (Tel: 767-445-7336) for exact dates.

October During the month of October people start gearing up for Independence Day with traditional dance and music competitions. The last week of the month you can attend Creole in the Park with all day musical events in the Botanical Gardens, Creole in the East, which takes place in La Plaine, and the three-night music marathon in Roseau called the World Creole Music Festival which attracts many prominent musicians. A full calendar of events can be found online at http://www.avirtualdominica.com/independence.cfm

Basics

Carnival

Carnival festivities usually start about a month before Carnival with Princess and Calypso shows, warm-up parades, feasts and street "jump ups." The Calypso shows are very entertaining as local musicians put on a big show and reveal songs written to poke fun at or address a current local issue. Towards the end of the season, there is a culminating event at the stadium in Roseau to crown the next year's Calypso King or Queen. The princess shows are similar but are full on beauty pageants that also culminate in an event held in the stadium to crown that year's Carnival Princess.

On the Sunday night before Carnival there are typically all-night events and concerts, as people gear up for J'ouvert (pronounced *joo-vay*), which starts at around 4am. People start to crowd the streets, dressed up in crazy costumes, with handmade goat-skin drums and traditional instruments forming a street "jump-up." As the sun comes up, the attention shifts to the big parade in Roseau. This is a wonderful event and all of the rich European and African traditions are still honored and make for a fun afternoon.

Tuesday is another parade but this one has more of the modern "bouillon" bands with giant stereos and a pulsating beat. A crowd of mesmerized partiers, all in matching t-shirts, bounce along behind the speakers.

On Wednesday night you can head to Dublanc on the west coast or the Carib Territory in the east to take part in Tewé Vaval. This is the symbolic burial of the spirit of Carnival. A coffin is crafted out of cardboard and an effigy is placed inside and paraded down the road while people sing in Creole, play drums, and carry torches made from bottles until they reach the culminating point in the night where a short ceremony is performed and the effigy is set on fire.

November Independence Day is on November 3 and National Day of Community Service on November 4, each of which are public holidays. There is a parade in the Botanical Gardens on Independence Day and a National Cultural Gala, which showcases some of Dominica's local talent and traditional foods.

December Christmas Day on the 25th and Boxing Day on the 26th are each public holidays. Christmas Eve is "shopping day" and everyone flocks to the capital where the stores are open late, street food vendors are out and it's a big celebratory party in the streets. Buses run late to accommodate this event.

Getting Married in Dominica

If Dominica is your wedding destination of choice, there are a few extra requirements necessary to get hitched here. At least one member of the party must be in Dominica for a minimum of two days prior to the ceremony. Birth Certificates and passports are required and if married before, a decree of divorce or death certificate of the former spouse must be produced. You must fill out necessary forms and pay a license fee of EC$300 (US$112) at the Magistrates Court. A visit to the Registry office is also required. For more information contact the Ministry of Community Development at 767-448 2401 or visit www.avirtualdominica.com/theknot.cfm

---

Places of Worship

One thing you won't have trouble finding in Dominica is a place to go to church. Each village has at least a Catholic Church and usually one or two other denominations as well, depending on the area. Most services start at 9am and last at least two hours, and some all day. Sevices typically start on time, so inquire beforehand about the start time to be sure you aren't walking in late. Dominicans take this opportunity to wear their best clothes and many of the women wear beautiful dresses and hats to church and the men wear button down shirts and slacks with closed toe shoes. So if you plan on attending a church, be sure to bring a dress with sleeves or appropriate menswear. Most people bring their own bibles and hymnals as the church doesn't always keep them in house.

Advice from Mom
You need to go to church!

If you have the opportunity and the inclination, attend a church service on Sunday morning. We went to a Protestant service in Calibishie and found it thoroughly enjoyable and inspiring. After the service nearly everyone introduced themselves to us and many invited us to a social gathering later that day. (A word about church etiquette: women shouldn't wear pants or a sleeveless blouse/dress as it's considered inappropriate attire.)

   "Won't forget it" moment: Two little girls in the pew in front of us turned around in their seats and stared at us through most of the service. I think they were amazed that foreigners knew the words to the songs they were singing!

Conduct & Customs

Dominicans are a laid-back people and are generally easy to get along with, especially if you follow a few simple guidelines. The pace of life here is slow and Dominicans begin every activity, even something as standard as walking into a store or a simple phone inquiry, with a greeting of "good morning," "good afternoon" or "good night" (yep, "good night" is a greeting here). Beginning with a greeting accompanied by a smile, even if you are feeling frustrated, will get any conversation off to a good start, not to mention keep the conversation going. Dominicans don't have much patience for stressed out and hurried tourists – they just can't relate. Remaining calm and pleasant will usually get you further than making angry demands if things aren't going your way. Be sure to greet those in authority or official positions as "mister" or "Miss" as a form of respect.

Try to look respectable, especially in Roseau. Dominicans take pride in their appearance and work hard to keep their clothes and shoes neat and clean. Going into Roseau is a big deal for many Dominicans and they wear their best clothes and get their hair done just for the occasion. This makes it difficult for them to understand why a foreign traveler, who they assume to have money, would walk around looking shabby and unkempt. Bathing suit attire should be kept to the beach and women who are traveling alone should be particularly mindful of dressing modestly so as not to garner unwanted attention. If you will be entering a church or dealing with government officials for any reason, it is especially important to dress nicely and conservatively.

Be courteous when taking photos and ask permission first. Most people will say yes and you may even make a new friend. Children especially love to pose for photographs and most will beg you to take more.

Sexual tolerance hasn't been embraced in Caribbean culture yet and many people are still very homophobic. Public displays of affection between two men or two women will likely be met with hostility. For more, see the box Gay Travelers in Dominica on page 67.

Accommodations

As a visitor, you will find a variety of accommodations to match your budget, personal tastes, or vacation plans. From locally owned guest houses to beach front villas, eco-lodges to resorts, you are sure to find something to suit your needs. If you want to maximize your time hiking in Morne Trois Pitons National Park, you may want to stay at one of the mountain top cottages in Roseau Valley. If you are looking for a relaxing vacation by the beach, then a villa on the west coast may be more suitable. You can also find an outstanding all-inclusive spa and yoga retreat center at one of the top rated eco-lodges in the Caribbean on the southeast coast. No matter where you stay, you are almost guaranteed to have an amazing view and will certainly get a taste of local life.

Locally owned guesthouses will likely be the cheapest and it is possible to get a room (although it will probably be less than ideal) for as little as US$20/night. The mid-range options are very suitable for most travelers and will be around US$60-$75/night. Top-end hotels and guesthouses are generally run by foreigners and are usually quite nice and very comfortable. They start at around US$100/night and go up from there and will typically include some meals. If you brought your camping gear, there are only a few places to camp but they are cheap and probably close to a clean river to make for nice bathing. As the Waitukubuli Trail gets established they will be setting up camping areas along the trail. Call Eric (Tel: 767-266-3593) at the forestry department to get more information. At the time of writing, a hostel is being built in the inside of an old fort that will soon be an affordable option for backpackers and those on a budget. It is important to note that many hotels may add on a 10% service charge as well as a 10% government tax (VAT). Please inquire when booking whether that is included in the price or added on at the end.

Another option is to sign up on **www.couchsurfing.com**, which is a great way to travel and save money while getting to know an area from a local perspective. The way it works is that people who have a couch or an extra room can sign up to host needy travelers. The travelers sign up and search for a place to stay. Emails are exchanged via the website and arrangements are made if it's a good fit for both. Afterwards, both parties leave public feedback on the website as to the quality of their experience with the other person. The traveler is responsible for bringing their own food and usually will compensate the host by cooking them a meal or some other nice gesture. It's a fun way to meet people and can really help save money.

Most accommodations in Dominica will have modern amenities such as electricity and hot running water. However you may want to inquire before booking if they have air-conditioning, internet, or TV, if that is a priority for you.

Accommodations in this book are listed by region and are categorized by price. Budget options will cost up to US$75, Mid-range from US$75-US$150 and Top-end will cost over US$150. Prices are graded according to the cheapest double room during high season (November-April). Prices will sometimes be lower in the off-season but you'll want to inquire first.

Advice from Mom
You must be a friend to make a friend (as my mother always said).

In other words, be friendly and Dominicans will respond in kind. We stayed in the small village of Riviere Cyrique and the communal water source was just across the road from our cottage. We sat out on the front porch in the morning while drinking our coffee and would say "hello" and speak to the people collecting their water for the day. After a few days our host told us that she heard we had been friendly and expressed her approval and that of our neighbors. One man told us he lived in the U.S. for a few years, residing in an apartment complex during that time. None of his neighbors befriended or spoke to him so he moved back to Dominica with the impression that Westerners just weren't friendly. Let's not perpetuate that image.

"Won't forget it" moment: Our traveling companion, Kenny, taught some neighborhood girls how to play four-square in the road by our cottage. They had a great time!

Food, Drink & Nightlife

With its wide array of fresh, locally grown tropical fruits, vegetables, herbs and spices, Dominica offers visitors a taste of the island in what is called "**Creole Food.**" Meals are usually comprised of stewed fish, chicken, pork, or goat meat served in a sauce with two types of starches. One of which will be root vegetables (called "provisions"), and the other will typically be mac n' cheese, fig pie, potato salad, or spaghetti. You will many times also get a small side of salad (generally just lettuce and a tomato slice) and beans. Although most Creole food probably won't send your taste buds into a state of rapturous bliss, you can get some excellent fresh fish most places, like at the **Fish Pot** (pg 227) in Pt. Michel. As the tourism industry grows, more restaurants are serving West Indian cuisine fused with international flavors. The result is really quite good and generally very healthy.

Basics

STAPLES AND SPECIALTIES

Provisions are ubiquitous and are essentially a variety of root tubers: dasheen, yam, tannia, sweet potato, as well as unripe green bananas, green plantains, and bread-fruit. Found on nearly every plate, these were once the weekly "provisions," which is where the name comes from, given to slave and estate laborers.

Bread is another popular carb that is quite delicious when freshly baked and straight from the bread shop. The best I've found is in the small village of Bellevue (pg 227) where it is baked in a wood-fired stove.

Bread on Dominica comes either in small or large baguette style (called mastif) loaves and is usually eaten in the evening as a dinner item. A popular, and the oldest, bread shop is Suki's, which is in Newtown just south of Roseau. They have several types of bread and pastries available in the main shop and in smaller shops around Roseau. Most villages also have a small bread truck that drives through the village every afternoon that delivers fresh bread. It typically looks like a small white van with no windows and will honk as it drives slowly down the road, stopping when people run outside to buy something off the truck. Try a coconut turnover if you get a chance.

Dominicans eat a lot of **meat**, particularly chicken, goat, pig and very occasionally cow. It often contains bones and is stewed in a tomato-based sauce. However you can mix things up by getting some excellent barbeque chicken on the weekends. You will find that locals eat animal parts you've never thought to eat before and if that makes you uncomfortable, you may want to ask before ordering something unfamiliar. *Souse*, in particular, almost always contains pig ears, pig feet, and sometimes tongue and you will also find that the back and neck of a chicken is very commonly included in traditional dishes.

Dominican Food Glossary

Accra- Deep fried fritter, sometimes with salted cod fish.

Agouti- Large rodent-type creature, eaten as a stewed meat dish.

Bakes- Fried semi-sweet dough eaten as a snack; called "dry bakes" when eaten plain and "stuffed bakes" when stuffed with cheese or fish.

Bazélik- a type of basil, used to make evening tea.

Bois Bandé-The bark of a local tree said to be an aphrodisiac, used to infuse tea and rum.

Breadfruit- Starchy fruit that grows on a tree. Eaten roasted, boiled, or fried.

Breadnut- Large nuts that grow on a tree similar to that of a breadfruit. Eaten raw or roasted.

Broth (or Braf)- A soup usually containing meat (or fish), vegetables, and seasoned broth.

Bush tea- Tea infused with local plants and herbs that is said to be medicinal in nature.

Bush rum- Cask rum infused with herbs, spices, fruit, or bark and used to make rum punch.

Callaloo- Dasheen or spinach leaf used to make a popular soup.

Canep- Small round green fruits sold in a bunch. Break open the thin green skin with your teeth and suck on the sweet white fruit inside.

Carambola- a sweet, sometimes tart star shaped fruit also called 5-finger fruit and star fruit.

Chatou water- Soup made with octopus.

Christophene- Green oval shaped vegetable with a soft white flesh. Eaten boiled or sautéed.

Coconut water- Liquid inside of a young "jelly' coconut. Very healthy and refreshing.

Cane-Refers to sugar cane that people chew on as a sweet treat.

Cassava-Also known as manioc, a root vegetable that is ground up, the liquid extracted, dried out, then typically made into a bread that is a traditional Carib staple.

Cocoa tea- A traditional type of hot chocolate made with cocoa beans, sugar, spices, and milk.

Custard apple- Green or pink bumpy fruit with sweet custard-like flesh and black seeds.

Dasheen- Starchy root vegetable, usually boiled, as a "provision."

Dolphin-A common fish (no, they don't eat Flipper here) also known as dorado.

Dry nut-Dry coconut

Dumpling- Flour, salt and water combo used in one-pots, soups, and stews.

Farine- Made from dried cassava-usually used as breakfast porridge.

Fig- Banana, also called "green fig" when unripe.

Goat water- Goat meat soup or stew.

Golden apple- Yellow or green skin with deep yellow very delicious flesh. Makes a good juice.

Guava- Authentic Arawak name given to small round green fruits with tiny seeds and pink flesh. Can be eaten raw or made into juice or jam.

Ice pops- Homemade ice cream served in a little plastic baggies. Bite off a corner of the bag to suck out the ice cream.

Dominican Food Glossary

Kako- Cocoa pod, once opened, eat the white flesh around the cocoa seeds. Very delicious.

Manicou- Like an opossum, the meat is used in stews.

Mountain Chicken (crapaud)- A very large frog that is endangered in Dominica. It is illegal to hunt them so refrain from ordering it if you find it on a menu.

Noni- A stinky and strange looking fruit, bumpy and off-white in color. Said to be very medicinal and used as a drink or rum infusion.

One-pot- A large soup or stew with anything and everything thrown in: meat, vegetables, lentils, and dumplings are the norm.

Passionfruit- Small round yellow fruit with a hard outer skin and jelly covered seeds inside. Used to make juice.

Pawpaw- Also known as papaya, a large orange or yellow fruit that lacks sweetness but is very nutritious.

Pear- A type of avocado that is very large and watery (as opposed to oily).

Pepper Sauce- Hot sauce made from scotch bonnet peppers.

Pelau- Seasoned rice dish typically made with chicken.

Plantain- In the banana family, but larger and less sweet. The unripe plantain is boiled and eaten as a provision and the ripe version is fried and very sweet.

Roti- Flat unleavened bread wrapped around curried vegetables and meat and usually served with fruit chutney.

Saltfish- Dried salted codfish.

Sancoch- Stew made with fish or meat, provisions, and coconut milk.

Scotch Bonnet Peppers- Very small and very spicy peppers.

Seagrapes- Small purple berries the size of a grape with a large seed.

Seamoss- A type of sea weed that is dried and reconstituted with milk to make a gelatinous drink that tastes good and is supposed to be very nutritious.

Sorrel- From the hibiscus family, the red/purple-ish flowers are boiled with spices and used to make a juice that resembles apple cider, only available around Christmas time.

Soursop- Dark green/brownish oval fruit with a white "wooly" flesh inside. Typically used in juice or ice cream.

Souse- Pickled pork parts (usually pig feet) served as an appetizer at events.

Sugar Apple- Much like the custard apple.

Sweetsop- Smaller version of a soursop.

Tablet- Sweetened dried coconut mixed with sugar and sometimes cinnamon.

Tamarind- Brown pods which hold three or four seeds covered in a thick and very tart pulp. Mixed with sugar to make "tamarind balls" or used to make juice.

Tannia- Starchy root vegetable, boiled and served as a "provision."

Titiri- Tiny fish, deep fried and served as accra or eaten whole.

Wax apple- Shiny pink, light weight, fruit shaped like a pear. Can be eaten raw for a refreshing treat.

Seafood is abundant here and usually very fresh. If you are cooking for yourself, listen for the sound of a conch shell in the early evening. After a full-day of spear or boat fishing, the fishermen drive through the villages in a truck piled with fresh fish and a scale and blow a conch shell to announce their sale. The most common fish you'll encounter is the tuna, dolphin (not Flipper, just a regular fish with the same name), marlin, and flying fish. You will also find dried saltfish for sale in nearly every market or small village shop. This is actually imported codfish that comes all the way from Europe and is a favorite that you'll find in many local dishes.

Many **spices** and seasonings are grown in Dominica so you will find a lot of the same flavors in many of your meals. These typically include bay leaf, thyme, cinnamon, nutmeg, parsley, and seasoning peppers. They don't add much salt or pepper to their meals nor will you find it on the table. Bland food is best spiced up with some pepper sauce (local hot sauce).

A good option for **dessert**, if you can find them, is an ice pop. These are a lot like ice cream or popsicles but are homemade and come in little plastic baggies that you typically buy from someone's home. Ask around the village you are staying in to find out who is selling them. Some of the best ice pops can be found in the village of Soufrière (see pg 222). As you enter the village and reach the main junction, go to the right and the second shop down on the right sells amazing ice pops. To eat an ice pop, you bite off a corner of the bag and suck the icy-goodness out of the baggie as it melts.

DRINKS

The tap **water** in Dominica is clean and safe to drink. In my years of living on the island, I have never heard of anyone getting sick from it. However, if there has been a very heavy rain the water may turn brown for a short period of time and in that case, stick to the bottled stuff, which is available at any market or shop, until it clears up. It's not unusual for the water to be shut off, especially right after a storm, for a day or two so it's always wise to have a couple extra large bottles of water around just in case. When it comes back on, if it isn't clear, just run the tap for a bit until it appears to be clean. If you are worried about the water, you can always boil it for several minutes before using it or just stick to the bottled stuff.

One thing you will not want to miss out on while you're here is the fresh squeezed **juice**, which will be offered at any restaurant and most snackettes and roadside stands. Depending on the season you may find passion fruit, guava, grapefruit, tangerine, carambola, mango, and lime. A winter specialty is *sorrel*, which is brewed from the flowers of a type of hibiscus. A range of other, lesser-known fruits that grow naturally on the island are also available and fun to experiment with. J.B. Juice Stand (pg 113) in Roseau has some of the best and if you're counting calories, you can request little to no sugar.

In addition to old school Coca-Cola, you can try some other, just as sugary, **soda** here too. Called "soft drinks" in Dominica, *Quenchi* is the most popular and comes in some interesting flavors with *Chubby* coming in a close second. A really good alternative for those who like "a little somethin' extra" in their soft drink is a Shandy. It's a mix between a beer and a soda that comes in a few different flavors, usually lime, lemon, ginger, and sorrel. Worth a try if you are getting tired of Kubuli.

Stemming from a history of British-colonial rule, **tea** is a popular beverage on the island and is usually drunk in the morning or evening. Most common types are cocoa tea, made from the local cocoa bean and is similar to a hot chocolate, and bush tea, which is made from local plants and herbs and is typically drank for health or medicinal purposes. You'll also find an abundance of regular bagged black tea. **Coffee** is also grown and roasted in Dominica and sold under the name *Café Dominique* in the stores. Somewhat surprising, coffee is not a common drink here and good coffee is hard to come by. Many places serve weak instant coffee instead so ask before ordering if that is unappealing to you.

The only local **brewery** on the island, located in Loubiere, makes a lager called Kubuli, which can be found at nearly all restaurants and roadside shops. If beer is not your thing, then the other option you have is rum (see box on pg 89).

Where to Get a Drink after 5pm

Dominica is not known for its nightlife or club scene and because Dominicans generally get up extremely early, you won't see much *sewo* (partying) late at night. The most common forms of evening entertainment are a laid-back dominos game in a shop or by the road or a drink at a local rum shop. However, if you are willing to travel a bit, you can find some kind of evening amusement most nights of the week. Here are a few to get your started:

Sunday: *Bar de Champ* (Picard): Sunset Dinner, 5:30-8:30pm

Monday: *Fort Young Hotel* (Roseau): Cocktail Party and International Buffet with a live steel pan band, 6-7pm.

Tuesday: *Bar de Champ* (Picard): Movie Night, 5pm.

Wednesday: *Big Papa's* (Portsmouth): Reggae Dance Party and dinner buffet, 7:30pm-onwards.

Thursday: *Symes Zee's* (Roseau): Live music and drinks, 9pm-onwards.

Cocoa Tea Recipe

If you want to take home a special treat to share with your friends when you return (other than rum, of course), cocoa tea is generally a crowd pleaser. You can get nearly all of the ingredients fresh off of the island, often sold in a package to make it even easier for you.

What you need to make one serving:

> ½ cup grated cocoa stick
> 2 cups water
> 1 cup milk
> Fresh grated nutmeg (to taste)
> 1 cinnamon stick
> Lime leaf or small amount of zest (optional)
> Sugar to taste

Bring water to boil along with a piece of cinnamon and optional lime leaf or zest. Boil for 15 minutes. Add grated cocoa stick and boil another 5 minutes. Lower heat and add milk and sugar to sweeten along with the rest of the spices. Stir and enjoy.

Friday: Friday is a big night in Dominica and you will have many options for how to spend your evening. Start with one of the many happy hours like at *Fort Young Hotel* (Roseau) which features a buffet and live music starting at 6pm. The *Evergreen Hotel* (Castle Comfort) has dinner and live jazz from 7pm to 11pm. *The Cove* (Canefield) features live music and drink specials starting at 8pm. After happy hour, get some barbeque from a local vendor then head down to Pt. Michel for a "lime" at *Melvina's* where you'll find drinks, delicious steamed fish, and dancing. If you would rather show off your vocal cords rather than your dance moves, go to the *Garraway Hotel* (Roseau) for some karaoke.

For those who are stationed near the north, head to *Peter's* or *Le Perroquet* in the Lagoon area in the northern area of Portsmouth. You'll find Latin music at *Le Perroquet* and Caribbean jams at *Peter's*.

Saturday: *Big Papa's* (Portsmouth): Caribbean Dance Party that lasts most of the night. Starts around 9pm.

Krazy Kokonuts (Castle Comfort): Dance party with a DJ or band beginning around 10pm.

Coconut Water

Coconut water is like Mother Nature's Gatorade: it's full of electrolytes, has more potassium than bananas, virtually sugar free (ok, that's where it deviates from Gatorade), cholesterol free, fat free and is full of important vitamins and minerals. It's great for re-hydrating – making it the perfect hangover cure – and gives you a natural energy boost. Since it has the same electrolyte balance as blood, it was given intraveneously as a substitute for plasma during WWII.

You can find small green coconuts being sold at the market, at beaches, and on the side of the road for only EC$1. The vendor will open the top for you with their machete and sometimes even supply the straw. When you are finished drinking it, hand it back and have them split it open for you. The white "jelly-like" flesh inside is also very nutritious and tastes pretty good, too.

FRUITS AND VEGGIES

Locals will tell you that it's impossible to starve on their island, and it's true. Everywhere you look you'll see some type of edible plant. **Fruit** and spice trees are abundant and you'll often see children or adults climbing around in the tops of trees trying to grab a ripe mango or orange as a snack. Almost any type of tropical fruit is available here, but only when it's in season. You'll likely encounter some fruits you've never seen before and this is a great opportunity to try something new. If you're unsure of how to eat it, don't be afraid to ask. One thing to note is that grapefruits and oranges are usually green, even when they are ripe. Also, some oranges are sour, and used only for making juice so inquire before you buy as to whether they are selling sweet or sour oranges.

Vegetables, on the other hand, aren't as easy to grow in the tropical climate and wilt very easily in the market. This is especially true with lettuce so buy it early in the morning if possible when it's fresh.

You don't have to worry about fresh foods being contaminated with dodgy water here. It is, however, a good idea to rinse everything off before you eat it so that you don't ingest anything funky that may have been climbing around the trees.

Yo, Ho, Ho, and a Bottle of Rum

"There's nought no doubt so much the spirit calms as rum and true religion"
— Lord Byron

The great thing about rum in Dominica is that it's easy to find and you'll have options when it comes to flavors and varieties. But first, let's start with the history of this sacred drink.

The prevalence of rum in the West Indies started from the earliest days of colonization. Once sugar cane was an established crop on the islands, rum soon followed as it is made from fermenting and distilling molasses, the by-product of sugar production. The British Navy gave their sailors rum as part of their rations in hopes that it would improve their health and make them fight harder. When rum gained popularity in England, it became a much sought after commodity and soon pirates battled over it, slaves were traded for it and wars were started because of it. Famous rum enthusiasts include Benjamin Franklin, Thomas Jefferson, and of course Captain Henry Morgan (yep, the Capitan Morgan), the governor of Jamaica who loved rum so much he drank himself to death.

In small villages of the Caribbean, the rum shop is often where the action is. Rum shops generally sell basic essentials – like rice, flour, eggs, salt, and of course, rum – and it's a place for people to gather, play dominoes, listen to music, and do a shot or two. Much of the rum available in village shops is "bush rum," also known as "spice rum," made from locally produced cask rum and infused with herbs or spices to make it go down a bit easier as it tends to be incredibly strong. The most common varieties of cask rum are *spice*, which is flavored with cinnamon, *bois bandé*, made from a bark that is said to have aphrodisiac qualities, *pueve* which is infused with herbs, and *fruit* or *rosemary* varieties.

Most restaurants make their own homemade variety of rum punch, and nearly all will claim to have the best on the island. The recipes differ but you can expect most to contain a healthy dose of bush rum, fruit juice, bitters, sugar, and grated nutmeg and is often mixed according to the old saying that goes "one of sour, two of sweet, three of strong, four of weak." Peanut punch is also a popular variety that is sort of like a peanut butter milkshake spiked with rum and served over ice. It's surprisingly delicious.

If you want to take some local rum home with you, I recommend stopping by *The Ruins*, a shop in Roseau that sells a large selection of infused rums in hand painted bottles. They have a huge variety of bush rum and you can ask to taste any of them before you buy. Larger bottles of rum punch are available at the grocery stores in Roseau. Macoucherie is the only rum made from sugar cane on the island and is produced in the traditional way. (See page 144 for information on production and tours.)

VEGETARIANS/VEGANS

Vegetarians will find the best options in the touristy and more expensive restaurants. Requests for something meatless from the small snackettes or local restaurants will most likely result in a plate of provisions with sauce (sometimes meat-based, so be sure to ask) and possibly a side of beans or salad, macaroni and cheese, a cheese and mayonnaise sandwich, or bakes (fried dough) stuffed with cheese. There are three vegan Ital restaurants open at the moment and at any hotel restaurant, if you give them a heads up, they can prepare you something according to your diet.

Ital (Rastafarian) Food

When Bob Marley sang the song "Dem Belly Full" in 1973, we can be assured that he wanted his belly to be full of ital food. So what exactly is ital food? You know that saying "you are what you eat"? Well Rastafarians take that to heart and believe that food directly affects your "Livity" or life energy. Therefore you won't find anything chemically modified in their food, including salt, coloring, flavoring, or preservatives. They believe that all food should be natural, pure and from the earth and they eat an almost entirely organic vegan diet, with the exception being honey used for sweetening. Cigarettes and alcohol are also out, but of course ganja (marijuana) is acceptable as it's an herb that grows naturally from the earth. The word ital comes from the word "vital" which is Jamaican patois for "pure." If you want to try some ital cooking for yourself, check out *The Rasta Cookbook: Vegetarian Cuisine Eaten With the Salt of the Earth* by Laura Osborne, which gives a comprehensive background of Rasta beliefs along with the recipes. As of now, there are three authentic ital restaurants in Dominica: *Rootz Healing Foods* in Roseau, *Strictly Ital*, in Wotten Waven, and *Natural Livity* in Picard.

GROCERY STORES/MARKETS

There are a few grocery stores on the island that have a decent selection of foods available. Whitchurch, Astaphans, Save-a-Lot and Brizee's Mart in particular have the most variety, including popular items from the U.S. It's wise to check the expiration dates on food before you purchase it because unpopular items can sit on the shelf for some time. There will be periods when the island "runs out" of certain things for a week or more, which can make it hard to cook your favorite dishes. But if you are cooking for yourself, you will become an expert at finding substitutes that work just as well. Baby items including food, diapers, and wipes are easy to find at the bigger supermarkets.

Get your produce at the outdoor farmers market rather than in the supermarket. It will be cheaper, fresher and there is much more variety. Also, you can feel good about giving your money directly to the farmers and their families. Typically the produce is cheaper inside of the market rather than on the outskirts. Vendors will also be more willing to make deals at the end of the day when they are trying to sell what they've got left before they head home.

Food Prices

If you will be cooking for yourself, here's what you can expect to pay at the grocery store or market on a few basic items. Prices fluctuate based on the season and the availability of a particular item.

Sliced bread: EC$4	Rice: EC$2/lb
Mastif bread: EC$1.25	Bottled Water: EC$2
Peanut Butter: EC$7	Kubuli Beer: EC$4
Eggs: EC$4/half dozen	Coffee 8oz: EC$15
Milk: EC$6/1 Litre	Rum punch: EC$20/bottle
Can of beans: EC$5	Soap: EC$3
Cheese: EC$11/lb	Toilet Paper: EC$3/roll
Yogurt: EC$13/15 oz	Carrots: EC$4
Jam: EC$7	Fish: EC$6/15 oz
Lettuce: EC$3	Chicken: EC$7/15 oz

RESTAURANTS & EATING OUT

As for now, the restaurant scene is rather inexpensive and unassuming, and most restaurants in the capital are small and locally owned. A few upscale restaurants have just started popping up but they do a great job of continuing to use recipes based on traditional Creole favorites that feature local ingredients.

Very few restaurants accept credit cards so be sure to have some cash. Tipping isn't common practice in Dominica but feel free to give your server an extra couple of dollars if you feel like they did an exceptional job. On that note, service in restaurants isn't the same as in the U.S. or Europe. Only more tourist oriented restaurants will have attentive and customer serive oriented waitstaff. That's just the norm here so patience is the best policy when eating out. Another frustration is the

---

Advice from Mom
Eat your vegetables.

We found the food in Dominica to be interesting and tasty. As a vegetarian, it was relatively easy to get meatless choices at restaurants. We especially enjoyed the Garage (pg 115), Jungle Bay (pg 212) was a wonderful splurge, and we loved Rose's lunch at the Carib Model Village (pg 193), all of which had vegetarian options. If you're "cooking at home" be aware that the only grocery store of any size is in Roseau, and the only large selection of produce is at the farmers market. On our first visit our host kindly provided us with some produce from her own garden and prepared a couple of meals for us – true homestyle Dominican cooking, and very delicious. And be sure to try the many variations of rum punch.

"Won't forget it" moment: We were super-excited to find fresh saffron for sale at the farmers market; a huge piece was only EC$1. Eventually we realized that it was actually fresh turmeric. Many foods are called by different names in Dominica, so don't be surprised when your pear turns out to be an avocado!

menu: it's unlikely that everything that is printed on the menu is what they actually have. Really, it's just a list of what they may, at some point, have or did have in the past. The best way to deal with this is to simply ask "What do you have to eat today?" This will save you the time and frustration of ordering non-existent items.

Fast food, as we know it, is almost non-existent on the island with KFC (which is wildly popular) and Subway being the sole exceptions. A more common type of fast food here is found in the **snackettes**. These are the tiny shops scattered along the road and in villages that serve fried chicken, fried fish, bakes, and sometimes french fries or sandwiches. You can typically get some juice, rum, or a soft drink here as well. It's a cheap, albeit not the healthiest, option when you're on the go.

Activities

HIKING

There is no escaping Mother Nature in Dominica and exploring the island on foot is one of the best ways to get a feel for the land. Over 60% of the island is protected forest and you would be missing out if you didn't attempt to see at least a portion of it. Most of the well-known hikes will deliver you either to a waterfall, hot spring, freshwater lake,

> Be sure to check out the Hiking section in this book on page 239.

picturesque river, secret beach, or a scenic peak. You can experience nearly all of those on the hike to the Boiling Lake, one of the most challenging and also most popular hikes in Dominica. This particular trek takes intrepid hikers past a small waterfall, across a river, over a peak, past some hot springs, through the "Valley of Desolation" and then to the world's second largest boiling lake.

No matter what your ability level, you will be able to find a hike or a stroll through the rainforest that allows you to engage with Dominica's most prized possession: the natural beauty of this Caribbean island.

DIVING

With its unspoiled reefs and dramatic terrain, Dominica is rated one of the top dive sites in the Caribbean. Because of the volcanic nature of the island, you can dive in an underwater caldera at Scotts Head, swim through warm bubbles at Champagne Reef, or explore a sheer cliff teeming with coral and sea life that falls to over a thousand feet below the water's edge. The dive companies in Dominica are extremely competent and well managed and the dive masters have become experts in helping you locate sea turtles, sea horses, eels, stingrays, and additional, otherwise

> There are several wreck dives just off the coast, including a World War I gun boat. If that's what you're looking for, be sure to make a request with the dive operator.

elusive, sea creatures. With some luck, you may even hear the sounds of whales or dolphins swimming nearby.

You can expect to pay around US$55 for a one-tank boat dive and US$80 for a two-tank. Shore dives are cheaper (around US$20 for a one-tank dive) but not available everywhere. Most dive operators offer PADI certified dive instruction including a short "discover scuba" course for those who just want to try it out but don't want to commit to the three- to five-day certification courses. The discover scuba courses cost anywhere from US$75-US$150 depending on how many dives you plan to do.

It's also important to note that until recently the closest recompression chamber was found on Martinique. In 2006, a new recompression chamber was installed in Dominica's main hospital, Princess Margaret in Roseau, but to my knowledge has yet to be used. You probably don't want to be the first to break it in, so please practice safe diving!

> **Dive Operators**
> For dive operators, see the Roseau, West and South chapters

Basics

SNORKELING

Like diving, there are a plethora of interesting and fun places to explore beneath the water around the coastline of Dominica and many of them don't require plunging too deep to see the good stuff. The Soufrière Scotts Head Marine Reserve is the best area for snorkeling on the island. Champagne Reef is the most developed and most popular which means that sometimes you'll see more legs than fish, particularly when a cruise ship is in town. To avoid the crowds, go on a day when a cruise ship is not in port and if that is impossible then go early in the morning or late in the afternoon after they have left. Other great spots include the Scotts Head peninsula and the area in front of the Soufrière Catholic Church. If you are stationed along the west coast, Rodney's Rock is a great place to find stingrays, lobster, and seahorses. Also, the Cabrits peninsula has some good snorkeling around the cruise ship berth and along the western edge. Douglas Point (between Douglas Bay and Toucari Bay) also offers some interesting snorkeling, including a cave system in the Toucari region, but it requires either a taxing hike or long swim so be sure you're up for the challenge before you set out.

Responsible Diving & Snorkeling

- Avoid touching or standing on living marine organisms or dragging equipment across the reef. Coral is extremely fragile and can be damaged or killed by even the gentlest contact. If you must hold onto the reef, only touch the exposed rock or dead coral.
- Be conscious of your fins and feet. Even without contact, the surge from fins near the reef can damage delicate organisms. Be careful not to kick up clouds of sand, which can smother organisms as well.
- Take care not to descend too quickly and thereby colliding with the reef; practice good buoyancy control.
- Throw trash and food scraps away in the appropriate bins. Trash left on the street or in the gutters will eventually be swept to sea and will end up in our marine environment. Plastics in particular are a serious threat to marine life.
- Do not feed fish or turtles.
- Do not harass any of the marine life and don't try to pet the turtles. They have been known to bite.
- Resist the urge to buy or remove any plant, animal, or shell from a coral reef. Even the smallest shells can be used as a home to tiny creatures.
- Help Dominica stay beautiful by picking up trash that you see on the beach or on the reef.

If you would like a guided snorkeling excursion or need to rent snorkel gear, contact any of the dive operators in the area you wish to go.

FISHING

Sport fishing for tourists is just starting to get off the ground in Dominica. Expect to pay around US$100 per hour to take a charter. In most cases, tackle, bait, and refreshments are provided and most require that you go out for a half- or full-day. Main catches include marlin, sailfish, barracuda, kingfish, and wahoo and if you are lucky you may snag a tuna, dorado, or mackerel. You can also ask around at your accommodation and many times they can connect you with a fisherman who would be happy to take you out. Shore fishing is also a possibility if you bring your own tackle and no permit is required. Fishing in rivers is restricted to locals only.

Island Style Fishing *Roseau; Tel: 767-265-0518, 767-613-1773; islandstylefishing@gmail.com, www.islandstylefishing.com; Cost: Half-day: US$550, Full-day US$1045 (max 6 people)*

Cabrits Fishing Carters *Portsmouth; Tel: 767-445-3010; cabritsdive@yahoo.com; Cost: Half-Day US$100/pp (+15% tax)*

Dive Dominica *Castle Comfort; Tel: 767-448-6088, 767-448-2188; dive@cwdom.dm; www.castlecomfortdivelodge.com/deepseafishing; Cost: Half-Day US$460, Full-day US$920 (1-6 people).*

JC Ocean Adventures *Salisbury; Tel: 767-449-6957, 767-295-0757; www.jcoceanadventures.com; Cost: Half-day: US$400, Full-day US$750 (max 4 people).*

Big Papa's Restaurant and Sports Bar *Portsmouth; Tel: 767-445-6444; Cost: US$100/pp, per hour*

BEACHES

Dominica tends to get a bad rap when it comes to beaches; it just can't compete with the idyllic white sand beaches that other islands boast. But Dominica uses this to its advantage. The beaches on Dominica aren't overdeveloped and full of tourists vying for a spot under a coconut tree. Instead you'll find magnificent pristine golden sand along the northern coast with groves of trees that you'll have all to yourself. Many also have crystal clear rivers flowing into them or waterfalls cascading onto the beach that makes for a great place to rinse off after a dip in the sea. At multiple spots along the west coast, especially around Portsmouth, there are black and light sand beaches with calm beautiful turquoise waters where one can take a relaxing dip in the sea. So don't be misled into thinking that a trip to Dominica means you have to sacrifice your beach time. In this case, you can have the best of both worlds.

HOT SPRINGS

One of the unique geothermal features of Dominica is its abundance of natural hot springs. The highest concentration of springs is in Wotten Waven (page 131) but you'll also encounter some around Soufrière, near the base of Trafalgar Falls, on the Layou River, and along the trail to the Boiling Lake from Laudat. Many of the springs have a high sulphuric content which is great for the skin and general well-being. Soaking in the springs after a long day of adventuring is the perfect way to relax and enjoy an evening under the stars.

RAINFOREST AERIAL TRAM

If you want to take a close look at the rainforest but aren't up for a long hike, the new aerial tram can bring you straight into the Caribbean's first UNESCO Natural World Heritage Site in comfort. Ride aboard a gondola with an expert naturalist by your side to explain the unique types of flora and fauna that you'll pass along the way. You'll get the chance to look for parrots and waterfalls as you pass through the canopy. There are also options to take a hike through the Vanilla Orchid Loop, the chance to walk over a 300ft suspension bridge, or take a stroll along the Chatannier Nature Trail if you are up for it. Reserve tickets in advance. *Laudat, Contact: Tel: 767-448-8775; or Roseau, Contact: 4 Castle Street, Tel: 767-440-3266; Cost: Adult US$64/pp, Child and Student US$46/pp.*

CANYONING

If you're tired of regular old hiking, then it's time you switch things up and give canyoning a try. It's a unique adventure that will make all other hikes seem lackluster in comparison. You'll enter some of the most stunning areas of Dominica that are otherwise inaccessible to humans. The trips are exceptionally well run by trained mountaineering experts and are rated as one of the top three activities on the island by visitor reviews.

You'll be equipped with everything you need to be safe: a harness, helmet, life

---

Fishing with the Locals *by Michael Farrell*

After living and working in the Carib Territory for several months, I became friends with some young men who, on occasion, would invite me to go spear fishing. This is the most popular way to catch fish in the rough Atlantic waters as boats could be difficult to navigate in the turbulent surf. Some of the locals would use homemade guns, carved out of driftwood with a rubber hose and some metal hardware attached.

With snorkel gear and guns in hand, we'd walk to the shore and would rub a type of bush onto our masks so they wouldn't fog up. Someone would always bring a plastic bag or a buoy with a long wire attached that was used to hold all the fish once they were caught. The buoy would have a string tied to somebody's body to keep it nearby. We'd dive down deep and swim behind the fish with all limbs as still as possible to not scare them off. Once we got within striking distance (five feet or less) we'd shoot. If you got it, you would unhook the fish from the spear, place it in the bag and move on. But if we missed, the spear would fall on the ocean floor, which sometimes was much deeper than where we were swimming.

We'd fish for lobsters, redfish, bluefish and brown fish (many times they only called them by their color) and lots of guys would also stand on the rocks and do line fishing, simply with a hand held piece of fishing wire, which they would throw out as far as they could with some kind of bait on the hook and just pull once they got a tug on the line.

After a successful trip, the custom would be to either cook a big pot that night with all the guys and all the fish (and a little rum of course) or we'd evenly divide the fish, even if one fisherman came back empty-handed.

jacket, wetsuit, and extremely competent guides. They'll lead you to your first rappel where you'll begin a series of descents through cascades and waterfalls, jumping into pools of water, scrambling over rocks, and wading through rivers. With guides above and below, your safety is ensured. Trips last around four hours and are catered to individual levels of ability and comfort. *Trafalgar, office located at Cocoa Cottages; Contact: Extreme Dominica Adventure Tours; Tel: 767-448-0412; cocoacottages@cwdom.dm; www.extremedominica.com; Cost: US$150/pp for 3-5 hours. Family and group rates availabl; 6 persons max.*

ATV OFF-ROADING & JEEP TOURS

Explore some of Dominica's isolated roads and dirt paths that interlace the island and travel to remote beaches, rivers and waterfalls, all along forested trails in 4WD jeeps and ATVs. Costs vary, but typically run around US$60 per person.

Highride Nature Adventures *Bellevue Chopin; Tel: 767-448-6296, 767-440-2117; highriders@cwdom.dm; www.avirtualdominica.com/highrideadventures*

Off the Beaten Trail *Roseau; Tel: 767-275-1317; adquatics@yahoo.com.*

Wacky Rollers Jeep Tours *Roseau; Tel: 767-440-4386; wackyrollers@yahoo.com; www.wackyrollers.com*

KAYAKING

Paddling through the calm Caribbean Sea is an excellent way to explore the shoreline and offers a great chance to spot a sea turtle or flying fish. Many of these excursions can be combined with a snorkeling excursion or a trip to secret beach for a fun afternoon.

Wacky Rollers Guided kayaking tour down the Layou River. *Roseau; Tel: 767-440-4386; wackyrollers@yahoo.com; www.wackyrollers.com; Cost US$65/pp*

Nature Island Dive Offers hourly rental, half and full-day excursions and guided trips. *Soufrière; Tel: 767-449-8181; natureidive@cwdom.dm; www.naturislanddive.com; Cost: Double kayak rental for US$25/hour, US$55/half-day, kayak/snorkel combo for US$70. Make reservation in advance.*

Wave Dancer *Coconut Beach, Picard; Tel: 767-245-2017, 767-445-5693; limbodancer@hotmail.com; Cost: Double kayak rental for US$20/hr, Hobie cat rental for US$50/hr.*

Calibishie Cove Kayak tour down Hodges Beach, River, and Treasure Island. Includes a hike and some snorkeling. *Calibishie; Tel: 443-987-6742, 767-265-1993; calibishiecove@gmail.com; www.calibishiecove.com/tours; Cost: US$45/pp, minimum of two or US$60 for one person.*

RIVER TUBING

If you want a lazy day, there is no better way to relax and beat the heat than to float down one of Dominica's beautiful rivers through the lush rainforest. There are virtually no large rapids and the guides are fun and competent, making for a great way to experience the rainforest without having to put forth much effort.

Wacky Rollers *Roseau; Guided river tubing tour down the Layou River; Tel: 767-440-4386; wackyrollers@yahoo.com; www.wackyrollers.com; Cost US$65/pp.*

Calibishie Cove *Calibishie; www.calibishiecove.com/tours; calibishiecove@gmail.com; Tel: 443-987-6742, 767-265-1993; "Tubing and Brews" Excursion: Two hour trip down the stunning Pagua River, beer breaks, and a visit to a beach; Cost: US$35 pp with two or more persons, or US$60 for one person.*

HORSEBACK RIDING

There are only two horseback riding centers on the island at the moment and they are both stationed in the north. They offer customized trips through the rainforest, to waterfalls, rivers, beaches, through farms and to historical sites. Horses are well kept and guides are very knowledgeable and experienced.

Brandy Manor Equestrian Center *Borne; Tel: 767-612-0978, 767-235-4801; brandymanor@ymail.com; Cost: US$55/1.5-2 hour ride.*

Horseback Riding with Rainforest Riding *Portsmouth, Tel: 767-265-7386, 767-445-3619; www.rainforestriding.com; rainforestriding@yahoo.com; Cost: Forest Ride US$40/pp, Beach Ride US$55/pp.*

BIRD WATCHING

Most bird watching tours will take place along the Syndicate Nature Trail, which is situated just east of Dublanc, at the base of Morne Diablotin. This trail is an easy walk and has the highest concentration of Dominica's indigenous and endangered parrots: the Sisserou and Jacko. The Layou River is a good place to see freshwater birds and sea birds can be found nesting on the cliffs at Scotts Head. See page 47 for more details about Dominica's bird species.

Bertrand "Birdy" Jno Baptiste Local forestry officer. *Tel: 767-446-6358; 767-245-4768; drbirdy2@cwdom.dm; Cost: Half-day: US$55, additional person US$20. Full-day US$80, additional person US$25. He can provide transportation and meals for an extra fee. Call ahead as Birdy is a busy guy.*

KHATTS Tours (Ken's Hinterland Adventure Tours) *Roseau; Tel: 767-448-4850; info@khatts.com; www.khattstours.com; Cost:US$60/pp for 4-5 hour tour.*

Calibishie Cove *Tel: 443-987-6742, 767-265-1993; www.calibishiecove.com/tours; calibishiecove@gmail.com; Meet guide at Syndicate Forest on the west coast, optional farm tour can be arranged; Cost: US$130/1-2 persons, with transportation US$210. US$40 per additional person.*

WHALE WATCHING

The two main whale watching operators are The Anchorage Dive Center and Dive Dominica, both of which offer excellent guided outings on Sunday and Wednesday afternoons. You will likely also see pods of dolphins that will swim right up to the boat, and you will get a wonderful view of the rugged outlines of Dominica. Expect an informative briefing before your boat departs and with the use of hydrophones you can usually expect to see at least one whale. That said, they can't guarantee sightings every time and money is not refunded if you are one of the unlucky few. Overall, it's a great way to spend an afternoon. See more info on whales and dolphins on page 47.

Anchorage Dive Center *Castle Comfort; Tel: 767-448-2638; www.anchoragehotel.dm; dive@anchoragehotel.dm; Cost: US$50/pp; Sundays and Wednesdays at 2pm.*

Dive Dominica, Castle Comfort *Tel: 767-448-2188; www.divedominica.com; dive@cwdom.dm; Cost: US$50/pp (children under 10 yrs: half price); Sundays and Wednesdays at 2pm.*

Kubuli Watersports Dominica's newest whale watching operator run by one of Dominica's whale watching pioneers, Andrew Armour, fondly known as the whale whisperer. *Tel: 767-275-3639, 767- 612-4401; Kubuliwatersports@gmail.com; Boat departs from the ferry terminal Sundays 9am and returns at 12:30pm. Cost: US$68 pp.*

Fort Young Hotel *Dame Eugenia Charles Blvd, Roseau; Tel: 767-448-5500, 767-448-5006; www.fortyounghotel.com, fortyoung@cwdom.dm; Cost: US$50/pp for adults, half price for children under 10.*

Island Style Fishing *Roseau; Tel: 767-265-0518; 767-613-1773; www.islandstylefishing.com; islandstylefishing@gmail.com; Cost: US$65/pp (min of 4 people).*

JC Ocean Adventures *Salisbury; Tel: 767-449-6957, 767-295-0757; www.jcoceanadventures.com; Cost: 2-3 people: US$100/pp, 4-6 people: US$50/pp.*

BOAT CHARTERS AND CRUISES

This tourism niche hasn't quite gotten off the ground in Dominica and remains expensive and unattainable for the average tourist. However, if you have the cash, cruising the perimeter of Dominica is an amazing experience and you'll get a genuine feel for the ruggedness of the terrain and may even make some dolphin friends while hanging out off shore.

Anchorage Dive Center *Castle Comfort; www.anchoragehotel.dm; dive@anchoragehotel.dm; Tel: 767-448-2638; Cost: Half-day Sunset sailing cruise US$70/pp, Full-day cruise with lunch US$90/pp, To Les Saintes US$2000, To Martinique US$3000, To Marie Galante US$2500, To Guadeloupe US$3000, 60' Catamaran Charter US$300/hr (max 50 people, min. 3 hrs), 75' Sailing Catamaran charter US$300/hr (max 60 people, min. 3 hrs).*

JC Ocean Adventures *Salisbury; Tel: 767-449-6957, 767-295-0757; www.jcoceanadventures.com; Offers sunset, sunrise and daytime cruises. Cost: US$100 per hour, 6 people max, 2 hours minimum.*

Wave Dancer *Coconut Beach, Picard; Tel: 767-245-2017, 767-445-5693; limbodancer@hotmail.com; Offers Hobie cat rental for US$50/hr, max 6 people.*

Island Style Fishing *Roseau; www.islandstylefishing.com; Tel: 767-265-0518; 767-613-1773; islandstylefishing@gmail.com; Boat charters; Cost: US$132 per hour (min 4 people, max 15 people).*

FARM AND ARCHITECTURAL TOURS

A growing trend in Dominica's sustainable tourism initiative is incorporating tours of the island's unique agricultural and cultural heritage as a way to allow visitors to interact with the people in the rural communities. These tours offer a glimpse into the organic farming tradition in the rural communities on the island. Spending an afternoon with the folks who provide sustenance for the island makes for a fascinating and informative outing. The architectural tour of Roseau is self-guided with a map and podcast provided by the Society for Heritage, Architectural Preservation & Enhancement (SHAPE).

Giraudel/Eggleston Community Farm/Flower Tour Located on the slopes of Morne Anglais, this area of the island is known for its agricultural products and abundance of flowers. Arrange a cooking or garden tour by emailing the tourism group well in advance. They can also arrange a homestay with someone in the village so that you can really get a feel for Dominica village life. *http://giraudelegglestonflowers.communitytourism.dm, giraudeleggleston@communitytourism.dm*

Bellevue Chopin Organic Farm Tour Enjoy either a one-day or three-day tour of this beautiful area of the south while learning about traditional and sustainable methods of farming on the island. The one-day tour takes you through four gardens where you'll learn about the fruits, vegetables, flowers, and medicinal herbs that thrive on Dominica's soil and meet the people who grow them. Price includes a traditional lunch. The three-day tour includes accommodation, airport/ferry transfers, two meals per day, and four farm tours. ATV, Horseback Riding, and hiking options available as well for an added fee. *Bellevue Chopin, Tel: 767-316-2710, 767-315-1175. 767-615-3310, http://bellevueorganicfarmers.communitytourism.dm; bcofmi@hotmail.com. Cost: One-day tour US$51/pp, three-day tour US$140/pp.*

Culinary Tour This tour was a finalist in the National Geographic Changemakers Geotourism Challenge and was designed by one of the most notable Domincans alive today, Atherton Martin. With a knowledgeable tour guide you will visit local farms and gardens and learn about sustainable organic agriculture, plant varieties on the island, and meet the farmers themselves who provide food for this community. You'll also hear traditional tunes played by local musicians. At the end of the tour, with Atherton's wife, Fae, a renowned cook who has been featured in several Caribbean publications, you'll learn to make a conventional meal out of the produce you encountered during your tour and enjoy fresh juice and a delicious lunch. *Giraudel; Tel: 767-448-8839; exotica@cwdom.dm; Cost: $US50/pp; 8 person minimum, 16 person max.*

SHAPE Society Self-Guided Roseau Walking Tour Maps are available at Cartwheel Café, Cocorico Café, and the Hotel and Tourism Association office on Castle Street for US$5. Podcast available for free on their website. Plans for a guided historical tour are in the works so contact SHAPE for more info if you are interested. Also, see page 105 for more on this tour. *Roseau; Tel: 767-275-5031, 767-440-3431; www.shape.dm, shapedominica@gmail.com.*

Small Axe Farm With a name inspired by the Bob Marley lyrics "if you are the big tree, we are the small axe, ready to cut you down," this farm represents what all large industrial farms don't: tranquil surroundings, organic production, and a personal touch by those who care deeply about the land and where their food comes from. The view from the farm is simply majestic and Nico, the owner, is a dynamic guy with a great sense of humor. He welcomes all visitors and volunteers, as long as they're willing to get their hands a little dirty. *Morne Jaune; Tel: 767-616-8606.*

Roots Farm Roots Farm has long been a leader in organic farm methods and when visiting this farm you'll see the experts at work. Karen Sutherland, co-owner and manager, makes all agricultural decisions on the basis of the long-term health of the land, people (both consumers and workers), and environment. They grow a wide variety of common and "exotic" fruits, roots, vegetables and herbs, which they frequently sell at the Roseau farmers market. *Cochrane; Tel: 767-449-3038; rootsfarm@cwdom.dm.*

Treehouse Farm Bakery Café This amazing vegan café sources all of its produce from the surrounding farm, which you can now tour. Walk through their lush garden paths to view tropical flowers, fruit trees, herbs, and vegetables. After the tour, hike down the river to take a dip beneath the nearby twin waterfalls or deep river pool. After your hike stop in the café to try some vegan baked goods like a

---

Advice From Mom
Go play outside.

Dominica is a gorgeous country, so get out and explore it. Hiking is a must and there are hiking opportunities for all different levels of ability. A word of caution, however: unless you are hiking a well-marked easy trail, do get a reliable guide. Ask for a recommendation from whoever is managing your accommodations. On one occasion we made the mistake of picking up a guide alongside the road near the trail. While he was a perfectly nice young man, he did not use good judgment and we found ourselves in a situation that had the potential for being somewhat risky. (However, it's a hike we'll never forget and has become a great story to tell at parties!)

"Won't forget it" moment: Walking back to the car in the dark over difficult terrain with only a cell phone to light our way.

plantain-mango bagel, cocoa cinnamon rolls, or eggplant pockets to name a few. Cabins for guests are in the process of being built. *Belles; Tel: 767-615-5813; www.treehousebakerydominica.com;.*

YOGA

For those interested in a vacation centered around health and wellness, you will find invigorating yoga classes as well as other healthful activities (massage, tai chi, watsu) offered at these locations. Rainbow Yoga is the only established center to offer private and group classes outside of an accommodation.

Rainbow Yoga Offers weekly classes of all ability levels, hiking and yoga excursions, yoga retreats, workshops, and private classes in the destination of your choice. Contact for prices. *Massacre and Portsmouth; Tel: 767-245-2474; rainbowyoga@yahoo.com; http://rainbowyogaindominica.wordpress.com.*

Jungle Bay Retreat and Spa, Offers yoga retreats and morning yoga classes. *Delices; Tel: 767-446-1789; www.junglebaydominica.com; info@junglebaydominica.com; skype: junglebaydominica.*

Rainforest Shangri-la Daily yoga is free for guests. *Wotten Waven; Tel: 767-440-5093, 767-616-9322; http://rainforestshangrila.com;shangrila@cwdom.dm.*

SCENIC FLIGHTS

Soar over Dominica's peaks and get a glimpse of rivers and waterfalls not attainable by foot. In the small six-person airplane operated by Extreme Dominica's Richard Metawi, you can also fly to Antigua, Monserrat, Guadeloupe and Martinique.

Extreme Dominica *Shawford; Tel: 767-295-7272; www.extremedominica.com; extremedominica@gmail.com; Contact Richard for pricing.*

Volunteer Opportunities

If you would like to get to the heart of Dominica and you have philanthropic leanings, consider volunteering. There's no better way to get to know the people and culture of Dominica and you can feel good about giving back to a country that could use a little help. Although Dominica is rich in nature and culture, there is a significant lack of resources put towards some significant areas of concern, especially when it comes to people with disabilities, youth at risk, and the elderly. For those interested in farming, there is only one farm registered with the World Wide Opportunity on Organic Farms (WWOOF) located in the Carib Territory. However, if you get to know a farmer on your own, I doubt any would refuse a helping hand on harvest days.

ORGANIZED VOLUNTEER EXPERIENCES

These organizations specialize in coordinating volunteer vacations exclusively in Dominica. All combine meaningful volunteer work with fun excursions so that participants have a well-rounded vacation and can gain insight into the country and culture that other travelers won't get. All three are highly recommended and run by individuals who have years of experience working with volunteers in Dominica.

Longé Dominica is an excellent volunteer organization stationed in the Carib Territory that is run by an outstanding group of professionals from Dominica and the United States. Longé, which means "reaching out" in Creole, offers interim/gap year programs and summer leadership programs for young adults, and volunteer vacations for adults groups any of which can be customized according to the participants strengths and interests. *Tel: 412-414-6891 (U.S.) or Tel: 767-225-8410 (Dominica); info@longedominica.com; www.longedominica.com*

Ready, Willing, Enable! Started by two former Peace Corps Volunteers who served in Dominica, RWE brings volunteers to Dominica to work with and teach persons with disabilities in a fun and supportive setting. Trips last approximately nine days and individuals or groups are welcome to participate. *Tel: 210-394-3637 (U.S.); info@rwenable.org; www.rwenable.org*

Home From Home Tina Alexander, a British social worker who relocated to Dominica in 1994, runs a comfortable guest house that can combine your relaxing vacation with opportunities to volunteer. She can cater your experience to match your skills and interests to include anything from education to construction to environmental protection. *Tel: 767-449-8593; enquiries@islandguests.com; www.islandguests.com/content/rent/goodwill.htm*

OPPORTUNITIES FOR YOUTH

Teenagers who would like to come to Dominica with an organized group to volunteer can sign up with **Longé** (see above) or with either of these two reputable organizations:

Visions Service Adventures Offers a four-week program in the Carib Territory providing service-learning opportunities coupled with customized tours of the island. *Tel: 717 567-7313 (U.S.); info@visionsserviceadventures.com; www.visionsserviceadventures.com*

Academic Treks For youth between the ages of fifteen and eighteen, this 21-day adventure offers service projects, inter-island sailing, and island exploration during the summer. *Tel: 919-256-8200 (U.S.); info@academictreks.com; www.academictreks.com*

INDEPENDENT VOLUNTEERING

If you would only like to spend an afternoon or two giving back, you may want to arrange something on your own with one of these non-profit organizations that could use an extra hand. I suggest contacting them before you arrive to give them a heads up that you may be stopping by.

Natural Vibes Organic Farm (WWOOF Independent Farm) Located in the Carib Territory, Keith will host guests in his modest eco-cottage (think small huts with no running water and pit toilets) and offers work on the organic farm in return. Meals cooked on site and Keith holds workshops on local food production such as making cocoa pods into chocolate. Rates are negotiable. *Sineku, Carib Reserve; Tel: 767-612-8215.*

Abilities Unlimited A craft enterprise for the blind and disabled that has been specializing in basket making and other local crafts making since 1964. Volunteers interested in local arts or working with people with disabilities may enjoy this opportunity. You can also support them by purchasing their crafts, which are for sale at their workshop in Goodwill and at the Old Market in Roseau. *Federation Drive, Goodwill; Tel: 767-448-2203.*

REACH (Reaching Elderly Abandoned Citizens Housebound) REACH provides much needed services and food to homebound elderly and they are actively seeking the assistance of volunteers. Activities could include sorting and delivering food, working in the office or on a construction project, or simply spending time with the elderly that they care for, which is a great way to get a fascinating perspective on the history of the island. *Roseau; Tel: 767-448-8096, 767-448-3404; reach@cwdom.dm; www.avirtualdominica.com/reach*

Operation Youth Quake The mission of OYQ is to provide day care, short term residential care, life skills training, individual and group counseling, and recreation to children and young people who are abused, deprived, neglected, or in crisis. Volunteers assist with educational work (homework, reading activities, science projects, or IT skills), recreational activities (sports, games, arts, cooking, or sewing) and life skills. Volunteers could also plan their own activity or come to simply hang out with the kids. Volunteers must, however, be over 21 years of age. *Roseau; contact Lennox Abraham at Tel: 767-448-4174; quakeyouth@hotmail.com; www.operationyouthquake.com*

Lifeline Ministries Lifeline facilitates community development by partnering with local entities to work in a number of areas: the environment, persons with disabilities, HIV/AIDS, homelessness and early childhood education. Volunteer opportunities include delivering meals, classroom assistance, website development, organic agriculture, and alternative energy equipment assistance. Their focus is on making a difference with integrity. Volunteers are accepted for short-term projects to year long internships. *Roseau; contact Tina Alexander at Tel: 767-449-8593; www.lifelineministries.dm; lifeline@cwdom.dm*

Roseau

Roseau, the capital city, holds 30% of the population in a small, compact district making it the densest area of the island. Called "Town" by locals, it is the heart of the country and its mosaic of modern and French colonial architecture houses the government headquarters, banks, supermarkets, businesses, restaurants, and numerous shops. The country's largest cruise ship dock is also here and the city is the staging grounds for most island activities. Roseau is still a glimpse into what many other Caribbean capitals used to be, before developers came in and gave everything an artificial makeover for the attraction of tourists. When you are visiting Dominica, it's almost unavoidable to end up in Roseau at some point so here's how to make the most of it.

If you came to do some sightseeing, try to come in the early morning when the town is waking up and coming alive. The heat is tolerable, the streets less crowded, and you can easily lose a couple of hours wandering around the cobbled roads lined with classic West Indian buildings of brightly painted wood. You will only need a part of a day to see the capital and you'll likely want to navigate it by foot. It's small enough to get across town in a few minutes and with the confusing one way streets,

TOP FIVES

Pick up a map and take a self-guided tour of the historic French Quarter of Roseau. Don't forget to download the podcast before you go! (pg 105)

Witness a centuries old tradition at the Farmers Market by the river and try some new tropical produce. (pg 110)

Roseau gets hot so be sure to hydrate yourself. Cool down with a drink from J.B. Juice or a homemade rum punch at The Ruins. (pg 113)

Discover all of Dominica's native tropical vegetation and visit the parrot sanctuary accessed by some easy walking trails in the Botanical Gardens. Want to kick it up a notch? Hike up the hill to Morne Bruce for some amazing views of the capital. (pg 110)

Visiting the "Whale Watching Capital of the Caribbean" is, as the name suggests, the opportune time to see these enormous and peaceful creatures up close. You're likely to encounter pods of dolphins as well. (pg 105)

incessant traffic, pedestrians, stray dogs, and lack of parking, it's not worth the trouble to try to drive around. Be warned, however, that walking around is not without its inconveniences. You'll be forced to step over large gutters, dodge children, vendors, and dogs; walk into the street (watch out for cars); cross the street multiple times when the sidewalks suddenly end. All this while being mindful of holes and steps in the middle of the walkway. You'll enjoy it more if you think of it as an obstacle course. Take it slow and enjoy the view and you'll quickly get used to the rhythm and pulse of the capital.

The bay front on **Victoria Street** is a good place to start if you want to get a feel for the town. It has a wonderful boardwalk with gorgeous views of the sea and surrounding green peaks of the south and Roseau Valley. Here you'll find the tourist information center and the **Dominica Museum** along with several tourist shops, and restaurants. At the end of the boardwalk, if you walk in the direction of the river, you'll end up at the lively **farmers market** where you can sample local produce or refresh yourself with fresh coconut water.

If you walk south from the bay front you'll pass the **Fort Young Hotel**, an 18th century stone fort that has been restored and made into modern accommodations. Continuing you'll come to the historic **public library**, beautiful **State House** and **House of Assembly (Parliament Building)**.

Coming back, walk up **Turkey Lane** to pass the old stone **Methodist Church** and **Roseau Cathedral**. Take a left to walk down **Independence Street**, another major thoroughfare where you'll pass the former residence of author **Jean Rhys** and several music shops where you can pick up a soundtrack to your vacation.

If you head straight inland from the cruise ship berth along **King George V Street**, you'll pass the **Old Market** and find yourself in the historic **French Quarter**. This is the original settlement of Roseau, with old two-story colonial structures replete with gingerbread trim, large verandas, and jalousie windows, many of which are still private homes. This road will eventually take you to the **Botanical Gardens** where you can catch a cricket game in action or enjoy strolling around the manicured gardens filled with local plants and flowers. If you need a time out from the chaos and heat of Roseau, this is a peaceful spot to relax and take a rest. For a little bit of a workout, you can climb up **Jack's Walk** to **Morne Bruce** for a bird's eye view of the capital.

SOME HISTORY

Roseau was not originally intended to be a capital city. The first capital was Portsmouth but because of the swampy nature of the area and the prevalence of mosquitoes, the capital was eventually moved to Roseau providing an easy access to a calm bay and a river leading to the interior. The Kalinago people, who established a sizeable settlement here, originally called the region *Sairi*. It wasn't until after the first French woodcutters arrived that the name was changed to Roseau, after the "*roseaux*" river reeds that were common to the area. They built homes along with the Kalinago in the early 1700s, centered around the Old Market. It wasn't until the British claimed control over the island that more aggressive development took place and the Kalinago retreated to the interior. With names like "Independence" and "King George V," the streets are a good indication of each area's development.

Roseau has seen its share of disasters since its inception. From attack and bombardment, to fires and hurricanes, the capital has gone through various stages of rebuilding. The most substantial calamity occurred in 1805 from a widespread fire that was ignited by the French during an attack. The capital went through another rough spot in 1979 from the destruction caused by Hurricane David.

NAVIGATING THE CITY

If you have to drive through Roseau, it's important to take note that nearly all streets are one-way. Look for the direction that cars are parked before you turn to be sure you aren't headed in the wrong direction, as most of the roads aren't marked.

Getting out of town to the southern villages can be tricky when a cruise ship is docked. Your best bet is to take Independence Street until it ends, and then take a right onto Bath Road. It will deposit you onto Victoria Street, where you can take a left and be on your way.

Traffic gets congested in the mornings around 7 or 8am, again around 1pm for lunch and around 4 or 5pm as work lets out.

Sights

Bayfront

This is where the action is on days when a cruise ship is in port. You'll find people drumming on the sidewalk (ask before you take a picture, they may want a small donation first), women braiding hair, small stalls set up selling trinkets, and tour guides waiting to load up passengers and wisk them off to a waterfall or other attraction.

Self-Guided Historic Walking Tour

This tour was put together by the Society of Heritage Preservation and Enhancement (SHAPE), which was formed in 1997 to help preserve Dominica's historical architecture. You can buy a self-guided tour booklet and map from local businesses in Roseau and learn about the history, architecture, and noteworthy buildings in the Roseau area. The tour should take around one to two hours. A free podcast is also available on their website (www.shape.dm). Maps are available at Cartwheel Café, Cocorico Café, and the Hotel and Tourism Association office on Castle Street for US$5. Plans for a guided historical tour are in the works so contact SHAPE for more info if you are interested. *Roseau; Tel: 767-275-5031, 767-440-3431; www.shape.dm, shapedominica@gmail.com.*

Whale Watching

Dominica's newest whale watching tour is run by one of the island's whale watching pioneers, Andrew Armour, who is fondly known as the "Whale Whisperer." His team specializes in locating sperm whales and their newest endeavor, which has garnered great publicity, is swimming and photographing some of the whales they've been studying for years. A trip with Andrew will likely be memorable and informative. *Kubuli Watersports; Tel: 767-275-3639, 767-612-4401; kubuliwatersports@gmail.com; Boat departs from the ferry terminal Sundays 9am and returns at 12:30pm. Cost: US$68.*

Roseau

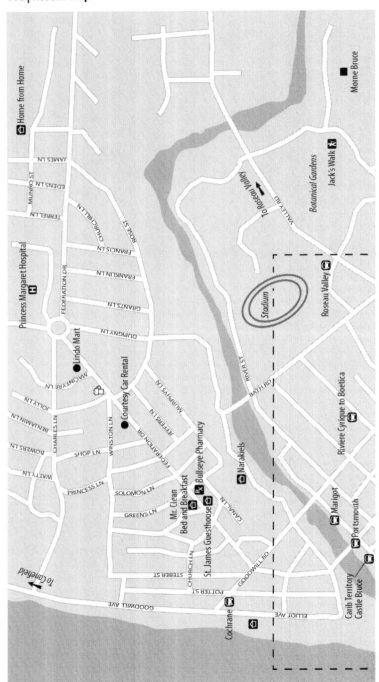

Roseau

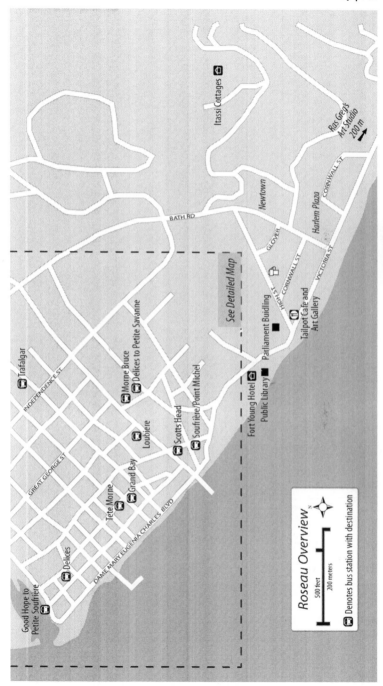

Itassi Cottages

Ras Greg's
Art Studio
200 m

Newtown

CORNWALL ST

Harlem Plaza

BATH RD

GLOVER

VICTORIA ST

HIGH ST

CORNWALL ST

See Detailed Map

Parliament Buidling

Tailpot Cafe and
Art Gallery

Trafalgar

INDEPENDENCE ST

Morne Bruce

Delices to Petite Savanne

Fort Young Hotel

Public Library

Soufriere/Point Michel

Scotts Head

Loubiere

GREAT GEORGE ST

Grand Bay

Tete Morne

DAME MARY EUGENIA CHARLES BLVD

Delices

Good Hope to
Petite Soufriere

Roseau Overview

500 feet

200 meters

Denotes bus station with destination

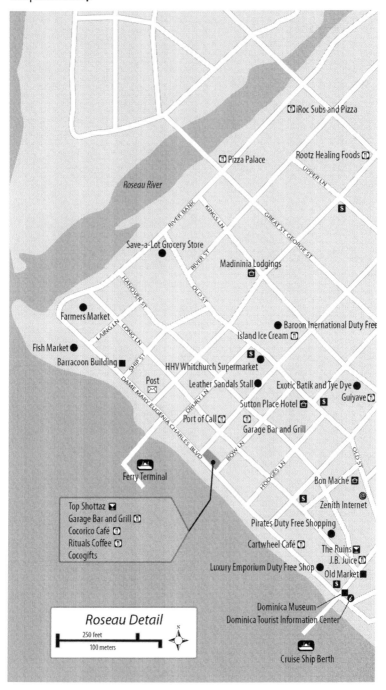

iRoc Subs and Pizza

Pizza Palace

Rootz Healing Foods

UPPER LN

Roseau River

RIVER BANK

KINGS LN

GREAT ST

GEORGE ST

Save-a-Lot Grocery Store

RIVER ST

Madininia Lodgings

OLD ST

HANOVER ST

Farmers Market

LAING LN

LONG LN

Baroon Inernational Duty Free

Island Ice Cream

Fish Market

SHIP ST

Barracoon Building

DAME MARY EUGENIA CHARLES BLVD

Post

HHV Whitchurch Supermarket

Leather Sandals Stall

Exotic Batik and Tye Dye

DRURY LN

Guiyave

Sutton Place Hotel

Port of Call

BON LN

Garage Bar and Grill

Ferry Terminal

HODGES LN

OLD ST

Bon Maché

Top Shottaz
Garage Bar and Grill
Cocorico Café
Rituals Coffee
Cocogifts

@ Zenith Internet

Pirates Duty Free Shopping

Cartwheel Café

The Ruins

J.B. Juice

Luxury Emporium Duty Free Shop

Old Market

Roseau Detail

250 feet

100 meters

N

Dominica Museum

Dominica Tourist Information Center

Cruise Ship Berth

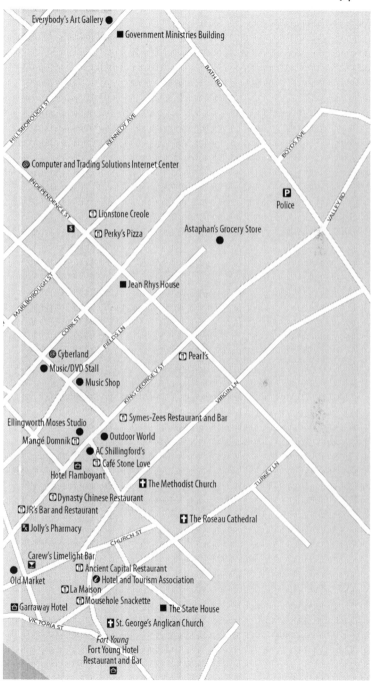

Everybody's Art Gallery ●

■ Government Ministries Building

BATH RD

HILLSBOROUGH ST

KENNEDY AVE

BOYDS AVE

@ Computer and Trading Solutions Internet Center

INDEPENDENCE ST

🅿
Police

VALLEY RD

🏧 Lionstone Creole

🅂

🏧 Perky's Pizza

Astaphan's Grocery Store ●

■ Jean Rhys House

MARLBOROUGH ST

CORK ST

FIELDS LN

@ Cyberland

● Music/DVD Stall

● Music Shop

🏧 Pearl's

KING GEORGE V ST

VIRGIN LN

🏧 Symes-Zees Restaurant and Bar

Ellingworth Moses Studio

Mangé Domnik 🏧

● Outdoor World

● AC Shillingford's

🏧 Café Stone Love

🏧
Hotel Flamboyant

🏧 Dynasty Chinese Restaurant

🏧 JR's Bar and Restaurant

✝ The Methodist Church

TURKEY LN

🏧 Jolly's Pharmacy

✝ The Roseau Cathedral

CHURCH ST

Carew's Limelight Bar

●
🏧
Old Market

🏧 Ancient Capital Restaurant

✪ Hotel and Tourism Association

🏧 La Maison

🏧 Mousehole Snackette

🏨 Garraway Hotel

■ The State House

VICTORIA ST

✝ St. George's Anglican Church

Fort Young
Fort Young Hotel
Restaurant and Bar
🏨

Roseau

Dominica Museum

This small and very interesting museum includes artifacts representing the history of Dominica. The museum covers the original inhabitants, the Arawaks, all the way to the present. *Dame Eugenia Charles Blvd, Roseau; Hours: M-F 9am-4pm, Sat 9am-12pm; Admission: US$3 adults, US$1 students.*

Botanical Gardens

Once considered the most beautiful gardens in the West Indies, these 40 acres, which were at one time used for sugar cane cultivation, were established around 1891 by the British Crown Government. It is divided into two sections: The Ornamental Section, which contains a variety of exotic tropical plants, trees, and shrubs, and the economic section where you will find tropical fruit and spice plants as well as those used for medicinal purposes. The garden was completely destroyed by Hurricane David in 1979, the evidence of which you can see from a school bus crushed under a giant boabab tree, but has since been redeveloped and is now the sight of weekly cricket matches, public ceremonies and festivals. In September it plays host to Creole in the Park, an outdoor music festival. With over 50 types of trees, a parrot conservation center (where you can get a close look at the island's Sisserou and Jacko parrots), beautiful open space, and a nice walking path amongst the labeled vegetation, this area is a great escape from the hectic city surrounding it.
www.da-academy.org/dagardens.html; Open 6am-7pm daily.

"Jack's Walk" to Morne Bruce Hike

This short, 15-mintue hike starts at the Botanical Gardens behind the Parrot Sanctuary and goes straight up a steep path to the top of Morne Bruce. Here you'll find a large historic cross that was erected in the 1920s, a cannon, and a shrine as well as a spectacular view of Roseau, the bay front, the valley, and the Botanical Gardens. If walking isn't your thing, you can also drive there from the southern end of Bath Road, enter the gates into the gardens by the cemetery and follow the road all the way up. This spot was once the main military garrison for Dominica because the location made it a natural post for the protection of Roseau. It is named after the the British Royal Engineer, James Bruce, who designed all of the original fortifications of the island. The old garrison graveyard still exists at Kings Hill and is reputed to have a ghost, the headless drummer, who at midnight can be heard playing his drum.

Historical Places of Interest

Farmers Market

A real farmers market that has been operating the same way for centuries – through the times of colonization, slavery, freedom, and independence. It is especially hopping on Saturday mornings when vendors come from all over the island to display and sell the best of their fruits, vegetables, flowers, and other marketable goods. Try an unfamiliar fruit or grab a roasted plantain or fresh coconut water for the road. This is a great way to see what types of produce the island has to offer and meet the people who grow it. The prices here are generally lower than the lackluster supermarkets and have a wider variety as well. The fish market can be found nearby at the fisheries complex where you can get portions of freshly caught mahi, tuna, marlin, dorado, and other types of seasonal fish.

Parliament Building

The ornate pink and white building that stands out as you drive down Victoria Street is the current House of Assembly. Built in 1811, it was once the old court house until 1979 when it was burned down during a civil unrest and was eventually restored to its current state in 1993.

The State House

This tenacious structure has survived a multitude of devestating events since its construction in 1766. The original structure was made of wood with a large wrap-around verandah but was completely destroyed by a hurricane in 1834. The new house was constructed in 1836, as a stone structure, and was extended several times throughout the late 1800s and early 1900s, which resulted in an eclectic mix of architectural styles. The building was again damaged in 1979 by Hurricane David and was renovated a year after into its current state. From the time it was initially built until Dominica gained its Independence it was used as the official residence of the Governor as well as an office, a place for entertaining, and a guesthouse for visiting dignitaries. It is now the setting for state functions and official receptions.

Jean Rhys House

Now labeled *Vena's Guesthouse*, this residence was established in the mid 1800s and takes up nearly an entire block. The Dominican-born novelist Jean Rhys (1896-1979) spent the first 16 years of her life here. Born to two well-known residents, one of whom owned the Geneva Estate in Grand Bay, she's most famous for her well known award-winning novel, *Wide Sargasso Sea*. Part of the book takes place in Dominica, specifically at Geneva Estate and Massacre. She never finished her autobiography but does write about a mango tree, which is still there today, in her garden in Roseau.

Roseau Public Library

Built in 1906 with financial assistance from Andrew Carnegie, the American philanthropist, the library has withstood hurricanes and uprisings and remains almost completely unchanged from its original structure. This library houses the best information related to the history, social patterns, and flora and fauna of Dominica. While you're there check out the Cannon Ball Tree that stands between the library and Fort Young. This was once the site of the first public gardens on the island.

Fort Young

When it became clear that the capital of Dominica would be Roseau, and not Portsmouth as was thought before, the construction of Fort Young began. Named after the British Governor, Sir William Young, the fort was established in 1770 and seven years later additions were made by the French. In the 1850s it housed the main police station until 1964 when it was bought and turned into a hotel. Hurricane David didn't spare this structure when it blew through in 1979 and much of the fort was destroyed. In its rebuilding they were able to retain the thick stone walls that were built for fortification and still use the original structure as hotel rooms today.

Old Market

Though you'll find this to be a peaceful spot today, this cobblestone square has had a long and turbulent history. Once called *La Place* in Creole the story of this bustling market dates back to the earliest French settlers who planned for this to be the nucleus of the island, with all roads branching out from the central plaza. In its earliest days this was where slave auctions, public executions, punishment, and lively political rallies took place and it continued for centuries to be the heart of the island as the main farmers market. In 1971 the market was moved to the riverbank and farmers moved their stalls there to sell produce. Today you'll find rows of craft booths selling T-shirts, spices, baskets, carvings, music, and "Made in China" souvenirs at the Old Market. The prices here are decent and can sometimes be negotiated. Inside of the building on the Old Street side is a great selection of unique handmade woven baskets which are of a different style than the traditional Carib baskets and are made locally and quite nice.

Barracoon Building

What is now the site of the Roseau City Council office was once a gloomy stone structure built in the 1760s in the style of West African architecture. It was originally used to hold slaves that were awaiting auction or who were to be sent to another island. In the 1800s it was again used as a holding spot, but this time for prisoners who were being sent to work on whaling ships. In 1999 it was completely restored and given a face lift and was recently used as the site of a memorial was held to commemorate 200 years of freedom from slavery.

Historic Places of Worship

The Roseau Cathedral

This building was originally made in the 1700s using wooden posts covered in thatched palm leaves in accordance to the Carib building tradition. It took over 100 years to become what it is today with the help of many diverse groups of people. The funds were raised by the levies of French planters, Caribs camped outside of Roseau for three months to help erect the first wooden ceiling frame, and convicts from Devil's Island (located off the coast of French Guiana) were forced to build the pulpit. There are beautiful stained glass windows, one of which is dedicated to Christopher Columbus, and ornate Victorian murals behind the side altars, which were painted by local artisans. The rock used to build it is volcanic stone and the structure was designed in the style of Gothic-Romanesque Revival, which was popular during that time. It was finished in 1916 and very little has changed about the church since.

The Methodist Church

The location of this church, so close to the Catholic Church, is the result of a strange twist of fate dating back to 1766. King George III gave the Catholic Church 10 acres of land and a 99 year lease to be used for purposes the church deemed fit. At the end of the lease, these Catholics asked the Crown for a freehold grant to keep those 10 acres indefinitely. The appeal was granted except for two small corner lots which had already been sublet to people who happened to later convert to Methodism. The Methodists eventually gave their land to the Wesleyan Mission and it was here that a church was built. During the late 1800s there was great disturbance due to the close proximity of these two churches that at one point turned into an all-out street riot over 100 years ago. Thankfully, all is now peaceful between the two churches.

St. George's Anglican Church

The first Anglican church was constructed near this site in 1768 and was originally made from wood. Because of the extreme climate, it soon fell into disrepair and in 1820 was rebuilt in square Regency style. Throughout the years, additions were built resulting in its current shape. Unfortunately, because of its proximity to the bay front, it was completely destroyed in 1979 by Hurricane David and some of its architectural style was lost in its rebuilding. The cemetery nearby contains some of the oldest tombstones on the island.

Eateries & Restaurants

 J.B. Juice An absolute must while in Roseau! J.B. has been serving up the best juice on the island for years. For only EC$5 you pick which fresh fruits you want and J.B. whirls them together into some kind of smoothie magic. You can request low or no sugar. *King George V Street, street stand across from the Old Market, Roseau; Hours: 10am-6pm M-Sa.*

Rituals Coffee Just like a real coffee house that we all know and love. It's air-conditioned, has wireless internet available and is one of the few places you can find espresso drinks and iced coffee. They also serve bagels and bagel sandwiches, paninis, pizza, sandwiches, burgers, quesadillas, and smoothies. *Dame Eugenia Charles Blvd, Roseau; Hours: M-F 7am-7pm, Sat 10:30am-7pm, Sun 10:30am-4pm; Tel: 767-440-22333; Cost: EC$5-$12 for coffee drinks, EC$10-$15 for food.*

Rootz Healing Foods This is the best vegetarian place in town run by a well-known herbalist. They serve only Ital food (see page 90), with items such as veggie burgers, ginger red beans, breadfruit balls, salads, veggie rotis, roasted plantain, and full Creole lunch plates, veggie style. A variety of drinks are available as well: teas, juice, coconut water, and even veggie juice. This rasta hang-out is the hub for healthy-living minded folks and you can pick up mango butter, honey, and blackstrap molasses for sale here as well. *53 Kennedy Ave, Roseau; Tel: 767-615-7414; Hours:M-Sa 8am-late afternoon; Cost: EC$15 for a lunch.*

JR's Bar and Restaurant You'll likely hear this place before you see it as they are almost always playing some type of lively music throughout their open-air plaza that draws a crowd. They serve local lunches of chicken and fish with all the regular fixings. There's not much of an option for vegetarians, but you may find macaroni and cheese some days. On Friday evenings you can enjoy excellent barbeque and a rum punch while you get to know the locals. *King George V Street, Roseau; Hours: M-Sat 7am until late, Sun 12pm-late; Cost: EC$15.*

Dynasty Chinese Restaurant When you get tired of Creole food and want a change, try one of the many Chinese restaurants in Roseau. They're all relatively similar but I prefer this one because the service is good and the location is convenient. Like all of the local Chinese restaurants it has a long, comprehensive menu that includes a vegetarian section. The dining area can be rather stuffy and hot but fans are sometimes available if you ask. *King George V Street, Roseau; Hours: M-Sat: 10am-10pm, Sunday: 6pm-10pm; Cost: EC$15-$50.*

Symes-Zees Restaurant and Bar The best reason to visit Symes-Zees is to learn how to play dominos with the locals in the evening over a Kubuli or to hear live jazz on a Thursday night (9pm-midnight). Located in a historic old stone building and infused with the air of a former hot spot, this restaurant and bar certainly didn't splurge on décor but the food is decent with the usual Creole fare including curried goat, sancoche, barbequed ribs, and rotis. They can make a vegetarian plate, although it will cost more. *King George V Street, Roseau; Hours: M- Sat 9am-late evening; Cost: EC$12 for breakfast, EC$18-25 for lunch/dinner.*

Roseau

Mangé Domnik A local crowd gathers here for lunch and snacks. Mangé is unique in that you can pick which items and how much you want on your plate for lunch. Choices include pork, fish, chicken, goat, a variety of salads, rice, beans, provisions, and macaroni and cheese. Each portion is about EC$3 and you can also get half portions of any of them. *King George V Street, Roseau; Hours: M-F 10am-5pm, Sat 10am-2pm; Cost: EC$15.*

Lionstone Creole This small, simple, open air restaurant is situated on a shaded patio and offers fresh ital vegan food along with some regular Creole food. The highlight is the music, especially on weekend nights when reggae dominates the playlist. *Great Marlborough Street, Roseau; Hours: Tu-W 11am-10pm, F-Sa 11am-12am; Cost: EC$15 lunch.*

Pearl's This is one of the best places if you want to get a local style lunch plate. Pearl's has been serving up an excellent and authentic local meals for over 20 years and they know how to do it right. The downstairs is always packed during the lunch hour with people getting takeaway orders of sandwiches, snacks, rotis and Creole food. The restaurant upstairs has open-air seating that is tastefully decorated and is popular among the local businessmen and women. The dishes offered vary by season so you can expect anything from rabbit to crab to callalou. Give their famous rum punch a try while you're there. *King George V Street, Roseau; Tel: 767-448-8707; Hours: M-Sat 9am-6pm (downstairs take-away), 12pm-6pm (upstairs restaurant); Cost: EC$6-$20 lunch.*

Cartwheel Café Dine in one of Roseau's original buildings (built circa 1840). The stone walls are over three feet thick which has successfully protected it from multiple destructive hurricanes, lootings, and fires. The restaurant is small, with only five indoor tables and a few on the crowded sidewalk outside, so get there before it fills up. They serve traditional Creole breakfast items of fish and pork and omelets (which you can get made without meat for vegetarians). For lunch you'll find a traditional Creole lunch or a selection of sandwiches. The bayfront location is rather charming and the service is great. *Dame Eugenia Charles Blvd, Roseau; Hours: M-F 8:15am-2:30pm, Sat 8:15-1pm; Cost: EC$7-$13.*

Carew's Limelight Bar Small and unseemly, this second floor spot is excellent if you just want to relax and drink a Kubuli or rum punch and look out over the bay front. A great place to chat with locals or catch a cricket game on TV and the owners are friendly and welcoming. They serve an inexpensive but good Creole lunch and on Saturdays make a fish broth and *peleau*. This has become a favorite local hang-out over the years. *Old Street, across from the Old Market on the 2nd floor, Roseau; Tel: 767-245-9036; Hours: M-Sat 8:30am-9:30pm (Open very late on Friday); EC$10-$15.*

Perky's Pizza The pizza here is good and they offer an interesting variety of toppings. The restaurant itself is very hot inside but they have an enclosed patio next door where you can grab a table. *Independence Street, Roseau; Tel: 767-448-1628; Hours: M-Tu 9am-10pm, W-Sat 9am-11pm; Cost: EC$5-$7 slice, EC$20-$55 whole pizza, EC$10-$16 sub.*

iRoc Subs and Pizza You'll find great pizza with a variety of toppings and subs made to order in this tiny shop. The seating area tends be crowded during busy times of the day but you can always get your food to go and eat it across the street by the river. Plenty of vegetarian options available. *River Street, Roseau; Hours: M-Sat 9am-10:30pm, Sun 4pm-10:30pm; Cost: EC$5-$7 slice, EC$20-$55 whole pizza, EC$10-$14 sub.*

Café Stone Love A tiny painted stone café with sidewalk seating. You can occasionally find vegan meals here, which tend to be soya chunks with the usual Creole fixins. Otherwise you can count on a Creole meal with chicken or fish. They also advertise teas and coffee but don't be fooled, the coffee is sometimes instant. *Cross Street, Roseau; Hours: M-Sat 8am-6pm; Cost: EC$12 lunch.*

Pizza Palace They have an extensive menu of mostly Creole food but the rasta crowd likes to come here for their interesting vegetarian pizza, which consists of whole wheat crust, lentils, cabbage, and shredded carrots with cheese on top. Definitely not like any pizza you've had at home but really very good! *River Street, Roseau; Tel: 767-448-4598; Hours: M-Sat 10am-late; Cost: EC$10-$15 full lunch, EC$5 pizza slice.*

Pumpkins This little spot next to the Roseau market is loved by locals and visitors alike. With friendly service, excellent local food, consistent vegan and vegetarian options and Kubuli on tap, there's no reason not to give it a try. Listen for the reggae and jazz coming from Pumpkins on Friday nights when they stay open late in order to feed and entertain the vendors who set up their stalls late at night before the market rush on Saturday. *40 Hanover Street, Roseau; Tel: 767-613-3645; Hours: M-F 7am-11pm, Open Saturday for lunch; Cost: EC$10-$18.*

The Ruins This is a fun place to buy local and imported spices, handmade bush rum and an amazing rum punch and you can sample for free before you buy. The café attached serves rum drinks out of bamboo cups with coconut lids and they occasionally sell snacks and exotic meat dishes. Friendly service and free wireless internet makes this a nice place to spend an afternoon. Stock up on homemade bush rum or hot sauce in a painted bottle before you head home. *Across from the Old Market, Roseau; Hours: M-Sat 8am-late, Open Sunday if a cruise ship is in port.*

Mousehole Snackette There are no signs to help you find this place so look for this hidden snackette beneath La Robe Creole just across from the round-about. They serve excellent pastries, breads, bakes, meat pies and fresh juice. Give their coconut turnovers and potato pies a try. *Old Street, Roseau; Hours: Daily 8am-4pm.*

Island Ice Cream A great place where locals go to grab an ice cream. Friendly staff and seating available. *Kennedy Ave and Kings Lane, Roseau.*

Sutton Place Restaurant Located in a stone courtyard attached to the hotel, this restaurant specializes in international fare as well as Creole dishes with a twist, using local ingredients. They will happily accommodate any diet. Come in on Wednesdays and Saturday for the best rotis on island. The service isn't great but the food makes up for it. *25 Old Street, Roseau; Tel: 767-449-8700; www.suttonplacehoteldominica.com; Hours: Daily 7am-10pm; Cost: EC$12-$20 breakfast, EC$25-$35 lunch, EC$30-$70 dinner.*

Balisier Restaurant and Old Jetty Bar Balisier serves both local and international cuisine for every meal with outdoor seating available on the bay front. Good food in a pleasant setting with friendly service and plenty of vegetarian options. Come in for karaoke every Friday night from 8pm-12am. *Located in the Garraway Hotel (1 Dame Eugenia Charles Blvd, Roseau); Hours: Daily 8am-9:30pm; Cost: EC$18-$40 Breakfast, EC$25-$30 Lunch, EC$85 for full dinner including soup, salad, main course, sides, and dessert. Dinner menu changes nightly.*

Port of Call An upscale restaurant that attracts the more affluent crowd in Roseau. They offer everything from sandwiches and salads to steak and lobster and have a full bar. Open later than most restaurants so if you find yourself in Roseau late and hungry this is a good bet. *Kennedy Ave, Roseau; Hours: M-F 10am-10pm, Sat 10am-11pm; Cost: EC$10-$80 (most items are at the higher end of the spectrum).*

Guiyave This eatery gets recommended more than most so it's worth checking out. The downstairs serves great pastries and you can get a regular ol' Creole lunch as well. If you want something with a little more pizzazz, try the very popular restaurant upstairs that has an attractive buffet for EC$40 and includes excellent traditional Creole fare. On Saturdays they have a special menu that includes *pelau*, goat water, broth, rotis and other local favorites. *Cork Street, Roseau; Tel: 767-449-2930; Hours: M-Sat 8:30am-2:30pm; Cost: EC$8-$40.*

Garage Bar and Grill A genuine sports bar and grill in the heart of Roseau. They have excellent paninis and skewers as well as salads, steaks, burgers and Creole food served up in a fun and inviting atmosphere. Happy hour is from 5 to 6pm when you can get two for one drinks. Definitely worth checking out! *Hanover Street, Roseau; Tel: 767-448-5433; Hours: M-Sat 10am-10pm (bar stays open later); Cost: EC$10-$50.*

Cocorico Café This bayside bistro is a tourist hotspot because of its vibrant atmosphere, excellent food and wireless internet. If you need a taste of home, you can find it in this French-American fusion style café. They have an extensive menu complete with mixed drinks, desserts, and espresso. Check out the local artwork that adorns the walls and take advantage of their outdoor seating area that has amazing views of the bay and the mountains. *Dame Eugenia Charles Blvd, Roseau; Tel: 767-440-8686; Hours: M-F 8:30am-4pm, Sat 8:30am-2pm; EC$15-$46*

Ancient Capital Restaurant This Asian-themed restaurant is a favorite among ex-pats who want something different from the usual Creole and Western food found most places. The menu is very extensive with everything from Thai food to sushi and a large selection of seafood, meats, and vegetarian options. The prices are steep (and don't include tax) but the service is excellent and food is great. *Church St, Roseau; Tel: 767-448-6628; Hours: M-Th 10:30am-9:30pm, F-Sa 10:30am-10:30pm, Sun 5pm-9:30pm; Cost: EC$30 for sushi roll, EC$35-$65 main course. (Cash only)*

Talipot Café and Art Gallery This new gem of a place is located just south of the Parliment Building, in an old cottage home replete with a stone courtyard, wrought iron fencing and a large veranda. Food is a creative mix of local Creole and international fare with items such as salads, soups, sandwiches, chicken, burritos, and shrimp, and a typical Creole lunch plate. Seating available indoors or out. Café is part of a formal art gallery that displays and sells local artwork and souveniers. Restaurant serves lunch daily and dinner (must call ahead) from Wednesday through Saturday until 9:30pm. *Victoria Street, Roseau; Tel: 767-276-3747; talipotgallery@gmail.com, www.talipotgallery.com; Hours: 11am-3pm; Cost: EC$40 for main course, appetizer and drink.*

La Maison This elegant French-Creole restaurant is located on a small side street in Roseau. The service is excellent with a soothing atmosphere and an extensive wine list. It is probably the most upscale eatery in Roseau and the French chef will take vegetarian orders if not listed on the menu. *Fort Lane, Roseau; Tel: 767-440-5287; Hours: Tu-Sat 5pm-late; Cost: EC$45-$85.*

Fort Young Hotel Restaurant and Bar You have a choice of three different restaurants and a bar at this hotel complex. The casual and central restaurant, called the Balas Bar and Café serves snacks, which include salads, pizza, fish, wraps, burgers and vegetarian options. The Waterfront Restaurant, a more up-scale option, has a set menu for lunch and dinner with a soup or salad, main course and dessert. The breakfast buffet here is excellent. The Boardwalk Café Bar is seaside and has a gorgeous waterfall in the patio area. Drinks are rather overpriced but the music and atmosphere are fun. *Dame Eugenia Charles Blvd, Roseau; Hours: Daily 8am-10pm; Cost: Snacks: around EC$20, Full Lunch: EC$40, Set Dinner: EC$50.*

Nightlife

JR's Bar and Restaurant Fun, lively atmosphere with a well stocked bar. Several tables are available in an open-air plaza. On Friday nights JR's fires up the barbeque grill and serves barbeque chicken, ribs, fish, and pork chops. A great place to get to know the locals during late night liming, however the music is generally so loud that a good conversation must be taken elsewhere. Be sure to give their rum punch a try. *King George V Street, Roseau; Hours: Open M-Sat 7am until late most nights. Open from noon onwards on Sundays.*

Top Shottaz Bar, Pool Hall, and Internet Cafe If pirates still roamed the islands, this is definitely where you'd find them hanging out. They cater to tourists during the day who want to stop for a Kubuli and enjoy the second story view of the bay front alfresco, but the beer odor that permeates the interior reveals that this place is hoppin' at night with the locals. They don't close until the last patron leaves. *Dame Eugenia Charles Blvd, Roseau; Hours: 10am-very late; Internet is EC$3.50/30 minutes.*

Carew's Limelight Bar Carew's stays open late and has some of the friendliest owners in Roseau. You'll find a relaxed atmosphere that's great for chatting with friends or getting to know the local crowd while you enjoy a Kubuli or a killer rum punch. Friday nights are best to come by when you'll potentially find some live jazz upstairs and barbeque being sold on the sidewalk below. *Old Street, across from the Old Market on the 2nd floor, Roseau; Tel: 767-245-9036; Hours: M-Sat 8:30am-9:30pm (Open very late on Friday),Open on Sunday if a cruise ship is in port.*

Garage Bar and Grill One of the more happening places in Roseau after hours, you can count on them to stay open late, especially on the weekend. Happy hour is from 5-6pm when you can get two for one drinks. On most Friday nights they clear the floor, hire a DJ, and put on a great dance party. *Hanover Street, Roseau; Tel: 767-448-5433; Hours: 10am-10pm M-Thrs, Open later on F & Sat.*

Fort Young Friday night happy hour is one of the best in town. From 5:30-10pm, pay EC$10 for entrance and you receive one or two free drinks. Enjoy the live jazz, drink discounts, and buffet (warning vegetarians, all they serve are meat and fries so eat beforehand!). *Dame Eugenia Charles Blvd, Roseau; Hours: Friday 5:30pm-10pm; Cost: EC$10.*

Garraway Hotel Come in for Dominican-style karaoke every Friday night from 8pm-12am. Food and drinks available from the bar. *1 Dame Eugenia Charles Blvd, Roseau; Hours: Friday 8pm-12am*

Grocery Stores

Farmers Market and Fish Market Located on the riverbank, in the northwest corner of Roseau, you can find any fresh local produce that is in season. Best days to buy are Wednesdays, Friday and Saturdays when everyone brings out the cream of the crop. Get there early for the best selection. Prices are sometimes negotiable. *River Bank Street, Roseau; Hours: M-F 7am-5:30pm, Sat 6:30am-3pm.*

Astaphan's Grocery Store Well stocked grocery store on the first floor and home goods department store on the second floor. *King George V Street, Roseau (near the Botanical Gardens); Tel: 767-448-3221; Hours: M-W 8am-7pm; Th-Sat 8am-8pm.*

Save-a-Lot Grocery Store Convenient location for dry goods, as you can get your produce next door at the farmers market without having to walk all the way across town. *River Bank Street, Roseau; Hours: M-W 8am-7pm, Th-Sat 8am-8pm.*

HHV Whitchurch Supermarket Well stocked grocery store with all of the basics. *Old St, Roseau; Tel: 767-448-2181; Hours: M-W 8am-7pm, Th-Sat 8am-8pm.*

AC Shillingford's Not as comprehensive as Whitchurch or Astaphans, but has the essentials and sometimes stays open later than the others. *King George V Street, Roseau; Tel: 767-448-2481; M-W 8am-7pm, Th-Sat 8am-8pm.*

Shopping

Outdoor World Carries swimsuits, sandals, fishing and hunting equipment and sometimes snorkels and masks. It's very expensive but may be the only place you can find some of these items if you accidentally left them at home. *King George V Street, Roseau; Hours: M-F 9am-5pm; Sat 9am-2pm.*

Cocogifts A gift shop that features arts, crafts, and other goods made by local artists. They sell high quality calabash carvings, bamboo artwork, Carib baskets and food items. It's definitely worth a glance inside. *Dame Eugenia Charles Blvd, Roseau; Hours: M-F 8:30am-4pm, Sat 8:30am-2pm, Sundays open if a cruise ship is in port (10:30-4pm).*

Exotic Batik and Tye Dye Probably the only place on island to get handmade batiks. Their selection really varies depending on when you come but occasionally you can find some really great and original pieces here. *Kings Street (at Cork Street), Roseau.*

Leather Sandals Stall Specializing in handmade leather sandals. You can also generally get a shoe fixed here. *Stall on Old Street and Kennedy Ave, Roseau.*

The Ruins A very popular and fun place to buy local and imported spices, homemade bush rum and an amazing rum punch. You can sample for free before you buy. Café attached that serves rum drinks and Kubuli and occasionally snacks and exotic meat dishes. Friendly service. *Across from the Old Market, Roseau.*

Old Market What was once a site for slave auctions is now a vibrant marketplace for vendors selling local and imported tourist items. This is where you'll find "made in China" types of goods like shot glasses, mugs, ash trays, tote bags, t-shirts, key chains, and tropical wraps with "Dominica" written on them. You can also find some locally made crafts, jewlery, and instruments. Inside of the building, on the Old Street side, there is a great selection of unique handwoven baskets and you can even watch them being made. *King George V Street and Dame Eugenia Charles Blvd, Roseau.*

DUTY FREE

Pirates Duty Free Shopping A new duty-free shop in a historic building, Pirates has wine, liquor, watches, cigars, jewelry, and sunglasses for sale in their convenient air conditioned location one block up from the bay front. *6 Long Lane, Roseau; Tel: 767-449-9774.*

Luxury Emporium Duty Free Shop Shop here for duty-free spirits, wine, leather bags and purses, belts, shoes, and local goods. *Dame Eugenia Charles Blvd, Roseau.*

Baroon Inernational Duty Free A small selection of clothing, souvenirs, and duty-free watches, jewelry, and pens. *Kennedy Ave at Prevost Cinemall, Roseau.*

Jewellers International Duty Free An upscale shop that sells Rolex and other high end jewelry. *Fort Young Hotel, Bayfront, Roseau; Tel: 76-440-3319; Hours: M-F 9am-5pm, Sat 9am-2pm.*

ART GALLERIES

View contemporary work at the following restaurants, hotels, and galleries:

Fort Young Hotel Local artwork on display and for sale throughout the passageways of the hotel. *Dame Eugenia Charles Blvd, Roseau; Tel: 767-448-5500, 767-448-5006; www.fortyounghotel.com, fortyoung@cwdom.dm.*

Talipot Gallery Located in a beautiful old house across from the ornate pink parliament building in Roseau, this formal gallery features local artwork, all of which is for sale. *Victoria Street, Roseau; talipotgallery@gmail.com; 767-276-3747; Hours: M-F 11am-3pm; www.talipotgallery.com.*

Cocorico Café Local artwork adorns the walls in the adorable café. Exhibitions change regularly and most artwork is also for sale. *Dame Eugenia Charles Blvd, Roseau; Tel: 767-440-8686; www.natureisle.com/cocorico; Hours: M-F 8:30am-4pm, Sat 8:30am-2pm.*

Everybody's Art Gallery Local venue for artists to display their work. *Hillsborough Street, Roseau; Tel: 767-295-7885, 767-277-1556; susancweeks@yahoo.com.*

Ras Greg's Art Studio Located south of Roseau in Newtown, this resourceful painter utilizes re-claimed media to create vivid scenes of Dominican history and lifestyle. He includes a strong emphasis on maroons, the escaped slaves of the islands. *Hours vary, best to just stop by.*

Ellingworth Moses Studio Located behind Mangé Dominik, follow the signs for local art down the hallway in the back you'll find **Ellingworth Moses,** a very popular and talented artist. He's a self-taught painter whose unique style captures local island landscapes. His paintings range in price from EC$750-$3,000 and are worth checking out. You'll see his work around town and it is regularly on display in hotels and restaurants. You can check out his website before you visit at www.emosesart.com.

Services

TOURISM INFO

Dominica Tourist Information Center *Located on Dame Eugenia Charles Blvd beneath the Dominica Museum, Roseau*

BANKS & MONEY EXCHANGE

Royal Bank of Canada *Dame Eugenia Charles Blvd; M-Th 8am-2pm, Fri 8am-4pm; ATM*

Cambio Man *Money exchange. Cork Street, Roseau; Tel: 767-440-0879; Hours: 8am-4pm.*

Scotiabank International *Hillsborough Street, Roseau; Tel: 767-448-5800; Hours: M-Th 8am-2pm, Fri 8am-4pm. ATM*

National Bank of Dominica (Roseau Branch*) Independence Street, Roseau; Tel: 767-255-2624; M-Th 8am-2pm, Fri 8am-4pm. ATM*

First Caribbean Bank *Corner of Cork Street and Old Street, Roseau; Tel: 767-448-2571; Hours: M-Th 8am-3pm, Fri 8am-5pm. ATM*

INTERNET

The Ruins (Wireless) *Across from the Old Market, Roseau; Hours: M-Sat 8am-late, Open Sunday if a cruise ship is in port.*

Computer and Trading Solutions Internet Center Offers copy service, scanning and faxing. *Independence Street, Roseau; Hours: M-F 8:30am-6pm, Sat 10am-7pm Cost: $3.50EC/30 min.*

Zenith Internet Café *Hanover Street, Roseau; Hours: M-F 8:30am-5:30pm, Sat 9am-5pm; Cost: $3 EC/30 min.*

Cyberland Cool off in the AC while you internet. *Great George and Cork Street, Roseau; Tel: 767-440-2650; Hours: M-F 8:30am- 6pm, Sat 10am-5pm; Cost: $3EC/30 min.*

Roseau Public Library (Wireless) *Victoria St, Roseau; Tel: 767-266-3341 Hours: M-F 9am-5pm, Sat 9am-12pm.*

Rituals Coffee House (Wireless) *Dame Eugenia Charles Blvd, Roseau; Tel: 767-440-2233/440-2633; Hours: M-F 7am-7pm, Sat 10:30am-7pm, Sun 10:30am-4pm; Cost: US$3/hr.*

Cocorico Dame *Eugenia Charles Blvd, Roseau; Tel: 767-449-8686; Hours: M-F 8:30am-4pm, Sat 8:30am-2pm; Cost: EC$5/30min.*

Top Shottaz Internet Café Only has two computers available for use. *Dame Eugenia Charles Blvd, Roseau; Hours: 10am-very late; Cost: EC$3.50/30 min.*

LAUNDRY

Lin's Dry Clean and Laundry *Church St, Roseau; Tel: 767-448-8988; Hours: M-F 8am-5pm, Sat 8am-12pm; Cost: EC$1.84/lb.*

PHARMACY

Jolly's Pharmacy The sign says open 24 hours, seven days a week. They don't sue for false advertising here so don't be fooled. They are only open during the hours listed below. A well-stocked store with most necessity items as well as medications and pharmaceuticals. Very friendly and helpful staff who will help you find what you need, even if they don't carry it. *Two locations in Roseau: 8 King George V Street and 36 Great George St; Tel: 767-448-3388 Hours: M-F 8:30-5:30 (Great George St Branch opens and closes a half hour earlier M-Sat), Sat 8:30-2:30.*

SHIPPING SERVICES

Western Union and DHL *Corner of Hanover and Kennedy Street, Roseau; Hours: M-F 8am-4pm, Sat 8am-1pm.*

Fed Ex *Corner of Cork Street and Old Street, Roseau; Tel: 767-448-0992; Hours: M-F 8am-4pm.*

UPS LIAT Ltd *64 King George V Street, Roseau; 767-448-3185.*

YACHTING & SAILING SERVICES

Several hotels, including Anchorage Hotel and Fort Young Hotel, will provide moorings and some services as well as the Dominica Marine Center. A well-done, online guide has additional information that is worth checking out before your arrival: www.doyleguides.com/domroseau.htm

Sea Cat Tours, *Roseau; Tel: 767-448-8954/245-0507; VHF: 16; seacat55@hotmail.com.*

Accommodations

Budget

Madininia Lodgings Located upstairs from the Yamaha shop, the Madininia has very basic, sparse accommodations. Rooms are, however, clean and there's a small common kitchen for guests to use. The hallway has a TV, but not really anywhere to sit comfortably to watch. *Amenities: AC, hot water, wireless internet. Hillsborough Street, Roseau; 6 rooms; Tel: 767-448-0849; Cost: US$60 dbl, US$90 tpl, US$150 five persons.*

Bon Maché Another small, budget friendly option. Three rooms have an ensuite bathroom and the other has its own bathroom next door. What it lacks in attractiveness and amenities it makes up for in price, convenient location, and an owner who is a real sweetheart. *Amenities: Fans, common kitchen and sitting room with TV and a large veranda for guests to use. 11 Old Street, Roseau; 4 rooms; Tel: 767-448-2083; Cost: US$30 sgl, US$40 dbl, US$50 tpl.*

Mid-range

Hotel Flamboyant You can spot this multi-colored, tall concrete hotel from a mile away. Rooms are colorfully painted concrete. It's simple but cute and well taken care of. The location on a main street in Roseau makes this a good choice for business travelers who want something nice but don't need a lot of frills. Staff is friendly and helpful. Restaurant and bar downstairs serves local style lunch and dinner and is open until 10:30pm. *Amenities: AC, TV, Hot water, private bathrooms, internet access, breakfast included, conference room available, tour arrangement. 22 King George V Street, Roseau; 16 rooms; Tel:*

767-440-7190, 767-616-7190; reservation@laflamboyanthotel.dm, www.laflamboyanthotel.dm; Cost: US$103 dbl, US$133 executive dbl (includes fridge and desk). Rates increase during high season.

Garraway Hotel Set on the bayfront at the south entrance of Roseau, Garraway is one of more upscale lodgings in the capital and is popular with the business crowd. Rooms are very spacious and comfortable and executive suites will also have a living room with a pull-out couch. Hang out at the Ole Jetty Bar downstairs on Friday nights for karaoke. *Amenities: Internet, AC, secretarial/facsimile service, mini fridge, cable TV, telephone, private meeting facilities, conference room, oceanfront restaurant, sidewalk café and bar and a rooftop terrace. Some rooms come with balconies. 1 Dame Eugenia Charles Blvd, Roseau; 31 rooms; Tel: 767-449-8800; garraway@cwdom.dm, www.garrawayhotel.com; Cost: US$100-$110 dbl, US$110-$140 suite (includes pull-out sofa); US$200 executive suite (includes extra sitting area).*

Fort Young Hotel This 18th century fort was turned into a hotel in 1979 and was recently expanded to include more luxury rooms and amenities. The small rooms inside of the actual fort are quite simple and basic, nothing special really except for the fact that you're sleeping in a fort. The new additions have gorgeous upscale rooms with amazing views and some of which have wrap-around balconies. Very popular spot with business people and travelers alike. *Amenities: AC, cable TV, coffee/tea maker, hair dryer, restaurant, bar, massage and wellness center, pool, hot tub, sun deck, duty free shopping, exercise room, business center and activity center. Oceanfront rooms have private balconies with sea views, Wi-Fi, mini-fridge, and large vanity area. Packages available. 71 rooms (standard, oceanfront, oceanfront deluxe, oceanfront suites); Dame Eugenia Charles Blvd, Roseau; Tel: 767-448-5500, 767-448-5006; www.fortyounghotel.com, fortyoung@cwdom.dm; Cost: US$115-$255 dbl (price is for one person; add $20 per additional adult, $10 per additional child).*

 Sutton Place Hotel Originally built in 1901, the old stone building was destroyed by Hurricane David and rebuilt into a residence and then a hotel. The rooms and suites are stylish, comfortable, and each room has a unique and charming personality, all with beautiful hardwood floors. Group rates can be negotiated. *Amenities: AC, TV, telephone, hair dryer, wireless internet and suites also have a kitchenette, dining area, and most have balconies, reserved parking. Rates include continental breakfast. 25 Old Street, Roseau; 8 rooms; Tel: 767-449-8700; sutton2@cwdom.dm, www.suttonplacehoteldominica.com; Cost: US$75 sgl, US$105 sgl suite; US$95 dbl, US$135 dbl suite.*

North of Roseau

POTTERSVILLE AND GOODWILL

These small, suburban communities are mainly residential and the people who live here generally work in Roseau or as fishermen. Staying in this area means you can be very close to town but without all the chaos of the city.

See page 106 for a map of this area.

Getting There

For Pottersville and Goodwill, which are situated just across the river from Roseau, you can either walk across the bridge or take a bus for EC$1.75.

SERVICES

Mr. Clean Laundry Services *9 Federation Drive, Goodwill; Tel: 767-448-4885; mrclean@cwdom.dm; Hours: M-F 7:30am-6pm, Sat 8am-12pm; Cost: EC$2.25/lb.*

Princess Margaret Hospital *Federation Drive, Goodwill; Tel: 767-448-2231.*

Courtesy Car Rental *Federation Drive, Goodwill; Tel: 767-448-7763.*

Roseau

Bullseye Pharmacy Has very basic necessities, a pharmacy, ATM and Moneygram. *Federation Drive, Goodwill; Tel: 767-449-8600; Hours: M-Sa 8am-11pm, Sun 9am-10pm.*

Riverside Gas Station *St. John's Ave (across the bridge from Roseau), Pottersville. Typically open in the evenings; Tel: 767-448-4259.*

Lindo Park Gas Station *Federation Drive, Goodwill; Tel: 767-448-2599.*

Lindo Mart Small grocery store with basic supplies and an ATM. *Federation Drive, Goodwill. Hours: M-Th 8:30am-8pm, F-Sa 8:30am-10pm, Sun 8:30am-2pm.*

ACCOMMODATIONS

Pepper's Cottage A self-contained studio apartment that was built behind "Pepper's" home right behind the sea wall. Small plunge pool on the back patio with patio seating. There is access to a rocky beach hidden behind a wall. The main attraction here is Pepper, a friendly, knowledgeable, and fun tour guide who treats his guests like family. *Amenities: Internet, AC, kitchen, fans, pool, tours available. 21 Eliot Ave, Pottersville. 1 cottage, sleeps 2; Tel: 767-440-4321, 767-245-1234, 767-616-4321; askpepper@pepperscottage.com; www.pepperscottage.com; Cost: US$60.*

Mr. Clean Bed and Breakfast Mr. Clean is located above a Laundromat and it lives up to its name. The rooms are clean and basic but also pleasant and spacious. *Amenities: AC, internet, TV, hot water, balcony, communal kitchen and dining area for guests to use. Continental breakfast included. 9 Federation Drive, Goodwill; 5 dbl rooms; Tel: 767-448-4885; mrclean@cwdom.dm; Cost: US$70.*

St. James Guesthouse This tranquil and comfortable guesthouse is conveniently located near Roseau and although the amenities are fairly basic, it's a good deal for the price. You'll find a small garden area near the rooms and a restaurant serving local Creole food. *Amenities: Wi-Fi, fans (some rooms have AC), hot water, breakfast included. Federation and Canal Street, Goodwill; 11 rooms; Tel: 767-448-7170, 767-276-5808, 767-265-1151; stjamesguesthouse@hotmail.com, www.avirtualdominica.com/st-jamesguesthouse; Cost: US$39 shared bath sgl, US$50 private bath dbl, US$70 trp (with AC).*

Home From Home This very comfortable, community-centered guesthouse is unique in that it offers "ethical holidays." Tina Alexander, who has lived and worked in the non-profit sector of Dominica for 15 years can arrange for guests to volunteer in a variety of places near Roseau. You can choose how much or how often you want to volunteer and Tina can arrange all of your tours and excursions for your downtime. Meals and airport transfers are included for volunteers.
Guesthouse is available for those who don't wish to volunteer for a slightly higher price (US$50-$70). Beautiful kitchen, dining area, living room and veranda. Some rooms share a bathroom. Tina also has long-term rental properties around the island. Check her website for prices and availability. *Amenities: shared bathroom, full kitchen, living room, dining room, balcony, fans, internet access. Jepson Road, Goodwill; 3 dbl rooms or whole apartment; Tel: 767-449-8593, 767-615-1353; www.islandguests.com, lifeline@cwdom.cm; Cost: US$50 dbl room with shared bath; Whole apartment (sleeps 6) US$200.*

Narakiels These stately and comfortable rooms are newly renovated and a great option for a stay in the Roseau area. Located a short walk to the capital on a relatively quiet street, on the top floor of an apartment building. Some rooms come with sofa beds for extra sleeping options. *Amenities: AC, cable TV, Wi-Fi, microwave, iron, coffee maker, fridge, fan, suites come with kitchenette and dining area. Can arrange tours, car rental, taxi service and airport pickup and drop off. St. John's Avenue, Pottersville; 7 rooms: sgls, a studio, a one-bedroom suite, and a two-bedroom suite; Tel: 877-281-4529 (toll free), 718-941-6220; narakiels@gmail.com, http://narakielsinn.com; Cost: US$68-$115.*

South of Roseau

NEWTOWN, CASTLE COMFORT & CITRONNIER

When you leave Roseau and head south you'll inevitably have to pass through the communities of Newtown, Castle Comfort, and Citronnier. This area is mainly residential with a few shops intermingled throughout and a large fisheries complex. As you enter Citronniere and Castle Comfort you'll find a string of hotels, most of which cater to the diving community. If you are around this area in the evenings you may spot fishermen bringing in their catch of the day, (which tends be a community affair when it's a big one) or happen upon a soccer game in the large playing field or a concert at Harlem Plaza.

Getting Here
You can easily walk to Newtown if you head south along the bay front. Pass Fort Young Hotel and the public library and continue on the main road. If you are heading all the way to the strip of hotels you may want to consider taking a bus. You can catch a bus on Kennedy Ave, across the street from the multi-colored Hotel Flamboyant. The bus fare is EC$1.75 from Roseau to Castle Comfort.

RESTAURANTS & NIGHTLIFE

Zam Zam's Mexican Restaurant This is probably the only place you'll find authentic Mexican food on the island. The shoreline atmosphere, organic foods, great music, and wireless internet make this an excellent choice for when you want to switch things up from the typical Creole fare. Menu includes quesadillas, mole, nachos, and pico de gallo made from scratch. *Citronnier, next to Anchorage Hotel; Tel: 767-440-7969, 767-612-7471; Hours: Wed-Thurs 4pm-10:30pm, Fri-Sat 4pm-12am, Sunday 4pm-10:30pm; Cost: EC$18/plate. Free wireless available.*

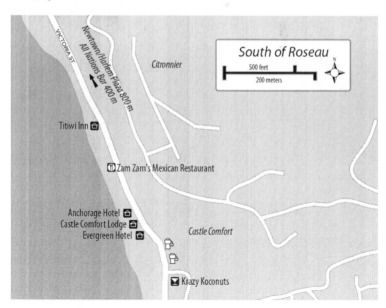

Evergreen Hotel Restaurant and Bar Upscale restaurant on the seafront that will cater to any diet. Come for "Happy Time" on Friday nights from 7-11pm for live jazz. Tickets can be purchased at the front desk. For EC$15 you'll get entrance and a free drink. For EC$10 more, you can also get appetizers. Buffet available as well. *Castle Comfort; Tel: 767-448-3288; Hours: 7:15am-9pm M-Su; Cost: Snacks: EC$8-$30; Lunch EC$70-$100; Dinner EC$75 - $113 (includes everything).*

Castle Comfort Hotel Restaurant and Bar Cute restaurant in a lush garden serving international cuisine at a decent price. Vegetarian items available. The rotis are top notch. *Castle Comfort; Tel: 767-448-2188; www.castlecomfortdivelodge.com; Cost: EC$20-$75 for lunch and dinner.*

Anchorage Hotel Restaurant and Bar Casual seaside restaurant and bar with an extensive snack and lunch menu. Plenty of vegetarian options available. Thursday night barbeque happens during the high season and many locals come out for the Creole breakfast that takes place every Sunday from 7-10:30am. Happy hour is from 5:30-6:30pm. *Castle Comfort: Tel: 767-448-2638; www.anchoragehotel.dm, Cost: EC$20 lunch, EC$7-$20 snacks (served all day).*

All Nations Bar Bar and snackette that stays open late and occasionally has live music on the back patio by the sea. Good place to get to know the locals. *Citronnier; Hours: 6pm-onwards.*

Krazy Koconuts Open every Friday for happy hour from 6pm until late. Sometimes hosts live shows. Restaurant serves rotis, sandwiches, and pizza. *Loubiere; Hours: 6pm-onwards.*

ACTIVITIES

Anchorage Dive Center One of the oldest dive operators in Dominica, they offer a variety of water sport activities for very reasonable prices. Services include boat dives, night dives, guided snorkeling and equipment rental, PADI dive courses, whale watching, inter-island sailing, and catamaran rides. *Castle Comfort: Tel: 767-448-2638; www.anchoragehotel.dm,welcome@anchoragehotel.dm; Cost: two-tank boat dive US$75, 1/2 day sailing US$70/pp, guided snorkeling US$30, snorkel equipment rental US$10, whale watching (Sundays and Wednesdays at 2pm) US$50.*

Dive Dominica Well established and popular dive operator offers boat dives, several PADI dive courses, guided snorkeling, equipment rental, and whale watching. Dive Dominica is also the only outfitter to offer nitrox diving. *Castle Comfort; www.divedominica.com, dive@cwdom.dm; Tel: 767-448-2188; Cost: two-tank boat dive US$80, guided snorkeling US$30/pp, snorkel equipment rental US$10, whale watching (Sundays and Wednesdays at 2pm) US$50 (children under 10 yrs: 1/2 price).*

Whale Watching

The Anchorage Dive Center and *Dive Dominica* both offer excellent outings on Sunday and Wednesday afternoons. In addition to whales, you will likely also see pods of dolphins (which will swim right up to the boat), sea turtles and flying fish, and you will get a wonderful view of the rugged outlines of Dominica. Expect an informative briefing before your boat departs and with the use of hydrophones you can usually expect to see at least one whale. Overall, it's a great way to spend an afternoon. For more on whale watching in Dominica, see pg 105.

ACCOMMODATIONS

Itassi Cottages Peaceful cottages with the convenience of being close to town (15 minute walk). The owner, a former Carnival Queen, is warm and welcoming and also owns Sutton Place Hotel and Restaurant in Roseau. Each cottage has a home-like feel and includes separate bedrooms, sitting area and kitchenette and amazing verandas with spectacular views of Roseau and the sea. Wireless is available on the veranda near the main office. Some cottages are more nicely furnished than others but all are comfortable. *Amenities: Fans, kitchenette, TV, access to Wi-Fi. Morne Bruce; 3 cottages; Tel: 767-448-4313, 767-448-3045; sutton2@cwdom.dm, Cost: 1-2 person cottage US$60 daily, $380 weekly; 3-4 person cottage US$90 daily, $570 weekly; 5-6 person cottage US$110 daily, $690 weekly.*

Evergreen Hotel The bright and airy rooms offer amazing views of the sea from the balconies. The honeymoon hut is a separate building next door to the bigger hotel. Packages available for honeymooners, divers, and large groups. Great upscale restaurant is on site with jazz on Friday nights. If you just want to go for a swim in their pool, non-guests can pay EC$11.50 for an all day pass. *Amenities: AC, cable TV, telephones, laundry service, swimming pool, conference facility, Wi-Fi, parking, fax and postal service, taxi, tour and scuba arrangement, restaurant and bar on site. Castle Comfort; 16 rooms; Tel: 767-448-3288; evergreen@cwdom.dm, www.avirtualdominica.com/evergreen.htm; Cost: Sgl: US$118, with sea view: US$136; Dbl: US$140, with sea view US$164; Honeymoon Hut: US$180.*

Anchorage Hotel Whale Watch and Dive Center The highlight of a stay at Anchorage is the access to island activities. It is known for its whale watching excursions and also offers many tours and activities throughout the island organized by their very own "experience coordinators." The rooms are colorfully painted concrete with tile floors and most are fairly spacious, albeit a bit plain. Some more expensive rooms have small balconies overlooking the sea. Hotel also organizes inter-island trips, if given enough notice, and offers yacht services. *Amenities: AC, internet, phone, cable TV, pool, balconies, restaurant/bar on site, tour arrangement available. Castle Comfort; 32 rooms; Tel: 767-448-2638; reservations@anchoragehotel.dm, www.anchoragehotel.dm; Cost: (low season- high season rates, accommodation only) US$60-$90 sgl; US$90-$110 dbl; US$150 - $165 tpl; US$140-$195 quad.*

Titiwi Inn Pleasant and cozy atmosphere with very friendly owners sets this apart from the bigger hotels on the strip. The three-bedroom apartment can sleep six or seven guests. The apartment is available as a whole or as individual rooms. Comes with common kitchen and living area and the owners are willing to buy groceries for you prior to arrival. There is a bar and dining area out back by the pool but the views of the sea are limited, as there is a wall between the property and the shoreline. *Amenities: Internet available, AC, pool, common kitchen and lounge area, TV, meals can be cooked for you upon request. Citronnier; 6 rooms or 3 bdrm apartment; Tel: 767-448-0553; info@titiwi.com, www.titiwi.com; Cost: Sgl or dbl: US$80-$104 (min 3 nights); 3 bedroom apartment: US$250.*

Castle Comfort Lodge and Dive Dominica Excellent choice for divers. Packages are comprehensive and include dives, land excursions, and some meals. Charming and comfortable rooms and a garden area that makes for a great place to relax, whether it be by the pool, hot tub, sun deck or the seaside bar. They offer a wide selection of water activities and tours as well as 24-hour access to dive equipment and unlimited shore dives. Restaurant with international cuisine on site. Closed for the month of September. *Amenities: AC, Wi-Fi and computer access, safe box, telephone, swimming pool, parking, balconies, cable TV, breakfast included. Castle Comfort; 14 rooms; Tel: 767-448-2188; dive@cwdom.dm, www.castlecomfortdivelodge.com; Cost: Packages range from US$235/pp for a weekend to US$1150/pp for a 7-day package.*

Roseau Valley

The dramatic silhouetted peaks of the Roseau Valley provide a stunning backdrop to the hustle and bustle of the the capital city. Crouched on the edge of Morne Trois Pitons National Park, a UNESCO World Heritage Site, this area is the epicenter of adventure activities with popular trails, roaring waterfalls, relaxing hot pools, and lush valleys and peaks begging to be explored. The Roseau River begins here, tumbling over Trafalgar Falls, writhing its way through the valley and down into the capital where it spills out into the sea. The tall reeds that frame the river in patches along its banks and are what gave the area the name "Roseaux," which is the French word for reed.

The road leaving Roseau to the east passes the Botanical Gardens before it branches out into four separate roads, each passing through small residential villages before rising into the heights of the valley and offering its own unique array of adventures. The northern road splits and, heading to the left, will take you to Laudat where you'll find the trail to the Valley of Desolation and Boiling Lake, the Aerial Tram, Middleham Falls, Freshwater and Boeri Lake, and Titou Gorge. If

> **Site passes** are needed for all of the sites except Titou Gorge. You can buy them from Roxy's Mountain Lodge, Café Mon Plezi or Didi's Mini Shop in the village.

TOP FIVES

Visit Trafalgar Falls where an easy walk takes you to a viewing platform and some hot pools and a slightly more challenging hike takes you to the base of the falls for a swim. (pg 131)

"Relax de bones" at any one of Wotten Waven's Hot Springs. (pg 133)

Swim through the movie set of *Pirates of the Caribbean 2* at Titou Gorge, a volcanic feature with hot and cold water and a waterfall when you reach the end. (pg 130)

Hike through the pristine rainforest to the stunning Middleham Falls. And if you are into stinky bat caves, you can find one those just off the trail. (pg 127)

Tired of hiking? Try canyoning where you will walk along rivers and repel through waterfalls to see some of Dominica's most perfect, untouched land. (pg 134)

you take the road to the right you'll pass Fond Cani and Shawford before you end up at Trafalgar where you can visit the twin falls and Papillote Gardens. The southern road also splits and journeys to Wotten Waven and the natural hot pools or the village of Morne Prosper, a residential and agricultural area with spectacular views and a recently opened alternate route to the Boiling Lake. A new road was just built between the villages of Trafalgar and Wotten Waven making it easier to access more of the valley without all the backtracking.

GETTING THERE AND BACK

Buses run (EC$3-4 each way) from Roseau very regularly to and from the valley. Buses run more frequently in the morning from 6:30am until about 9am and in the evenings from 4 to 6pm with scattered buses throughout the rest of the day. Pick up a bus to Trafalgar on King George V Street, near the front of Astaphans. Buses to Laudat can be found at the entrance to the Botanical Gardens and run less frequently because there is only one bus for the village. If you are catching this bus to hike the Boiling Lake get to the bus stop by 9am for the first bus.

If you are driving, the roads have just been fixed throughout most of the valley so it's much easier to get here. You should still be cautious as roads are very curvy and there can be lots of traffic during high tourist season. At the time of writing, the road to Laudat was still under construction, resulting in long traffic delays to reach the village. However, once these roads are finished, it will make for a much easier journey to this popular destination.

Roseau Valley

Laudat

A small but active village of 300 residents, Laudat rests on the top of a ridge at over 2,000 feet above sea level, making it the highest village on the island. This was once an important resting point for those walking from the east coast along the **Chemin Letang Trail** (see hiking detail on page 290) on their way to Roseau before there were motorable roads. Because of its elevation, this was once the location of a successful coffee and citrus estate, run by Pascal Laudat, a Frenchman for whom the village is named.

Just north of the village is the trail to **Middleham Falls** (see hiking detail on page 255), one of the most beautiful falls on the island. If you are taking the bus, be sure to tell your driver where you're headed and he'll assist you in getting a site pass before you take off down the trail. If you are driving, get your site pass at the Forestry Office in Roseau before you leave or you'll end up having to drive all the way up to the village to get one. These falls are really spectacular and the hike there and back is long but not all that difficult. If you want to change things up a bit you can hike out the other side of the falls and you'll end up in the village of Cochrane. Look for the stinky bat cave on your way out. You'll likely smell it before you see it.

> If you are staying in Laudat, be sure to bring a jacket, as it can get pleasantly cool in the evenings.

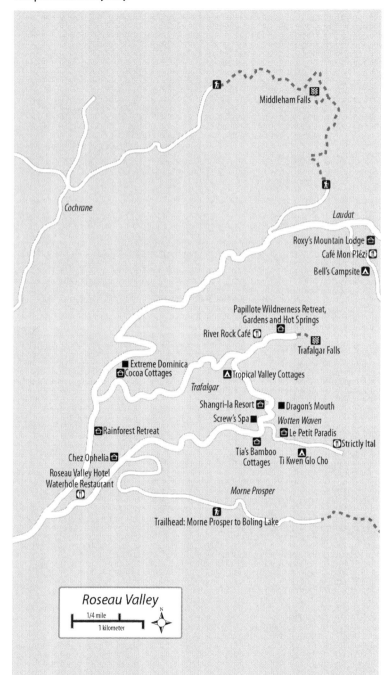

Middleham Falls

Cochrane

Laudat

Roxy's Mountain Lodge

Café Mon Plézi

Bell's Campsite

Papillote Wildnerness Retreat,
Gardens and Hot Springs

River Rock Café

Trafalgar Falls

Extreme Dominica
Cocoa Cottages

Tropical Valley Cottages

Trafalgar

Shangri-la Resort

Dragon's Mouth

Screw's Spa

Wotten Waven

Rainforest Retreat

Le Petit Paradis

Strictly Ital

Chez Ophelia

Tia's Bamboo
Cottages

Ti Kwen Glo Cho

Roseau Valley Hotel
Waterhole Restaurant

Morne Prosper

Trailhead: Morne Prosper to Boling Lake

Roseau Valley

1/4 mile
1 kilometer

N

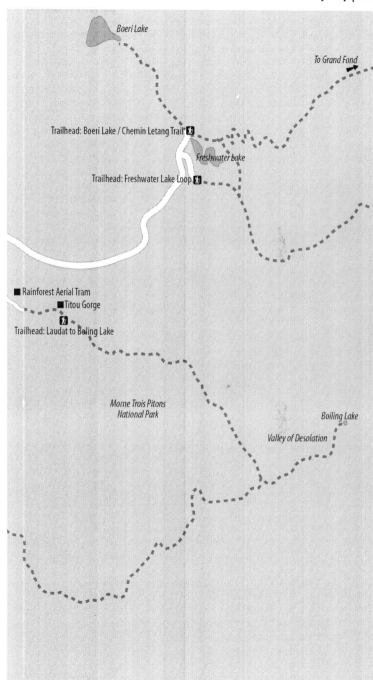

Boeri Lake

To Grand Fond

Trailhead: Boeri Lake / Chemin Letang Trail

Freshwater Lake

Trailhead: Freshwater Lake Loop

Rainforest Aerial Tram

Titou Gorge

Trailhead: Laudat to Boiling Lake

Morne Trois Pitons
National Park

Boiling Lake

Valley of Desolation

Roseau Valley

Head to **Freshwater Lake** and **Boeri Lake** for a cool misty mountain hike. This area is so high that it's frequently covered by clouds and fog creating an enchanting and breezy environment and is a good place to get away from the heat. Freshwater Lake is the first lake you come to and has a large parking lot and what was formerly a visitor's center which is currently closed down. The lake itself is a beautiful expanse of glassy clear water with your choice of three trails. One trail runs along the outer edge of the lake and although it is well maintained it does have some challenging areas. The other newer trail is a one-hour loop that takes you up a small summit with great views of the lake. The third takes you through the cloud forest to Boeri Lake with amazing views along the way that allows you to see all the way to the coast. The lakes are also the start of the Chemin Letang Trail that leads you down the historic path to Grand Fond. It rains frequently at this elevation so come prepared. For details on these hikes, see page 290.

Follow in Johnny Depp's footsteps and swim through **Titou Gorge**, one of the filming sites for *Pirates of the Caribbean 2*. It can get very busy on cruise ship days and you'll end up having to wait in line to access the gorge. If you arrive early enough, though, this magical spot will be all yours. The water is chilly but conveniently, there's a hot stream of water running out of a pipe on one side of the pool to warm up in. Swim through the narrow deep chasm, formed by volcanic activity millions of years ago, to reach the end where you'll find a small waterfall that you can swim all the way up to.

Titou Gorge is also the starting point for the popular and very challenging trail to get to the second largest **Boiling Lake** (see hiking detail on page 252) in the world. The journey is half the fun as you hike through rainforest, watch for parrots, cross a river, climb a peak with incredible views, descend into the "Valley of Desolation" and scramble over rocks to reach a lake that is, most definitely, boiling. The hike is long (average time is seven hours) and you'll need a guide. The gorge makes a great place to refresh your weary muscles after a hike to Boiling Lake.

> If you'd like to see the rainforest but don't really want to exert yourself then jump on board the **Aerial Tram** (Pg 95) and soar over the canopy while your knowledgeable guides point out all the good stuff.

Getting Back

If you are taking the bus back to Roseau, it's imperative that you get back to the main village road by 5pm to get a ride back down. If not, you'll find yourself exhausted and walking back or waiting a long time to hitch a ride.

Trafalgar

With its close proximity to Roseau and very accessible waterfalls, this was Dominica's first developed tourism site and continues to be the most popular (which is why you should avoid it on cruise ship days). Way before it became such a hot tourist destination, Trafalger was a coffee and sugar estate and at one point supplied most of the produce to Roseau. Today, many villagers make their living by working in Roseau or in the tourism industry, taking advantage of what their natural surroundings have to offer.

Trafalgar Falls, which is what draws the tourists, is located at the end of the road at the very top of the village. Pass the hydro-electric plant and you'll find a parking lot, craft and food vendors, and a visitor center with restrooms and changing facilities. Site passes are sold here, too. The short 10-minute walk takes you to the viewing platform via a well-established trail where you can get photos of the twin falls. You can continue on the trail past this point and reach natural hot sulphur pools that form several basins going down to your right. A minute further and you'll have to climb around some large boulders to reach the base of the falls where you can take a swim and find hidden pools and natural jacuzzis. Don't forget to take a dip in the hot pools on your way back.

> **Olma's Shop** (near the top of the village) or **Franco's Shop** (by the playing field) are good choices for a drink or to watch a dominoes game go down.

A great compliment to Trafalgar Falls is a stop at **Papillote Gardens**, which is located on the other side of the hydro-electric plant, down the hill. You can take a self-guided tour of the gardens or pay a bit more for a local guide who will explain the traditional uses of the huge array of indigenous plants on their grounds. With four acres of waterfalls, hot pools, cold mineral creeks, orchids, bromeliads, helico-nias, ginger-lilies, medicinal herbs, spice and fruit trees, and an array of ferns, you'll get your money's worth at this well established and internationally acclaimed garden. Stick around and soak in the hot and cold pools or have a rum punch or Creole lunch in their open-air restaurant.

Be sure to stop by **Mr. Nice's Fruit Stand** on your way to Trafalgar. His personality lives up to his name and he will send you on your way with a belly full of delicious fresh fruit, coconut, or sugar cane and is a wonderful source of entertainment.

Fete Kai Che

If you're around the first week of August, stop by Trafalgar during the village feast called **Fete Kai Che** (meaning "Feast of the House of Che," Che being the former estate owner in Traflagar). The feast happens the first weekend of August but for the week preceding there will be dances, discussions, and early morning "jump-ups" with big bands playing all night and into the morning.

Wotten Waven

With the pervasive smell of sulphur hanging in the air around the village and strange volcanic fumaroles spurting out of multicolored rocks, it's a wonder what the initial attraction to this area was when a British family established a coffee estate here in the 18th century. They named the area after a town in England and despite the smell coffee flourished in the fertile land and was successful until a spreading disease destroyed the coffee plants. Sugar then became the crop of choice until the early 19th century when the estate was divided up into small plots of land and sold to local families and emancipated slaves.

> Research is being done in this area to see if it could be a possible source of geothermal energy.

Roseau Valley

Although the smell seems to be strong in some areas, you get used to it quickly and will hardly notice it when you're luxuriating in the developed (but not too developed) hot baths and relaxing under the steamy skies with the sounds of the river singing in the background. People have been attracted to these natural sulphur

> Avoid wering a light colored bathing suit to the sulphur springs! The water in these hot pools is a rust color, which will stain.

springs, of which there are many, for centuries hailing the therapeutic benefits of a soak in the rich mineral water. As they have garnered more attention, more people have taken advantage of the hot water they find on their land and have made some very impressive and beautiful areas for locals and tourists to "relax de bones" after a hard day of work or play. A visit to Wotten Waven and the springs is the perfect way to end your day in Dominica. After the sun sets, head into the cool heights of the Roseau Valley, grab a rum punch, and enjoy a beautiful evening under the stars. Visit Screw's Spa, Tia's Bamboo Cottages, Ti Kwen Glo Cho, or Shangri-la Resort to enjoy a soak in the sulphur pools (see following section for contact information).

If you are just passing through the area, you can make a quick stop at **Dragon's Mouth**, a fumarole that has recently been developed as a tourist attraction by Rainforest Shangri-la Resort. A short walk down an established trail will take you to the opening of a grumbling steam cave that burps out thick clouds of steam from the boiling water down below. There is also a short and popular trail just before the entrance to the resort with a wooden viewing platform situated over a stinky hot bubbling stream with small pools that spurt boiling water into the air.

If you take the road between Trafalgar and Wotten Waven you'll pass **Tropical Valley Cottages** and a gorgeous river. Nathaniel, who owns the cottages, is a talented craftsperson who is happy to show you around and demonstrate how he makes his crafts (which you can purchase from him directly). He's also constructed a small wooden cottage by hand using local wood that is essentially just a basic shelter right by the road. It can be rented for US$25 a night. He plans to build more, further into the bush, which will be a bit more elaborate. Just beyond the cottage is a trail leading to a large pool in the river where you'll find an ideal spot for a river swim.

Morne Prosper, one of the smaller villages of Roseau Valley is known for its

Benefits of Sulphur

Sulphur has been used medicinally since ancient times. Yet many wonder how something that smells so bad really be so good? It's because approximately 0.25% of our bodies are composed of sulphur and it is found in every cell of our bodies. It is most concentrated in our hair, skin and nails and helps our bodies produce collagen, the substance that keeps our skin looking young, which is why it's called "nature's beauty mineral." Bathing in mineral rich sulphur springs can be very beneficial for skin problems, especially rashes, eczema, bug bites (I know you have some if you've been on island for more than a day) and acne. The warm baths are also good for treating arthritis, muscle aches and menstrual pains. Plus something has to be said for the psychological effects of sitting in a warm bath in the middle of the rainforest, gazing at millions of bright stars in completely peaceful surroundings.

organic farms, which produce a lot of the vegetables that are sold in Roseau. The steep and narrow road will take you up to the top of a ridge where you'll have amazing views of the surrounding area. A stroll along the road, talking to the farmers in the morning, is also quite fun. Recently a trail was opened from here to the **Boiling Lake** as an alternate route. The trail is of equal length and equally difficult, but is less established and you'll likely have it to yourself until it meets up with the main trail just before you enter the Valley of Desolation.

Organized Activities

Papillote Gardens, Hot Pools, and Butterfly Boutique
Started in 1969 by Anne Jno Baptiste, these mature and unique gardens stretch over four acres and contain a wide variety of Dominica's decorative, herbaceous and edible plant life. You can take a guided garden walk with a very knowledgeable guide for US$10 or pay a donation and do a self-guided tour. A network of hot springs are interlaced throughout the gardens with several semi-private hot pools to bathe in. The waterfall pool, aptly named after the 60 foot waterfall that flows behind the pool, has both hot and cool water. Massages are available by appointment. The Butterfly Boutique carries a unique variety of locally made high-quality crafts. *Trafalgar; Tel: 767-448-2287; Hours: Daily 8am-5pm; Cost: Waterfall pool: US$8, Restaurant pool: US$4; Massage US$60/hour.*

Screw's Spa
Expect to be warmly welcomed by Screw himself who loves to talk to his guests about the history of his establishment and the surrounding area, which includes a network of hot pools interspersed throughout lush gardens. Lava scrubs and mineral wraps are available. Changing rooms, shower facilities, bathrooms, hammocks, and bar are on site. *Wotten Waven; Tel: 767-440-4478; Hours: Mon-Sat 10am-10pm, closed Mondays; Cost: US$10 for 1 hour.*

Ti Kwen Glo Cho
Extensive gardens spread out over three acres with one big hot pool and three smaller tubs. Bathes are flushed out after each use. A walk through the gardens leads you to a

"Glo Cho" means hot water in Creole.

fish pond, the Kabwit waterfall, sulphur mud pools, and campground areas. Water is piped through bamboo in order to take out some of the copper color and also regulates the temperature of the water. This site also has "African Fire" smoked meats, which you can place an order for. Bush rum made on site for purchase. *Wotten Waven; Tel: 767-285-9131, 767-612-9761; Hours: Daily 8am-midnight or later; Cost: EC$10 per person or US$5.*

Tia's Hot Springs
Two private hot pools located inside of a bamboo hut and three public pools at the bottom of a lush hill next to a river. Water flows continuously through bamboo pipes and each pool is a different temperature. Night bathes are especially nice as you can star gaze while soaking in the pools. *Wotten Waven; Tel: 767-448-1998; Hours: Daily 9am-11pm; EC$10/pp for public pools (unlimited); EC$10/pp for private pool for 30 minutes. www.avirtualdominica.com/tiasbamboocottages*

Roseau Valley

Wotten Waven Community Tour

Wotten Waven has both a one-day and three-day tour option. The one-day tour starts with a three hour hike up a sulfuric river where you'll encounter submerged fumaroles, champagne bubbles, natural steam vents, porous volcanic rocks and volcanic mud which is hot and rich with minerals. You will have the option of taking a warm or cold river bath along the way before you head back for lunch in the village. The afternoon is spent in one of the natural spa facilities where you can relax in a hot pool completely surrounded by nature. The three-day tour is the same and includes accommodation, meals (two lunches and one dinner), ferry/airport transfer, and the tours. *Tel: 767-440-6678; wottenwaven@communitytourism.dm, Cost: One-Day Tour: US$41/pp, Three-Day Tour: US$186/pp.*
http://wottenwaven.communitytourism.dm

Holistic Therapy

Rainforest Shangri-la Resort offers aerobics, qi-gong, tai-chi, yoga, massages, and an on-site natural hot mineral water pool all of which can compliment a vacation meant for relaxation and natural healing. ***Wotten Waven**; Tel: 767-440-5093, 767-616-9322; shangrila@cwdom.dm, www.rainforestshangrila.com.*

Rainforest Aerial Tram

Soar over the Caribbean's first UNESCO Natural World Heritage Site in comfort, aboard the Rainforest Aerial Tram gondola with an expert naturalist by your side to explain the unique types of flora and fauna that you'll pass along the way. Look for parrots and waterfalls as you explore the rainforest canopy that most never experience on foot. You'll have the option to take a hike through the Vanilla Orchid Loop, walk over a 300 foot suspension bridge – which crosses over the Breakfast River Gorge – or take a stroll along the Chatannier Nature Trail. Reserve tickets in advance. *Laudat, Tel: 767-448-8775; Roseau Office: 4 Castle Street, Tel: 767-440-3266; Cost: Adult US$64/pp, Child/Student US$46/pp.*

Canyoning

If you're tired of regular old hiking, then it's time you switch things up and give canyoning a try. It's an adventure unlike any other and you'll be begging to do it all over again once you're back on dry land. You'll be equipped with everything you need to be safe: a harness, helmet, life jacket, wetsuit, and extremely competent guides. They'll drive you to your first rappel where you'll start a series of descents through cascades and waterfalls into large pools of water. Guides are stationed above and below you to ensure your safety. Trips last around four hours and you'll enter into some of the most beautiful areas of Dominica that are otherwise inaccessible to humans. The trips are exceptionally well run by trained mountaineering experts and are rated as one of the top three activities on the island by TripAdvisor. ***Trafalgar**; Extreme Dominica Adventure Tours; www.extremedominica.com; Tel: 767-448-0412; cocoacottages@cwdom.dm; office located at Cocoa Cottages, Cost: US$150/pp for 3-5*

Eateries

 Papillote Rainforest Restaurant Covered terrace overlooking the extensive gardens makes for a tranquil dining experience after a trip to the falls. Excellent international cuisine with lots of seafood and specialized local dishes. They fire up the grill every Wednesday and you can get an all-inclusive dinner for EC$90. *Trafalgar; Tel: 767-448-2287; Hours: Daily 6:30am-10pm; Cost: Bkfst EC$10, Lunch EC$25-$30, Dinner EC$50-$90.*

River Rock Café A short walk down from the falls, on the side of the road, this spot usually sells lunches which are a bit overpriced. It's a good choice if you are on the go and want to grab a local dish or quick sandwich on your way down the hill. *Trafalgar; Cost:EC$40-$50.*

Rainforest Shangri-la Resort You can choose to eat indoors or on the veranda surrounded by lush vegetation. Specializes in local and international cuisine with plenty of vegetarian options. *Wotten Waven; Tel: 767-440-5093; Hours: Daily 8am-10pm; Cost: EC$20-$80 (breakfast, lunch, dinner).*

Tia's Restaurant If you plan to visit the pools and want to grab a meal before or after, call Tia's ahead of time to make a reservation. They serve mainly local Creole dishes and can make up something vegetarian if requested. Open air patio dining. *Wotten Waven; Tel: 767-448-1998; Hours: 9am-10pm (closed Wednesday and Sunday) by reservation only; Cost: EC$40 for full meal.*

Le Petit Paradis Family operated restaurant that serves mainly local dishes on their open-air deck with beautiful views of the valley. You can request a special Creole breakfast or choose to have something more continental. Dinner is served by candlelight (reservation only). Try "The Bullet," their signature rum punch, or buy a bottle of their homemade bush rum to take back with you. *Wotten Waven; Tel: 767-440-4352; www.petitparadisdominica.com; Cost: EC$45 (dinner), EC$16 (breakfast), EC$26 (lunch).*

Roseau Valley Hotel Waterhole Restaurant Indoor restaurant on the first floor of the hotel specializing in organically grown food, taken directly from their backyard garden and local farms. Dinner is a three-course affair and vegetarian friendly. *Shawford; Tel: 767-449-8176; rosevale@cwdom.dm; Open by reservation only; Cost: US$10-$25.*

 Strictly Ital Vegetarian Restaurant A bit of a walk up the hill from the hot pools, but definitely worth it. One of the only strictly vegetarian restaurants serving authentic ital food (pg 90), prepared in the healthiest way possible. Very friendly and knowledgeable owners. The restaurant is quite small and is located in front of the family's house. You can sit down for a local organic lunch or just grab some veggie pizza (not like any you've ever had) or baked goods to go. *Wotten Waven; Tel: 767-440-7449; Hours: M-F 10am-6pm, Sat 10am-4pm; Cost: EC$10-$25.*

Café Mon Plézi A good place to get a bite to eat (which will usually be a Creole lunch) before or after the Boiling Lake hike. They host a barbeque on weekend nights with music and drinks. A popular spot with locals. *Laudat, near Boiling Lake Trailhead; Hours: M-W 8am-6pm, Th-Sat 8am-1am; Cost: EC$8-$12.*

Roxy's Mountain Lodge Restaurant Full and continental breakfasts to choose from. Lunch is mainly sandwiches and dinner is Creole style and heavy on the meat (vegetarians you won't find much here). Not something to drive all the way up to Laudat for but will provide a decent meal if you are headed to the area and need a bite to eat. Can provide packed lunches for hikes and excursions. Reservation only so be sure to call ahead. *Laudat; Tel: 767-448-4845, 767-265-3065; roxys@cwdom.dm; Hours: 7am-10pm; Cost: EC$30 (breakfast), EC$15 (lunch), EC$65 (dinner).*

Accommodations

Budget

Le Petit Paradis These simple cottages are a great option for backpackers passing through this area. The lower-end cottages have a separate bathroom called the "rustic washroom," but all are very close to the hot pools. The restaurant and bar make their own unique rum punch called "The Bullet" that is quite popular and they also sell homemade bush rum on site. *Amenities: fans, tour arrangement, internet available, restaurant and bar on site. Showers have cold water only. Wotten Waven; 3 dbls, 1 cottage; Tel: 767-440-4352, 767-276-2761; lepetitparadis200@hotmail.dm, www.petitparadisdominica.com; Cost; US$45 dbl, self-contained cottage with 3 dbl rooms US$45 (sleeps 6) or rooms can be rented individually for US$20.*

Tia's Bamboo Cottages A stay in their simple bamboo and reed structures puts you right in the thick of the rainforest, amidst the network of hot pools, which you'll have almost exclusive access to as a guest here. Hot pools consist of two private pools and three large public pools with varying degrees of warmth. Restaurant on site that serves local Creole food and can accommodate vegetarians on request. *Amenities: En suite bathrooms, verandas with hammocks, and wireless internet. Wotten Waven; 3 rooms, all dbl; Tel: 767-448-1998, 767-225-4823; tiacottages@hotmail.com, www.avirtualdominica.com/tiasbamboocottages; Cost:US$60.*

Ti Kwen Glo Cho Campsite The translation "Little Corner of Hot Water" sums this place up nicely as it's a beautiful little area tucked into the hills with natural hot springs and its own waterfall. Price includes access to hot pools and rinsing station and food is available on site. *Wotten Waven; Tel: 767-440-3162, 767-612-9761; Cost: US$19.*

Bell's Campsite Owned by Paul and Kanita Bell, this private campsite is in a great spot for backpackers who want to hike Boiling Lake and get an early start. River and spring on site with outdoor toilet. Owners are currently building a six person bungalow to be finished soon. *Laudat, at entrance to Titou Gorge/Boiling Lake; Tel: 767-615-7183; Cost: EC$10 per tent.*

Mid-Range

Roxy's Mountain Lodge The highest hotel on the island, Roxy's sits at 2,200 feet, which means it's nice and cool during the day and chilly at night. Designed to have a log cabin feel, the rooms are plain but with exposed beams and balconies with great views of the surrounding mountains. This is a great place to stay before or after the Boiling Lake hike as it's very close to the trailhead and the owners will arrange a guide for you and send you with a packed lunch. *Amenities: hot water, common lounge with TV, computer access, tour arrangement, restaurant/bar on site, common garden sitting area, sells site passes. Special group rates. Laudat; 16 rooms (sgl/dbl); Tel: 767-448-4845, 767-265-3065; roxys@cwdom.dm, www.avirtualdominica.com/eiroxys.htm; Cost: US$56 sgl; US$75-$85 dbl; US$117deluxe dbl; US$103 quad.*

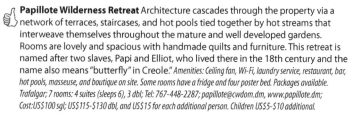**Papillote Wilderness Retreat** Architecture cascades through the property via a network of terraces, staircases, and hot pools tied together by hot streams that interweave themselves throughout the mature and well developed gardens. Rooms are lovely and spacious with handmade quilts and furniture. This retreat is named after two slaves, Papi and Elliot, who lived there in the 18th century and the name also means "butterfly" in Creole." *Amenities: Ceiling fan, Wi-Fi, laundry service, restaurant, bar, hot pools, masseuse, and boutique on site. Some rooms have a fridge and four poster bed. Packages available. Trafalgar; 7 rooms: 4 suites (sleeps 6), 3 dbl; Tel: 767-448-2287; papillote@cwdom.dm, www.papillote.dm; Cost:US$100 sgl; US$115-$130 dbl, and US$15 for each additional person. Children US$5-$10 additional.*

**Cocoa Cottages** A mix of nature, comfort, and beauty, these unique and inviting cottages blend seamlessly with the environment. Each room also acts as an art gallery, displaying work by local artists. Most cottages come with an outdoor

swinging bed as an extra sleeping option. One newly built room is an actual treehouse with a 360 degree view of the rainforest and two levels that sleep six guests. Restaurant on covered patio serves breakfast and dinner family style. Also the home of Extreme Dominica, which offers canyoning tours (discounted for guests). *Amenities: Wi-Fi, fans, library, common TV lounge, breakfast included, canyoning discount, restaurant on site, tour arrangement. Trafalgar; 6 rooms (sgl, dbl, family house); Tel: 767-448-0412, 767-276-2920; Cocoacottage@gmail.com, www.cocoacottages.com; Cost: US$110 sgl, US$130-150 dbl, US$240 family treehouse (6 person), US$30 extra person in room.*

Chez Ophelia Named after the owner who is also a famous singer in Dominica, this accommodation consists of five colorful cottages set atop a small hill near the main road to the valley. Each cottage has two apartments, which can sleep up to four guests, and each has a small kitchenette. Apartments have adjoining door to accommodate large groups. Ophelia herself is likely put on a show for lucky dinner guests when the restaurant has a full house. With the friendly hosts and good location, Chez Ophelia gets regular return guests and lots of recommendations. *Amenities: TV, Wi-Fi, and fans in each apartment as well as cell phone rental. Can arrange tours and meals. Copt Hall; 10 rooms; Tel: 767-448-3438, 767-615-6518; chezophelia@cwdom.dm, www.chezophelia.com; Cost: US$72 sgl, US$83 dbl, US$98 tpl, US$111 quad. Discounts available for large groups.*

Top-End

Rainforest Shangri-la Resort With a bubbling sulphur spring and natural hot pools on site and a short hike to a waterfall this accommodation begs its guests to get out and explore. The cottages are nestled behind high Roseau reeds and the yoga center, and massage cabana are a short walk through the surrounding gardens, which cover over 18 acres of land. The rustic wooden duplexes include a family room with two bunk beds and a king size bed in a separate room with two bathrooms. Kitchen is accessible for guests use or you can choose to eat at their open pavilion restaurant. Reiki, tai chi, watsu, qi gong, meditation and chiropractic services are available and open to the public. *Amenities: hammocks, hot pools, yoga classes, laundry service, Wi-Fi in reception area, access to common kitchen. Packages and tours offered. Wotten Waven; 7 rooms: 5 dbl, 2 duplexes (sleeps 6); Tel: 767-440-5093, 767-616-9322; shangrila@cwdom.dm, www.rainforestshangrila.com; Cost: US$150 dbl.*

Rainforest Retreat Located at the junction between the road going to Trafalgar and the road to Laudat, Rainforest Retreat makes for a very convenient location if you are planning on taking advantage of hikes in the valley. The guesthouse offers three spacious rooms (all double) with balconies that sit above a yoga studio and dining area. The cottages are cute and airy and include a kitchenette, sitting area, screened in porch, which can be converted to a kid's room, and outdoor shower. The accommodations are laid out over a large garden area with a variety of fruit and spice trees that surrounds a sizeable swimming pool. A separate kitchen is available for use by guests and meals can be requested. *Amenities: TV, fans, balconies, airport transfer, continental breakfast provided, group rates, long term rates and meal plan available. Shawford; 3 dbl rooms (in guesthouse), 2 cottages (1 1/2 rooms); Tel: 767-449-9540, 767-448-7059; Rachel@ourdominica.com, www.ourdominica.com; Cost: US$70 sgl room (one week minimum), US$175 dbl cottage.*

West Coast

The west coast is the most populous area on the island and also the most accessible because of the well-built roads. Small villages, usually located alongside rivers, dot the entire coastline as do black and golden sand beaches and strings of colorful fishing boats. The West Coast lies in the shadow of the interior and therefore is much drier than the rest of the island (as the rain doesn't always make it over the peaks). Because of this it tends to be hot, brown and scrubby during the dry season and in some places you'll even find cacti along the hillsides. The best beaches for swimming are found here as the water is incredibly calm, warm, sparkly blue and inviting.

The West Coast is rich in history and geological features that are unique to this area. Because the West Coast was the last area of the island to rise from its submersion in the sea millions of years ago, you may be able to see the layers of volcanic ash, evidence of coral, and ancient sea shells and debris in the strata where the road was cut into the cliffs, sometimes over 100 feet above sea level. Some of the biggest estates were established on this coast and important historical events took place here, the evidence of which can be found at Massacre and the Cabrits National Park in Portsmouth. Look for the national flower, the Bwa Kwaib, between February and June. It is a tree with scarlet flowers is typically only found on the West Coast.

Because of the well-maintained roads and frequent buses, many of the west coast

TOP FIVES

Take a swim in the exquisite Layou River and soak in the natural hot pool at Glo Chaud. (pg 142)

Stop by one of the black volcanic sand beaches on the west coast for a swim in beautiful placid waters.

Find the elusive trail or take a boat ride to the magical hidden Secret Beach. (pg 148)

Learn about Dominica's heritage of plantation life at the Old Mill Cultural Center. (pg 149)

Walk up the Syndicate Trail to see some of Dominica's rare indigenous parrots and take a side trip to the Syndicate Falls while you're there. (pg 150)

residents (who aren't farmers or fishermen) commute to either Roseau or Portsmouth for work. They work in offices and restaurants and many of those in the northwest villages like Colihaut, Bioche, and Dublanc, are employed at Ross University (pg 34). Being employeed at Ross is considered a prestigious, well paying job.

Eat Fish Day

At the end of the Independence season, typically the second Sunday of November, rotating between the villages of Coulibistrie, Colihaut, Bioche and Dublanc is a cultural celebration of fish. All the different cultures represented on Dominica participate and prepare fish in their own traditional way. There are cultural performances by local groups and at night local bands perform.

GETTING HERE AND BACK

Canefield buses (EC$2.50) pick up at the Texaco station, just across the bridge. Wait by the road and you'll get a bus very quickly. For any destination past Canefield (EC$3.00 to EC$5.00), you'll pick up a bus by the Independence Street bridge in Roseau. Drivers will be yelling "Portsmouth"from their buses and probably mistake you for Ross Medical student. Take any of these Portsmouth buses if you are going further than Canefield. West Coast buses leave frequently from Roseau, as soon as the bus is semi-full. Coming back is fairly easy but buses run much less regularly after 6pm so you may have to wait quite awhile to ge t home. Finding a hitch isn't difficult but because west-coasters are accustomed to Ross students, they might try to charge you a taxi price for a hitch. The rate will most likely be overpriced, so decide what a ride is worth beforehand.

Driving

The road up the west coast is new and in good condition except for certain areas such as Mahaut and Massacre where the road is narrow and has a lot of traffic. Watch for speed bumps as you get closer to town, they aren't well marked and are very difficult to see at night.

Canefield to St. Joseph

Heading north from Roseau, you'll first pass **Canefield**, which once held one of the largest lime and sugar estates on the island and is home to the **Old Mill Cultural Center**. Stop by for a tour of the mill to learn the entire process starting with the harvest of sugar cane to the final product: rum. You can also walk around the interior to check out work by local artists and if you time it right, you can occasionally catch a dance or steel pan drum performance here.

Donkey Beach is found at the southern end of Canefield (when approaching from Roseau, turn left at the AID Bank sign and keep following the road as it heads west). This is a popular spot with locals on Sundays and holidays, although it is right by the airport so it's not the most peaceful location.

If you take a detour to the right near the Old Mill Cultural Center and go up the hill, following the rugged road, you'll eventually end up in the village of **Cochrane**, which hosts the annual **Rabbit Fest** every August. This is not an opportunity to snuggle and play with little bunnies, however. This is the time of year when rabbits are stewed, skewered, and roasted into a whole variety of local delicacies. If you are vegetarian minded then skip the rabbit fest and head over to **Roots Farm** (page 99) for an organic farm tour. This is also where you can pick up the trail to **Middleham Falls** (pg 255).

To get a bus here, you must first get to Canefield and then wait on the road at the bottom of the hill. A bus picks up there around 9:15am, 1:30pm and 5:15pm to take people up the hill. There is also a bus stop in Pottersville, on Goodwill St across from Hayden's Supermarket, but the buses only stop there at 9am and 5pm.

Just as you are enjoying the straight and wide roads going up the west coast, you'll reach the village of **Massacre** where driving gets a little more tricky. As you try to squeeze through the narrow lanes, take care to not end up in the gutter or run over stray dogs. When you enter the village, look to your left to see a recently renovated mural depicting a historical account of the drama that unfolded here. As the story goes, in 1674 the popular Carib chief, "Indian Warner," who was the product of an affair between the Englishman, Sir Thomas Warner, and a Carib woman, was working hard to help his people and make Dominica a permanent safe haven for all Carib people. But unfortunately for him, his English half-brother, Phillip, did not like this idea and conspired against him. Phillip, being British, told the Caribs that the fighting between them and the British had to stop and that he was interested in a truce and was willing to sign a treaty. To celebrate, he invited his brother and some Caribs onto his ship for a party. At the climax of the revelry, he killed his brother, which was a signal to begin a massacre of all of the Caribs, hence the name of the village.

Once you get through Massacre, enjoy the view for a minute before you get to the next pinch, which is the village of **Mahaut**. This is a very lively area and the party never seems to stop on this stretch of road. As you're stuck in traffic here, enjoy the local music emanating from bars and shops.

Just north of Mahaut is **Belfast Estates**, home to Dominica Coconut Products, which is owned by Colgate Palmolive and employs a lot of people in this area. They make an excellent soap using local coconut oil called *Refresh* and can be bought in nearly any shop in Dominica.

For a water-filled hike, follow the signs for Mahaut village resources to the **Belfast River Canyon** trailhead (pg 286). This newly recognized hike takes you past seven waterfalls, the largest one being **Soltoun Falls**, on a challenging undeveloped trail, a third of which involves hiking in a river (expect waist-high water in some places). A guide is highly recommended as the trail can be hard to find, especially on the Campbell side. You'll be deposited in the interior a mile north of Pont Casse.

> "Mahaut" comes from the name Amerindians used for plants that could be used to make ropes. These plants were absolutely essential to their daily life for everything from roofing to hammocks to anchor ropes and fishing nets.

Located on the coast, near the village of **Tarou**, is **Rodney's Rock**. Just as you approach it you will see small round huts, picnic tables and a gazebo on the side of the road by the beach. This volcanic rock that sits off the shore is another area of historical significance, although the legend of the rock is now thought to be just a myth. Supposedly the English Admiral Rodney, after winning the Battle of the Saints in 1782, decided to come back to Dominica, which was being occupied by the

West Coast

French at that time, to pursue the retreating French fleets. The French knew he was coming and in order to delay his arrival, dressed the rock with lights and sails to look like a French ship. Rodney, being fooled, allegedly spent all night firing cannons at the rock, confused as to why this strong ship wasn't sinking.

Just off the shores and in the direction of the rock are prolific reefs that make for good snorkeling. This is one of the best places to spot seahorses and other tiny marine creatures that use this area as a juvenile nursery. Local vendors selling crafts and goods sometimes occupy the round huts and occasionally you'll find bands playing at the gazebo on weekend nights. It's best not to hang out here at night unless there is an event though.

> Snackette and snorkel rental are open from 8am-10pm, Mon-Sat. Snorkel equipment can be rented for US$5/hour. Showers and bathrooms available for US$1.

Heading north you'll eventually come to a bridge that crosses over Dominica's longest and most popular river, the **Layou**. After crossing, you have the option to take a right and follow the road inland alongside the river. This is an opportunity worth taking as the Layou has some really magical spots that will charm your socks right off as it lures you into the river. The best and most accessible place to start out is just past the single lane bridge that re-crosses the river on that inland road. Find a place to park and head into the water. Here you'll find a **natural hot pool**, locally called "Glo Chaud" on the opposite side of the river with stones built up around it, keeping it warm and providing a place to sit and relax. There are deeper pools around the bend so take some time to explore the absurdly clear, clean water. Locals all have their favorite secret spots on the Layou where they come to swim and relax so if you run into folks near the river, ask them where they recommend you go and you might find a new favorite spot as well.

If you can't get enough of the Layou, take a water-tubing trip with **Wacky Rollers** (pg 149). They transport you upriver and send you on your way down some gentle rapids and lazy pools with some fun and knowledgeable guides and then give you some strong rum punch to finish the day.

Back on the coast and heading north you'll enter the tightly packed village of **St. Joseph**, made famous (sort-of) by the movie *The Seventh Sign*, an American horror flick that was filmed here in 1987. If you decide to stop in St. Joseph, be sure to take a stroll past the large and very pretty **Catholic Church**, which is situated on the southern side of the river. The people of St. Joe are very friendly and welcoming and it's worth strolling around the village to get a feel for what west coast living is all about. During Carnival this is one of the best places to be as local groups perform on the weekends.

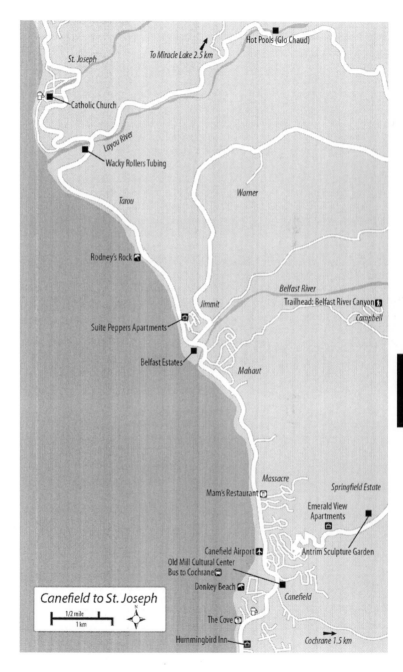

Hot Pools (Glo Chaud)

St. Joseph

To Miracle Lake 2.5 km

Catholic Church

Layou River

Wacky Rollers Tubing

Tarou

Warner

Rodney's Rock

Belfast River

Trailhead: Belfast River Canyon

Jimmit

Campbell

Suite Peppers Apartments

Belfast Estates

Mahaut

Massacre

Springfield Estate

Mam's Restaurant

Emerald View
Apartments

Canefield Airport

Antrim Sculpture Garden

Old Mill Cultural Center
Bus to Cochrane

Donkey Beach

Canefield

Canefield to St. Joseph

1/2 mile

1 km

N

The Cove

Cochrane 1.5 km

Hummingbird Inn

West Coast

Mero to Salisbury

Mero, which was once a Carib village with the name Merocaille, is centered around one of the most popular **beaches** on the island and attracts folks from every corner of Dominica on weekends and holidays. This is partly due to its convenient location and partly because of its wide expanse of black volcanic sand, very calm waters, and fun beach atmosphere. There are plenty of snackettes and shops along the beach road where you can get barbeque chicken, fresh fish, and killer ice cream. They have bathrooms, changing rooms, and shower facilities available for a small fee. This beachfront area was originally developed centuries ago when freed slaves took up fishing over farming and started settling along the calm shoreline. Those who stuck with farming moved into the heights of Mero and produced vanilla, cocoa, oranges and limes there.

Macoucherie isn't much of a village and is really just made up of a few guest-houses and a beach. Its notoriety comes from having the only (official) rum distillery in Dominica to produce the archetypal Caribbean spirit made from local sugar cane, which is grown on the surrounding Macoucherie estate. What used to be a slave operated estate that produced sugar, rum and molasses, is now the in the capable hands of the Shillingford family as it has been for generations. They produce 10,000 gallons annually and up to four varieties of rum the old fashioned way using a 10-foot waterwheel that grinds the cane – a process that is similar to small-scale moonshine operations. You can arrange a tour (US$3/pp for a

> This rum is often used as the base for homemade bush rum and rum punch around the island.

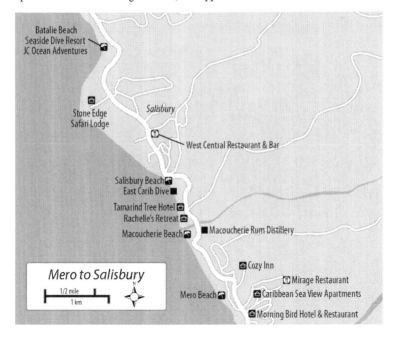

Batalie Beach
Seaside Dive Resort
JC Ocean Adventures

Stone Edge
Safari Lodge

Salisbury

West Central Restaurant & Bar

Salisbury Beach
East Carib Dive

Tamarind Tree Hotel
Rachelle's Retreat
Macoucherie Beach — Macoucherie Rum Distillery

Cozy Inn

Mirage Restaurant
Caribbean Sea View Apartments

Mero to Salisbury

1/2 mile
1 km

Mero Beach

Morning Bird Hotel & Restaurant

30 minute tour) by calling 767-449-6409.

The aforementioned **beach** is directly west of the **Macoucherie Rum Distillery** but takes a bit of effort to locate. If you go to Rachelle's Retreat Guesthouse (located just before Tamarind Tree Guesthouse) you'll find a path that will lead you down the hill. The sand is a nice golden color and the beach is surrounded by coconut trees and a freshwater river where you can rinse off after your swim.

Just up the road, in **Salisbury**, the main attraction is the **beach**, which is home to **East Carib Dive** and their beach bar, "Chez la Douche." This sandy beach is used by fishermen to dock their boats and you can buy fresh fish from them if you time it right. Salisbury River flows into the sea here and snorkeling is decent with some warm bubbles and an occasional sea horse sighting. The village itself hugs a road that goes up to the right into the heights and surrounding farmland. This area grows a lot of the island's citrus fruits, making for a nice drive into the interior and through the farmland.

Nearby, in the village of Morne Raquette is **Batalie Beach**, another option that is located by the property of Sunset Bay Club Beach Resort. The sand is black and the water is calm and good for swimming and exploring. Fishermen dominate the northern area of the beach so the southern end will offer more privacy (not to mention snorkeling opportunities). There are three reefs that are easy to access including one right by the shoreline.

Morne Raquette sits in the shadow of Morne Diablotin and it is possible to drive up through the village and onto the crest of the minor ridges, although the road is steep and not maintained so please take caution and only drive up if you have a 4WD jeep. The views above are really astounding and you can see the far ends of the islands from the top.

Coulibistrie to Dublanc

Driving into **Coulibistrie**, you can stop and fill up on gas or take a stroll through the village that straddles a river to check out the old stone Catholic Church. It's an interesting and attractive structure with stained glass windows and a bell tower that sits by the coast, in this delightful little village.

The main road will deposit you straight through the center of **Colihaut**. Before slaves were ever brought to Dominica and the Caribs still had control of the land, Father Breton sailed to the island and lived amongst its people in an attempt to convert the Caribs to Christianity. The first church was built here in Colihaut but to the disappointment of Father Breton, Christianity didn't take hold until almost one hundred years later when the French took control of the island.

Colihaut is the starting point for the hike to **Kachibona Lake**. You probably won't hike this trail for the lake itself, as it's really not that impressive after being filled in by landslides and rubble, but let the dense jungle, parrot sightings, and the island's largest and most majestic gommier tree be your inspiration for embarking on this mildly difficult and sometimes muddy hike.

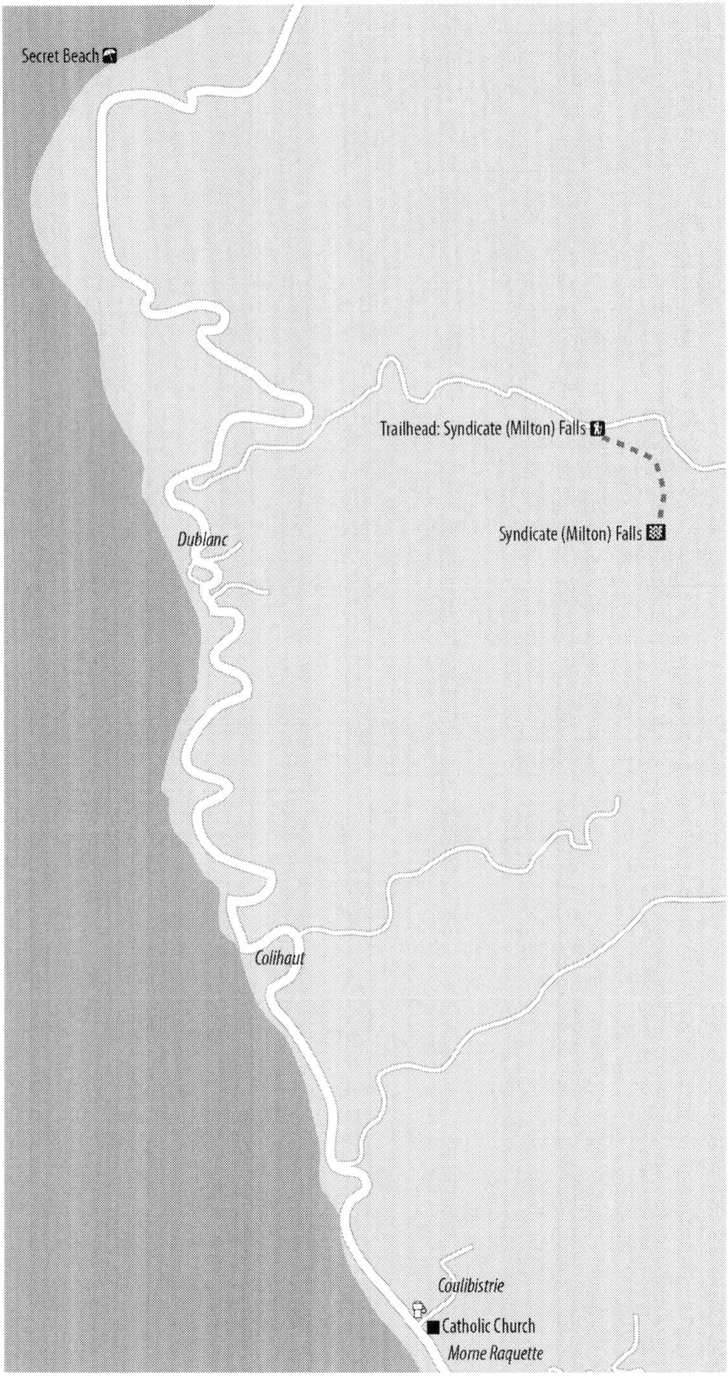

Secret Beach 🏖

Trailhead: Syndicate (Milton) Falls 🚶

Dublanc

Syndicate (Milton) Falls 🏞

Colihaut

Coulibistrie

⛪ Catholic Church

Morne Raquette

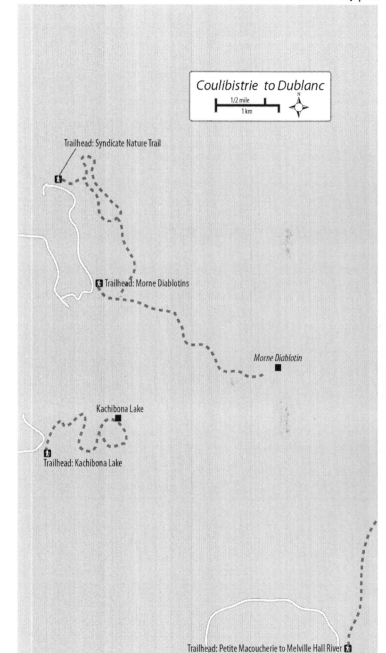

Coulibistrie to Dublanc

1/2 mile
1 km
N

Trailhead: Syndicate Nature Trail

Trailhead: Morne Diablotins

Morne Diablotin

Kachibona Lake

Trailhead: Kachibona Lake

West Coast

Trailhead: Petite Macoucherie to Melville Hall River

You can drive to the heights of Colihaut (4WD needed) on farm roads to pick up the start of segment 9 of the Waitukubuli National Trail (pg 243). This is one of the toughest stretches of trail on the island that requires a full body workout. You'll hike in the shadow of Dominica's tallest peak, Morne Diablotin (see hiking detail on page 258), through some very remote stretches of primary forest with extensive uphill climbs, including some hand climbing. The payoff for this

> If all that hiking made you hungry, there is a very good (and cheap!) restaurant in Colihaut called Western Delights that sits right on the main road. It's all local cuisine, which costs around EC$7 for big portions of chicken or fish with all the fixings.

hard work is being in the middle of a rich wildlife and parrot habitat in remote unspoiled rainforest. The trail conveniently ends at the start of the Kachibona Lake trail if you want to continue to explore the area. A guide is highly recommended.

Dublanc is the last village you'll drive through before the onslaught of Ross Medical School development. This is one of two places where you can access the ever elusive "**Secret Beach**" which is the perfect spot to be if you're tired of the cruise ship crowds, aren't ready for the general public to see you in your swimsuit, or just like some solitude with your beach. Getting to the beach isn't easy (which is why it maintains the name "secret") and requires either a very steep hike on a relatively unmarked trail or a short boat ride around a point of land from Picard or Dublanc. If you are driving north from Roseau you will pass through Dublanc, where you can ask around for someone who is willing to take you by boat (and potentially get a good deal that way). If you want to hike there you'll keep driving through the village and a bit longer until you come to the first house on your right. (If you reach Picard then you've gone too far.) Park there and look for the trail on the left side of the road going down (it may be behind some construction). Be careful on the way down as the trail is really steep, especially at the very end.

If you fancy yourself adventurous but not *that* adventurous, then you can go to **Indian River** and talk to the tour guides who have boats at the dock or call up the

West Coast

The Wild Wild West

Katchibona Lake's name comes from the Carib word for maroons, or escaped slaves, "katchiona." This region was the hiding place for a tribe of maroons and their fearless leader, Pharcelle who would camp out in the heights of these mountains and come down to raid Colihaut's plantations and estates in an effort to reclaim their freedom. If you chose to hike to Kachibona Lake, be sure to bring a local guide as the trail is not clear and it's easy to get lost in the dense forest.

This wild west atmosphere continued when the nonconformist French revolutionaries, who stuck around after the British gained control of the island, decided to stage an uprising and recruited the local maroons to help them overthrow the British. Their plight was unsuccessful but their rebelliousness continued and in 1828 they had 12 billiard tables and 16 taverns, which was and continues to be unheard of in Dominica.

Stemming from this turbulent history, Colihaut is known for its Bann Mové cultural group that wear masks and wild costumes during Carnival season as a nod to the maroons who struggled here.

folks at Wave Dancer (Tel: 767-245-2017 or 767-612-5903) and ask for a boat ride from them. They are stationed at **Coconut Beach** and will rent kayaks and catamarans for really reasonable prices. It takes about 10 minutes to get there from the beach by boat. Swimming and snorkeling are possibilities if

Just past Dublanc is the start of the **Syndicate Trail**, which also leads you to the start of the **Morne Diablotin** hike (pg 258).

the water isn't too rough. The pain of getting there is absolutely worth it to see this gem of a place. If you have someone take a boat, it will likely cost you around EC$100. Kayak rental is EC$20 and catamaran rental is EC$50 for an hour and fits about six people.

Sights & Activities

Old Mill Cultural Center
Located on a former sugar and lime estate that produced rum and Roses Lime Juice, this property lay idle for many years until 1988 when it was transformed into a museum and cultural center. The building now houses Dominica's cultural division. You can arrange your tour of the mill in advance or stop by for a look at their art gallery that exhibits work by local artists. *Canefield, Roseau; Tel: 767-449-1804; www.culture.dm; Hours: Daily 8am-4pm Mon-Fri; Cost: small donations accepted.*

Wacky Rollers
A well-established adventure tour company that usually caters to the cruise ship crowd but all guests are welcome. Tours include river tubing down the Layou, a jeep safari coupled with a hiking option, a high-ropes adventure course, and river kayaking. Tour guides at Wacky Rollers are very fun, safe, helpful and knowledgeable. Each tour ends with some (strong) rum punch and fresh fruit. Kids are welcome on most tours. *Office: #8 Fort Street, Roseau, however most tours begin in Layou; Tel: 767-440-4386, wackyrollers@yahoo.com, www.wackyrollers.com, Cost: US$60/pp.*

Mahaut/Rodney's Rock Community Tour
Although you could technically snorkel for free here, if you pay a little extra you'll get a half-day guided snorkeling tour around this historic spot. If that wasn't enough, lunch is included while a traditional music group plays onsite. *Cost: US$37/pp; Contact via the website: http://rodneysrock.communitytourism.dm.*

Mero Community Tour
Located about 30 minutes north of the capital, this beach community is easily accessed and one of the favorite spots for locals and tourists alike. The community offers one- and three-day tours. The one-day tour (US$62) includes a tour of a rum factory, hike to a waterfall, lunch, a trip to the beach and ends with an optional tour of a bat cave. The three-day tour (US$153) includes the same plus a panoramic tour from the heights of Mero, airport/ferry transfer and two additional meals. *Mero; Tel: 767-615-5723, 767-277-3424; mero@communitytourism.dm; http://mero.communitytourism.dm.*

Layou Community Tour

This village sits on the banks of the longest river in Dominica, the Layou, about 20 minutes north of the capital on the west coast and is an area ripe to be discovered and explored. The one-day tour (US$88) includes a trip to Dominica's newest natural feature: Miracle Lake, which was formed by landslides in 1997. You'll come back for lunch and then head down the Layou via kayak or river tube and end at the sea. The three-day tour (US$326) includes the same with an additional day of fun at Wacky Rollers Adventure High Ropes Course, accommodation, four meals, and airport/hotel transfer. *Layou; http://layou.communitytourism.dm; layou@communitytourism.dm; Contact Lazare Julien Charles at Tel: 767-245-2086 or lazare_charles@hotmail.com.*

Bird Watching Tour

Your guide on this adventure is Bertrand "Birdy" Jno Baptiste who is a local Forestry Officer, lecturer, guide and one of the foremost experts on birds in Dominica. He also has a knack for calling and locating even the most hard to find birds. He can conduct the tour anywhere but the most popular spot is on **Syndicate Trail** where you are more likely to see the the two species of rare parrots on Dominica (see pg 47 for more on birding). Bertrand works during the week so tours are only available on the weekend. He can also arrange botany tours with an officer for those who are interested. Whichever you choose, be sure to call ahead as Birdy is a busy guy. *Tel: 767-446-6358, 767-245-4768; drbirdy2@cwdom.dm; Cost: Half-day: US$55, additional person US$20. Full-day US$80, additional person US$25. Birdy can provide transportation and meals for an extra fee. www.natureisland.com/bird+bot.html*

Antrim Valley Sculpture Studio and Gardens

In 1974, Roger Burnett gave up his secure lifestyle as an engineer to become an artist, setting sail in a 30-foot canal barge for a transient lifestyle around Europe with his wife and two-year-old daughter in tow. Fast forward to 2005 when Burnett, after gaining international attention for his expressive figurative sculpture, water colors, and illustrated books, settled into the Antrim River Valley of Dominica. With the assistance of his wife, Denise, they have created two and a half acres of beautiful gardens exhibiting every type of flora interlaced with bronze sculptural works and quiet walking paths. There is also the possibility of hiking to an 18th century water mill for those interested in the history of the site. Artwork and gift items are available for sale at the gallery. *Antrim River Valley (between Canefield and Pond Casse, half a mile down the road from Springfield Estate); Tel: 767-449-2550, 767-225-5470; sculptor@cwdom.dm, http://sculpturestudiodominica.com; lunch available with prior reservation. Cost for tour and refreshments: US$15.*

SNORKELING & DIVING

East Carib Dive French owned dive shop that offers boat diving, offshore diving, PADI dive training, night dives, and snorkel equipment rental (and can even arrange accommodations). Restaurant on site serves French cuisine made from local ingredients. Relax in a hammock on the beach between dives; they provide the snacks. Showers and changing rooms are available on site. They can also provide moorings for boat stays. *Salisbury; Tel: 767-449-6575; www.east-carib-dive.com, eastcaribdive@yahoo.de; Cost: 2 tank boat dive: US$79.*

JC Ocean Adventures A small water sport adventure company with personalized service. They offer boat diving, diving instruction, deep sea fishing, whale watching, guided snorkeling, and boat cruises. Because they're a small operator, they are a bit pricier but you will get excellent service in return. Cash only, reservation required. *Office in Mero, Boats in Salisbury at Batalie Beach; Tel: 767-449-6957; 767-295-0757; www.jcoceanadventures.com; Cost: 2 tank boat dive: US$85, guided snorkeling: US$100/pp, half-day fishing: US$400, costal cruise: US$200 (2 hours).*

Seaside Dive Resort Located at Sunset Bay Club Resort, this dive operator is more expensive than others on the island but they do have packages available for guests who are staying at the resort. Services offered include: diving, PADI dive courses, snorkeling, and whale watching. *Sunset Bay Club, Batalie Beach; Tel: 767-446-6522; www.sunsetbayclub.com; sunset@cwdom.cm*

The Cove Water Sports Rental Jet skis, kayaks, snorkeling, knee boarding, sports fishing, and banana boats are available for rent. Prices are steep but it's one of the only places on island to find many of these activities. *Road between Roseau and Canefield; Tel: 767-440-2683; Hours: M-W 8am-5pm, Th-Sun 8am-late.*

Eateries

The Cove This big colorful complex sits by the sea on the main road between Roseau to Canefield. They serve up local dishes as well as seafood, ribs, steaks, salads, pizza and burgers. Good food and great service and it turns into a club at night with a full bar available. Saturdays are the nights to come if you want to get your dance on. *Canefield; Tel: 767-440-2683; Hours: M-W 8am-5pm, Th-Sun 8am- late; Cost: EC$10-$30.*

Mam's Restaurant and Supermarket This large popular restaurant serves local Creole food and fresh baked breads. Supermarket is adequate if you are staying in the area and need to pick up some dry goods or driving through and in need of a snack. They have a few rooms for rent as well, however they aren't well established yet. *Massacre; Tel: 767-449-1390; Hours: Restaurant M-Sat 7am until 8pm, Supermarket: M-Sat 7am-9:30pm, Sun 7:30am-2pm; Cost: EC$13-$20.*

L n' O Restaurant, Bar and Internet Cafe Orine and Loftus, the owners, have been cooking up meals all over the Caribbean and can make a mean fish lunch plate. Very popular lunch and night spot with the locals and great prices to boot. They have accommodations available as well but you'll want to check them out first before you book. Two computers available for use (EC$3 for 30 minutes). *Mahaut; Tel: 767-449-1357; Hours: 7:30am-11:30pm; Cost: EC$10-$35.*

Morning Bird Restaurant Located on the bottom floor of the Morning Bird Hotel, you'll need to call ahead if you plan to eat here but it's worth the hassle. "Chef" has been cooking in over 18 countries and has created some amazing meals along the way. He specializes in Caribbean fusion and is also a cooking tutor for other restaurants on the island. Restaurant has a nice atmosphere with great views from the veranda seats. *London Road, Mero; Tel: 767-449-7401; www.morningbirdhotel.dm, morningbirdhotel@gmail.com; Cost: US$8 (breakfast), US$10-$18 (lunch), US $20-$25 (dinner).*

Mirage Restaurant Located just off the main road past Mero beach, this is a great spot to get dinner after a day at the beach. Menu specialties range from East or West Indian to French to North African and Asian, all made with local ingredients. You can get crepes or a salad in addition to a selection of seafood and other local dishes. The open-air structure has great views of the sea and a nice breeze. Open for dinner only. *Mero; Tel: 767-449-6676; mirage.mero@gmail.com, Hours: Thu-Tues 5pm-11pm, Sun noon-9pm; Cost: EC$65-$75.*

West Coast

West Central Restaurant and Bar Probably the only place on island to get a gourmet burger or a veggie burger. Outdoor lounge is a great place to watch the sunset, which makes this a popular date spot on the weekends. If burgers aren't your thing, you can also get steaks and seafood or get a party platter to please everyone. Full bar and desserts available. *Salisbury; Tel: 767-449-7979; Hours: Tues-Sun 6pm-10pm; Cost: EC$20-$50.*

Stonedge Safari Restaurant and Bar Come by to grab a great lunch with a view on the restaurant's large wooden veranda overlooking the sea. Food is made using all natural ingredients with a set menu every night for dinner. They serve an international fare with options such as fresh seafood, crepes, and salads. Full bar. Breakfast, lunch and dinner all by reservation. *Salisbury; Tel: 767-277-3607, 767-449-6536; http://stonedge.free.fr, stonedge@free.fr; EC$12-$75.*

Sunset Bay Club & Seaside Dive Resort The main draw of this indoor/outdoor restaurant is that it sits close to the beach and has a very extensive menu (including a kids menu) but the food itself isn't all that outstanding. You'll find lots of seafood options and vegetarians have a few choices as well. Full bar and wine menu. *Batalie; Tel: 767-446-6522; www.sunsetbayclub.com; Hours: Sun-Th 7:30am-9pm, F-Sat: 7:30am-10pm; Dinner by reservation only; Cost: US$10, (breakfast), US$15 (lunch), US$30 (dinner).*

Chez La Douche Café Located at the home of East Carib Dive, the French owned dive shop. Café serves French cuisine made from local ingredients with a set menu daily that usually includes fresh fish. Relax in a hammock on the beach after your meal. It's a good idea to call ahead if you plan to eat here. *Salisbury; Tel: 767-449-6575; www.east-carib-dive.com, eastcaribdive@yahoo.de; Cost: EC$34.*

Services

Brizee's Mart Supermarket that has an excellent selection of imported foods, fresh local meats, produce, and house wares. Plus a playground and ice cream for the kiddos. *Canefield, Tel: 767-448-2087, Hours: M-Th 8am-8pm, F-Sa 8am-9pm.*

Mam's Supermarket Mostly dry goods and a small amount of produce. *Massacre; Tel: 767-449-1390; Hours: M-Sat 7am-9:30pm, Sun 7:30am-2pm.*

West Indies Gas Station *Canefield Tel: 767-449-1352, Hours: M-F 7:30am-4:30pm*

St. Joseph Gas Station *Tel: 767-449-6329; Hours: M-Sa 7:30am-7pm*

There are also gas stations in Canefield, Jimmit, St. Joseph, Coulibistrie

Accommodations

Budget

Morning Bird Apartment Hotel This is a good place to stay if you want to spend some time on the beach as it's just up the hill (a long steep hill) from Mero. Apartments contain kitchens and dining areas. This place is not very extravagant but the rooms have good views from the balconies and there is an excellent restaurant on site. *Amenities: fans, TV, internet, cell phone rental, can arrange tours, packages available. London Road, Mero; 5 apartments, sleeps 2-4 people depending on type of room; Tel: 767-449-7401; www.morningbirdhotel.dm, morningbirdhotel@gmail.com; Cost: US$60 sgl, US$80 dbl, US$115 trpl.*

Cozy Inn Good choice if you want something cheap and close to the beach. The rooms are very simple and nothing to write home about, but are clean and will the do the trick if you are on a budget. *Amenities: Fans, some rooms have TV, hot water; Mero; 13 rooms: 5 sgl, 8 dbl; Tel: 767-449-6969, 767-225-7691; Cost: US$46.*

Caribbean Sea View Apartments These extremely spacious and inviting apartments have it all: great views, comfortable living room and dining areas, four-poster beds with mosquito nets, and are a close walk to the beach at Mero. Great value for large groups as most of the apartments have sofa beds as well. Discounts available for longer stays. *Amenities: Full kitchen, verandas, laundry on site, Wi-Fi, tours can be arranged. Mero; 4 apartments (sleeps 1-6 people); Tel: 767-449-7572, 767-276-4238; www.caribbeanseaview.com, info@caribbeanseaview.com; One bdrm: US $50/$60, Two bdrm plus fold out bed: US$110/$130, (Rates are for 2-6 nights and prices drop the longer the stay).*

Stonedge Safari Lodge This unique accommodation is rustic and charming and a great deal for those on a tight budget as they offer dorm-type rooms for US$10 per person. The main wooden house has a few rooms upstairs and they also have colorful cliff-top cottages (some with bunk beds) with great views of the sea. The only real frills are the strange miniature golf course on site and a great restaurant/lounge area in the main house. Camping available. *Amenities: Computer available for use, fans, organized tours, hammocks. Salisbury; 8 rooms: sgl, dbl, tpl; Tel: 767-277-3607, 767-449-6536; http://stonedge.free.fr, stonedge@free.fr; Cost: US$10 dorm, US$25 sgl, US$40 dbl.*

Suite Peppers Apartments Small studio apartments (bedroom and kitchen are in close quarters) are neat and clean, albeit simple, on the road to Pond Casse, up the hill from Jimmit. "Pepper," the owner and a popular tour guide, is the highlight of this place. He treats his guests like family and will go out of his way to make your stay enjoyable. *Amenities: AC, Wi-Fi, cable TV, full kitchen, washing machine, common porch, tours available. Jimmit; 2 apartments (dbls); Tel: 767-440-4321, 767-616-4321, 767-245-1234; www.pepperscottage.com, www.sweetdominica.com; Cost: US$60.*

Mid-Range

Hummingbird Inn Family-run since 1993, these cute cottages are up the hill from the main road and a beach (although the beach is rocky and on a main thoroughfare). Rooms are well-designed, some better than others, with handmade quilts and mosquito nets. Honeymoon Suite includes a kitchenette and 4 poster bed. Peaceful and close to Roseau. This is also an iguana habitat, so be sure to stick around during the day to see them feeding. Hummingbirds and butterflies are easy to spot here as well. *Amenities: fans, balconies, continental breakfast included, dinner can be arranged. Morne Daniel Cliffs, Canefield; 7 dbl rooms; Tel: 767-449-1042, 767-614-9967; hummingbirddominica@gmail.com, www.thehummingbirdinn.com; Cost: US$89 dbl, US$130 honeymoon suite.*

Emerald View Apartments Located up the road from Canefield in the direction of Pond Casse, this is a good deal for folks who want to be in a peaceful location that's relatively close to Roseau. Spacious apartments are self-contained with a kitchen, dining room and lounge area both with balconies that have views of the sea. Not much in terms of ambience but clean and comfortable. *Amenities: A/C, cable TV, Wi-Fi. Imperial Road (1 mile up from Canefield); 2 apartments (each sleeps 4 or more); Tel: 767-276-1404, 767-449-3462; Colombo104@hotmail.com; Cost: US$80/$100.*

Tamarind Tree Hotel Friendly Swiss and German owned hotel with colorful but basic rooms that all have views of the sea from the shared verandas. Great garden area to relax or sunbathe in and a small freshwater pool on site. You'll find two beaches a short walk away and a dive center just down the beach. Outdoor restaurant serves international Creole fusion with Kubuli beer on tap. Summer program for children available. *Amenities, All rooms include: Fans, telephones, fridge, pool, hot tub, Wi-Fi. Superior rooms have AC. Restaurant and bar on site. Breakfast included in the rate. Salisbury; 12 rooms dbls; Tel: 767-449-7395, 767-449-7007; www.tamarindtreedominica.com, hotel@tamarindtreedominica.com; Costs, standard: US$80/$98 sgl; US$95/$113 dbl; US$110/$128 tpl; US$142/$170 family; Costs superior: US$110/$128 sgl, US$135/$153 dbl; US$160/$178 tpl; US$203/$230 family.*

Rachelle's Retreat This guesthouse is an extension of Rachelle's own house, which is in a great spot on a hill over looking the sea. The guesthouse feels just like home and the spacious veranda is a great place to enjoy a meal or to lounge on one of the many comfy chairs. Great deal for a family or a big group and has a sizeable well-equipped kitchen and large garden area. Owner is also willing to rent a single bedroom (dbl) for US$45 with access to her own kitchen. *Amenities: Fans, washing machine, hot water, TV, Jacuzzi bathtub, short walk to river and beach. Macoucherie; 3 bedroom/2 bath house; Tel: 767-449-6160, 767-276-3849; philmambo@hotmail.com, www.dominica-the-nature-island.com; Cost: US$80 (for 4 people, add $20 per additional person).*

Sunset Bay Club & Seaside Dive Resort Rooms are small and a bit plain but amenities abound. Good place to stay if you want to dive on the west coast and be on the beach and is one of the only all-inclusives in the area. *Amenities: Wi-Fi, fans, safe box, covered porch, tour arrangement, breakfast included, laundry service, pool, sauna, gardens, massages available, iguana sightings. Beach on site. All-inclusive includes 3 meals, snacks, and drinks. Batalie; 12 rooms/bungalows (sgl/dbl/tpl/quad/suite); Tel: 767-446-6522; sunset@cwdom.dm, www.sunsetbayclub.com; Cost: US$89/$99 sgl; US$132/$147 dbl; US$161/$179 tpl; US$183/$204 dbl; US$112/$124 suite sgl; US$162/$178 suite dbl; All-inclusive plans from US$141 to $411; Children under 12 stay free.*

Portsmouth & Picard

If you are feeling homesick and a little out of sorts, then head to **Picard**. Home to Ross Medical University, an off-shore American medical university, Picard features nicely paved sidewalks, familiar food, and residents with an American accent. Because of the success of the school, this area is being developed at a dizzying rate as apartments, restaurants, strip malls, and grocery stores are being built and everyone is attempting to get a piece of the American wealth that is brought in with the students. If you travel to this area, locals will most definitely ask you if you are a Ross student.

There are excellent beaches in this area, including the **Picard/Coconut Beach.** It is less crowded than the popular Purple Turtle Beach in Portsmouth but with the same great sand, sunsets and swimmable waters. You can get to it by following signs for the Coconut Beach Hotel (which has been closed down for years so don't worry about any crowds here). This is also the beach where you can rent a boat or kayak to get to "**Secret Beach**" (page 148).

Just north of Picard is the former capital of Dominica, **Portsmouth**. Because of its prime location on a two mile long protected bay, this seemed the obvious choice to place the capital of the island. However the settlers eventually got tired of battling the swampy lands and the mosquitos and moved the capital south to Roseau. Portsmouth still remains the second largest village in Dominica and because it hasn't

---

TOP FIVES

Take a leisurely boat ride up the Indian River to see rare and magnificent mangrove trees and glimpse Dominica's wildlife as your guide paddles you through the lush vegetation. (pg 156)

Get a feel for life in the 18th century by visiting the garrison at Cabrits National Park. Check out Ft. Shirley and stroll the easy trails, enjoying views off the west coast. (pg 158)

Visit one of the sandy beaches for a relaxing swim in the blue waters of the Caribbean.

Ride on horseback through the rainforest, to rivers, waterfalls, and beaches with knowledgeable guides. (pg 159)

Get a feel for local nightlife by spending an evening at Big Papa's. (pg 161)

been fancied up for tourists, it retains its authenticity and has an exuberant character.

You'll find plenty to keep you busy in this area from the **Indian River** tour to the 18th century fort at **Cabrits National Park**, to a swim in the gorgeous harbor. Most of the activities here are also very family friendly. But if you want to ditch your family and go out dancing or get some drinks, this is a great place to do that as well. The nightlife is more prolific here than anywhere else on the island and many of the bars and clubs are located on the beach and stay open late.

The main beach in Portsmouth sits in Prince Rupert Bay, locally known as **Purple Turtle.** It is very lively and popular with views of Prince Rupert Bay, Cabrits, and the nearby peaks. Make it a point to stick around for sunset. There is a bar and restaurant with restroom access on site and they occasionally hire bands on the weekends. You'll find some decent snorkeling around the Cabrits cruise ship dock and the western end of the peninsula.

The other, less crowded option is **Douglas Bay,** located on the other side of Cabrits from Portsmouth and this bay is quiet and relaxing and just as sandy as the others in the area. There's good snorkeling around a reef about 30 yards out with plenty of sea life and sand dollars to be discovered..

GETTING HERE AND BACK

You can easily get a bus (EC$9.50) to Portsmouth and Picard by the Independence Street bridge in Roseau. As you walk in that direction up the riverfront you'll hear drivers yelling "Portsmouth" at you from their buses. Jump in the one that has the most passengers, as it will likely be leaving first. West coast buses run frequently from Roseau, until about 6pm, after which time you may have to wait for awhile to get a ride. Although hitchhiking is easy, some people will try to charge you taxi rates since this area is accustomed to Ross students. It's your choice to either deny the ride and wait a bit longer or negotiate a price to get where you're trying to go.

Sights

Indian River Boat Trip

A trip down this mangrove-fringed river, named after a former Carib Indian settlement in the area, is a great way to spend a relaxing afternoon and enjoy what feels like an Amazonian adventure. As you reach the Glanvillia area of Portsmouth you'll see colorful wooden boats along the shore of the river beneath a bridge. Park near the bridge and the guides will direct you to where you can buy your site pass. As your trained guide paddles you down the one-mile stretch of placid water, you'll learn about the history, flora and fauna of the area. It's not uncommon to see iguanas, kingfishers, herons, large colorful land crabs as well as remnants of the set from the swamp scene in the second *Pirates of the Caribbean* movie. At the end of the river you can enjoy some juice, rum punch, and snacks at the small refreshment stand. Afterwards, take a walk around to get a closer look at the flowers that line the bank and Bwa Mang trees. The trip usually takes around an hour and a half and is best to do in the early morning or late afternoon if you want the river to yourself. *Glanvillia, **Portsmouth**; Tel: 767-445-5352; Cost: US$15 and US$2 site fee.*

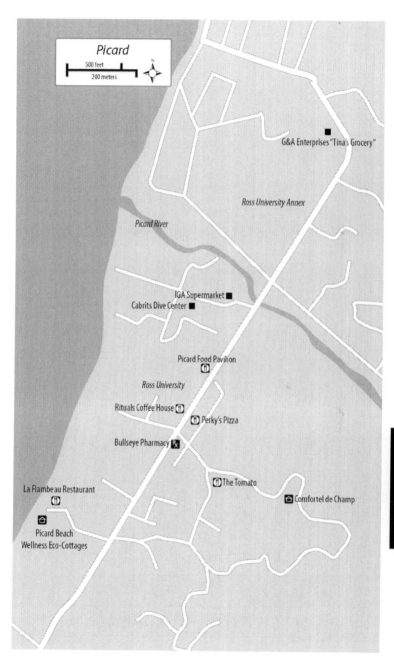

Picard

500 feet
200 meters

N

G&A Enterprises "Tina's Grocery"

Ross University Annex

Picard River

IGA Supermarket
Cabrits Dive Center

Picard Food Pavilion

Ross University

Rituals Coffee House

Perky's Pizza

Bullseye Pharmacy

The Tomato

La Flambeau Restaurant

Comfortel de Champ

Picard Beach
Wellness Eco-Cottages

Cabrits National Park and Fort Shirley

Built to protect Dominica from pending attacks by the French, Fort Shirley, an 18th century garrison, is now part of the Cabrits National Park which was formed in 1986 to protect the historic fort. The headland is the remnants of a volcanic crater and gets the name "Cabrits" from the French and Portugese name for "goat" (dating back to when goats and pigs were allowed to run wild in the area in order to supply meat for the sailors). The fort itself housed over 700 troops as well as the officer's quarters, kitchens and mess, guardroom, powder magazines, cisterns, artillery and ordinance stores until it closed down in 1854. Restoration of the fort began in 1982 under the guidance of Lennox Honychurch, a local historian. An excellent visitor center sits at the entrance to the park, which is located about one kilometer north of Portsmouth. After you soak in the history, geography, and flora and fauna of the area, explore the West Cabrits trail which leads to the edge of the peninsula where you can check out some old cannons. This is also an excellent vantage point to take in the great views of the area and surrounding islands. Currently a hostel is being built in the old fort and is scheduled to open in summer 2012. Refreshments are available outside of the visitor center. *Interpretive Center open M-F 8am-4pm; Site fee: US$2.50/pp.*

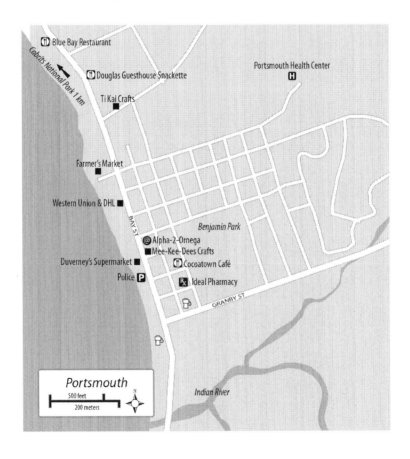

Portsmouth Community Tour

A great way to get a sampling of what this area has to offer in one comprehensive package. The one-day tour starts with a trip down the Indian River with lunch at the Indian River Restaurant followed by a tour of Cabrits National Park and Fort Shirley Garrison. The tour ends with a nice dip in the sea at Purple Turtle Beach. The three-day package offers the same plus airport/ferry transfer, two night accommodation, one lunch, and an additional tour of Syndicate Trail to catch a glimpse of the native Sisserou Parrot. *http://portsmouth.communitytourism.dm; Cost: One-day tour: US$54/pp, Three-day package: US$165/pp.*

Horseback Riding with Rainforest Riding

Explore the surrounding rainforest, Indian River, Cabrits National Park, local beaches and farms with Valerie, a Canadian ex-pat who owns and runs Rainforest Riding. Customized trips and riding lessons available. There is a maximum of eight persons per group and reservations are required. ***Portsmouth***, *Tel: 767-265-7386, 767-445-3619; www.rainforestriding.com; rainforestriding@yahoo.com; Cost: Forest Ride US$40/pp, Beach Ride US$55/pp.*

Activities

DIVING & WATER SPORTS

Big Papa's Deep Sea Fishing and Tours Located at Big Papa's Restaurant and Bar, Big Papa himself will take you fishing around the Portsmouth area. He can also arrange tours of old estates in the area and birdwatching excursions. *Portsmouth; Tel: 767-445-6444; Cost: 2 people for US$75 per hour, whole day rates available.*

Cabrits Dive Centre Located near Prince Rupert Bay, this five-star PADI dive center offers 2 tank dive trips in the morning and a one tank trip in the afternoon. A little pricier than the dive shops in the south but the service is good and owners are very friendly and helpful. They can provide snorkel gear rental and guides as well as dive courses. Open from 10am-6pm between Nov and May. Can accommodate yachters. *Picard; Tel: 767-445-3010, cabritsdive@yahoo.com, www.cabritsdive.com, skype: cabritsdivecenter.*

SAILING & YACHTING

There are several companies that can assist those looking to get out on the water (this includes excursions on Indian River). A few are listed below and you'll find more under the Portsmouth section of this well-done on-line yachting guide: www.doyleguides.com/domiportsmouth.htm

B&B Yacht Services *Portsmouth, Tel: 767-445-6444.*

Cobra Tours (Andrew O'Brien) Comes highly recommended and does a variety of water-based tours in the area. *Portsmouth; Tel: 767-445-3333, VHF: 16; info@cobratours.dm.*

Providence Boating (Martin Carriere), *Portsmouth; Tel: 767-445-3008, VHF: 16; carrierre@hotmail.com.*

Eddison Tours and Yacht Services *Portsmouth; Tel: 767 225 3626; www.eddisontours.dm; info@eddisontours.dm.*

Early Bird (Jefferson Benjamin) *Tel: 767-254-9159, 767-445-6987; VHF:16; earlybird_79@hotmail.com.*

Portsmouth & Picard

WATERSPORTS EQUIPMENT RENTAL

Wave Dancer Kayak and catamaran rental. Look for the eccentric funky shack that says "Jah Love" on the beach. Friendly operators are happy to provide tours as well. *Located on Coconut Beach, just north of Picard Beach Wellness Eco-Cottages; Conctact Clint at Tel: 767-245-2017, 767-265-3654 or Shorty at Tel: 767-612-5903, 767-617-3502; Open daily; Catarmaran rental EC$50/hr, Kayak rental EC$20/hr (plus tax).*

Restaurants & Nightlife

The Tomato This American-owned café is a hot spot for Ross Medical students and American ex-pats who want a break from Creole food. You can find some of the best sandwiches, burgers, and wraps here and vegetarian options abound. Desserts, wine and liquor are also available. Restaurant is cute but small and can be crowded during the lunch rush so try to grab a table on the balcony when you arrive. To get there, take the road directly across from the Ross University entrance and follow signs. *Picard; Tel: 767-445-3334; www.thetomatocafe.com; M-Th 9am-9pm, F-Sa 9am-10m, Sun closed; Will deliver locally; Cost: EC$40/entrée. Wi-Fi available.*

Natural Livity Rastaraunt This wonderful ital (pg 90) restaurant serves delicious snacks (try the accra) and vegan lunches using local ingredients. You'll find items such as lentils with provisions, pizza, veggie burgers, salad, vegetable pies, and stuffed bakes. Healthy and very reasonably priced. Although their menu is extensive, they sell out of most items during the busy lunch hour so getting there early is advised. *Picard; Tel: 767-613-4860; naturallivityrastaraunt@yahoo.com, Hours: 11am-late afternoon; Cost: EC$15 (lunch).*

Picard Food Pavilion Located just north of Ross University, these stalls make their best attempt at Mexican, East Indian, and North American food using local ingredients. It's generally very good and you can take care of that craving for a burrito, pizza, chicken tenders, sandwiches, and burgers (including veggie burgers) for a really reasonable price. One stall sells excellent local juice and iced coffee. Creole food available as well. Seating is found up the stairs that are located between two stalls on the left side. Picnic tables tend to get crowded during lunch time. *Picard; Hours: M-Sat 11am-3pm; Cost: EC$10-$15.*

Rituals Coffee House Just like a coffee house that we know and love in the States or Europe. It's air-conditioned, has wireless internet available and is one of the few places you can find espresso drinks and iced coffee. They also serve bagels and bagel sandwiches, paninis, pizza, sandwiches, burgers, quesadillas, and smoothies. *Picard; Tel: 767-445-4223; Hours: M-F 7am-7pm, Sat 10:30am-7pm, Sun 10:30am-4pm; Cost: EC$5-$12 for coffee drinks, EC$10-$15 for food. Wi-Fi available.*

Perky's Pizza The pizza here is good and they offer an interesting variety of toppings. The restaurant tends to be hot inside so you may want to take your food to-go. *Picard, Opposite Ross University; Tel: 767-445-3281, 767-445-4745; Hours: M-Sat 8am-10pm, Sun 12pm-8pm; Cost: EC$5-$7 for a slice, EC$25-$50 for a whole pizza, EC$10-$16 subs.*

La Flambeau Restaurant and Bar Large beachfront restaurant with patio seating and an extensive American-style menu including salads, burgers and veggie burgers, quesadillas, fish, steak and lobster. Great place to sit on the beach and enjoy a drink or some ice cream. *Picard; Tel: 767-445-5142; pbh@cwdom.dm, www.avirtualdominica.com/pbh.htm; Hours: daily 7am-10pm; Cost: EC$13-$50.*

Comfortel de Champ Restaurant and Bar You'll find an amazing American style breakfast here, which is the pride of the owners. Their lunch and dinner are pretty good as well with mostly International fare such as burgers, salads, and fresh fish. The service is attentive and they have a full bar and excellent bartender on site.

Sunday night they serve a three course dinner for EC$50 (by reservation only). Theme nights throughout the week including a trivia night and movie night makes this a popular spot for Ross Medical students. *Picard; Tel: 767-445-4452, 767-275-3660; info@godominica.com, www.comforteldechamp.com; Hours: 7am-10pm (closed Wed) Open late on weekends; Cost: EC$15-$30.*

Blue Bay Restaurant This seaside location attracts a gathering around sunset when people come from boats and land to watch the sun go down behind Fort Shirley and Prince Rupert Bay. The prices are on the higher side but the meals are excellent (try the fish or pork) which is why you'll find a lot of locals like to come here for special occasions. Serving mostly seafood, chicken, and beef dishes, there isn't much for vegetarians besides ice cream and cocktails. Look for signs on the main road north of Portsmouth and a short walk through an alleyway will take you to the restaurant. *Portsmouth; Tel: 767-445-4985, 767-225-5428; Hours: Mon-Sat 5pm-late (call 24 hours in advance to make a reservation); Cost: EC$30-$82.*

 Big Papas Restaurant, Sports Bar, and Nightclub Whether you come for a seafood lunch, to watch a game on the big screen, to use the free Wi-Fi, or to show off your moves on the dance floor, you'll love the atmosphere and vibe of the open-air beachfront setting at this one stop shop. They serve fresh seafood that is caught daily as well as a wide variety of international fare such as sandwiches, pizza, burgers, kabobs, and vegetarian options. The coconut curry lobster is worth a try as are the Jamaican dishes. You'll find pool tables, a bar, big screen TVs and a dining area upstairs and a bar, restaurant and dance floor downstairs, right on the beach. Wednesdays are Reggae Night with a buffet from 7:30-10:30pm. You can get groovy on the dance floor to some of the best reggae jams around from 10pm onwards. On Sundays they host a barbeque dinner. You can also arrange tours to go deep-sea fishing, parrot watching, and hiking through local estates here with Big Papa himself. *Portsmouth; Tel: 767-445-6444; Hours: daily 8am-11pm; Cost: EC$20/entrée.*

Douglas Guesthouse Snackette Located directly across from the bus terminal in Portsmouth, this place sells some of the best ice cream on the island as well as other snack food. *Bay Street, Portsmouth; Hours: M-Sa 8am-6pm.*

Cocoatown Café Located next to the Benjamin Park playing field, just across from the bleachers, this is a great spot to get a cheap but good Creole lunch on the go. *Rodney St, Portsmouth; Hours: M-Sa 9am-10pm; Cost: EC$15 lunch.*

Services

FOOD & GROCERIES

IGA Supermarket Soon to be the biggest supermarket in Dominica, this IGA will be located on "Lizard Trail," off the main road just south of the Picard River. Still being built during the writing of this book and is slated to open early 2011.

G&A Enterprises "Tina's Grocery" Good selection of basic and imported food items and sometimes you can even find some Ben and Jerry's ice cream here. *Picard; Tel: 767-445-4865.*

Portsmouth Farmers Market Farmers in the area converge at the wee hours here to sell their best produce on Saturdays and the earlier you get there the better as the good stuff goes fast. You'll find veggies, fruit, fresh coconuts, and fish for reasonable prices. Market happens Tuesdays and Fridays as well but Saturdays are the biggest days and you will likely hear some jammin' Caribbean music and can buy some tasty barbeque'd treats such as grilled plantain. *End of Bay Street, Portsmouth; Tues, Fri, Sat 4am-3pm.*

Portsmouth & Picard

Duverney's Supermarket A small but decently stocked grocery store to get basic items. *2 locations on Bay Street, Portsmouth; Tel: 767-445-5017.*

INTERNET

The Tomato (Wireless) *Picard; Tel: 767-445-3334; www.thetomatocafe.com; M-Th 9am-9pm, F-Sa 9am-10m closed Sun; Cost: free for customers.*

Bar De Champ (Located in Comfortel de Champ Restaurant) (Wireless) *Picard; Tel: 767-445-4452, 767-275-3660; info@godominica.com, www.comforteldechamp.com; Cost: free for customers and guests.*

Alpha-2-Omega Computer Resource Center *Bay Street, Portsmouth; Tel: 767-445-3370; Hours: 9am-10pm Mon- Sat; Cost: LAN EC$3/30 min; wireless EC$5/30 min.*

BANKS

Western Union Money Transfer *HHV Whitchurch Travel, Michael Douglas Blvd, Portsmouth; Tel: 767-445-4531; Hours: M-F 8am-4pm, Sat 8am-1pm.*

National Bank of Dominica *Bay Street, Portsmouth; Tel: 767-445-5430; Hours: M-Th 8am-2pm, Fri 8am-4pm. ATM.*

OTHER SERVICES

Police Station: *Bay Street (just as you enter Portsmouth from Picard); Tel: 767-445-5221, 767-445-5222*

Portsmouth Health Centre *Portsmouth (take Bay St. all the way to the market, then turn right and go up the hill to the end of the road.); Tel: 767-445-5237, 767-445-5016.*

Gas Station *Bay Street (at entrance of Portsmouth from Picard); Usually open late.*

DHL *HHV Whitchurch Travel, Michael Douglas Blvd, Portsmouth; Tel: 767-445-4531; Hours: M-F 8am-4pm, Sat 8am-1pm.*

SHOPPING

Ti Kai Crafts Great place to buy beautiful local crafts and other goods to take home as souveniers. *Lagoon, Portsmouth (area north of town, over the bridge); Tel: 767-445-3787; Hours: Daily 9am-4pm.*

Mee-Kee-Dees Crafts and Business Training Center Internet Café Attractive hand-carved items by local artist, Michael Valentine. Specializes in picture frames as well as decorative pieces. Internet available here as well. *Bay Street, Portsmouth; Tel: 767-445-3727*

LAUNDRY

Hannah's Laundry *On Banana Trail Road across from Ross University entrance, Picard; Tel: 767-445-5421; Hours: M-F 7am-7pm; Cost: EC$20/load.*

Mr. Clean *Banana Trail, Picard; Tel: 767-445-5606; Hours:M-F 7am-5pm, Sat 8am-2pm; Cost: EC$5/kilo.*

PHARMACY

Bullseye Pharmacy *Ross Blvd, Picard; Tel: 767-445-3600 Hours: M-F 9am-5pm, Sat 9am-4pm.*

Ideal Pharmacy *Harbour Lane, Portsmouth; Tel: 767-445-3038 Hours:M-F 8:30am-4pm, Sat 8:30-1pm.*

CAR RENTAL

Silver Lining Car Rental *Michael Douglas Blvd, Glanvillia, Portsmouth; Tel: 767-445-3802, 767-445-5502; silverlining@cwdom.dm, www.silverliningrental.com. Online reservations available.*

Valley Rent-A-Car *Lagoon, Portsmouth; Tel: 767-445-5252;* valley@cwdom.dm, *www.valleyrentacar.com. Online reservations available.*

Island Car Rentals, Ltd. *Picard; Tel: 767-235-7368, 767-255-6844; reservations@islandcar.dm, www.islandcar.dm.*

JX Rent-A-Car *Portsmouth; Tel: 767-445-3498; jxrentals1@hotmail.com.*

U Save Rent-A-Car *Portsmouth; Tel: 767-445-6931, 767-245-1174.*

Accommodations

Budget

Fort Shirley Hostel Scheduled to open in the summer of 2012, this hostel is being built to accommodate around 40 guests across three floors in the old soldier barracks of this 18th century garrison. The top floor will house two self-contained apartments. Dormitories will be on the second floor and divided into male and female. Bathroom facilities will be in the basement. The historic kitchen will also be restored to provide an old-style barbeque, oven and cooking range. For more information, stop by the visitor center at the entrance to Cabrit's National Park *Portsmouth; Tel: 767-245-5866, 767-445-6009; lennoxh@cwdom.dm.*

Mid-Range

Comfortel de Champ Hotel and Bar This Belgian owned hotel is a very popular choice for the Portsmouth area so book far in advance. The rooms are beautifully decorated with multi-jet showers, local artwork adorning the walls, balconies with great views, and wonderful hosts that treat their guests like family. The restaurant on site is lively and has themed nights such as trivia, movie night and Sunday three course dinners. *Amenities: A/C, fans, Wi-Fi, flat screen TV, mini-bar, safe box, tea/coffee maker, private balconies, breakfast included, restaurant and bar on site, tours available, laundry service, currency exchange, airport transfer available, and welcome drink. Jacuzzi coming soon. Picard; 5 rooms (dbls, one w/ sofa bed); Tel: 767-445-4452, 767-275-3660; info@godominica.com, www.comforteldechamp.com; Cost: US$125 superior, US$100 garden.*

Picard Beach Wellness Eco-Cottages These small wooden beach cottages are named after the actors and executives that stayed in them during the filming of the *Pirates of the Caribbean 2*. All the cottages have a kitchen, living room (with single bed that doubles as seating), a bathroom, and a bedroom that sleeps two. All have a porch out front. The only difference between standard and superior is the proximity to the beach (which is minimal) and the size of the porch. Be sure to leave valuables at home or have the front desk hold onto them as there have recently been thefts in this area. *Amenities: Cable TV, kitchens, Wi-Fi, beach chairs, verandas, fans, A/C, tours, diving, restaurant on site, spa facilities and yoga, beach on site, cell phone rental, private pier, snorkeling on site. Picard; 18 cottages (tpls); Tel: 767-445-5131, 767-315-7663; www.avirtualdominica.com/picard.htm, picardbeach@cwdom.dm; Costs: US$80/$100 standard beachview, US$120/$180 superior beachview, US$120/$180 standard beachfront; $180/$220 superior beachfront.*

Portsmouth & Picard

The North

In 1567, six vessels of a Spanish fleet crashed off the northwestern tip of Dominica leaving behind millions of pesos in treasure. Caribs supposedly salvaged the treasure, hiding it in nearby caves. It is said that pirates searched for this treasure for years after the wreck but to this day, it was never found. What the pirates didn't realize is that there is still plenty of booty to discover in the north – it is in the form of dazzling beaches, sparkling azure water, and lush emerald rainforests. All this is making the north a favorite starting point for tourists coming to Dominica.

The north starts just north of Marigot on a stretch of road that moseys along the northeastern shoreline, until it splits and one road continues west, cutting off the peninsula and eventually ending in Portsmouth. The other road veers off to the right and becomes the Northern Link Road (NLR) that reaches up through the heights of the peninsula and comes back down the other side. With hidden beaches, a drive-through volcano, swimming holes, amazing viewpoints, and diverse hiking trails, both roads offer a plethora of sites and activities that could keep you busy for days.

You'll find that some people in the northeast speak "cockoy" (English patois) instead of French Creole. This is due to the influx of laborers that came over from British-controlled islands to help work the estates when slavery ended. This distinctly different culture spills over into religion – most people are Methodist as opposed to Roman Catholic and have a slightly different heritage than the rest of the island.

TOP FIVES

Stop for lunch in Calibishie and soak in the beautiful views. (Pg 169)

Jump off the cliffs into the turquoise waters at Chaudiere Pool in Bense. (Pg 170)

Drive up the Northern Link Road and stop for a picnic at the Connor (Canna) Point in Capuchin and if you have some energy to burn, hike to Pennville from here.

Take a break at one of the beautiful and remote beaches along the northeast coast.

Take a hike around the gorgeous Red Rocks at Pointe Baptiste. (Pg 169)

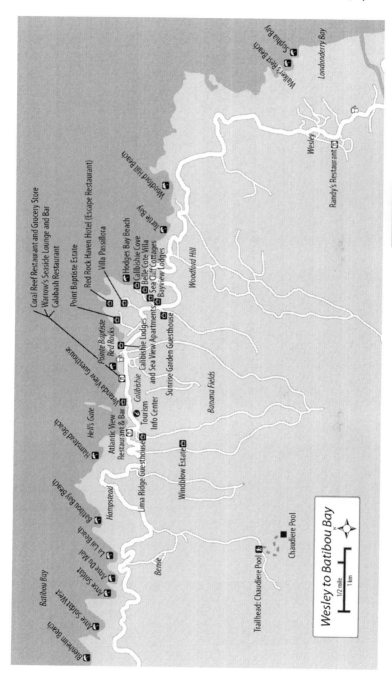

The North

Wesley to Batibou Bay

Londonderry Bay

Sophia Bay

Wake's Rest Beach

Wesley

Randy's Restaurant

Woodford Hill Beach

Woodford Hill

Turtle Bay

Hodges Bay Beach

Calibishie Cove

Belle Cote Villa

Sea Cliff Cottages

Bayview Lodges

Villa Passiflora

Red Rock Haven Hotel (Escape Restaurant)

Point Baptiste Estate

Coral Reef Restaurant and Grocery Store

Warro's Seaside Lounge and Bar

Calabash Restaurant

Pointe Baptiste

Red Rocks

Veranda View Guesthouse

Calibishie Lodges
and Sea View Apartments

Sunrise Garden Guesthouse

Calibishie

Tourism
Info Center

Banana Fields

Hell's Gate

Atlantic View
Restaurant & Bar

Lima Ridge Guesthouse

Windblow Estate

Hampstead

Hamstead Beach

Batibou Bay Beach

La Cai Beach

Anse Du Mai

Anse Soldat

Anse Soldat West

Blenheim Beach

Batibou Bay

Bense

Chaudiere Pool

Trailhead: Chaudiere Pool

Wesley to Batibou Bay

1/2 mile
1 km

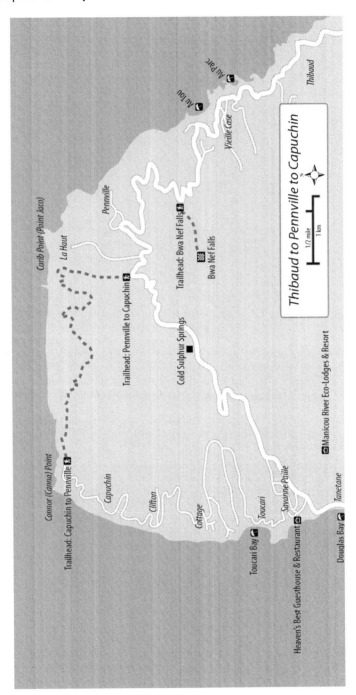

Thibaud to Pennville to Capuchin

The North

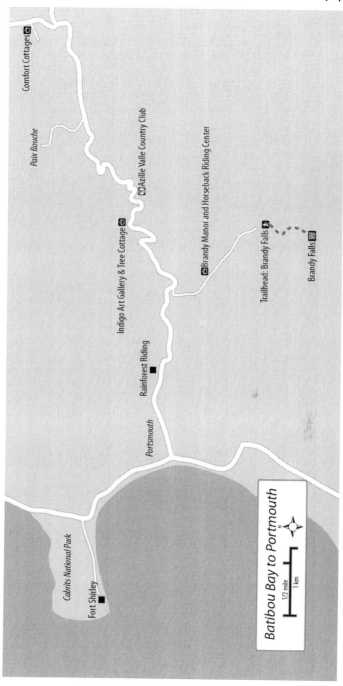

Comfort Cottages

Paix Bouche

Azilie Valle Country Club

Indigo Art Gallery & Tree Cottage

Brandy Manor and Horseback Riding Center

Trailhead: Brandy Falls

Brandy Falls

Rainforest Riding

Portsmouth

Cabrits National Park

Fort Shirley

Batibou Bay to Portmouth

N

1/2 mile
1 km

GETTING THERE

Getting to various spots around the north can be a bit of a labyrinthine affair. Starting from Roseau, catch a Portsmouth bus at the outgoing bridge in Roseau and transfer at the Portsmouth bus terminal. There, take a Calibishie or Marigot bus (EC$4.50) if you want to take the interior route. The buses to Paix Bouche (EC$3.50) leave from the northern side of the playing field, just east of the bus terminal. You can tell your driver where you are headed and they will help you find your connection. If you are headed north, up the peninsula, go to Portsmouth then walk up the road a bit to the market and ask the drivers where they are headed before you jump on as they don't all do the entire loop. They'll direct you to the correct bus. All of these buses run quite a few times a day from about 7am to 7pm.

Wesley to Portsmouth

WESLEY

As you pass the airport and head north, you'll notice **Londonderry Bay**, a handsome expanse of golden sand, to the east until the road shifts inland and you enter Wesley. Wesley is a larger village, by Dominican standards, with a population of about 1,700. The village was named after either an eccentric woman shopkeeper from the mid-1800s named Ma Wesley, or after the founder of Methodism (there is a debate as to which it is). Whichever may be the case, Wesley maintains the feel of a sleepy little rural community. If you're in need of some fuel for yourself or your automobile, you'll find both here. There is a gas station on the hill and a very good restaurant called **Randy's** (follow signs on the bus stop) where you'll find authentic Creole dishes and entertaining conversation with the jovial and welcoming owner.

Copra
The northeast is known for its production of *copra*, a product made from dried coconut meat that is exported and used for its coconut oil or turned into beauty products. Locally, copra is used to make coconut milk and as food for cattle and livestock as it provides high quality protein. There is a good chance you'll see people gathering and shelling dried coconuts as you pass along the road in the region.

WOODFORD HILL

The first beach you encounter as you reach the northern coast is a slice of attractive terrain that has been in high demand for centuries. A large Amerindian village sat at the mouth of Woodford Hill River around 1,400 years ago. When the French eventually arrived they claimed it for themselves until the British swiped it and sold it to Mr. Napleton Smith (which is where its local name comes from as "simit" is the cockoy name for Smith).

In 1795, the French tried to reclaim the area but due to the protection from a small fort built near the harbor, they were unsuccessful.

During the 19th century the "sugar king of Dominica," as Smith became known, ran a large estate on the gently sloping land, the ruins of which are still visible near the shore. After emancipation the newly freed slaves settled between Woodford Hill and Hodges, and would eventually take ownership of the small farms on the surrounding hills.

Before you reach Calibishie there are two places worth visiting on this stunning coast. One is **Hodges Bay Beach**. Its not right on the road so its easy to miss but this also means that it's frequently unpopulated and feels very secluded. To get there, take the path down to the right from the road that houses Sea Cliff Cottages and Villa Bellecote. It's a short

> **Woodford Hill Beach** is a very accessible beach that is one of the best places to take a swim in the north, which is why it can become crowded.

hike down and well worth it. A ring of small islets and reefs act as protection against the northern surf, which makes it a good spot for swimming and even a bit of snorkeling. Except for the occasional fisherman or tourist, you are likely to have this beach to yourself. There is also a river that flows out through the beach that is a nice spot for bathing after a dip in the sea.

Once back on the main road and heading west, you'll reach a fork in the road. If you stay to the left you'll reach Calibishie, but if you want an adventure, take the one that goes to the right and stay on it until it ends.

If you follow the footpath in the same direction you'll reach the **Pointe Baptiste Red Rocks**. The unique headlands are made of soft red rock that has been molded and sculpted by the wind, rain and sea into deep gullies and rounded protrusions. It's a very impressive area with expansive views of the northeast and surrounding islands with easy and moderate walking paths. Climb around the rocks to discover hidden caves and birds nests. Be careful, however, when it's raining as it can be slick. **Pointe Baptiste Beach** can be accessed just past Red Rock Haven Hotel and Spa. For more privacy, walk around to the eastern side of the beach. This is a beautiful spot to spend an afternoon.

CALIBISHIE

Calibishie has just recently started becoming a tourism mecca (by Dominican standards, that is) due to the allure of being a picturesque seaside village with a mile long barrier reef just off of the coast and golden sand that glitters beneath a string of palm trees. In the past few years the number of hotels and guesthouses has multiplied, with some of the more upscale places on the island are located here. It has also seen a sizeable influx of foreigners who have built homes and live here for at least a portion of the year. Despite this, it still has the feel of a rural fishing village and the approximately 1,000 villagers who reside here remain as friendly and amiable with tourists as ever. That said, the new arrival of wealth consequently means a rise in thefts. Dominica is a very safe place, by most standards, so there is no reason to be particularly paranoid, just be sure to keep your valuables locked up somewhere safe while you are out site seeing.

While you are here, stop by **Escape Bar and Grill** on the property of Red Rock Haven Hotel for lunch, a drink, and a relaxing afternoon where you can sink your toes into the soft sand. Or stop by **Veranda View** for a coffee and enjoy true Caribbean ambiance while you watch fishermen cast their nets into the far-reaching shallows. There are a few great snackettes and rum shops on the main strip but the one with the best vista is Atlantic View at the west end of the main road which will put you in the perfect spot to see **Hell's Gate**, two islets off the coast that were once an archway that collapsed in 1954. A nice hike or drive up Windblow Road or

Calibishie Ridge Road through banana fields and up into the heights behind Calibishie make for a good early morning or evening activity to get marvelous views of the coast and interior and see some local farms. If you come upon a farmer harvesting his crops, don't be shy – ask about the process. They will be pleased that you are interested and you'll be amazed at what it takes to grow the perfect banana.

HAMPSTEAD

Hampstead Estate contains both a piece of history and a beautiful secluded yellow sand beach. You can access **Hampstead Beach** (also known as "Number One Beach") by a rugged one-mile track down from the main road. It is only a short 15-minute walk down and may be easier than driving. You can find the track on the north side of the road at the mid-point of a turn. Look for two small wooden posts and there is generally a space to park on the side of the road there. At the western end of the beach you'll stumble on a gorgeous placid river that flows into the sea and is deep enough for a swim. If you're a *Pirates of the Caribbean* fan, you may recognize this spot as the place where Jack Sparrow is running away from the mob of cannibals down a long stretch of beach in the second movie.

The same river that you see here was once used to power a large sugar mill and the waterwheel equipment is one of the best examples in existence of the 18th century estate machinery on the island. You can locate the old stone building, waterwheel, and workings when you pass over the river on a bridge with yellow striped sides between Calibishie and Bense. Once sugar production ended, the area modified its crop production to lime and cocoa and then to coconut and copra, which is still the main produce in this area.

BENSE

You'll know it when you reach Bense as they have recently erected a nicely painted sign pointing you in the right direction to get to what you really came here to see: **Chaudiere Pool**. One of those hidden jewels that will make you want to stay in Dominica forever, this dazzling deep river pool is part of Hampstead River and sits between two cliffs, surrounded by lush vegetation, with a short cascade that surges into the translucent water. To find it, walk or drive through the village of Bense until you reach the top and the road will turn into a farm access road. You'll pass through banana farms and meadows and will eventually reach a sign that points you to a trail on your left. Zig-zag down through the rainforest until reaching a river below. Cross this river and walk around to the right to find the pool, which is upstream of the adjoining river. The cliffs are a prime location to jump off into the pool. Either side is an easy climb up from small trails and you can even use the tiny waterfall as a slide. It's fast enough that you likely won't touch the rock. If you are more inclined to hang out on the sidelines, then be sure to keep your eyes and ears open for parrots, which are known to frequent this area.

BATIBOU BAY

Although it's not easy to find, it's well worth the trouble as this is, in my opinion, one of the best beaches on the island. If you are heading west from Calibishie, you'll pass over a bridge with yellow stripes on the sides and then you'll do a large U-turn to your left. Just after the turn, locate a small dirt road to the right that veers off of the main road. If you don't have a stellar 4WD vehicle (and even if you do), I recommend walking down the track, which will take roughly 30 minutes. One benefit of walking is that you'll pass a small trickling fresh water spring, which is located on the left side of the road on your way down, that always attracts beautiful hummingbirds. This beach is decent for swimming as it has a shelf where the waves are gentler and is protected by land on either side. You'll most likely find the beach deserted, except for possibly some farmers coming to harvest coconuts.

Staying Safe

When visiting the more secluded areas, such as the beaches in the northeast that attract tourists and sightseers, it's wise not leave valuables out in the open, or even bring them with you at all, as it would be easy for someone to walk down and quietly snatch your wallet or purse while you're out frolicking in the waves. This isn't a common occurrence but is always something to keep in mind when traveling.

The North

Anse Du Mai and **Anse Soldat** are two small bays that stand as beautiful portraits of Dominica's coastal life, albeit with an unfortunate history. Anse du Mai received its name from the Creole word for bay, "Anse," and from the French Captain Du Mé who in 1635 came ashore and led a massacre against Caribs living in the area. Over the years the spelling has shifted to Du Mai. It is now a port of entry for private boats and has a very basic customs house and concrete jetty. Anse Soldat is really quite lovely and is worth at least a drive through (the name Anse Soldat is the Creole word for soldier and refers to soldier crabs found in this area). The bay has incredibly clear water with colorful wooden boats sitting on top, nodding over the gentle waves. Take a right off the main road to reach the village. Most of the men here earn their income from fishing which makes this a great spot to buy fresh fish and to get to know the fishermen who catch it. The fish, generally mahi mahi or tuna, are sold at a table near the shore.

> Day trips to Marie Gallant can be arranged here.

After you pass the bays, you will be heading inland and on your way to Portsmouth. At one point you'll pass a colorful bus stop on the left with a road leading uphill to the right. This road will take you to the small residential village of **Paix Bouche**, which translates to "shut your mouth" in Creole. Not to give the impression of bad manners, this name comes from the steep hill you must climb to reach the village; meaning it would be hard to talk for those who need to save their breath. Most villagers here are either farmers or work in Portsmouth. The main attractions of the village are the views of surrounding mountains, including **Morne Trois Piton**, a UNESCO World Heritage site, and glimpses into rural village life.

If you continue on the main road, you'll pass **Indigo Art Gallery** which is a really magical art gallery run by a French artist full of beautiful paintings for sale on site. Soon after that, you'll reach **Brandy Manor Equestrian Center** and **Rainforest Riding**, which are two very well run horseback riding centers that will take you on a customized day trip to beaches, rainforest, waterfalls, or historical places of interest. As you reach Brandy Manor, in the village of Bornes, you can pick up a 45-minute trail that leads you to the 300 feet tall **Brandy Falls**, a beautiful cascade of water that often attracts the local parrots. It's a challenging hike that will take you upstream, along a narrow ridge top through deep mature rainforest, past gardens, and across two rivers that ends at Brandy Falls where you can refresh yourself for the hike back in the pool below. The trail to this hike is incredibly hard to navigate so your best bet is to call up Jasmin or Lincoln at Brandy Manor to ask for a guide.

Thibaud to Pennville/La Haut

The alternative and more scenic route to reach Portsmouth is through the heights of the upper-peninsula and back down again. After passing the bays and beaches of the northeast, take a very sharp right (almost feels like a U-turn) and head north to the farming and fishing village of **Thibaud**. Named after a French settler, Louis Thibaud, who bought 10 acres off of the Caribs in the 18th century, this village holds the last beach area before reaching Portsmouth, called **Sandwich Bay**. Surprisingly, this beach was not named for its prime picnic location but rather after the Fourth Earl of Sandwich who was an important member of the Board of Trade in England.

Au Parc and **Au Tou**, near the village of Vieille Case, have recently been developed as community tourism sights so that locals can share their favorite village spot with visitors on the island. Au Parc consists of small pools that locals love to relax in while benefiting from what they believe are the therapeutic properties of the water here. In the past, parents would bathe their babies in this pool because of a myth that the water from the pool would give their children strong legs and help them walk sooner. Au Tou, meaning "the hole," is a precarious launching area for fishing boats that houses a deep cave and a "blow hole" where you can go to hear the sounds of the sea. This was once the landing spot for Caribs, missionaries, and French settlers. Above Au Tou was a pre-Columbian settlement and is now used as an archaeological site.

Hazardous Driving
Driving in the peninsula, you'll notice that the roads get progressively steeper and more twisting as you head north and west. This is because the road was originally created using pick-axes and shovels along steep inclines and drop-offs. The result being severe turns and vertical roads that can make you feel as if you are on a theme-park ride.

VIEILLE CASE

Called "Itassi" by the Kalinago, Vieille Case is a village with a noteworthy past. It was the last Carib stronghold after 200 years of fighting, the first Catholic mass was held in its church in 1646, and thanks to the current prime minister of Dominica being from Vieille Case, the roads just got a makeover. The area from Vieille Case to Pennville has strong connections with the islands of Les Saintes and Marie Galante and until rather recently, many people lived and worked in Marie Galante and had more contact there than with Roseau. Because of this history, many Vieille Case families have French, African and Carib ancestry.

BWA NEF FALLS

Continue from Vieille Case as the road squirms its way north, until you see a sign for the falls on the left side of the road. The track is very narrow and it takes approximately 30 minutes each way. The waterfall is high and it cascades gently down the inky rocks forming a small pool below. Bwa Nef is the perfect place to experience

Dominica's natural beauty while still having privacy and serenity. It's one of the hidden charms of these rural northern communities.

PENNVILLE

As you drive past the small village of Pennville, stop by the adorable little church to stretch your legs. You can also take in some views of Marie Galante, the flat pancake-like land that feels incredibly close from this point. If you want to journey to the northern most point in Dominica, continue west a bit and you'll reach a road on the right that takes you to the village of **La Haut**. Ask around for the trail leading you to the northeastern tip of the island called Carib Point and also known as Point Jaco. The trail is relatively short but not that easy so be cautious but enjoy the view.

Pennville to Capuchin

Driving west from Pennville, you'll pass over some crazy roads as you enter into the crater of the northern volcano, Morne aux Diables. Be sure to stop at the **Cold Soufrière (Sulphur) Springs**, which is a short and easy walk from the road and is well signed. Like the other sulphur pools on the island, this one also smells like rotten eggs but it's worth holding your nose to see Mother Nature at her strangest. The small brown pools of water do indeed bubble and are indeed cold. It's weird, interesting and only a five minute walk to reach.

Morne aux Diables "Devil's Peak"

Morne aux Diables is just one of Dominica's nine active volcanoes. The unique feature of this particular volcano is that you can drive straight through the crater. Except for the fact that you pass the cold sulfur springs, you would never know you were in the middle of a one and a half million year old pile of block and ash flow from previous volcanic activity. The crater sits at 2,826 feet (848 meters), which is small in comparison to its closest volcanic neighbor, Morne Diablotins "Little Devils." There has been no volcanic activity at Morne aux Diables in recorded history although it does produce small earthquakes on a regular basis, so small in fact that most are imperceptible.

After passing through the crater, you'll meet the west coast and if you head north, you'll pass into the village of **Toucari**. This is the main sandy **beach** north of Portsmouth and it is a beautiful bay. Plan to be there around sunset as it is really breathtaking. The best places to swim are immediately after the bridge into the hamlet and to the north near the church, the rest of the coastline is rocky and taken up by the fishermen. **Toucari Bay** also boasts some excellent **snorkeling** locations at the very northern end (where you'll find caves that are great for skin divers) and the southern end of the bay. Divers frequent this bay to see the sunken wreck of a First World War German vessel that hides beneath waters. There are a few shops in this area selling basic food staples, snacks and drinks. In the center of Toucari there is also a restroom that can be used by asking the adjacent shop for access (expect to pay a small fee).

The unfinished jetty is visible in the water and there are plans to start developing Toucari into a harbor for yachters as an alternative to Prince Rupert Bay in Portsmouth. If you time it right, you can watch the fishermen cast their nets into the bay and draw them in. They all come together and help each other to pull the catch ashore and haul it into coolers then head up the road, blowing their conch shells, to let people know there is fresh fish for sale.

As the road continues north, it passes through two sweet little villages, Cottage and Clifton, before reaching **Capuchin**, the northernmost village on the western edge of the peninsula. This tiny village carries a lot of history and significance. Drive up as far as the road goes then park your car and hike the short trail to **Connor (Canna) Point**, a national heritage center, where the Capuchin monks, for whom the village is named, established their first settlement. From there you will have a breathtaking view over Guadeloupe, Marie-Galant and Les Saintes. There are ruins from both an Amerindian village as well as an 18th century gun battery as this was a great spot to keep watch over the islands of Les Saintes and was also used as a signal station to send messages down the western coast. It is an ideal place for a picnic and is the start of the **Capuchin to Pennville Trail** (see hiking detail on page 274), a nice walk that takes you past old estates, across a river and affords incredible views nearly the entire way.

For a close up view of the sea, head down to the bay, just south of the village. This is where the fishermen depart to either fish, pick up their fish pots or to take boatloads of agricultural produce over to Les Saintes to trade. Bring your waterproof shoes (because of the rocky beach) and wade in to enjoy the beautifully warm and transparent turquoise Caribbean Sea. This short section of sea is full of multicolored fish and sea creatures, just within the first few feet off the shore.

If you chose to turn south once you hit the west coast you'll end up driving through **Savanne Paille** and then down to **Tanetane** and **Douglas Bay Beach**. Located on the other side of the Cabrits peninsula, this is a smaller beach than Purple Turtle (pg 156), but it is quieter and just as nice and sandy. There are a few bamboo structures where you can have a picnic or escape the sun. The recently completed road and sea wall in Tanetane has a nice sidewalk that allows one to walk along the bay from Douglas Bay and enjoy the view of Cabrits. You can also take the sidewalk and continue up the road a few more minutes to Poonkie's, a quiet bar located on a small river that was once a small mill for processing bay leaves into bay rum. Some good snorkeling exists at the very northern end of the bay.

Sights & Activities

Calibishie Tourism Center
You can't miss this colorful building on the side of the main road in Calibishie and it's worth a quick stop if you are spending a few days in the area. They can guide you to some of the best attractions, help you find tour guides, and make any other necessary arrangements during your stay. They also specialize in selling local real estate for those who decide not to go home. *Calibishie; Tel: 767-445-8344, 767-275-3406; www.calibishiecoast.com, ctdc@cwdom.dm, dreamsdominica@hotmail.com; Hours: M-F 9am-4pm.*

Itassi Community Tour
In the village of Vieille Casse, once called Itassi by the Carib Indians, there are two spots that people in this area have held dear for generations. Au Tou, once considered to be an area where the villagers' ancestors would speak to them, contains a swimming hole, a cave, and a traditional fishing area. Au Park, where a Carib market

was once held, is now a popular swimming area with water that is thought to have therapeutic properties. Your one-day tour will take you to both of these locations and includes lunch for US$37 per person. *Vieille Casse, Contact tour operators via their website: http://itassi.communitytourism.dm.*

Scenic Drive

The North Coast Road starts in Portsmouth and runs through Pennville, Vieille Case and Thibaud. This stretch of road is worth the detour with gorgeous views over the sea and the neighboring islands as well as interesting natural formations and small friendly villages.

Begin your drive by heading north from Cabrits and turn left at Savanne Paille. You will find yourself going up a steep mountainside with sweeping views of Portsmouth and the French Islands in the background. You will see lands being farmed on both sides with banana, coconut, and citrus trees as well as ground provisions, nutmeg and cocoa trees. At the crest of the mountain, which is in fact a volcano, you'll find yourself entering the crater. You can smell the sulfur in the air and, on the left (look for signs for the **Cold Sulphur Springs**) a short trail takes you to a bubbling cold sulfur creek. It's an interesting spot and worth the short walk to see. The locals take away bottles of the water to drink, as they believe it cleans the digestive system.

Further, down the road, after you pass the entrance to the **Pennville to Capuchin Trail**, you enter Pennville, a quiet farming community. Keep an eye out for the small waterfalls on the side of the road and the sweeping view over Marie-Galant by the **Pennville Church**. The road then meanders along the coast and through Vieille Case, which is where the current Prime Minister is from. The road has recently been widened and resurfaced but the corners are still as tight as ever. On the left, after the village, there is a viewing platform and a seawater pool that locals like to come and bathe in. When in season, there are a profusion of colorful flamboyant trees along the next portion of the road, which crests another hill and then heads down into Thibaud, right on the sea.

Now on the Atlantic Ocean side of the island, the sea is rougher. There are two sandy beaches in Thibaud, divided by a small peninsula, but the currents are strong and the waves high so use them cautiously. Past Thibaud, the North Coast Road goes past Paix Bouche and back down to the main road, which links Portsmouth to Marigot and Melville Hall Airport. The whole loop, from Portsmouth to Portsmouth, will take most of an afternoon but it is definitely one of the roads less traveled and well worth the detour.

A Brief Detour

If you are enjoying the drive and want to explore even further you can take the road heading north past Toucari Bay and through the tiny villages of Cottage, Clifton, and Capuchin until the road eventually dead ends. Leave your car there and take a five-minute walk to Connor (Canna), a national heritage center, where the Capuchin monks, for whom the village is named, established their first settlement. From there you will have a breathtaking view over Guadeloupe, Marie-Galant and Les Saintes. There are ruins from both an Amerindian village as well as an 18th century gun battery here since this was a great spot to keep watch over the islands of Les Saintes and was also used as a signal station to send messages down the western coast. It is an ideal place for a picnic and is the start of the Capuchin to Pennville Trail (pg 274).

The North

Calibishie Cove Tours

If you're not one for exploring on your own and would like some guidance to make sure you've seen and done it all, Calibishie Cove offers a wide variety of tours that are based out of the north. Some are rather pricey, especially if you go by yourself since the prices are quoted for one to three people, but there are a few that are a great deal. Try the "Tubing and Brews" excursion which takes you down the Pagua River to some stunning swimming spots while you sip on some Kubuli beer for only US$30 a person. Another favorite is the kayaking tour on Hodges River that takes you along the beach to Treasure Island for a hike and some snorkeling for only US$45 a guest. *Contact: Jenner Robinson at Tel: 767-276-4659 or via the website:* *http://www.calibishiecove.com/tours.html.*

Sea Turtle Watching

Although the most popular spot for watching sea turtles lay their eggs is on the east coast, you will likely also find them around the beaches in Marigot, Wesley, Londonderry, and Calibishie between March and August after sundown. If you go on your own, pick a moonlit night for the best chances to get a good view and don't get too close so as not to disrupt them in this special process. Call the Sea Turtle Hotline at 767-616-8684 or 767-225-7742 to find out more and arrange a guided tour.

Brandy Manor Equestrian Center

Yasmin and Lincoln will take you on an amazing riding adventure through farms, rainforests, mountains, waterfalls, an old fort, or to the beach. Horses are gentle and the guides are knowledgeable and accommodating making the rides comfortable and enjoyable even for the most novice rider. ***Borne**; Tel: 767-612-0978, 767-235-4801; brandymanor@ymail.com; Cost: US$55 for a 1.5-2 hour ride.*

Beaches

Dominica gets a bad rap for not having an abundance of beaches. Those naysayers, however, have likely never ventured to the northern coast where the beaches are untamed, unspoiled, undiscovered and often breathtaking. Many of them require either a very bumpy drive or short hike to get to but it's worth it to have a yellow-sand beach, fringed with coconut groves and a spectacular view all to yourself. Many also have freshwater rivers alongside so you can rinse off after a dip in the sea before you head back.

Eateries

 Randy's Restaurant and Bar While Randy's lobster, crayfish, and curried chicken are good and plentiful, the best reason to eat here is Randy. He's a real entertainer and a fabulous and friendly host who loves to talk to his guests and share his knowledge of the island. Follow the signs on the bus stops of the main road to this highly recommended restaurant. Stop by on a Wednesday after 7pm for Reggae Night that includes a DJ, dancing, drink specials, an EC$10 menu featuring steamed fish, pork, and other Caribbean specialties. It's a really good time. *Wesley; Tel: 767-315-7474, 767-614-3443; Hours: Daily 8am-10pm; Cost: EC$12-$30.*

 Veranda View Restaurant This excellent restaurant is situated directly on the beach with amazing views of the surrounding islands and has a real Caribbean ambiance. The international breakfast is amazing. Call ahead for dinner and request some of the fresh seafood. Don't miss the homemade desserts. *Calibishie, Main Road; Tel:*

767-445-8900, 767-613-9493; www.lodgingdominica.com; Hours: Daily 7:30am-9:30pm; Cost: EC$25 (breakfast), EC$85 (dinner).

Coral Reef Restaurant and Grocery Store Located directly on the beach with amazing views of the surrounding cliffs, you can get lunch or dinner, local style with chicken, ribs or fish for a very reasonable price. Ask ahead for special items such as shrimp, steak or hard to find seafood. Full bar available as well. *Calibishie, Main Road (behind the telephone booth); Tel: 767-445-7432; Hours: M-Sat 8am-10pm, closed Sun except for brunch by reservation; Cost: EC$12-$15 (lunch).*

Warrow's Seaside Lounge and Bar Restaurant on the main strip in Calibishie serving local Creole food. Once a month they host special events with music, dancing, and fish dishes. Can accommodate vegetarians. *Calibishie, Main Road; Tel: 767-285-7100; Hours: Daily 8am-11pm; Cost: EC$30.*

Bamboo Restaurant and Bar Located pool-side on the property of Calibishie Lodges, they serve excellent international cuisine using only fresh local ingredients. Chef is on site for lunch and dinner and snacks are available all day. Try the fresh fish or a banana milkshake. *Calibishie, Main Road; Tel: 767-445-8537; Hours: Daily 7:30am-9pm; Cost: EC$15-$75.*

Atlantic View Restaurant and Bar Very small restaurant located high on the main road by the west entrance to the village. Serves up Creole style food with chicken, fish, pork or octopus and local drinks and juice. Great place to sit and check out one of the best views on the island. *Calibishie, Main Road; Tel: 767-277-0893; Hours: Daily 9am-9:30pm; Cost: EC$25-$30.*

Escape Bar and Grill Chef on site cooks up some mean sweet potato fries and excellent fresh fish dishes. However the best part of this dining experience is the atmosphere. Tables sit beneath a garden canopy on a white sand beach. Eat with your toes in the sand and watch the waves lap the shore. Full bar available as well. *Calibishie, Red Rock Haven Hotel; Tel: 767-445-7997, www.redrockhaven.com; Hours: Wed-Sun lunch and dinner by reservation; Cost: EC$25-$60.*

Heaven's Best Guesthouse & Restaurant Chef and owner, Heskeith Clark, has been practicing the art of fine cooking for over 30 years and prides himself not only on his excellent food but also on his ability to make guests feel at home. The menu is mostly high-end steak and seafood dishes with one or two options for vegetarians. Located just a few miles north of Portsmouth. *Savanne Paille; Tel: 767-445-6677; www.heavensbestguesthouse.com; Hours: M-Sat 7:30am-9pm (reservations recommended); Cost: EC$60 for entrée.*

Azille Valle Country Club The owner, John Baptiste Azille, is a musician and entertainer and loves nothing more than a house full of people, good music, and good food, which is why he recently opened the Azille Valle Country Club. Beyond the full bar and restaurant, which serves local Creole dinners, you will find a large stage that hosts local musicians, a disco downstairs with DJ equipment, and apartments which will soon be available for rent. Friday and Saturday nights are the time to come if you want to hear live music and don't be surprised if you run into the Prime Minister who is known to show up for a *lime* on occasion. *Borne; Tel: 767-445-5568, 767-245-7888; Hours: daily 2pm-late; Cost: EC$45 (dinner).*

Calabash Restaurant This new upscale restaurant offers indoor and outdoor fine dining in a beautiful location, right by the sea. Fish, steak, chicken, and pork are the main items on the dinner menu along with appetizers, a wine list, dessert and coffee. *Main Road, Calibishie; Tel: 767-445-8438, 767-277-6031; info@calabashonline.com; www.calabashonline.com; Hours: Open daily for breakfast (7am-10am), lunch (11:30am-2pm) and dinner (6pm-late); Cost: EC$15 (breakfast), EC$20 (lunch), EC$60 (dinner).*

The North

Services

Internet: Calibishie Lodges (Wireless) *Calibishie, Main Road; Tel: 767-445-8537; Hours: 7:30am-9pm; Cost: EC$10/hr.*

Coral Reef Grocery Store This small shop has very basic items, mainly dry goods. *Calibishie, Main Road (behind the telephone booth); Tel: 767-445-7432; Hours: M-Sat 8am-10pm.*

Accommodations

Budget

Heaven's Best Guesthouse & Restaurant Small but comfortable tiled rooms come with kitchenettes, wonderful verandas and some have beautiful handmade quilts. Owners pride themselves on having excellent service and great food. Being just two miles north of Portsmouth makes this a convenient but peaceful location. *Amenities: A/C, cable TV, Wi-Fi, swimming pool, irons, verandas with sea views, cell phone rental, laptop rental, breakfast included. Savanne Paille; 7 suites (dbl/tpl); Tel: 767-445-6677, 767-277-3952; www.heavensbestguesthouse.com, reservations@heavensbestguesthouse.com; Cost: US$65/$85, extra US $30/$35 per night for 3rd person in room.*

Mid-Range

Brandy Manor and Horseback Riding Center This peaceful spot is perfect for the horseback riding enthusiast who wants to really get away from it all. Lodging is set up farm-house style with three rooms in the upstairs of the main wooden house that all share a bathroom (which is a very interesting part of the house). There is a separate cottage for rent with a loft bed that is rustic and was built by hand out of local wood. At the moment, the only bathroom is in the main house but owner hopes to build a bathroom in the cottage soon. Owners are friendly and welcoming and delight in making guests feel at home. *Amenities: breakfast included, horseback riding packages, tour arrangement, river access (note: no electricity but owner has a generator that she runs when needed). Borne; 4 rooms (dbls); Tel: 767-612-0978, 767-235-4801; brandymanor@ymail.com; Cost: US$75.*

Indigo Tree Cottage This rustic and handsome cottage will have you feeling like you are "roughing it" in comfort. The cottage has only three walls, allowing guests a stunning view of the surrounding mountains, and can technically sleep three as the sofa converts to a single bed. Owned and operated by two artists – Marie, from France, and her Dominican Rastafarian husband, Clem – who double as chefs and amazing hosts. You'll find yourself surrounded by their beautiful nature-inspired artwork. The bathroom (a pit toilet) and shower are outside and a short walk from the cottage itself. Be sure to treat yourself to an outstanding breakfast or dinner while you are there, prepared by Marie. To top it off, this place is recommended by Johnny Depp, Kiera Knightly, and Orlando Bloom who enjoyed their time here while filming *Pirates of the Caribbean. Amenities: Mosquito net, Wi-Fi, double hammock, kitchen (note: there is no electricity in the cottage, however lanterns are provided). Borne; One cottage; Tel: 767-445-3486, 767-277-6859; www.indigo.wetpaint.com, marie_clem@hotmail.com; Cost: US$100 sgl (1-2 nights), US$85 sgl (3 or more nights), US$115 dbl (1-2 nights), US$100 dbl (2-4 nights), US$85 dbl (5+nights), US$25 extra for third person.*

Windblow Estate American owned cottages on a hill overlooking Calibishie and the sea. Tastefully decorated and comfortable, units have one and two bedrooms, living room, well-supplied kitchen, and veranda. Property also has a sunbathing/viewing deck where you can see the neighboring island of Marie Galante and star gaze at night. Close to two of the best beaches on the island as well as a river. *Amenities: Fans, TV, internet access. Windblow Road, Calibishie; 3 cottages; Tel: 767-445-8198;*

skype: islandtwo; islandtwo@windblowestate.com, www.windblowestate.com; Cost: US$80-$110 one bedroom, US$90-$135 two bedroom.

Lima Ridge One of the more budget options in Calibishie and one of the few Dominican owned accommodations in this area. These self-contained units are very basic with one and two bedrooms and a small kitchenette, dining table, and a few have a fold out couch. *Amenities: TV, fans. Calibishie; 4 rooms; Tel: 767-277-0984, 767-445-7644; Cost: US$80/$90 dbl.*

Veranda View Bed and Breakfast Located along the main strip of Calibishie, this is one of the best places to sit in the morning with a cup of coffee and enjoy an amazing view of a turquoise blue sea. Aptly named, the downstairs veranda houses the restaurant and has direct access to a gorgeous golden sand beach. The rooms themselves are plain compared to the cute, colorful restaurant but just outside of the rooms you'll enjoy a huge shared upstairs balcony where you can enjoy the view and possibly spot a whale or dolphins out at sea. *Amenities: maid service, Wi-Fi, laundry service, airport transfer. Calibishie; 2 rooms; Tel: 767-445-8900, 767-613-9493; www.lodgingdominica.com, reserve@lodgingdominica.com; Cost: US$85/$95 dbl, US$95/$105 tpl.*

Calibishie Lodges and Sea View Apartments Highly rated and award winning apartments and cottages on the east side of Calibishie. The rooms are comfortable and elegant with natural décor and beautiful verandas with a view. Suites fit two adults and two children or three adults. Each suite has a separate bedroom, kitchenette and comfortable sitting area, some with a pull-out sofa bed. Seaview apartments are up the road from the cottages, situated on a hill over looking the sea. All are comfortable and self-contained with maid service available if requested. Specials for long-term rentals. You'll want to rent a car if you choose to stay in the apartments as the road is very steep. *Amenities: Wi-Fi, fans, flat screen TV, swimming pool, safe deposit box, kitchenette, tour arrangement, bar/restaurant on site, and sundeck. Meal packages available. Calibishie; 6 cottages, 5 apartments; Tel: 767-317-1843, 767-316-9258; info@calibishie-lodges.com, www.calibishie-lodges.com; Cost suites: US$110-$145; Cost apts: US$85 dbl, US$95 quad; Cost luxury suite: US$220 dbl (2 children under 12 can stay free).*

Point Baptiste Estate Old World charm meets Caribbean design in this delightful 40-year-old family run estate. Set out over 25 acres with amazing views, gardens, access to three beaches, and everything you need for a comfortable stay, this is a great choice for large groups and long-term visitors. House and cottages are self-contained, spacious and comfortable. Book far in advance as this is one of the oldest-run and most popular guesthouses in the area. *Amenities: Internet, tour arrangement, fans, mosquito nets maid and cook available for hire. Calibishie; 1 cottage, 1 house; Tel: 767-445-7368, 767-225-5378; manager@pointebaptiste.com, www.pointebaptiste.com; Cost dbl cottage US$90/$110; Cost house (sleeps 6-8) US$270/$350.*

Sea Cliff Cottages These five distinct cottages are spread out along a road leading to the sea, each surrounded by manicured lawns and gardens with close proximity to a beach. Cottages themselves are simple but comfortable and fully equipped with all of the modern conveniences. Each has a balcony with a view of the sea and full kitchen. Owners live nearby and are there when you need them but also allow you complete privacy if that is what you desire. Solar panels were recently installed to have a more gentle impact on the environment. *Amenities: TV, Wi-Fi, mobile phones for rent, washing machines, barbeque grills. Calibishie; 5 Cottages with 1-2 bdrms each; Tel: 767-445-8998, 767-265-3473; seacliff@dominica-cottages.com, www.dominica-cottages.com; Cost one bdrm: US$80/$110; Cost two bdrm: US$110/$155; Special rates for longer stays and weekly rates available.*

Belle Cote Villa Large and pink, this comfortable house sleeps 6 without feeling crowded. House is fully furnished with a kitchen, living room, and three bedrooms that give you that "at home" feel. Close to beaches and a river with beautiful views from the balcony. Great value for a large family. *Amenities: Washer, dryer, dishwasher, TV, DVD,* *safe, barbeque, fans, A/C, and swimming pool. Calibishie; 1 house with 3 bedrooms, 2.5 baths; Tel: (USA) 703-754-1964, 571-213-2272; bellecotevilla@gmail.com, http://bellecotevilla.com; Cost: US$180/$250.*

 Calibishie Cove Picturesque rooms displaying local artwork open up to a wrap around veranda that allows guests to be completely enveloped by their natural surroundings with views of the sea from most of the house. You can choose between individual double rooms or a penthouse suite with full kitchen and dining room and plunge pool. It is also possible to rent the entire villa for around US$500 per night. Calibishie Cove also acts as a tour operator that can take guests to any island destination. *Amenities: Wi-Fi, local cell phone use, hair dryer, refrigerators, coffee/tea maker, snorkel equipment, hardwood floors, kayak and bike rental, board games, and amenities for kids and babies including babysitting services. Massages available in-room or with a view. Calibishie; 4 rooms; Tel: (USA) 443-987-6742, 767-265-1993; calibishiecove@gmail.com, www.calibishiecove.com; Cost: US$135/$145 dbl, US$200/$240 penthouse, US$490/$550 whole villa.*

Bayview Lodges Modern and stylish self-contained apartments come with one double bedroom plus a fold-out couch, a well-equipped kitchen, and large bathrooms. Each has an enclosed porch with amazing views. Close to beaches and snorkeling, this accommodation comes highly recommended. *Amenities: Wi-Fi, TVs, cell phone rental, and fresh bread delivered daily (except Sundays). Calibishie; 2 apartments; Tel: 767-245-8370, 767-245-8705; enquiries@bayviewdominica.com,www.bayviewdominica.com; Cost: US$80/$100.*

Sunrise Garden Guesthouse A "just like home" feel permeates these apartments. Kitchens are incredibly well supplied for easy cooking at home but don't worry about making juice as the caretaker frequently makes and brings it over for guests. Each apartment has large balcony with amazing sea views. Gets frequent return visitors. *Amenities: Wi-Fi, fans, modern laundry facilities, security system, discount on long term stays. Calibishie Ridge Road, Calibishie; 2 apartments (1 bdrm lower, 2 bdrm upper); Tel: (USA) 727-862-3481, 767-445-7604, 767-276-2600; sargeman1@msn.com, www.calibishiesunrise.com; Cost: US$100 one bdrm, US$130 two bdrm.*

Top-End

Manicou River Eco-Lodges and Resort Beautifully appointed eco-lodge that is passionate about providing comfort for guests while simultaneously preserving the natural environment. Gorgeous modern cottages are situated on a ridge high above Douglas Bay and are made from local wood with stunning views of the mountains and sea from the extensive decks. Each cottage has a fully equipped kitchen and eco-friendly bath products are provided (no outside products allowed). They use only ceramic filtered rainwater and energy is solar powered. They provide natural beeswax candles for lighting as well. Trails have been built around the property and are nice to explore to find the organic fruit trees inters-persed throughout the land. *Amenities: Wi-Fi, maid service, laundry service (for a fee), shopping and cooking service available, cell phones for rent, airport transfer. Tanetane; 5 cottages (dbls/tpl); Tel: 767-616-8903, 767-317-0650; manicou_river_restort@fastmail.com; www.manicouriverresort.com; Cost: US$185 (sleeps 2-3).*

Comfort Cottages You will know you've arrived at this American-style accommodation when you come around a turn to see a beautifully manicured lawn and several small cottages sitting atop a hill. Each cottage is set up to feel like home and is equipped with one and two bedrooms, a well-stocked kitchen, living room, entertainment center, and each cottage's own plunge pool. Restaurant and bar with inexpensive international cuisine on site and vehicle rental, airport transfer, and barbeque pits for guests' use. *Amenities: A/C, international phone line, Wi-Fi. Terre Platte, Blenheim (between Thibaud and Paix Buche); 4 cottages that sleep 2-4; Tel: 767-445-3245, 767-616-3325 Overseas Tel: 732-298-7081; comfortcottages@cwdom.dm, www.comfortcottages.com; Cost: US$200 one bdrm, US$245 two bdrm.*

Red Rock Haven Hotel and Spa Tucked away in a coconut grove by the sea is the new Red Rock Haven Hotel and Spa and Escape Restaurant. The hotel consists of one large house and three smaller cottages. Each charming unique cottage consists of wood and stone and blends beautifully with its natural surroundings. The larger house is elegant and very spacious with a large infinity pool that overlooks the sea on the veranda and small heated plunge pools that are connected to each of the three bedrooms. Beautiful stonework and stunning design permeate throughout. Restaurant on the beach has a full bar and serves outstanding meals with breakfast included. Excellent swimming beach with deck chairs on site. *Amenities: Spa services, Wi-Fi. Calibishie; 4 cottages, 1 house; Tel: 767-445-7997; www.redrockhaven.com, info@redrockhaven.com; Cost dbl cottages: US$225; Cost house: US$650.*

Villa Passiflora This unique and visually stunning house was built with an appreciation for the outdoors and is situated on a hill overlooking the sea. The open design and large verandas accent the best of both the indoors and outdoors at once. Comfortable surroundings and beautiful architecture and decor allow you to relax and feel at home while the vistas, sounds of the sea and steady breeze of the trade winds put you in a Caribbean state of mind. The house includes a full kitchen, infinity pool and patio, housekeeping services, on-site caretaker and optional meal service for your convenience. *Amenities: Wi-Fi, mosquito nets, hammocks. Calibishie; 4 bdrm/ 3 bath house; www.villapassiflora.com, parkneur@comcast.net; Cost: US$1955/week; Sleeps 6 adults, 2 children; One week min, Basement studio available for separate rental.*

The East

Dominica's eastern road rises, dips and twists its way from Melville Hall airport in the north hugging the rugged coastline through villages and farmland all the way down to Petite Soufrière. Although this stretch of land is technically only about 15 miles, you'll find plenty of diversity in its string of coastal villages – from the populated Marigot and Castle Bruce to the sprawling rural Carib Territory to the tiny fishing village of Saint Sauveur. Because of the steady trade winds, this area generally receives more rain than the rest of the island and you'll likely find the best swimming is in a river as opposed to a beach. There are quite a few interesting and unique lodging options here and the east coast is a great place to station yourself if you are interested in learning more about the people and culture rather than lying on a beach.

GETTING HERE AND AROUND

The east coast as a whole is not easy to reach by bus (fares will run between EC$9 and EC$11) as they run very infrequently and the trip is rather long. Take the Marigot bus if you are headed to Concord or Hatton Garden, which leaves from the east bridge in Roseau and at the bus station in Portsmouth. They only run a few times a day, generally in the afternoon and again around 5pm. Buses to Castle Bruce

TOP FIVES

Learn about the way the indigenous people of Dominica lived off the land at Kalinago Barana Aute and take the opportunity to purchase handmade baskets made exactly as they have been for hundreds of years. (pg 193)

Drive down to the picturesque fishing village of Saint Sauveur and get a glimpse of rural village life on the east coast. (pg 191)

Hike over horseback ridge and go for a swim in Basen Majo, a beautiful pool in the Pagua River. (pg 188)

Stop by the Cassava Bread Bakery in the Carib Territory to get an authentic taste of a historic Dominican staple. (pg 188)

Taste some homemade bush rum and enjoy the turquoise vistas at Islet View Café in Castle Bruce. (pg 190)

and the Carib Territory can be found on the riverside at the junction of Kings Lane and River Bank Street and run about the same time as Marigot's. To get to Saint Sauveur and Petite Soufrière you'll have to pick up a bus behind the Market on the riverside. They run even more infrequently and the last bus leaves around 3:30 or 4pm. Check in with a driver beforehand to be sure you don't miss it.

Driving to these places will make your life easier, especially since a lot of the interior roads are getting a makeover. The road from Pond Casse to Marigot, however, is still narrow with essentially just one lane and people tend to drive fast. If a car is approaching and you are able to, the best thing to do is to pull over and let them pass or a game of chicken may ensue.

The other road going in this direction (from Pond Casse) will take you to through the interior where you will eventually come to an intersection with a purple bus stop on the corner. Turn left here and you will pass the very popular **Emerald Pool** and will end up in Castle Bruce. Once you reach Castle Bruce you can either go north and head towards the Carib Territory and Marigot or south to the small villages of Good Hope, Saint Sauveur, and Petite Soufrière. The road south will eventually dead end as it turns into a footpath used to reach Rosalie. It is always a good idea to rent a 4WD jeep if you can because many accommodations are quite far off the main road and potholes flourish in this area.

GETTING BACK

Buses go to Roseau just as infrequently as they come. The first round of buses usually leaves very early, around 6 or 7am and again around noon. On the slower days there may only be one bus in the afternoon and then your best bet is to hitch a ride. If you find yourself stuck in the area and in need of a ride (either hitching or bussing), the Hatton Garden junction, the Castle Bruce bus stop, or the junction east of Pond Casse (that goes north to Emerald Pool or east to Rosalie) with the purple bus stop are the best places to wait. Once you get a ride to either of these spots, you likely won't have to wait long to get a ride to Roseau.

Marigot to Castle Bruce

MARIGOT

As the largest settlement in the northeast (population 2,700) and home of the fisheries complex and largest airport, Marigot is becoming progressively more developed while at the same time maintaining its unique culture. Following the abolition of slavery, a large amount of labor was required to sustain some of the large estates around Hatton Garden, Marigot, Wesley, and Woodford Hill. Workers were recruited from several surrounding islands including Antigua, Montserrat and Anguilla, which were all under British-rule. Because of this, the people in the Marigot region have a markedly different heritage and predominately speak an English patois, as opposed to the rest of the island that speaks a French-influenced patois. Also, this area is mainly Methodist while the majority of Dominica is Roman Catholic.

There is a wonderful hidden beach in Marigot, **Sandy Bay Beach**, located just behind My Father's Place Guesthouse. A short climb down a steep trail (some scrambling required) puts you on this beautiful sandy beach, which is separated into three bays by rocky protrusions. There is good snorkeling here and just a short swim around the rocks will lead you to the other two beaches.

If you want easier access to a beach, **Londonderry Beach** is a good option. This long and beautiful black sand beach is adjacent to Melville Hall Airport. This is the beach where a scene from *Pirates of the Caribbean 3* was filmed (when Jack's Crew lands on shore and finds the body of Kraken who was shot here). As with all beaches on the Atlantic, beware of currents and undertow as swimming can be dangerous on this side of the island.

ATKINSON

Located at the northern end of the Carib Territory, Atkinson is small village of only about 450 people. The main source of income in this area is farming (primarily passion fruit and banana) and construction. This area was historically known for growing limes, but a disease destroyed most of the lime trees on the island. There are several eco-tourism sites in Atkinson that the village council is in the process of developing and promoting. **Big River** is made up of pools of warm water that are formed on lava rocks overlooking the Atlantic Ocean. Waves come over the rock and fill the pools, which warm up in the sun. Locals frequently go to this area to "relax the bones" in the warm sea water and the young boys go to these rocks for spear fishing. Close by is an area known as **Dragon's Mouth**, where waves crash through a small opening in the rocks and spray upward, making a loud noise. You can get to this site by going down the road next to the Atkinson Bus Stop (which overlooks the playing field and primary school, a good place to watch a cricket game on Sundays). Go down this road and turn onto a small extension of it on your right. Follow a mud track that leads you through farmland and down a slope with cinnamon "spice" trees to the opening of the lava rocks. It's a short walk from the road but be cautious on the rock as it has moss (thus slippery) and is volcanic rock (thus, very sharp and rough).

Antrizle Beach is located near Atkinson. Look for the Antrizle Bus Stop, which has a mural of the beach painted on it and take this road to get down to the small black sand beach. Like most beaches on the east coast, swimming isn't advised as there is sometimes a strong undercurrent. The village council is currently expanding and paving this road to make it accessible to vehicles. Until then, you can park by the bus stop and walk down the road, which is no more than a 10-minute stretch of trail. Locals frequent this beach on weekends.

A little further on, you will be able to see **Antwistle Rock.** There is a Carib legend that says if you can climb to the top of this rock and pick a blue flower, you will be able to have magical powers over the one you love. To find it, look for a lone rock perched atop the hill and a platform that occasionally has people selling crafts. Although for some it may be tempting, I would not recommend walking up this steep cliff to reach the rock because of the prevalence of loose rocks and falling trees. While the rock itself is very crumbly, it does make for a good photo op.

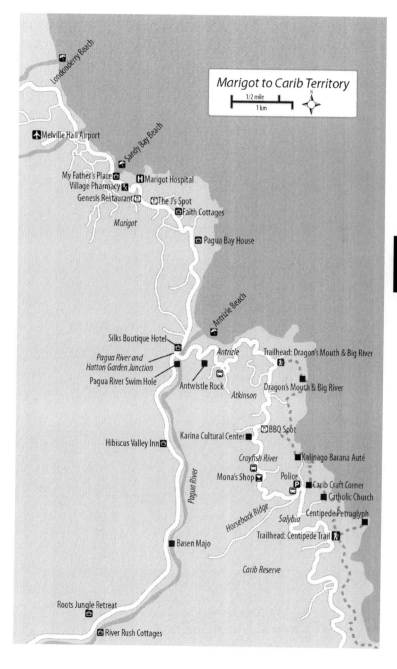

The East

Marigot to Carib Territory

1/2 mile
1 km
N

Londonderry Beach

Melville Hall Airport

Sandy Bay Beach

My Father's Place
Village Pharmacy
Genesis Restaurant
Marigot Hospital
The J's Spot
Faith Cottages

Marigot

Pagua Bay House

Antrizle Beach

Silks Boutique Hotel
Pagua River and
Hatton Garden Junction
Pagua River Swim Hole
Antrizle
Antwistle Rock
Atkinson
Trailhead: Dragon's Mouth & Big River
Dragon's Mouth & Big River

Hibiscus Valley Inn
Karina Cultural Center
BBQ Spot
Crayfish River
Mona's Shop
Police
Kalinago Barana Auté
Carib Craft Corner
Catholic Church
Centipede Petroglyph
Salybia
Horseback Ridge
Pagua River
Basen Majo
Trailhead: Centipede Trail

Carib Reserve

Roots Jungle Retreat
River Rush Cottages

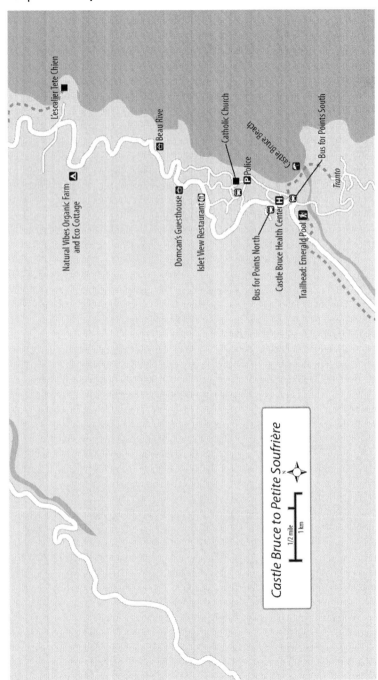

Castle Bruce to Petite Soufrière

Lescalier Tete Chien

Natural Vibes Organic Farm and Eco Cottage

Beau Rive

Catholic Church

Castle Bruce Beach

Police

Bus for Points South

Tranto

Domcan's Guesthouse

Islet View Restaurant

Bus for Points North

Castle Bruce Health Center

Trailhead: Emerald Pool

1/2 mile
1 km

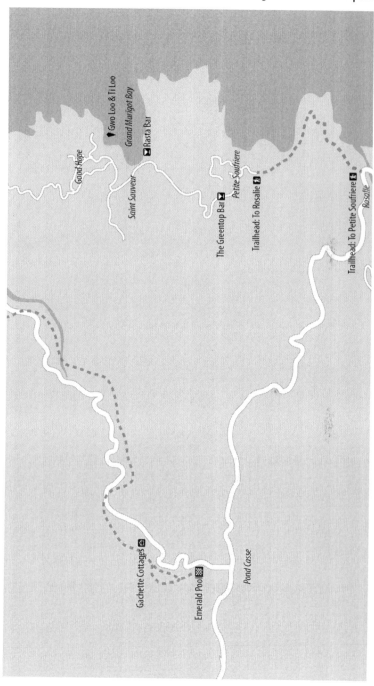

Gwo Loo & Ti Loo

Grand Marigot Bay

Rasta Bar

Good Hope

Saint Sauveur

Petite Soufriere

The Greentop Bar

Trailhead: To Rosalie

Trailhead: To Petite Soufriere

Rosalie

Gachette Cottages

Emerald Pool

Pond Casse

The East

Just behind the trees at the **Pagua River** and **Hatton Garden** junction is a nice calm river that people frequently stop to bathe in. You can usually find some small seashells here and will see wild almond trees growing along the banks.

Hatton Garden was once a 300-acre estate, named after a street in London known for its shops and diamond trading. The ruins of the mill, sugar and lime factory are still evident on the property of **Silks Boutique Hotel,** which sits right at the junction. The mill, at one time, produced over 160,000 pounds of sugar and over 5,500 gallons of rum.

For a great hike that takes you through a large section of the Carib Territory on foot, check out segment 6 of the **Waitukubuli National Trail** (pg 243) that runs from **L'Escalier Tete Chien to Dragon's Mouth** (see hiking detail on page 276) via the main road and smaller farm roads, hugging the coast the entire way. Start this hike early in the morning to avoid the heat (unlike other hikes, you won't have the cover of rainforest to block the sun) and to catch a spectacular sunrise.

CARIB TERRITORY

Stretching from Bataka in the north to Sineku in the south, the Carib Reserve consists of eight villages stretched over 3,785 acres of communal land. This is the only reservation for the Carib people, also known as the Kalinago, in the entire Caribbean region. The rugged landscape of Dominica helped the Carib people maintain a foothold for many years during colonization. Although the approximately 2,200 people who live here today are almost entirely of mixed ethnicities, you can still see evidence of their heritage in their long black hair.

> If you are on-island in September, you may want to stop by during **Carib Week**. It's a great event celebrating the culture and traditions of the Carib people. Call the Carib council office (Tel: 767-445-7336) for exact dates.

Several years ago the former Carib Chief, Charles Williams, made an effort to preserve the heritage of the Carib community by attempting to implement a law that any Carib person who had a child with a non-Carib would be forced to move outside of the territory. The law wasn't popular and was never enforced during his term as chief. Despite the lack of support for this law, the Carib people are proud of their heritage. There are two groups that make an effort to preserve some of the rich traditions of their people. One is the **Carina Cultural Group**, whom you can find performing traditional song and dance at the Carina Cultural Center in Bataka near the community hall. The other is the **Karifuna Cultural Group** (Karifuna is the Carib word for women). They hold performances at the Kalinago Barana Auté (pg 193). Both groups have traveled extensively and are internationally recognized for practicing the preservation of Carib culture for over 30 years.

The administrative center of the Carib Territory is in the village of **Salybia** where the primary school, health centre, Catholic Church, police station, library and Carib Council Office are located. The territory is governed by an elected Carib Chief, who is the head of the Carib Council, and one parliamentary representative that is chosen to represent the territory at the House of Assembly in Roseau. **Horseback Ridge** also originates in this area. This is a farm access road that will take you up into some of the banana farms and gardens of this region. The road is rather torn up so driving up will require a 4WD. If you follow the path down the other side of the gazebo, it will lead you to the **Pagua River** and some amazing river pools, such as **Basen Majo**, that are great for a swim.

To get to Basen Majo from the end of the trail, take a right on an established road as you pass a banana shed. Walk on this road for about 15 minutes until you come upon a large empty field with a concrete building. Go left along the south side of the field until you reach the edge of the river. Look for a footpath to your left that goes down through the brush and you'll know you're there when you see a clear pool and a huge rock. If you end up in the river and you don't see the large rock, head upstream a bit and you'll find it.

Just south of Salybia is the village of Saint Cyr and the start of the **Centipede Trail**. This short trail takes you down a well-maintained path to a rocky outcropping at the edge of the Atlantic. Once you climb out onto the rocks, look behind you at the colored pattern in the rocky cliff, which the Caribs believed resembled a giant centipede that crawled out of the ocean and stuck onto the rocks. Stick around to enjoy the amazing views of the rugged eastern coast.

Because the land is communal, it cannot be bought or sold to anyone or used as collateral for a loan. This is one of the reasons that the territory continues to be one of the poorest areas on the island. Many families have no running water and rely on the rivers to bathe and do their laundry and the natural springs for their drinking water. But what they lack in material wealth they make up for by having some of the most fertile soil and optimal weather conditions for growing plants, fruits, and vegetables. Often times you can get fruit here that is not in season anywhere else on the island and many people rely on subsistence farming for almost their entire supply of food.

When passing through the Carib territory you will find that it looks like most of

Cassava Bread

Brought over by the Kalinago people more than 1,000 years ago, this root tuber has one of the highest concentrations of carbohydrates of any plant in the world. It was an essential and daily part of the Amerindian diet for centuries and is still being made in the Carib Territory today. The process for making cassava is important because the plant contains toxic chemicals that must be released from the tuber before consumption. To do this, the cassava is peeled then shredded using a large wheel that is lined with an aluminum or jasper grater. The ground cassava is dropped into a container as it's grated and then water is poured over it to separate the fiber from the starch. The liquid is squeezed out of the fibers (which removes the toxic properties) and is then dried in a large metal cylinder over a fire. The resulting dried material is called farine and is often mixed with a bit of starch to create a dough that is then flattened into pancake-type shapes (and is often mixed with dried coconut and cinnamon for flavor). The dough is then cooked on a large metal surface over a fire, with the end result being a tasty dense bread.

When you pass through the territory and reach Crayfish River in the northern end, look for the cassava wheel and bakery on the side of the road. Several afternoons a week, locals will make a fresh batch and sell the baked treats hot off the griddle.

the other rural villages in the east but with one notable difference: **Carib crafts** being used or sold around every corner. The making of these crafts has been handed down through generations. Many of the craft makers in the territory rely entirely on their sale of these goods for their livelihood and buying a basket or calabash bowl is one of the most authentic Caribbean souvenirs you could possibly bring home with you.

Carib Baskets

Carib basket weaving is a time-honored craft that dates back thousands of years and is still an essential source of income for many Carib families in Dominica. It is thought that the Kalinago brought the larouma reed with them from the Orinoco River delta in South America over a thousand years ago. The basket making process starts with the women going into the rainforest to cut down the reeds. They haul them back to the village, slice them into thin malleable strips and then lay them in the sun to dry. To create interesting designs, the weavers will dye the reeds by submersing them in mud or rubbing them with plants and flowers creating shades of yellow, brown, black and pink. Historically, these baskets were waterproofed and used as vessels to carry food, catch fish, and for any number of everyday tasks. Today, the tradition remains much the same and one can find baskets in every shape and size in the Carib Territory. You will find stands and shops selling baskets and other handicrafts throughout the Territory and there is a wonderful selection at Kalinago Barana Auté, where you can also watch the weavers at work.

If you want to learn more about how the Kalinago lived and used the land in the time before Columbus, visit the **Kalinago Barana Auté** (pg 193), a Carib Model Village by the Sea. The excellent guides will lead you through the customs, architecture, use of plants, and legends that the Kalinago used to survive and flourish on this island.

CASTLE BRUCE

This broad river plain, once called Kouanari by the Caribs, was settled first by the Amerindians over 2,000 years ago who used the area's fertile soil, brackish lagoon, and ocean access to provide their community with plenty of sustenance. After colonization, Captain James Bruce, for whom the village is named, brought over 150 slaves from West Africa, which he used to established a coffee and sugar cane estate. It wasn't until the 1970s, after a major labor dispute, that the land was divided up into small individually owned plots that are now almost entirely banana farms.

As you approach Castle Bruce from the north, you'll pass a large school with a mural on the outside wall. This is the secondary school used by most of the east coast students of high school age. It is the largest school in the entire region which makes Castle Bruce a bustling spot in the early mornings and late afternoons as students rush about. The playing field is across the road from the school, which holds regular cricket games with music and refreshments.

One of the highlights of this area is the long **black sand beach** at the south end of the village with a view of two islets sitting just off the coast. There is a river with a deep pool flowing into the ocean that is popular with locals who come here to bathe and do their laundry. You can usually find someone who is selling "jellies" (young coconut water) on the beach and for a small payment (around EC$2) they will climb up a coconut tree, bring one down, and slice it open with a cutlass for you. Turtles are sighted here both during the day and at night when they come to shore to lay eggs.

To get a feel of the land and people around Castle Bruce, start at the beach, walk the length of the shore, ford the river (find a waist deep spot in normal river flow), and find a dirt road at the south end that winds up into the hamlet of Tranto. Pause here at one of the shops to "check your vibes" and chat with colorful locals. Then, turn right on the main road and wind back down the hill, cross the main bridge over the river (dip in again here) and return to the playing field and snackettes to enjoy some local specialties (Edith's roast fig and saltfish is excellent). Don't forget to check out the playing field where soccer, cricket or rounders games usually last the entire day.

Castle Bruce is also known for having excellent **bread**. You can find it in the area known as "Glou Glou" (the flat area between the bus stop and the old health center). One shop is behind the building next to the Catholic Church and the other is found in the little white shack next to the bus stop, run by a friendly woman named Augustine. They also sell fresh juices, cakes, fried chicken and fish, fish broth, bakes, and ice cream.

You can pick up segment 5 of the **Waitukubuli National Trail** (pg 243) here, just south of the Secondary School that follows the old Carib Trace Trail to Emerald Pool. This historic walking path is an easy, slightly uphill walk that was used before roads were built to link the east coast with Roseau. You will even pass over cobbled stone pathways that were laid in 1828 and still remain.

Good Hope to Petite Soufrière

GOOD HOPE

Good Hope is a small village of about 300 people. The village is supported mainly by subsistence farming and fishing and many young men go spear fishing off the east coast and catch crayfish in the rivers and streams. At the very bottom of the steep village there is a nice spot to sit by the bayside and watch the rough Atlantic crash into the rocks below. Even when the surf is low, it is stunningly beautiful. If it is not too rough, the brave can go for a swim out to **Ti Loo** and **Gwo Loo** (meaning, "small rock" and "big rock" respectively), which are perched in the bay. They are prime spots for jumping off of into the warm ocean. But beware as the water can be very rough. The locals can tell you if it is a good day for swimming or not. Many women do their laundry near this bayside spot so prepare to be greeted when you arrive. It also is a great place for a picnic.

SAINT SAUVEUR

This picturesque fishing village, located on the Grand Marigot Bay, is worth the drive down as it's one of the most beautiful spots on the island. In the afternoon and early evening, you can watch the fisherman bring in their catch while people gather to buy fresh fish. Be sure to check out the beautiful Catholic Church on the bayside (services are held on Sunday if you want a look inside) or drive by some of the old bay leaf factories, a few of which are still in use today. Take a break from all the driving at the **Rasta Bar**, which has an excellent patio that overlooks the bay. Like most typical snackettes, you can get rum, bakes and beer here. If you are around in

June, be sure to stop by for the **Feast of St. Isidore**, a traditional annual festival that celebrates the harvest of the season. You'll see people from the surrounding villages dressed up in bright traditional Creole clothing parade out of the old church and walk through the village balancing baskets full of their best fruits and vegetables on their heads. Another interesting festival called **Fete La Saint Pierre** also happens in June in San Sauveur and other fishing villages. It generally starts at the church, where people will present an offering of fish, and is followed by a procession to the bay for the blessing of the decorated and colorful fishing boats, hoping to guarantee an abundant fishing season. Usually, against the best wishes of the priest, the villagers will celebrate into the night with drinking and dancing, going from house to house in the village. To get the exact dates of these festivals, call the San Sauveur Village Council (Tel: 767-446-0880).

Historical Ties

If you came through San Sauveur 2,000 years ago you would have found an Amerindian village where the current school and playing field now stand. Many families in this region are descendents from those first people who eventually mixed with the French and Africans that settled here. Fast forward to the 1770s and you would have found a plantation called the Grand Marigot Estate. All that remains, however, are the foundation and stone entrance and stairway of the house. The site of the present day village health centre once housed the watermill and sugar factory of this estate but they also were eventually destroyed by hurricanes and decay.

PETITE SOUFRIÈRE

With a population of only roughly 500 people, Petite Soufrière is located at the end of a less-traveled road and is one of the more rural villages on the island. Most people earn their income by farming, specifically bay trees, which cover the surrounding hills, and there are a handful of small, old style bay factories still in use. Processing the bay leaf is generally a long process that often continues through the night and involves a lot of rum drinking. If you head to the bottom of the village you'll find two trails: one leads to a small rocky beach and the other trail takes you from **Petite Soufrière to Rosalie** where a road is planned to someday be built (and thereby connect the east coast and create a loop around the exterior of the island). The moderately easy trail from Petite Soufrière to Rosalie takes you along the coast to the black sand beaches of Rosalie and is around 45 minutes each way. As you walk, notice the small streams of fresh water that trickle along the path. This is natural spring water and Dominicans in the area collect it to drink in their homes. **The Greentop Bar** is located at the top of Petie Soufrière and is one of the few places on the island that has a pool table. The owner of the bar, Beltina, is a friendly woman who enjoys talking with foreigners and has a personality strong enough to handle the rum drinkers of the village. She has an excellent collection of bush rum, as well as beer and on the weekends she serves chicken, fries and bakes. If you are interested in checking out some local crafts, ask around for a man named "Black" – his shop is near the Greentop Bar. You can watch him make some really remarkable wood carvings right there and he is usually willing to sell them when he's finished.

Sights & Activities

Sineku Community Tour

This half-day tour will take you to two of the Carib Territory's magical spots that are as beautiful as they are rich with legend. You'll start by hiking down a short trail as you learn about some of the area's flowers and medicinal plants until you reach the head of L'escalier Tete Chien (also known as Snake's Head). A hardened lava formation reaches out into the sea and was believed by the Caribs to be a snake that followed the Caribs from South America and entered the island here, only to hide in a cave and eventually emerge as a white man. If the water is calm, this is a nice place to relax in the natural pools of water at the base of L'escalier. The second half of the trip involves another hike to the Manjini pool, which is part of the Waitukubuli National Trail. This area was once believed to house mermaids because of the deep pools, which also makes it a nice spot to take a refreshing swim. Lunch is provided at the end of the tour. *Cost: US$42/pp; Contact via website to schedule: http://sineku.communitytourism.dm.*

Salybia Catholic Church

If you are driving through the territory, it's worth your time to stop and take a look at this very unique Catholic Church. Built in 1991 in the Kalinago style, it has painted murals thoughout and a traditional Kalinago canoe acts as an alter. The murals were done by local historian and artist Lennox Honychurch and a former Carib Chief, Fuastulus Frederick. The outside mural depicts the scene of Columbus's arrival to the island, which forever changed the course of the Kalinago's way of life. The mural inside was done by Frederick and shows a traditional village scene, featuring the images of notable Caribs including former Carib chiefs. The regular Sunday service is from 10am-12pm and visitors are welcome to attend. If you would like to see the church but skip the service, come before or after the service or you can also try to drive down and ask one of the nuns on the property for a look inside. *Salybia, Carib Territory*

Kalinago Barana Auté (Kalinago Cultural Village By the Sea)

An excellent 30-minute tour that takes you through an interpretation center and down a circular path where you will learn about Kalinago history and their way of life. From their housing, to their traditions, boat building, dances, myths and legends to the fruits and medicinal plants that are still in use today. End the tour by visiting the craft shops where local craftswomen make their living by weaving baskets from larouma reed. Just across from the craft shop is a café where you can get one of the best Creole lunches on the island, served in a Calabash bowl for EC$25. *Crayfish River, Carib Territory; Tel: 767-445-7979; www.kalinagobaranaaute.com, kbamanager@cwdom.dm; Hours: Daily 10am-5pm; Cost: US$10 (EC$26), kids half price.*

Eateries & Nightlife

Islet View Restaurant and Bar This small bamboo restaurant has one of the best views on the island. The local Creole style food is decent and but the real highlight is the 70+ types of bush rum and one killer rum punch. Definitely worth stopping by for at least a drink. *Castle Bruce; Tel: 767-446-0370; Hours: Daily 9am-10pm; Cost: EC$25.*

The East

Kalinago Barana Auté (Kalinago Cultural Village By the Sea) Cafe Even if you don't have time to take the tour, you should make a point to stop and have lunch at the historic village. Rose, the cook, makes an outstanding traditional Creole lunch that typically includes fish or chicken, provisions, rice, beans, green banana salad, plantains, and a green salad. If bringing a large group, it's a good idea to call ahead. *Crayfish River, Carib Territory; Tel: 767-445-7979; www.kalinagobaranaaute.com, kbamanager@cwdom.dm; Hours: Daily 10am-5pm (lunch and snacks only); Cost: EC$25.*

Silk's Royal Hatton Restaurant One of the classier places to eat on the east coast so be sure to call ahead to make reservations. The chef blends traditional Creole fare with modern international flavors and the outdoor patio dining makes for a nice atmosphere. Be sure to inform the restaurant ahead of time if you have special dietary restrictions. *Hatton Garden; Tel: 767-445-8846; silkshotel@gmail.com, www.silkshotel.com; Hours: 8am-9pm daily; Cost: EC$21.50 (breakfast), EC$80 (dinner).*

River Rush Restaurant Mo, the owner, has a team of excellent chefs that make an outstanding Sunday brunch for her weekly "Jazz in the Jungle" event. You'll find Mo playing the sax, but she always makes a point to walk around and talk to her guests during intermissions. On the last Friday of every month, she fires up the barbeque and hosts another fun event called Moonlight Party. Starting around 8pm, as the crowd grows a DJ comes on board and dancing ensues until late into the night. *Concord; Tel: 767-295-7266; mo@river-rush.com, www.river-rush.com; Hours: Sunday brunch: 11am-2pm, Dinner by reservation from Thursday to Saturday; Cost: EC$40(brunch).*

Pagua Bay Bar and Grill Located just five minutes from the airport, this is an excellent spot to grab lunch and enjoy a fantastic view of Dominica from the sun deck before you make your way off the island. Chic, modern architectural style makes use of typical regional materials with big TVs inside to catch a cricket match. The menu includes salads, sandwiches, burgers, pizza, tacos, and snack items as well as a full bar menu. Dinner is more extensive and by reservation only. This new restaurant is quickly becoming a favorite among locals and ex-pats on the island. Wireless internet available. *Marigot; Tel: 767-445-8888; paguabaybarandgrill@cwdom.dm; Hours: Mon closed, Tues-Thur 12pm-9pm, Fri-Sat 12pm-10pm, Sun 12pm-7pm; Cost: EC$15-$20 (lunch), EC$70 (dinner).*

The J's Spot Restaurant and Bar This small snackette is just off the main road in Marigot and is usually a hoppin' spot at night. They serve fried chicken and *paleau* but the real reason to come here is for the bakes; some of the best on the island. *Marigot; Tel: 767-245-4904; Hours: Open 10am-late; Cost: EC$2-$5*

Genesis Restaurant Located just below the pharmacy, this snackette sells fish broths, fried chicken, codfish and fresh juice. They also hold a fish market every afternoon around 2pm or 3pm where you can have the fish scaled and cut for EC$1 extra per pound. *Marigot; Tel: 767- 445-7725.*

Rum Shops

Strung along the many rural roads in Dominica are tiny rum shops that double as convenience stores and sell only the basic necessities for rural villagers (flour, rice, eggs, etc). One thing that almost all of them have in common is that they carry the village's supply of rum and each makes their own version of local bush rum, which is generally strong and flavorful. If you want to fit in with the local guys, stop by a shop in the evening and try a shot. You'll likely be invited to stay for a second round. One such shop is **Mona's** in Crayfish River. Look for the tiny wooden shack on the side of the road at the northern end of the village.

Friday Night Barbeques

As soon as the sun begins to sink below the horizon on a Friday evening, villagers get ready for the weekend by turning up the music and firing up their barbeques. You'll probably hear and smell them before you see them and it's definitely worth a stop when you encounter one. Prices are reasonable for some chicken and a beer, and you're bound to get to know the locals in a very authentic way.

Services

Marigot Gas Station *Marigot; Open till 7pm; Tel: 767-445-8942.*

Western Union *Marigot, Marigot Credit Union; Tel: 767-445-7155; Open M-F 8am-4pm.*

Marigot Hospital *Marigot; Tel: 767- 445-7091.*

Internet: Pagua Bay Bar and Grill *Marigot; Tel: 767-445-8888; paguabaybarandgrill@cwdom.dm; Hours: Tues-Thur 12pm-9pm, Fri-Sat 12pm-10pm, Sun 12pm-7pm; Wi-Fi.*

CAR RENTAL

Courtesy Car Rental *Melville Hall Airport; Tel: 767-445-7677.*

Discount Car Rentals *Melville Hall Airport; Tel: 767-445-8291; 225-2654; 277-1935.*

Bonus Rentals *Melville Hall Airport; Tel: 767-448-2650.*

Budget Rent A Car *Melville Hall Airport; Tel: 767-445-7687.*

Island Car Rental *Melville Hall Airport; Tel: 767-255-6867.*

The East

Carib Crafts

As you enter the Carib Territory you will find that around every corner there are crafts hanging out of windows, stacked on top of tables, and being presented to you at every opportunity. Deciding who to buy from isn't easy as they are all fairly similar, so your best bet is to spread your money around. The crafts men and women in the territory work hard and for many, their entire family income is based on the amount of crafts they sell. Some of the best places to buy crafts are at **Kalinago Barana Auté**, where there is a good variety of items and some of the best baskets, the **Carib Craft Corner,** where you'll see tables set up on a corner at the southern end of Crayfish River, or at some of the smaller shops by the road in that same area. All of the items are hand crafted and at Barana Auté you can actually see them being made and learn the long process associated with basket-making that includes of harvesting the reeds, dying them with mud and weaving them into beautiful vessels. You will also find masks made from the tree fern (Fwijé), wood carvings, calabash bowls, jewelry made from natural beads and shells, and other various items. Buying crafts here is like buying a little piece of Dominican history. The tradition of basket making has been passed down for centuries and little has changed since its inception. You can get a good-sized basket for a mere EC$35.

Shopping

Village Pharmacy A small pharmacy where you can get some basic health items. As an added bonus, they often sell locally bottled honey, which is tucked away behind the counter. *Marigot; Tel: 767- 445-8176.*

Shalom's Mini Mart Located on the main road this small market carries mainly non perishable food and various household items. *Marigot*

Shop-N-Save Grocery A decent sized grocery store where you can buy a wider selection of food, mostly non perishable goods, and other household items. *Marigot; Tel: 767-445-8400; Hours: M-F 7am-7pm, Sat 7am- 8pm; closed Sun.*

Accommodation

Budget

Gachette Cottages A cluster of small octagonal cabins sit on a slab of concrete just off the main road near Castle Bruce. Each cabin is set up like a small studio apartment with a kitchenette, bed, small table and a stone or tiled floor. Good location if you want to explore the interior or east coast of the island. *Amenities: solar hot water, kitchenettes, TV. Castle Bruce; 8 cottages (dbls); Tel: 767-446-0700; info@gachettecottages.com, www.gachettecottages.com; Cost: US$60/70.*

Domcans Guesthouse These spartan but spacious apartments come with a full kitchen, living room, bedroom, and veranda with a table and excellent views of mountains and ocean. Harry (from Canada) and Grace (from Dominica) treat their guests well and the price really makes this a great deal. *Amenities: Cable TV, fans, Wi-Fi, 10% discount at restaurant. Castle Bruce; 3 self-contained apartments; Tel: 767-445-7794; domcanrestaurant@hotmail.com, www.domcansguesthouse.com; Cost: US$60 dbl.*

Hibiscus Valley Inn and Adventure Center There are rooms for every budget here. For those who are looking for something on the cheaper end, there are the Economic Cottages, which are very small wood structures containing simply a bed, closet, fan, and hammock and share an outdoor bathroom. The Nature Bungalows, which are small and simple octagonal cottages, are rustic but comfortable enough. Finally, the Semi-Deluxe rooms are very spacious, beautifully decorated and furnished well. There is also one self-contained cottage on site that comes with a kitchen and large veranda. River on site makes for good tubing and a nice beach is a short walk away. Great tour packages available and group discounts apply. *Amenities: verandas on each room, hammocks, safe box, fans, mosquito nets, restaurant on site and tour packages available. Semi-Deluxe rooms also have: AC, fridge, TV, deck seating. South of Hatton Garden; 11 rooms (sgls, dbls, tpls); Tel: 767-445-8195, 767-275-8195; info@hibisucusvalley.com, www.hibiscusvalley.com; Cost economic houses: US$33 dbl; Cost nature bungalows US$65 dbl/trpl; Cost semi-deluxe US$121 dbl; Cost self-contained US$150 dbl.*

Faith Cottages This is a good option for people on a budget who have an early flight and want a ride to the airport. The owner is friendly and welcoming and is working on some improvements to the place. Overall this isn't an ideal long-term stay option. Some of the cheaper rooms are windowless and have to share a small bathroom. Others have odd layouts that don't make for a pleasant bathroom experience. But since this place is usually not full, you can probably have your pick of a room so just choose one that's more to your liking. *Amenities: Kitchenettes (not all rooms), hot water, TV, owner is a tour guide, free airport transfers. Marigot; 10 rooms; Tel: 767-614-8837, 767-277-7120; Cost: US$25-$55 sgl/dbl.*

My Father's Place Another budget option if you need a place to stay close to the airport. Bedrooms in the main house are small and basic with only a bed and a mosquito net and small side table. The three rooms share a common bathroom. Apartments are well equipped and comfortable with tiled floors throughout, a kitchen, dining table, lounge and bed with mosquito net. The sun deck above the apartments is a great place to watch the sunset but the best part about this place is that is right above an amazing secluded beach that's just a short walk away. *Amenities: Apartments have AC, TV, hot water, and full kitchens. Rooms in house have fans, Wi-Fi, common library and lounge,* *dual voltage plugs, access to common kitchen. Marigot; 3 apartments (dbls), 3 rooms (sgl/dbl); Tel: 767-445-7215; www.myfathersplaceguesthouse.com, info@myfathersplaceguesthouse.com; Cost: Apartments US$80, rooms US$30/$40 sgl/dbl.*

Natural Vibes Organic Farm and Eco Cottage This rustic set-up is meant for those who want to get their hands dirty working on the owner's farm, and don't mind roughing it a bit. The three small huts are made from bamboo and local wood with thatched roofs and consist of only a bed and a table. A communal kitchen is available and as well as a separate communal pit toilet. There is no running water; guests must carry their own up from the stream. The sole source of electricity is from a solar battery that can be used to charge cell phones. He also has a campsite higher up on his land for those who brought their own tents. Discounts on food and lodging are available for those who work on the farm and the owner will also provide workshops on local food production (such as turning cocoa seeds into chocolate). *Sineku, Carib Territory; rootsnaturalvibes@gmail.com; Tel: 767-612-8215; Cost: US$40. To make reservations, Keith, the owner, recommends texting him your name, the dates of your stay, and how many people plus your contact info to the number above.*

Mid-Range

Roots Jungle Retreat This unique eco-lodge is tucked into the rainforest, completely off the grid and the owners, Staci and Pat, do their best to be kind to the environment while making your stay enjoyable. Each cabin (called a Kai Pai) is built to replicate the design of the original Kalinago peoples' housing. The lodge, in fact was built by Kalinago descendents using traditional tools and materials: local bamboo, wood from surrounding forests and thatched roofs. The Kai Pais are situated deep in the jungle next to the Bamboo River with close access to deep river pools and a waterfall. Staci is an excellent cook and meals can be arranged with her. If you are renting a car, be sure to get a jeep or the drive down will be brutal in a car. *Amenities: telephone modem for internet, kitchenettes, breakfast included, tours available, hot water possible. Concord; 2 Kai Pais (small sleeps 4, large sleeps 6), 1 dbl guest room; Tel: 767-265-3806, 767-275-6000; www.rootsjungleretreat.com, www.rootsjungleretreat@gmail.com; Cost: US$85 guest room, US$100 small Kai Pai, US$125 large Kai Pai; Additional person is US$25 per night.*

Top-End

Beau Rive This highly recommended, guest-centered lodging was built by hand through the sweat of an Englishman named Mark. He's an excellent host with a special affection for Dominica that comes out in every aspect of the accommodation. The rooms are stylish without being overdone, and Mark caters to each guests' needs individually. The restaurant uses only local ingredients and, like the guesthouse, each meal is made from scratch by hand with special attention to detail. *Amenities: Ocean view, veranda, tea/coffee maker, ceiling fan, swimming pool, common lounge, library, restaurant on site, continental breakfast included. North of Castle Bruce; 10 rooms (dbls); Tel: 767-445-8992; www.beaurive.com, info@beaurive.com; Cost: US$180.*

Silks Boutique Hotel Formerly a rum distillery, this unique and charming hotel is spread out over 1.2 acres of river and gardens with a nearby beach. The tower of Josephine room is the gem of the hotel with a spiraling staircase, arched doorways, candlelit stairs, a four-poster bed and interesting nooks and crannies. It was purported to be built by Napoleon as a room for his precious Josephine (hence the name). Decorated with a mixture of history and modernity, the rooms are all spacious, elegant, and natural. They have big expansions in the works for the coming year. Closed in September. *Amenities: AC, coffee/tea maker, Wi-Fi, in-room safe, swimming pool, library, kayak rental, massages available, tour organization, restaurant on site, communal lounge/library. Hatton Garden; 4 rooms; Tel: 767-445-8846; silkshotel@gmail.com, www.silkshotel.com; Cost: US$220 dbl, US$275 family room (sleeps 4).*

River Rush Cottages Situated between two beautiful rivers (great for river bathing) the large wooden cottages are minimal but stylish and open to allow full views of the rivers, forest, and natural surroundings. The bedrooms contain merely a four-poster bed with mosquito net and a beautifully designed bathroom. The owner, Mo, does a great job of combining simplicity, elegance and nature. The restaurant, bar and hot tub are central to the cabins and on Sundays you can find Mo playing the saxophone for the weekly "Jazz in the Jungle" brunch. *Amenities: Continental breakfast, tours available, internet available, hot tub and restaurant/bar on premises. Concord; 4 cottages (3 dbls, one cabin sleeps 4); Tel: 767-295-7266; mo@river-rush.com, www.river-rush.com; Cost: US$150.*

 Pagua Bay House Located just minutes south of Melville Hall Airport, these simple, stylish and modern rooms are infused with bright Caribbean color, inspired by traditional banana sheds. Rooms have an outside deck with hammocks, beach chairs, and absolutely stunning views of the sea. Bathrooms are upscale and environmentally sensitive products are provided. *Amenities: AC, fans, flat-screen TV with cable, Wi-Fi, complimentary cell phone usage, safe, coffee maker, mini bar, dual voltage outlets, cleaning service, laundry service, airport transfer, iron, hair dryer, water sports equipment, tour coordination. Marigot; 4 cabanas (dbls, two can be joined for a family); Tel: 767-445-8888; paguabayhouse@cwdom.dm; www.paguabayhouse.com; Cost: US$150-$250 dbl; US$275 joined cabanas (sleeps 4).*

The Southeast

Traveling through the southeast offers towering interior peaks to the west and the surging Atlantic to the east. The road soars to frighteningly high points, nuzzles into the valleys, and skirts along the coast as it runs through the lush humid landscape, nodding in and out of villages along the way.

Because of its distance from the capital, a shortage of public buses, and the challenging roads separating it from the rest of the country, this region is one of the more remote and rural areas of the island. Surprisingly, though, the southeast has some of the most interesting and diverse accommodations on the island to choose from and with plenty of things to experience, it's worth stationing yourself here for a few days.

If you came to Dominica to swim beneath waterfalls, this is the place to be. Several large rivers flow down from the heights of Morne Trois Piton, gathering water and speed until they spill over cliffs, creating a spectacle that can only be seen by those who are willing to do the work to get there. Here, unlike many of the interior falls, you are likely get the waterfall to yourself. While waterfalls can be truly magical, it is important to remember that visiting a waterfall can be very dangerous after a large or extended rain as flash floods are common here. If you are unsure, call the Forestry Department (Tel: 767-266-3817) or ask a local guide about a safe time to visit.

TOP FIVES

Witness the ancient act of Leatherback Sea Turtles coming ashore to lay their eggs on the beach, as they've done for over a millennium. (pg 202)

Hike through rivers and streams to swim beneath the elegant Sari Sari Falls. (pg 205)

Muster up your courage to visit the secluded and hard to reach Wavine Cyrique Falls where you can swim in the ocean and under a waterfall simultaneously. (pg 204)

Walk through farms and forest to the breathtakingly beautiful Glassé Point. (pg 206)

Do yourself a favor and treat yourself to lunch at Jungle Bay. Stick around for a yoga class or a massage while you're at it. (pg 212)

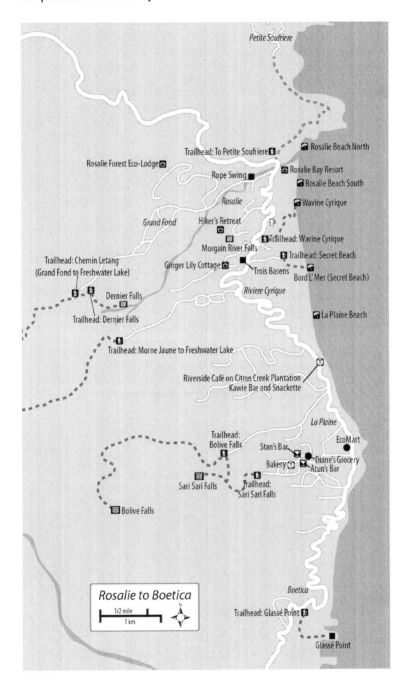

Petite Soufriere

Trailhead: To Petite Soufriere

Rosalie Forest Eco-Lodge

Rope Swing

Rosalie

Grand Fond

Hiker's Retreat

Morgain River Falls

Trailhead: Chemin Letang
(Grand Fond to Freshwater Lake)

Ginger Lily Cottage

Trois Basens

Dernier Falls

Trailhead: Dernier Falls

Trailhead: Morne Jaune to Freshwater Lake

Rosalie Beach North

Rosalie Bay Resort

Rosalie Beach South

Wavine Cyrique

Trailhead: Wavine Cyrique

Trailhead: Secret Beach

Bord L' Mer (Secret Beach)

Riviere Cyrique

La Plaine Beach

Riverside Café on Citrus Creek Plantation
Kawie Bar and Snackette

La Plaine

Trailhead:
Bolive Falls

Stan's Bar

Bakery

Sari Sari Falls

Trailhead:
Sari Sari Falls

Bolive Falls

EcoMart

Diane's Grocery
Atun's Bar

Boetica

Trailhead: Glassé Point

Glassé Point

Rosalie to Boetica

1/2 mile
1 km

N

GETTING THERE

Buses pick up passengers on Kennedy Street, across from Subway, for villages in the northern part of the Southeast (from Rosalie to Boetica) and should cost EC$7 to EC$11. The bus stop for Delices to Petite Savanne is on Cross Street. Buses only run a couple of times a day. You'll likely get one around noon and again around 4pm or 5pm, but it's wise to check with the driver beforehand to be sure you don't miss it.

There are two ways to drive here: You can take an interior road through Pond Casse and then take the road east to Rosalie and head south. Or if you are going to one of the southern villages, you can take the road from Roseau through Grand Bay and then head north up the coast. This road is not in great condition and is insanely steep, so take care when going in this direction. Keep your camera handy as there are great views when you reach the top and at one point, on the Delices side, you can even see Victoria Falls shooting out of the side of the mountain and the rising steam from Boiling Lake.

GETTING BACK

Buses leave the southeast early in the morning (before 9am) to take workers and students to Roseau. If you miss that round, you won't catch any until the next group

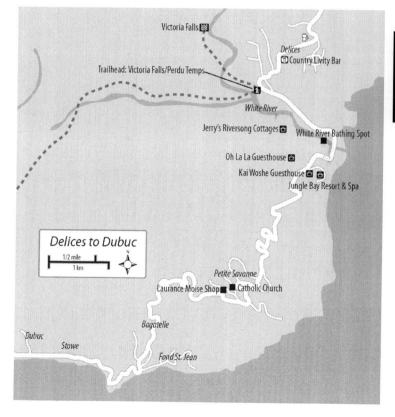

of buses heads out around 2 or 3pm. Hitching is the most common way to get to Roseau on the off hours, but traffic is pretty limited so keep your day open.

Rosalie

Rosalie is ideally located near a river, beach, and a main road. Despite these attributes, it is no longer much of a village due to events dating back to the time of emancipation. This area once held one of the largest estates on the island, producing sugar, cocoa, limes, bananas, and coconuts, the remains of which can still be seen by the river. In 1785 the Maroon chief, Balla, led an attack on this estate, triggering the government to start a massive campaign to get rid of the Maroons. This affront resulted in the eventual capture and public execution of Balla. Not long after, emancipation was enacted and a village began to develop around the estate. But when the estate changed hands, the new owners made the villagers dismantle their homes and move to the surrounding villages of Grand Fond and Riviere Cyrique where their descendants remain today.

> A new four-star resort, *Rosalie Bay Resort,* has just been built by the river and will likely attract more development of this area in the future.

The long, sandy **beach** that sits on the edge of the river is quite picturesque with gardens and a coconut grove that contrast the black sand. The current here can be severe, so be cautious when diving into the surf. Try to find a flat shallow area if you want to get in a quick dip. Climb the rocks and rinse off in the nearby natural freshwater lagoon or the river. **Sea turtles** frequent this beach nearly every night during the nesting season, which is most active from June through September. Please, however, be mindful of their eggs from March through October.

The **Rosalie River**, which streams down the eastern slope of Morne Trois Pitons, offers great bathing and swimming holes along its path and especially as it gets closer

---

The Long Journey Home: Turtle Watching

From late March to September the eastern beaches of Dominica play host to some very special guests. Three types of sea turtles follow the paths of their ancestors and return to the place they were born – some coming from as far away as Africa – to lay their eggs on the beach. While in many countries you would have to pay a lot of money to watch rare and endangered sea turtles come to the beach, in Dominica it's completely free. Enlist a certified guide from the Dominica Sea Turtle Conservation Organization (DomSeTCO), to get a closer look at nature in action. Leatherback, Hawksbill, and Green Turtles come to Dominica's coasts, all of which are endangered globally and protected in Dominica. Leatherbacks are the biggest, weighing about a ton and sometimes growing over eight feet long. They are most commonly sighted in June and July. Come after dark (moonlit nights are best) to the beach in Rosalie or La Plaine to see these rare creatures. Be respectful of the guides and their rules as they are working to protect the turtles. For more information on turtle watching, call the sea turtle "hotline" at 767- 225-7742. *For more information on the turtles, check out www.marinecreatures.com and www.widecast.org.*

to the beach. If you're coming from Pond Casse, cross the bridge and take the road to the right along the river that leads towards Grand Fond. Go slow and look to your right to find some foot paths that lead to the river. If an essential part of your tropical vacation is jumping off trees and flying through the

> If you head north from the bridge, you'll find a footpath that leads up to Petite Soufrière and the rest of the eastern villages.

air via a rope swing, you can check that off the list here. To get to the swing, locate a path that is up a slight incline about 100 yards down the road from the bridge. If you see some local kids around, they can tell you exactly where it is and will probably show you a thing or two about rope swingin'.

Is Something Missing?

Many visitors are shocked by the concrete bridge that lacks railings or protection as it crosses the Rosalie River. But the bridge isn't in disrepair; it lacks supports out of necessity. Whenever there is a big storm, the river floods and debris is carried over the bridge toward the ocean. The absence of side rails allows debris to flow easily over the bridge without damaging it or clogging the river. Just take care and drive slowly as you cross it.

Grand Fond

This tiny village sits high on a ridge and is literally at the end of the road. Getting here by bus is sometimes impossible as there is only one and it doesn't always run. If you are driving to Grand Fond, you will almost certainly be asked for a lift. If you are coming here to hike, be sure to fill up on water before you get to the village as there is no running water from early morning until dusk in the upper area, called Boulva.

What it lacks in water, it makes up for with some of the best peanut rum punch on the island at Jacklyn's Shop. Jacklyn also plays host to a dominoes game most evenings with a group of older gentlemen. If you ask nicely they may let you play, but probably won't let you win.

The end of the road here is the beginning of the historic **Chemin Letang Trail**, which was once the most frequented footpath on the island as it connected the east coast to Roseau via the Freshwater Lake before roads were built. It's always interesting to talk to the older folks who live on the east coast to hear their stories about traversing the interior peaks weekly, carrying their goods all the way to Roseau to sell at the market. You can still hike the Chemin Letang Trail and loop back on a different trail to finish at the village of Morne Jaune (just south of Riviere Cyrique). (See the hiking guide on page 290 for more details.)

From Morne Jaune, you can hike the 30-minute trail to **Dernier Falls**, which can be found via a small sign in the village (just ask around if you can't locate it). Follow the narrow dirt path through gardens, down a steep descent, through a rain forest to a riverbed. Head right, scramble over a few boulders and encounter a large pool of clear, cool water with a smallish waterfall that you can swim right up to.

The Southeast

Riviere Cyrique

Although Riviere Cyrique is a small village of less than 300 people, unique natural sites and activities abound in this area comprised of waterfalls, beaches, river pools, and the 1,000-pound sea turtles that visit the shores here. There are several small shops in the village that carry basic necessities. For not-to-be-missed evening entertainment, join the local guys for a game of dominoes. Find them at any of the shops around the Pentecostal Church near the village center.

It's a short and relatively easy hike to **Morgan River Falls**, which is just off the main road coming into the village from the north (if you get to the sign for Wavine Cyrique, you've gone too far). The path crosses a stream and small river so wear sturdy sandals that can get wet. The falls are pretty, and it is possible to hike all the way to the base of the falls for a swim.

TROIS BASEN

This is the perfect place to cool off and take a dip in a secluded pool beneath a small cascade of clean cool water. To reach it, enter a small path on the right side of the road when you are heading south towards La Plaine. You'll find it just past the Cable and Wireless sign that says "Thank you for visiting Riviere Cyrique," and just before an orange and black concrete wall along the side of the road. The path takes you down to a small stream, which you follow up (to the right) for a short distance, taking care to avoid slipping on the rocks. Arrive at a moderately sized pool, which is about five feet deep and is fed by a small waterfall. There is a narrow path going up on the left side of this pool that reaches the ledge in the middle of the cascading waterfall. A quick scramble over the ledge will take you to a smaller and more secluded pool just above. Visitors with some scrambling skills and good water shoes can continue ascending the series of water cascades and pools for at least half a mile up the stream, but these first two pools are the only ones really suitable for bathing. The hike to the first two pools is five minutes or less, and not at all strenuous. However, the rocks can be slippery, so proceed slowly and wear water shoes. The site is the perfect place to relax and cool off during the day, and both pools look almost as if they were intentionally constructed to create a bathing spot amidst perfect rainforest scenery.

WAVINE CYRIQUE

This unique location with a waterfall flowing onto a beach is an all-time favorite. After a laid-back, half-mile hike along a dirt path, the route becomes more challenging (mentally rather than physically) as you begin to descend the side of a cliff via roots, ropes and ladders that will bring you to the island's only waterfall that pours directly onto the beach. Because it's difficult to locate, you won't find swarms of tourists here and you can enjoy rinsing the sea water off under a cascading waterfall. Beware of swimming out very far as the currents are swift and unpredictable. The terrain beneath the waterfall changes frequently as the surf rearranges the rocks and sand. If you get down and notice that the sea is rough and has reached the cliff face (which is very rare), it's not a wise idea to stay and hang out. (See the hiking guide on page 297 for more details.)

BORD L'MER "SECRET BEACH"

Although it is often confused for Wavine Cyrique, Bord L' Mer is a completely separate place that is comprised of a black sand beach with a small river running into it. Getting to Bord L'Mer requires a walk down a small road next to Magdalene's Shop (you can ask locals if you can't find the entrance). The path at the bottom of the hill enters the "bush" on the right. A large white sign marks the entrance to the 1,000 steps down to the black sand beach. The waves here can be unpredictable, so be cautious when close to the water. Rock cliffs surrounding the cove can be climbed by the more adventurous. A small river stream is perfect for rinsing off after swimming in the ocean. This is a great place to sit and read or totally relax. Leatherback Sea Turtles come here to lay eggs in the spring and summer, so be mindful of their eggs between March and August.

La Plaine

La Plain, the largest village in the southeast with over 1,000 residents, was built on a broad, flat rocky outflow from ancient volcanoes of the Grand Soufrière hills. Many estates were once located here and all had names that indicated that their owners enjoyed the area: Pleasant, Bliss and Golden Hills, for example. In 1893, the calm was disrupted by riots after villagers refused to pay land tax. A war ship was sent over by the British marines in an attempt to evict those who refused to pay. Four persons lost their lives in the resistance. Today, there is a memorial dedicated to this event located in the now peaceful village.

> **Creole in the East** is a fun event if you happen to be here in October during the same week as World Creole Music Festival. Bands perform late into the night, celebrating the musical traditions of the Caribbean.

There are several places to eat or pick up some essentials in La Plaine. **Stan's Bar** is up the road from the main junction and attracts a mellow crowd with its pool table and frequent games of dominoes. **John's Bar** is just off the main junction in the center of La Plaine. John personally cooks up some amazing barbeque chicken on weekend nights. **Atun's Bar** ("Point 1 Disco") can be found at the main junction in the center of La Plaine. Not only does this bar/club have the most happening "action" on Friday and Saturday nights, they generally sell fried chicken, bakes, chips, and other local dishes for a very reasonable price. **EcoMart** and **Diane's Grocery** are also both located on the main road and are great places to grab a snack before you head out to the beach or a waterfall.

Bout Sable Bay "La Plaine Beach"
La Plaine beach is accessed right off of the road as you come into the village from the north. Although this isn't a good area for swimming, it's one of the most popular places to sight turtles during the nesting season.

SARI SARI FALLS

Sari Sari Falls, located at the western end of the village, is one of the most beautiful spots on the island and is not terribly difficult to get to. You'll hike about 30 minutes

The Southeast

amidst dense tropical plants and flowers with a few relatively easy river crossings. The falls themselves are tall and form a deep clear pool for swimming below and have some rocks around the outer edge from which courageous individuals can jump into the water below. (See the hiking guide on page 260 for more details.)

BOLIVE FALLS

Until recently, hiking to the remote **Bolive Falls** was nearly impossible unless you found someone who knew the area well. In the past few years the trail has been restored and more guides are familiar with the hike so getting to these gorgeous and elusive falls is more of a possibility for those who are up for a challenge. The hike is around four hours round trip, and the trail traverses some steep and difficult terrain. Your efforts will be rewarded when you can swim in a large clear pool beneath 20-foot falls that sit above double falls that cascade below with gorgeous mountain views in every direction (think nature's infinity pool). The trailhead is found near the village of La Plaine, but don't attempt to find it on your own. A guide is a must for this one. (See the hiking guide on page 288 for more details)

Boetica

Boetica is the very small village that sits on either side of the road just south of La Plaine and is the start of the trail to **Glassé Point**. The trail is well-marked and easy to follow: the path winds through farms and forest and ends at a stunning rocky point that juts dramatically into the sea. Here you'll find small perfectly circular deep pools that have formed in the rocks at the edge that were carved by the surf splashing up over the peninsula. Some even contain sea life that was deposited with the surf over the rocks and now has made a home in the pools. This is a great place to bring a picnic and witness the power of the ocean as it collides with the rocky coast. Caution, however, should be taken as the waves can be strong in some areas and potentially wash a person out to sea.

Delices

Named by the French settlers after the French word "delight," the village of **Delices**, unfurls along a green ridge several hundred feet above the Atlantic Ocean. Small garden plots of sweet potato, yam, and passion fruit vines wind their way down to the water. Rum shops and the area's only petrol station dot the roadside, and reggae radio hits vibrate from the shops, joining crowing roosters early each morning.

Once a major producer in Dominica's "banana belt," Delices farmers now cultivate mostly root crops like dasheen, sweet potato, and tania for local and wider Caribbean markets. In particular, toloma (or arrowroot), a gnarly tuber that farmers grind and rinse into a fine white powder, is a mainstay of the agricultural market. Locals frequently use this powder as a thickening agent instead of cornstarch or mix it with water or milk for baby porridge. Any visitor passing through the village during toloma season (harvest occurs every six months) will see groups of women gathered around heavy bags of toloma, deftly knifing dirt and cutting the skin from the roots. Driving along the village's main road, a visitor might smell another of Delices's major crops: bay leaves. Farmers process these eucalyptus-scented leaves in several local distilleries in order to extract its oil. Locals know to add a few drops of bay oil to their mopping water as a natural mosquito repellent.

At dusk, community members gather at the petrol station to fill up on gossip as well as gasoline. A boisterous crowd attends Sunday cricket and rounders games on the village's playing field, which is in the lower part of Delices, near the ocean.

Local **crafts** produced here include basket and mat weaving, as well as wicker traps for catching crabs. An active sewing group produces beautifully embroidered quilts and pillowcases. You can find many of these local crafts for sale in the gift shop of Jungle Bay Resort. Many elders have an impressive knowledge of "bush" remedies and the medicinal uses of local plants. One such man is Moses, a Rastafarian who lives with his family down in a valley by the entrance to Victoria Falls.

The **White River**, which originates at the Boiling Lake, tumbles down Victoria Falls and passes through Delices on its way to the Atlantic. If you didn't get enough of it at the lake or the falls, you can enjoy a dip in this milky-white river (the color is a result of the sulphur in the water) by the village of Delices. When the road passes Jungle Bay and nears the coast, a small bridge passes over the river. Locate parking near the bridge and walk upstream a bit to find some pools in the river that are great for bathing and cooling off. Due to its mineral properties, the water is said to have therapeutic qualities. There are also some very nice secluded spots for swimming where the Perdu Temps trail crosses the river. Be sure to take off any jewelry before you jump in as the sulphur will tarnish your silver.

VICTORIA FALLS

Located just south of the village, these falls can be accessed by the same path as the Perdu Temps trail. Just past the start, the trail splits and a turn to the right will start you on this challenging journey. The hike is tough, which keeps the crowds away, but it also means you really need a guide for this one. There are several difficult deep river crossings that aren't obvious unless you are with someone who knows the way and can help you get over the slippery rocks.

Victoria Falls are the highest falls in Dominica, with an impressive volume of water falling into the wide pool below, which makes for an exhilarating place to swim. As with all waterfalls, don't attempt this hike after a heavy rain. The river will be high and fast and flash floods do occur here. If you don't already have one, you can find a tour guides at the Country Livity Bar in Delices (just past the Perdu Temps trailhead, see hiking detail on page 264).

PERDU TEMPS

The hike can be attempted from either the village of Grand Bay (which is said to be the easier route) or from Delices, using the same entrance as Victoria Falls. The trek is less than five miles, but plan on it being an all-day adventure. The trail gets steep, reaching 1,800 feet, but you'll be rewarded with some great views of Jack's Falls, one of Dominica's tallest waterfalls – it's most impressive during during the rainy season. Since the path follows the Perdu Temps River and the White River, you'll get plenty of opportunities to take a swim and cool off. (See the hiking guide on page 295 for more details.)

Petite Savanne

Petite Savanne, or Ti Savanne as it is fondly called by its approximately 850 residents, is nestled near the coast between two tall ridges over which you have to pass to get into or out of the village.

If you arrive in Petite Savanne from the direction of Grand Bay, the first building you'll pass before entering the village is a plain concrete structure on the right side of the road home to a skilled furniture-maker and craftsman named **Laurance Moise**. This is a great place to stop if you're looking for unique, handcrafted local souvenirs. Laurance turns out beautiful wooden bowls, cups, candlestick holders and plates, all made from local, sustainably harvested tropical hardwoods. Prices range from about US$5 for a penholder to US$50 for a set of large serving platters and plates.

Continuing on into the village proper, you'll come to the **Catholic Church**. The main road to the left will take you through the village in the direction of Delices. The concrete road to the right will take you down a steep path to Petite Savanne Bay, passing bay leaf and rum distilleries (the village's main agricultural product) and the three-story primary school. On a clear day, there are opportunities to see Martinique, the French island to the south of Dominica.

The **bay** itself is a picturesque rocky beach with strong waves rushing in from the Atlantic. Swimming is not advised, as the undertow can be quite strong. On the far left of the bay is a natural spring coming out of the rocky hillside. Locals have rigged a bamboo spout so that the water, which is fresh and potable, can be used to shower or stored and taken to their homes for those who don't have running water.

As you head back up to the village, you'll notice a path leading off to the right into some bushes. This path will take you to the village's overgrown, less-than-level cricket pitch, which is now mainly used for grazing a few cattle or goats. Continuing along the path across the pitch, you'll cross a small stream and the path will eventually take you along a slightly precipitous ridge. Round a corner and arrive at the edge of a picturesque rocky outcropping with the Atlantic Ocean crashing below. From here, you can see all the way up the coast to the village of Delices. This hidden gem is mostly used by fishermen and is one of the most beautiful parts of Petite Savanne.

Bay Leaf Production

Bay leaf is the largest source of income for most families in Petite Savanne, and many families either own their own stands of bay trees or work for a neighbor or relative in exchange for a share of the income. For a lot of people, bay supplements other income, whether from farming or from working in Roseau. During harvest season you will likely see bundles of bay leaf branches tied together on the side of the road and piled on the backs of trucks.

Petite Savanne's biggest bay leaf distillery is run as a cooperative. It is the only distillery to be run on electricity and processes about half of the total amount of bay oil that is produced in the village. Other smaller, wood-burning distilleries produce the rest. Bay leaf is cultivated twice a year, once in August and once in December (the processing is timed to provide extra money for school necessities and Christmas presents). At these times, the big distillery runs 24 hours a day, and the entire village is infused with the scent of bay.

Bagatelle, Fond St. Jean, Dubuc & Stowe

Just south of Petite Savanne, you'll find yourself in the village of **Bagatelle**, a small friendly village streched out along the main road as it travels up the ridge. Near the southern tip of the village, you'll pass a concrete school house and beside it is a road leading towards a playing field. There are excellent views of the area from here and just past the field are the ruins of an old mill that was once used to process sugar cane. There are two main shops in the village on the main road that offer snacks or drinks, and you can usually catch a game of dominoes at either shop, especially in the evening.

As you travel further south, you'll come to another junction with the option to go right or left. To the left is the picturesque fishing village of **Fond St. Jean** where you'll see colorful wooden boats lining the shore and extremely friendly people sitting by the road chatting and watching fishermen bring in their catch. If you are lucky, you'll find a woman who sells really amazing ice cream out of a cart on the main road in the village. Continue along this road past the bay headed east for some incredible views of the southern end of the island.

Backtracking west, you'll eventually run into the village of Stowe and Dubuc. It's possible to hike up through the village of **Dubuc** and follow the path to the very small series of trickling falls. In the dry season they are fairly unimpressive but the hike there is fun and not too strenuous. Just after you pass **Stowe** (a very tiny fishing village) and start to climb the hill, there are really amazing views of Grand Bay and on a clear day, Martinique. This is a wonderful place to watch the sunrise if you are an early riser.

Sights & Activities

Southeast Community Tour

The southeast abounds with amazing hikes and waterfalls, and these tours do their best to fit in as much of what the southeast has to offer as possible. The one-day tour starts with a guided hike to Victoria Falls where you can bathe in the rich mineral water that originates from the Boiling Lake. You'll then refuel with a traditional lunch in the village and continue your day with a hike to the stunning Glassé Pools and enjoy one of the best views on the island. The three-day tour packs in a little more and includes both of those hikes plus a trip to a Creole garden, a bay leaf production site, or the beach at Bout Sable Bay. On the third day you will also be able to visit Sari Sari Falls and have the option (and for an extra fee) go to either Wavine Cyrique or Bolive Falls. Three-day package includes transfer to Airport (or Ferry), two nights of accommodation, lunch each day, and tours. *Cost: One-day tour US$79, three-day tour US$184; Contact tour operator via their website: http://southeast.communitytourism.dm.*

Fregates View Trail Community Tour

This unique two-hour, self-guided community tour of Riviere Cyrique will give you a window into rural village life in the southeast. You'll have the chance to sample local food, buy crafts, honey and produce from farmers and artists, hear about local history and folklore, and learn how to process cocoa, coffee and cinnamon-the natural way. Pick up a map at a shop in Riviere Cyrique or contact Nature Enc-

The Southeast

hancement Team, Inc. *Riviere Cyrique; Tel: 767-277-1608, 767-613-6049; mynetto-ti@gmail.com.*

Nature Enhancement Team Tours

This local team of tour guides offers tours that highlight everything the area has to offer. Pick from local hikes (Wavine Cyrique, Secret Beach, Denier Falls, or Frigate View Drive) or take a farm and cultural tour that focuses on local cuisine, historical sites, or farm life. From March to September, you can participate in watching giant leatherback sea turtles nesting. *Riviere Cyriques; Tel: 767-277-1608, 767-225-7742; mynettoti@gmail.com; Cost: US$10-$30.*

Eateries & Restaurants

Jungle Bay Restaurant A giant royal palm grows straight up through the middle of this open-air restaurant overlooking the ocean. Like all things Jungle Bay-related, the food is excellent and done with exceptional attention to detail. The breakfast buffet has everything one could possibly want and the lunches are light and fresh with lots of variety. Dinners are a creative mix of everything the island has to offer, often with amazing fresh fish. Friday nights you can catch a special cultural presentation with traditional music and dancing. *Point Mulatre, Delices; Tel: 767-446-1789, 767-446-1090; www.junglebaydominica.com, info@junglebaydominica.com; Hours: 7am-10pm; Cost: EC$20 (breakfast), EC$30 (lunch), EC$50 (dinner).*

 **Riverside Café on Citrus Creek Plantation** This new little gem of a restaurant was opened by a couple from Guadeloupe who believe in fresh, local ingredients prepared with French flare. Besides the fantastic food, the atmosphere is comfortable and charming. Dining is on an outdoor covered patio next to the Taberi River. You can go for a river bath after lunch or sit in a hammock and take advantage of the free Wi-Fi. *La Plaine; Tel: 767-446-1234, 767-277-9585; riverside@citruscreekplantation.com, www.citruscreekplantation.com; Hours: 10am-5pm; Cost: EC$25/breakfast, EC$68/lunch, A La Cart dining: EC$20 (average); Dinner by Reservation only.*

Kawie Bar and Snackette Nuzzled in the corner of a river and the sea, just north of La Plaine, this large snackette sits in a beautiful stone and wood building with a wrap-around porch for seating. The menu is very basic serving mainly snacks, chicken, rum, and beer, although they do host barbeques on Friday and Saturday nights. *La Plaine; Tel: 767-245-2350, 767-616-3150; Hours: M-Th 11am-9pm, F-Sa 11am-1am.*

Services

NP Gas Station *Delices, Hours:M-Sat 6am-7pm*

EcoMart Grocery Located on the main road as you enter the village, the EcoMart carries a decent selection of basic food items and serves as a good place to grab snacks before and after a hike. *La Plaine*

La Plaine Bakery Though it sometimes sells out in the morning, La Plaine's only bakery serves piping hot bread loafs for EC$1. Head up the road, past Stan's bar and take a left when you get to "Smokey Corner." You'll smell it before you see it! *La Plaine*

Diane's Grocery At the main junction in the center of La Plaine. A good place to get snacks and basic food items. *La Plaine*

Accommodations

Budget

Rosalie Forest Eco-Lodge Formerly known as Three Rivers, this is about as eco as it gets. Jem, the owner, can cater to any type of guest from backpackers on a budget who just need a patch of ground to lay their head on to those who desire a more pampered eco-friendly experience. The rugged shelters will bring to mind your youthful treehouse fantasies. A bamboo covered shower is even built into the root system. The property is in the midst of being revamped, so check the website for updates. Be sure to take a dip in the mermaid pool or hike to one of the many waterfalls in the area. Rustic outdoor kitchen available for use or you can arrange meals with Jem. *Amenities: phone and internet services, laptop rental, restaurant on site, communal kitchen, tours available, river access, sustainable living workshops. Rosalie; Camp site rentals, dormitory stays, self-contained wooden cottage; Tel: 767-446-1886, 767-275-1886; www.rosalieforest.com; Cost: US$15-$90.*

Ginger Lily Cottage This quiet rural area is the home to the only accommodation on the road south of Rosalie, tucked into the tiny village of Riviere Cyrique. With a modern, comfortable home as your base, you'll get a feel for village life here. Your host Fernanda will help you experience the daily rhythm of Dominicans. Sit on the veranda to drink your coffee in the morning and say hello to the locals as they pass by on their way to get water from the village pipe. If you came to Dominica for the hikes, waterfalls, and an occasional beach, then a stay at Ginger Lily will put you in a good place to get started. *Amenities: Full kitchen, laundry facilities, cable TV, telephone, hiking guide arrangement. Riviere Cyrique; 2 bedroom house (sleeps 4); Tel: 767-446-1170; gingerinfo@hotmail.com, www.ginger-lily.com; Cost: US$60-$100.*

Kai Woshe Guesthouse Kai Woshe means stone house in Creole, and the guesthouse is aptly named. The five guestrooms are spartan but comfortable. One room has an ensuite bathroom; the other four guestrooms have a shared bath. Restaurant on site uses mostly local ingredients and breakfast is included in the price, making Kai Woshe an affordable option for big groups and families. *Amenities: restaurant/bar on site, fans, internet available, can accommodate parties, private groups, meetings, and weddings, telephone, TV in common lounge area, breakfast included. Point Mulatre, Delices; 5 rooms (dbls); Tel: 767-446-1849, 767-265-8757; kaiwoshe@hotmail.com, http://kaiwoshe.hotels.officelive.com; Cost: US$65-$90.*

The Southeast

Advice from Mom
Make yourself at home.

On our first trip to Dominica we rented Ginger Lily Cottage in Riviere Cyrique. It is located in a neighborhood in a typical village. I highly recommend this arrangement. It allows you to get closer to Dominican life and interact with locals. Also, the cost was quite reasonable. Our host (Fernanda) couldn't have been kinder or more accommodating.

"Won't forget it" moment: On our first night in Dominica Fernanda took us to the local grocery store in Riviere Cyrique. It was basics only. Our dinner was a can of baked beans and mac 'n cheese made with water only! Things looked up in the morning when Fernanda walked up the steep hill to our cottage and greeted me with a kiss and provisions for breakfast and lunch.

Mid-Range

Zandoli Inn These spacious rooms are bright, airy, and colorful and they open up to one of the best views on the island. Situated on six acres of trails, a short walk to the ocean, and close to the small fishing village of Fond St. Jean, this is a nice spot to relax and enjoy a bit of what Dominica has to offer. *Amenities: balconies with sea view, plunge pool, sun deck, restaurant and bar on site, fans, mosquito nets, laundry service, hair dryers, Wi-Fi, tour arrangement. Stowe; 5 rooms; Tel: 767-446-3161; zandoli@cwdom.dm, www.zandoli.com; Cost: US$135 sgl, US$145 dbl.*

Oh La La Guesthouse This brand new, intimate, and upscale luxury villa is really a great deal. Rooms are very modern, stylish and comfortable with a living room, flat screen TVs, dining area, full kitchen and comfortable beds. The common entertainment area feels like someone just dropped a beautiful lounge right in the middle of the rainforest and equipped it with a movie screen, bar, games, and pool/sun deck next door. Debra and her husband Jules, a native Dominican, are wonderful and friendly hosts who can arrange special packages for romantic getaways, adventure/fitness tours, agriculture tours, or any other special request. Very family friendly as well. Be sure to check out their Friday night barbeque. *Amenities: AC, Wi-Fi, tour arrangement, kitchen, groceries upon arrival, entertainment lounge, swimming pool, trampoline, bar on site, meal arrangement available, yoga and aerobics classes, first mornings breakfast, laundry service, spa services. Point Mulatre, Delices; 3 rooms (dbls with extra sofa bed), soon expanding to 6 rooms; Tel: 767-446-1283, 767-616-6840; ohlaladominica@me.com, http://web.mac.com/ohlaladominica, skype: debra charles mark; Cost: US$80-$200.*

Jerry's Riversong Cottages Built in 1970 in traditional African roundhouse style, these charming little stone and wood cottages are straight out of a storybook. The circular guest cottage has a bed with mosquito net, couch and table. The bathroom is in a separate room just outside of the cabin and is easily accessible. The kitchen cottage and living room cottage are next door and can be utilized by guests as well. If you are renting a car, be sure to hire a jeep as the road down is rough and the cottage is tucked far into the forest. *Amenities: Internet available, kitchen available, common living room, outdoor dining area, continental breakfast can be provided. Point Mulatre, Delices; 2 rooms (dbl); Tel: 767-446-0224; windsong@cwdom.dm, www.travelbarefoot.com/Hotels/riversong; Cost: US$89-$99.*

Top-End

Rosalie Bay Resort Typical resort style accommodation (and at the moment the only one of its kind in Dominica) with nine cottages spread out along a piece of land that lies between a river and the ocean. Everything you need is on site: restaurant, bar, pool, beach, exercise room, spa, and nature trails so be sure to make a point to get out and see the rest of the island by taking advantage of their tours. Located next to a beach that is a prime leatherback sea turtle nesting spot from June to November. *Amenities: Wi-Fi, fans, spa services, maid services, beach on site, laundry services, on site activities, meeting room, fitness center, laptop rental, babysitting services, tours, airport transfers. Rosalie; 28 rooms (mostly dbls); Tel: 767-440-4439; info@rosaliebay.com, www.rosaliebay.com; Cost: US$150-$500*

Jungle Bay Resort and Spa If you want to treat yourself during your stay on Dominica, then treat yourself to a visit to Jungle Bay. Opened by Sam Raphael, a native Dominican, Jungle Bay has since been a huge success and is the recipient of many prestigious awards for its eco-friendly focus and unique features and accomodations. The cottages are built by hand from local materials, and they will give you the feeling of camping in luxury. Consider the all-inclusive package with all meals, daily excursions (of varying ability levels according to your preference), daily spa treatments, morning yoga classes, and airport transfers included; this package is a great deal. The customer service is the best on the island and the food can't be beat. A feel-good bonus is that Jungle Bay gives back a portion of their revenue to aid the nearby Carib community. *Amenities: Swimming pool, gym, mini-fridge,* *coffee/tea maker, veranda with hammocks, fans, business center, telephone, safe boxes, tours, restaurant/bar on site, spa, game room, library, gift shop, yoga center, sun deck, outstanding service. Point Mulatre, Delices; 35 cottages; Tel: 767-446-1789, 767-446-1090; www.junglebaydominica.com, info@junglebaydominica.com, skype: junglebaydominica; Cost: from US$179 (basic) to US$283 (all inclusive).*

Hikers Retreat This beautiful stone and wood house acts as your staging grounds for hiking adventures on the island with your hosts, Clement and Carol, as your personal guides. The stay is all-inclusive with organic dinners prepared on-site and guided island adventures. The rooms are cozy and welcominig with a private wrap-around veranda that offers beautiful views of mountains and valleys that surround the house. *Amenities: Organic meals, fans, Wi-Fi, laundry service, airport transfer, library. Riviere Cyrique; 2 bdrm 2 bath house (sleeps 5); Tel: 767-446-1076; www.hikingdominica.com; hikersretreat@hikingdominica.com; Cost: US$200/pp*

The South

The South covers a diverse spectrum of environments. From the farming villages of Giraudel and Eggleston to the fishing villages of Soufrière and Scotts Head, the South offers a range of very accessible activities for visitors. This region is the second most populous area and because of its proximity to Roseau, it tends to also be more affluent with a lot of the residents working in white-collar positions in the capital. Point Michel, Soufrière and Scotts Head dot the edge of the southern marine reserve making them great diving and snorkeling areas. Due to the scores of fishermen in this region, the southern coast is a wonderful place to get fresh fish. Giraudel and Eggleston are agricultural areas as the fertile land is well suited for plants that are more difficult to grow in other areas. If you time it right, you might catch the Giraudel Flower Show, which is an event that happens every couple years. Grand Bay, which is nestled in a stunningly beautiful valley, is the "cultural capital" of the island and you are guaranteed to hear lively conversations in the local patios language if you take a stroll down the main strip, "L'allay." There are only a few accommodation and restaurant options in this area but because it's close to the capital, you can come and go from the south easily without having to make it your homebase.

TOP FIVES

Get a taste of the culinary traditions and cultural heritage of Dominica by taking the Giraudel Culinary Tour. This tour was recently a finalist in the National Geographic Changemakers Geotourism Challenge. (pg 225)

Hike from Tete Morne down a well-maintained trail to Soufriere Hot Springs and enjoy a soak in the therapeutic baths to reward you for your efforts. (pg 221)

Snorkel through the warm bubbling underwater air vents at Champagne Reef (but not when a cruise ship is in port or you won't see the fish). (pg 222)

Snorkel around the rim of an ancient volcanic caldera formed over five million years ago at the base of Fort Cachacrou in Scotts Head. (pg 226)

Take a look inside one of the oldest and most beautiful Catholic Churches on the island in Soufrière and sit in the hot pools on the edge of the surf directly in front of it. (pg 222)

GETTING THERE

Getting around the South is relatively easy. Buses (EC$3-6) run frequently and you can get a ride until about 7pm (although you may have to wait a bit). After that, it is very easy to hitch a ride if you wait at the round-a-bout in front of Fort Young for any bus going south. The roads are pretty good for most of the villages in the south, the only really tricky spot is Point Michel in which the road is very narrow and runs very close (and without protection) alongside the sea. If driving, take caution and go slow through this village. Drive carefully through Pichelin (between Belle Vue and Grand Bay) as well as the road is narrow and buses tend to drive fast through this village. Getting back to Roseau is quite easy by bus as well.

The south is situated on three different paths. The road to Giraudel and Eggleston is a loop that starts off of Victoria Street, south of Newtown. Turn onto the road that runs between the two gas stations, West Indies and Texaco, and immediately turn to the right, taking the road directly behind the Texaco station. The road will continue going up and will pass through Giraudel then will start heading north, passing through Eggleston and eventually goes back down the mountain to Victoria Street and the bay front.

The path to Loubiere, Pt. Michel, Soufrière and Scotts Head is more straightforward. You just continue heading south from Roseau and follow the coastline. After passing Irie Safari, south of Pt. Michel, the road goes over a mountain pass and back down to the coast again, to Soufriere. At the junction, take a right to get to the coast and then a left, which will follow the shoreline and deposit you at the southern tip of the island.

If you want to drive to Galion, take a left at the junction when you enter the village of Soufrière and then take the first road to the right as it snakes around and ends in Galion. (You should feel free to ask villagers if you are unsure of the road as they will point you in the right direction.) If you are taking a bus there, wait at the main junction and ask a driver to take you up. They should charge around EC$2.

If you are heading to Bellevue Chopin, Grand Bay or just want to take the southern route to the southeastern villages, drive south from Roseau and as you reach Loubiere you will pass over a small bridge and you'll see a curving stone wall to your left. This is the Loubiere junction. Take a left and follow that road as it goes over a mountain pass, through Bellevue Chopin and back down through Pichelin, ending at the Grand Bay junction. Take a right to get to the village of Grand Bay or continue straight past the school and Geneva Estate to get to the southeastern villages.

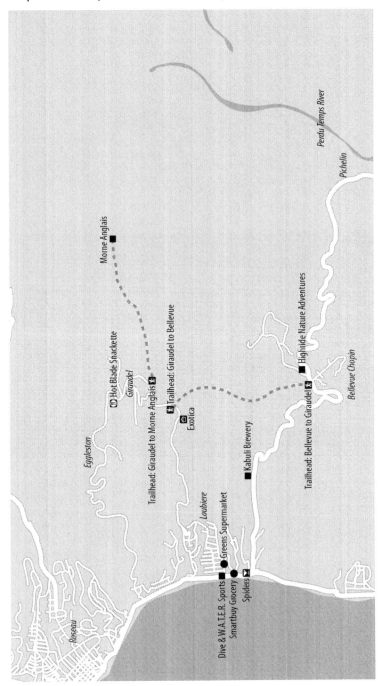

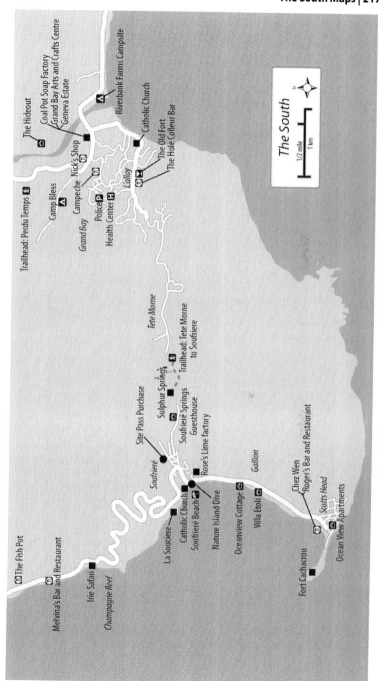

The Hideout

Coal Pot Soap Factory
Grand Bay Arts and Crafts Centre
Geneva Estate

Riverbank Farms Campsite

Campeche · Nick's Shop

Catholic Church

The Old Fort
The Hole Colieur Bar

Lalay

Camp Bless

Trailhead: Perdu Temps

Grand Bay

Police
Health Center

The South

½ mile
1 km

Tete Morne

Sulphur Springs

Trailhead: Tete Morne
to Soufriere

Site Pass Purchase

Soufriere Springs
Guesthouse

Rose's Lime factory

Soufriere

Chez Wen
Roger's Bar and Restaurant

Gallion

Scotts Head

Catholic Church
Soufriere Beach

Nature Island Dive

Oceanview Cottage

Villa Etoli

La Souciere

Ocean View Apartments

Fort Cachacrou

The Fish Pot

Melvina's Bar and Restaurant

Irie Safari

Champagne Reef

The South

Giraudel/Eggleston

If you need to relax and cool down from a hot day in Roseau, head to the heights of Morne Anglais and to the sister villages of Giraudel and Eggleston. Because they sit at around 1,500 feet above sea level, the air is much cooler, especially in the evenings. This region has gained recognition because of their flower show, usually held in Giraudel. The climate and rainfall at this height makes growing flowers and agricultural products somewhat easier here and the local talent is happy to show off their skills. Try out one of the excellent **community and culinary tours** that take you through some of the farms and flower gardens and will give you an authentic taste of the produce and heritage of this region. As you drive the loop around these villages, be sure to take time to check out some of the impressive views of the surrounding mountains and sea to the west. The **Hot Blade Bar and Snackette** is a hoppin' place in the evenings and hosts a farmers market on Saturdays.

Giraudel is the starting point to the **Morne Anglais** summit hike, which has extraordinary views from the top and is about two hours each way. You can also pick up a **trail to Bellevue Chopin** from this village that is a fun and less strenuous hike and part of the Waitukubuli National Trail. This is a great option if you are planning to check out the community farm tours in these villages.

Loubiere to Grand Bay & Tete Morne

LOUBIERE

As you turn at the junction and head up the road you'll pass Dominica's only brewery, which crafts the omnipresent Kubuli beer, Kubuli Shandy's and bottles Loubiere Spring Water.

The road winds and twists up a mountain with almost constant dramatic views of lush green valleys as it climbs to **Bellevue Chopin**, which very fittingly means "beautiful view." The tradition of farming is rich here and has been passed down for generations. Many people still farm today in the same manner that their ancestors did, living off of the land and using only organic methods for crop cultivation. To see this in action, take a community tour and get a first-hand look at how Bellevue provides much of this area with food and sustenance. When you reach the top of Bellevue, pull over and enjoy the view of Roseau from above. If a cruise ship is in port, the sheer size of the ship will be able to give you some perspective on just how small of an island you are on. There is a very good snackette right there and across the street, in the tiny wooden shack, is some of the best bread on the island. If it is open, it's in your best interest to spend EC$1 to try a loaf of bread or pastry. You won't regret it.

GRAND BAY

Continuing down the mountain you'll pass through the tiny village of Pichelin, past some farms and the trailhead to Perdu Temps until you reach a junction at the west end of **Grand Bay**. Take a right to get to the main village and L'allay, or continue straight to reach the coast.

You Say You Want a Revolution....

"Sout City," Berekua, Geneva, and Coulibri are all names given to the third largest village and cultural capital of the island, Grand Bay. This area has also been the site of a lot of historical drama dating all the way back to the 1700s. During the early 18th century, Jeannot Rolle, a free black from Martinique, made deals with the Caribs, who at that time were very wary of outsiders, to acquire timber. This ended up being a sneaky way to quietly take over portions of land and use it as plantations. As Rolle occupied larger sections of land, he invited the Jesuits to set up a mission and convert the Caribs to Christianity. During their stay, Rolle constructed a stone cross for the mission called "La Belle Croix" in 1720. (Today, it is the oldest cross on the island and now sits atop the Catholic Church's cemetery and the "sinners' burial grounds.")

English creditors swept up the land for themselves and started importing a large number of slaves. Maroons began to escape these estates, hiding out in the heights of Bellevue and the surrounding mountains. The rebellious activity continued amongst the slaves eventually making Grand Bay the sight of continuous rebellions, revolts and uprisings.

The resistant spirit continued over the years to include riots in 1844 by villagers who were opposed to a census taking. **The Geneva Estate** frequently bore the brunt of these revolutions. The estate, which originally produced sugar, molassas, and rum, changed hands several times and eventually received its name from a Swiss family, the Bertrands, who named it after their home city. In the 1820s the family of the author Jean Rhys acquired the property. After Rhys's great-grandfather passed away in 1837, his widow was left to run the estate.

During the riots in 1844 the home was raided and all of their possessions were burned in the front yard. Later, in 1930 when the estate was somewhat idle, it was burned again by arsonists. Jean Rhys visted the estate soon after and based a famous scene (the burning of Coulibri) on the destruction in her book *Wide Sargasso Sea*.

In 1974 the ongoing national dispute over landrights came to a head in Grand Bay. The large estate owners refused to sell small plots of land to farmers in the community even though the land lay dormant. In response, farmers squatted on the land, taking over thousands of acres. The owner of the Geneva Estate, Elias Nassief who purchased it in 1949, attempted to evict the squatters and convert the estate into a coconut and copra production plant. During the Carnival celebrations in Grand Bay that year, emotions ran high and during the festivities the roads to Roseau were blocked, shops were looted, telephone lines were cut, and estates were vandalized. Geneva Estate suffered its final blow when it was burned to the ground and its owners and workers driven off the land. After some time, when things settled down, the estate was handed over to the government and divided and sold as small plots to villagers in the community. You can still see the burned shell of the estate building on the Geneva historical site.

Some claim that the movement for independence from Britain was started in Grand Bay and because of this rebellious spirit, Dominica is its own country today.

The South

Grand Bay was originally called Berecoua ("*coua*" being the name of a white land crab found in abundance) by the Caribs who lived here over 2,000 years ago. The name has since changed to Berekua yet can still be found written that way on many maps today.

As you enter Grand Bay you'll first come to a well-signed junction that will point you to the right to get to the village. Just as you begin to climb the hill you'll pass **Campeche**, a small bar and restaurant with very welcoming and friendly owners. This is a great place to stop for a drink or a bite to eat. They also have rooms available in the back for rent that are still in the process of being developed. Continuing on this road, you'll pass some residential housing and a large community center. Eventually you will come to a T-intersection. Turning right takes you up the mountain to Tete Morne and turning left will deposit you onto **L'allay** – the congested and very spirited village center. There are a number of snackettes, shops, and old and new homes that line this narrow strip of road and you'll be sure to see people outside chatting in Creole, playing dominos, braiding each other's hair, selling their produce, or just lounging about. This village isn't called the "cultural capital of the island" for nothing and these are all perfect examples in one convenient location of some cultural traditions in Dominica.

As the buildings begin to thin out and the road starts to curve towards the bottom of the hill you will come to the coast and Pierre Charles Boulevard, named after the former Prime Minister from Grand Bay. A short walk down the boulevard, will lead you to the **Catholic Church** and cemetery. This is a very beautiful church made from stone with colorful stained glass windows. If you have any interest in going to church while on island, this is a nice one to attend as you will never feel more spiritual than when you gaze out the louvered windows to witness a breathtaking view of the sea and surrounding mountains. Behind the church are an old cemetery and the "sinners' burial grounds," on top of which sits the old bell tower and "Le Belle Croix," the oldest crucifix on the island.

Continuing on that road you'll come to a round-a-bout where you can continue straight on a path to reach a river or take the road that goes left past the **playing field**. Many important cricket, soccer, and rounders matches take place on this playing field as it is one of the largest and best maintained fields on the island. Feel free to stop and watch a game if you have the time.

At the playing field, you'll reach a T-intersection. Go left to see the historic

Coal Pot Soap

One of Dominica's most successful grassroots projects, the Coal Pot, was started in the early 2000s by a U.S. Peace Corps Volunteer alongside a tenacious Dominican, Avriel James. Built on the historic Geneva Estate, they now manufacture over 20 varieties of natural homemade soaps, creams, massage oils, mud masks, facial products, bath salts, skin ointments, and candles – some of which are sold in Kalinago woven containers. The products are eco-friendly and available for sale throughout Roseau. Avriel always enjoys visitors, but be sure to call ahead to arrange a time, as it is a small manufacturer without a designated public affairs person. *Grand Bay, Tel: 767-446-4685; www.coalpot-soaps.com, info@coalpot-soaps.com.*

Geneva Estate, where the **Coal Pot Soap Factory** (see box) and **Grand Bay Arts and Crafts Centre** are located.

Also referred to as GTEC, Grand Bay Arts and Crafts Centre is located in a small stone building with orange shutters and houses the woodcarvings and crafts of several local artists. Come by in the afternoon to see the artists at work. The hours of operation are supposedly 8am-4pm Mon-Fri but they can be rather irregular here so give Hilroy a call (Tel: 767-316-5788) if you want to stop by and no one is arround.

Continuing in this direction will bring you back to the junction that will lead you to Roseau.

Grand Bay hosts a lively village feast called the **Feast of St. Isadore,** which takes place in May. Activities include parades, concerts, and a lovely church service in which everyone dresses in traditional Creole attire and brings the best of their produce to the service to offer as thanks for a fruitful season. Many cultural activities with music and dancing take place throughout the day and a Creole lunch is available after the service. Contact the village council at 767-446-3307 for exact dates.

Spotlight on Local Talent: Michele Henderson

If you spend enough time at the Old Fort Bar on L'allay you are bound to eventually run into Michele or her musical husband who often relax and have a drink between their hectic travel schedules. Born and raised in Grand Bay, Michele is a Dominican superstar whose musical talents - that include zouk, rhythm and blues, jazz, reggae, and retro soul - have won her numerous awards throughout the Caribbean and beyond. She's always on stage at the World Creole Music Festival in October and has been asked to perform in venues as far away as Estonia and Los Angeles. She's an incredibly talented woman and is the pride of Dominica. You can hear samples of her music and purchase an album at www.michelehenderson.com

---

The **Perdu Temps** trailhead (see hiking detail on page 295) starts just outside of the village on the road going towards Roseau. Starting from this side is said to be the easier than beginning in Delices, and you'll get to end your hike at the beautiful White River or Victoria Falls, which is a nice way to reward yourself for finishing a challenging hike. Be sure to stop at Brother Pump's farm at his amazing highland homestead about half-way through.

TETE MORNE

If you head uphill from L'allay, you will pass through tiny hamlets, farms, and old estates until you reach the top and the village of Tete Morne, which means "head of the mountain." There are portions of road in these heights that retain their original state for their historical importance as they were built by slaves using huge rocks carried all the way up from the bay below.

You will notice that the weather here is very cool but still very humid. This makes for good agricultural conditions and farming is a popular occupation in Tete Morne. There is a wonderful hike from the village, down through forest and farms, that will put you right in the middle of the **Soufrière Hot Springs** pools. As you reach the trailhead and before you head down there is a spot where a bench was put in that allows you to see the Caribbean Sea and Atlantic Ocean at the same time. It's a wonderful place to stop and have a picnic. This pleasant downhill hike may require

The South

sturdy knees but for the effort, you'll be humbled by a grove of soaring Gommier and sprawling Chatanierre trees.

Getting to Tete Morne isn't easy if you don't have your own transport since there is only one bus and most of the people who live there don't have a car so the bus is always full. You actually have a better chance of picking up the bus in Roseau than in Grand Bay and hitching a ride can take a really long time as well. Walking is sometimes the best option.

Point Michel to Scotts Head

POINTE MICHEL

You can't miss Pointe Michel as you drive down the coast. It will be the place where you feel like your life may be in danger when you try to squeeze your way through the narrow piece of road with a 20-foot drop into the sea on one side and a giant car-eating gutter on the other. Don't worry. Loads of people drive through here daily and I have yet to hear about a disaster. And although it would be nice if they fixed this road, it's nearly impossible to maintain since storms and high waves errode the road constantly. So drive with care and enjoy this fun fishing village as you drive slowly through.

What is now an energetic village comprised of fishermen and farmers, 200 years ago was made up of coffee plantations owned by the French. In 1902, after the volcanic eruption of Mt. Pele, refugees from Martinique fled their island by boat and many ended up on the shores of Pt. Michel and settled in the village. If you pass through this area around sundown, be sure to stop by the **Fish Pot** where fresh fish is steamed or fried and served up nightly with fried plantains and a juice or Kubuli. This spot makes for an absolutely wonderful dinner and great place to watch the sunset.

After leaving Point Michel, just as the road turns left to head uphill you will pass **Irie Safari**, the home of **Champagne Reef**, the most popular snorkeling spot on the island because of the warm bubbles and abundance of underwater creatures. Coming here when there are cruise shippers afoot will only end in disappointment. Get here in the early morning or early evening to escape the crowds and actually see the fish and turtles.

SOUFRIÈRE

When you descend the windy road and just before you reach the village of Soufrière, you'll pass over a cliff and popular dive site known as **La Souciere**, or "The Sorceress." Legend has it that Carib men threw their adulterous wives off of this cliff and the ill-fated women put a curse on this site, which they continue to haunt to this very day. Another name for the cliff is Carib Leap and the story goes that Carib warriors would jump off of the cliff to their death rather than endure enslavement by their colonist captors. But murder, haunting, and suicide aside, this really is a great dive site with a vertical wall and a plethora of marine life and coral to discover.

As you arrive in Soufrière you'll come to a junction. Take a right to get to the village and coast, which sits on the edge of a volcanic caldera. You could easily spend the entire day in Soufrière as there is plenty to see and do in this small village of 900. Start by checking out the **Catholic Church**, one of the oldest churches on the island that sits on the right hand side of the road as you enter the village proper. You can take a look inside and admire the beautiful murals – painted by the local historian, Dr. Lennox Honychurch – depicting village life by the sea. The church is in the process of undergoing some much needed renovations so be sure to drop some change in the donation bucket if you stop by.

There is a **cave** at the foot of the cliffs by the church where some of the earliest settlers may have found refuge. Archeologists have found artifacts here dating back to some of the very earliest Amerindian tribes in this area. There is now a small shrine above the cave and an alter in front of it that is sometimes used for services.

In front of the church is a natural hot pool that is nice to relax in during high tide. Locals usually build up rocks around the hot area to form a **natural hot tub,** which also makes it easier to locate. Bring your sandals as the beach in this portion is rocky and can be very hot. There is good **snorkeling** (away from the crowds) about 300 feet in front of the church and a nice **swimming** spot is just off of the main dock in the village where the water is calm. You'll surely be entertained by local children doing flips off of the dock. Across from the dock is Nature Island Dive, the local dive operator that also provides kayaking excursions, snorkeling trips, and occasionally bike tours. The staff is very friendly and helpful should you just need some guidance.

Just past Nature Island Dive are the **ruins of the old Rose's Lime factory**. Rose's Lime Company was one of the most successful businesses ever based in Dominica, bringing prosperity and employment the villages of Soufrière and Scotts Head. In the 1970s they pulled out of the country because of the economy and the political upheaval that was occuring during that time.

The **Sulphur Springs**, for which the village is named, were originally built by the French for use by their soldiers when they occupied the island. From the main junction where you first arrive, head left and follow signs to the baths. Check out the Interpretation Center before you enter the springs to learn about history, geology, and indigenous plants and wildlife of the region. Walk down the path to a large cement pool or continue to a few

> If you are visiting Soufrière in the winter, you will notice the distinct smell of nutmeg on this road. This road is lined with nutmeg trees and as the seeds fall and get run over the entire area smells of sweet spice.

smaller private pools. Trails loop around the area for easy walking and the chance to bath in a warm waterfall. Picnicking area, changing rooms, and bathrooms are on site. Buy your site pass at any designated spot before entrance (you will see signs outside of shops that sell the passes).

This is also the start of the trail that heads up the mountain to **Tete Morne** (about 1.5 hours).

A fun side trip while you are in Soufrière is to head up to the tiny and adorable village of **Gallion**. You can get to Gallion by either asking a bus driver to take you up from the main junction for a nominal fee or by taking a left at the junction (when you enter from Roseau) and then taking a right down a narrow road and following it a short distance to the village. This is a wonderful lookout point and great place for a picnic and to watch the sunset. There is a hike (see hiking detail on page 282) to this village starting at Scotts Head with an optional side trip to Crabier, another *Pirates of the Caribbean* filming site. The trek offers beautiful hilltop pastures with gardens, fruit trees, and wonderful views of Martinique.

Diving Fest

If you came to Dominica to Dive or are interested in giving it a try, plan your trip to overlap with **Dive Fest** in July. Most of the activities take place in the Soufrière/Scotts Head area and are likely to include treasure hunts, photography competitions, canoe races, and lots of introductory scuba lessons for the novice diver. You can find specific dates at http://dominicawatersports.com/divefest.cfm.

SCOTTS HEAD

The road between Scotts Head and Soufrière is a little over a mile and makes for a nice walk along the sea. Be sure to wear a hat as there is no shade along the road. The village itself is home to roughly 900 people and is predominantly a fishing commu-

> Contrary to rumors, this village is not named after a Scottsman who had his head chopped off here!

nity, though a number of people also work in Roseau. As you walk through the village past the fisheries complex you will pass colorfully painted wooden boats and see fishermen sitting in the shade repairing their nets and traps.

At the end of the village when you walk across the narrow strip of land that is straddled by the Caribbean and Atlantic you'll reach **Fort Cachacrou**. The Carib name, *Cachacrou*, means "hat which is being eaten" (by the sea) and is a historical place of interest and the southernmost point of the island. Although now almost completely in ruin, this was once an important lookout point and line of defense for the British military in its attempts to protect the island from the French coming through the Martinique Channel. Named after Lieutenant Governor George Scott, it was constructed in 1765 and included gun batteries placed at various levels, soldier's barracks, kitchens, cisterns, a powder magazine, and a jetty. This was also a signaling station that would be the starting point for sending messages up the western coast. The most notable action at the fort happened on 7 September 1778 when the British were defeated by the French. The villagers of Cachacrou aided the French by getting the British soldiers drunk at a party the night before and then spiked the cannons with sand. Much of the fort has slipped into the sea since it closed in 1854.

Just below the fort is a wonderful **snorkeling area** with a dramatic drop off where turtles are sometimes sighted as well as calm shallow reefs. These cliffs are also the sight of seabird nesting areas so look for them as you swim around the bay. Local children love to come here and may even help you find conch sells and sand

---

Nutmeg and Mace

Both of these spices are products of the same fruit. When the round, yellow fruit is ripe, it splits open to reveal a lacy, bright-red seed, under which can be found the hard brown shell that holds the nutmeg. To harvest the nutmeg you can pick the fruit and easily pull out the red seed once the fruit spilts on its own. Let it dry out in the sun until the waxy red outer covering (which is actually mace) has dulled to nearly a brown color. The outer shell can then be removed and the little ball inside that you hear rattling around is the nutmeg. The seeds keep for a long time so if you happen across some, bring it home and have fresh spice year round! It takes more than 300 pounds of nutmeg to yield one pound of the spice!

dollars. However, because this is a marine reserve, politely decline their offers as it is illegal and unhealthy for the environment to take any shells or coral.

There are a number of restaurants and shops where you can get a good local lunch, one of the more popular ones being **Chez Wen**, which is on the main road in the village. Another popular spot across the street from the bay front is **Roger's.**

Sights & Activities

Bellevue Chopin Organic Farm Tour

Enjoy either a one-day or three-day tour of this beautiful area of the south while learning about traditional and sustainable methods of farming on the island. The one-day tour takes you through four gardens where you'll learn about the fruits, vegetables, flowers, and medicinal herbs that thrive on Dominica's soil and meet the people who grow them. Price includes a traditional lunch. The three-day tour includes accommodation, airport/ferry transfers, two meals per day, and four farm tours. ATV, Horseback Riding, and hiking options available as well for an added fee. *Bellevue Chopin, Tel: 767-316-2710, 767-315-1175, bcofmi@hotmail.com; Cost: One-day tour US$51pp, three-day tour US$140/pp; http://bellevueorganicfarmers.communitytourism.dm.*

Giraudel/Eggleston Community Farm & Flower Tour

Located on the slopes of Morne Anglais, this area of the island is known for its agricultural products and abundance of flowers. Arrange a cooking tour or garden tour by emailing the tourism group well in advance. They an also arrange a homestay with someone in the village so that you can really get a feel for Dominican village life. *giraudeleggleston@communitytourism.dm; Tel: 767-616-9335; http://giraudelegglestonflowers.communitytourism.dm.*

Culinary Tour

This tour was a finalist in the National Geographic Changemakers Geotourism Challenge and was designed by one of the most notable Domincans alive today, Atherton Martin. With a knowledgeable tour guide you will visit local farms and gardens and learn about sustainable organic agriculture, plant varieties on the island, and meet the farmers themselves who provide food for this community. You'll also hear traditional tunes played by local musicians. At the end of the tour, with Atherton's wife, Fae, a renowned cook who has been featured in several Caribbean publications, you'll learn to make a conventional meal out of the produce you encountered during your tour and enjoy fresh juice and a delicious lunch. *Giraudel; Tel: 767-448-8839; exotica@cwdom.dm; Cost: $US50/pp; 8 person minimum, 16 person max.*

ATV Through the Rainforest

Located in the rainforest on the hills of Morne Anglais, **Highride Nature Adventures**, an ATV tour company, will take you through forests, farms, and into some of the more remote areas of Dominica where you can stop and look for many of the island's unique plants, birds, and animals. Great rainy day activity as the tour runs rain or shine. They provide helmets, goggles, raingear, and lessons. *Bellevue Chopin; Tel: 767-448-6296, 767-440-2117; www.avirtualdominica.com/highrideadventures, highriders@cwdom.dm; Cost: US$65/pp for 1 hour.*

The South

Snorkel at Scotts Head

Scotts Head has become a very popular place to snorkel for both locals and tourists. To get there, drive to the end of the road and park your car on the narrow strip of land the lies between the ocean and the sea. If you are taking the bus, just let them know where you are going and they'll drop you at the end of the road. Walk along the Caribbean side of the small peninsula (called Cachacrou) until you come to a cement wall and rocky beach. As you swim out you'll find a shallow reef and eventually you'll reach a dramatic drop off. Baracudas and rays can be sighted in this area as well as small colorful reef fish. Swimming around the western end of the point (be mindful of the current) also has some shallow reefs that are great for snorkeling. Keep in mind that there is no safe spot to leave your valuables in this area. The fisheries warden may ask for a marine reserve fee of US$2 for using this area.

Soufrière Snorkeling

A lesser-known snorkeling area where you are more likely to have the place to yourself is right in front of the Soufrière Catholic Church, about 300 feet out to the Soufrière pinnacles. Turtle sightings are somewhat common as well as lots of colorful fish. If you notice that some areas are warmer than others it can be attributed to warm bubbles from the underground volcanic gasses that sometimes seep up through the ocean floor.

WATERSPORT OPERATORS

Nature Island Dive Located right on the Soufrière/Scotts Head Marine Reserve, this small and well-reputed dive shop prides itself on its personalized service. Offers a variety of PADI certification courses, as well as snorkel gear rental, dive packages, and kayaking excursions. Be sure to call a day in advance to arrange. *Soufrière; Tel: 767-449-8181; natureidive@cwdom.dm, www.natureislanddive.com; Cost for two tank dive: US$80.*

Al Dive & W.A.T.E.R. Sports Small and friendly family-owned dive shop that offers very personalized service in a safe and welcoming environment. Billy and Samantha will create an aquatic adventure catered to you or your group for a very reasonable price. Services include dive certification, guided snorkeling, kayaking, fishing, whale/dolphin watching, and yachting services. *Loubiere; Tel: 767-440-3483, 767-275-3483; aldive@aldive.com, www.aldive.com; Cost for two tank dive: US$80.*

Irie Safari Snorkel Adventures This popular snorkeling hot spot is home to Champagne Reef, a geothermal area where volcanic gasses seep up through the sea floor in the form of warm bubbles and, as some say, makes one feel like they are swimming through a glass of champagne. When not completely overtaken by tourists, you may encounter sea turtles, squid, sea horses, and a variety of colorful fish. If a cruise ship is in port, however, you are likely to see more tourists than sea life. Knowledgeable staff can help you identify any unknown fish and direct you on the best places to check out on the reef. Diving also available if arranged in advance. Snackette, showers, changing rooms, bathroom, and bag storage on site. Try their rum punch after your dip in the sea and look for iguanas roaming the property. *Champagne; Tel: 767-440-5085; iriesafari@cwdom.dm; Hours: daily 9am-4:30pm; Cost: US$12 for snorkel equipment rental.*

Eateries & Nightclubs

Melvina's Bar and Restaurant This seaside hot spot is a favorite among locals on Friday and Saturday nights, and is also open as a restaurant during the day. Starting around 10pm you can find rum punch flowing, locals dancing, and get some incredible steamed fish (it sells fast!). Melvina is known for her juice and rum punch and has been recently featured in a cookbook. She also rents vacation property and snorkel gear. *Located on the road between Point Michel and Champagne; Tel: 767-440-5480; Hours: 9am-very late Friday and Saturday, 12pm-onwards on Sunday.*

Fish Pot Locals flock to the Fish Pot in the evenings, located at the southern end of Pt. Michel, to get some of the best fresh fish on the island. Caught that day and steamed in a banana leaf, it doesn't get better than this. Red fish and Mahi Mahi are the favorites. If you get there by 6pm, you can snag a seat outside on the bench and watch the sun set while enjoying a great evening sea breeze. *Pt. Michel; Hours: 6pm-onwards.*

Chez Wen Its seaside location makes this a great lunch spot after a day of snorkeling at Scotts Head. You can watch the fishermen bring in their catch or enjoy a picturesque sunset while dining on reasonably priced fresh fish, Creole food or sandwiches. Vegetarian options are limited to egg or cheese sandwiches and fries. *Scotts Head; Tel: 767-448-6668; Cost: EC$12-$35.*

Roger's Bar and Restaurant Small bar/snackette on the beachfront across from the fisheries complex in Scotts Head. Serves Creole lunches and sandwiches and is popular with the locals. They have a porch where you can eat your lunch and watch the fishermen repair their nets and bring in their catch. *Scotts Head; Tel: 767-448-7851, 767-265-1839; Hours: 10am-8pm; Cost: EC$8-$25.*

Nick's Shop Located at the junction when you initially enter Grand Bay from Roseau, Nick's shop is the one with the large red Kubuli sign on top. Although it's essentially just a snackette, the grilled bread and cheese is cheap and delicious. Nick, the shop owner, is a friendly and very knowledgeable guy who also happens to be a hiking guide and can tell you whatever you want to know about the area. He also owns a campsite on his property, which you can rent for very reasonable prices. A good place to grab a bush rum or Kubuli while you wait for a bus. *Grand Bay Junction.*

The Old Fort One of the classier joints in Grand Bay and located centrally on the main drag, L'allay, you can't miss it. They host shows and parties here on the weekends but in general it's just a great place to grab a drink. You may even run into local celebrity and musician, Michele Henderson (pg 221), who resides in Grand Bay and frequents Old Fort when she's not on tour. *L'Allay, Grand Bay; Hours: 5pm-late.*

The Hole Colleur Bar This snackette is a great place for a cheap but tasty Creole dinner. Located directly across the street from the Old Fort, tucked away in a hole (hence the name) with a full line up of provisions, chicken, fish, and snacks and friendly service. Vegetarian options available. *L'Allay, Grand Bay; Hours: 11am-late; Cost: EC$12.*

Spiders If you find yourself at the Loubiere junction late in the evening and want a drink or bite to eat, the fish pies here are surprisingly tasty. Don't let the dark atmosphere scare you off – this is a great place to have a drink and socialize with some very friendly locals. *Loubiere Junction; Hours: 10pm-onwards.*

Bellevue Bread Shop If you are driving through Bellevue and you happen to see, on the crest of the hill, a very large woman in a very small shack and a lot of folks milling around outside, then you have just found some of the best bread on the island. It's cooked in a wood stove by the large woman's husband and brought over straight away to be sold in the tiny shack. You can get a loaf for EC$1 or larger for EC$2. She also sells a variety of baked treats like banana muffins and small cakes. *Bellevue Chopin; Hours: flexible but usually M-F 10am-4pm.*

Services

Greens Supermarket A relatively comprehensive grocery store, with basic supplies. *Loubiere; Hours: M-Sa 8am-8pm.*

Smartbuy Grocery Small grocery store with only very basic dry goods and snacks. *Loubiere; Hours: daily 8am-9pm; Tel: 767-440-6540*

Accommodations

Budget

The Hide Out Quaint, rustic, and charming wooden house tucked away next to the Geneva River. Swiss-Dominican Rastafarian owners, Rahel and Octave Joseph, are very welcoming hosts who love to share their knowledge of the island and its flora and fauna with guests. Octave is a tour guide and will happily gather and share whatever fruit is in season. A great place to get away from the daily grind while being completely enveloped by nature. *Amenities: Full kitchen, barbeque grill, deck, river access; Note: Solar powered lights but no electrical outlets. You may, however, use the owners' home outlets as needed. Grand Bay; 1 cottage that can sleep up to 6; Tel: 767-446-4642, 767-277-8750, 767-277-8751; www.hideout.ch; seedatriva@yahoo.com; Cost: US$60 dbl, US$80 quad, US$100 six person (discounted weekly rates available).*

Riverbank Farm Campsite Campsite run by friendly and knowledgeable local tour guide, Nick Jacobs, near the Geneva River in Grand Bay. No real amenities here (meaning you will be bathing in the river) and you must provide your own tent. You can usually find Nick working at the Kubuli shop at the Grand Bay junction when you first enter the village, and can make arrangements with him there. *Grand Bay; Tel: 767-446-4141, 767-225-8866; Cost: US$5.*

Oceanview Apartments These self-contained studio apartments are located up a steep hill from Roger's Bar and are a good budget option if you want to stay in the Soufrière/Scotts Head area. The apartments themselves are small and a bit rundown but for the price and location it's a good deal. Apartments are surrounded by gardens with a great view of the sea and surrounding area. Owners supply fresh juice and fruit from the fruit trees on the property. *Amenities: fans, mosquito nets, veranda, hammock, cable TV, Wi-Fi. Scotts Head; 3 apartments (sleeps 3-4); Tel: 767-449-8266; www.avirtualdominica.com/oceanview_apts, oceanview_apts@hotmail.com; Cost: US$50 sgl, US$60 dbl.*

Oceanview Cottage If you prefer falling asleep to the sound of waves rather than having lots of amenities, then here is your spot. This self-contained cottage is located on the main road (with regular fast moving traffic) between Soufrière and Scotts Head directly across from the sea. This spacious wood and stone cottage is in a convenient spot if you plan on spending a lot of time diving in the marine reserve. Take advantage of the open-air patio and hammocks in the evenings when the sun is setting. *Amenities: fans, radio, hot water, mosquito nets. Soufrière; 2 bedroom cottage (sleeps 4); Tel: 767-449-8266; oceanview_apts@hotmail.com; Cost: US$60 sgl/dbl, US$15 for each extra person (max. 2).*

Soufrière Springs Guesthouse This very simple guesthouse is located on the road to the sulphur springs in a very quiet area, removed from the village itself. These plain but clean and tidy rooms consist of a tiled floor, double bed, small closet, and table. You get what you pay for here (please note there is no hot water). *Amenities: fans, porch, restaurant on site. Soufrière; 2 rooms (dbls); Tel: 767-440-4926, 767-449-8281; Cost: US$34.*

Camp Bless Campground Located on a farm access road just north of Grand Bay, this friendly vegan farmer will open up his lower field to hikers and travelers. Not much here in the way of amenities but it's not a terribly far walk to get to a river. *Grand Bay; Tel: 767-614-0846; Cost: EC$20.*

Top-End

Villa Etoli This two bedroom, two bath house is very spacious, bright, comfortable, and inviting and in a great location if you want to spend time diving and snorkeling. Having all the sporting equipment in your rental and at your disposal makes this a fun rental option. Definitely one of the best options for the area. *Amenities: A/C, cable TV, internet, barbeque grill, outdoor gazebo, mountain bikes, kayaks, and snorkel gear for guests use. Scotts Head; 2 bedroom villa (sleeps 4) and separate cottage available upon request; Tel: 767-448-6961, 767-265-9028, 767-225-0751;aetienne@vipowernet.net; Cost: US$150 dbl, US$200 quad, US$250 villa.*

Exotica Cottages Situated high on the slopes of Morne Anglais, these quiet and comfortable cottages are a great escape to get away from it all. The front of the cottages open up almost completely to the surrounding mountains to allow for the indoors to mingle with the out. The living room contains sofa beds to allow for family accommodation. The owners are exceptional hosts and their culinary tour was a finalist in the National Geographic award for being one of the best geo-tours in the world. *Amenities: verandas, Wi-Fi, fans, hairdryer, telephones, tours, car rental arrangement, airport transfer arrangement, long-term rates available. Giraudel; 8 cottages (sleeps 2-4); Tel: 767-448-8839, 767-448-8849; exotica@cwdom.dm, www.exotica-cottages.com; Cost: US$110 sgl, US$160 dbl.*

The Interior

Stretching through the island's central interior region and covering nearly two-thirds of the land, approximately 40,000 acres of rainforest make up the most peaceful and serene area on the island. The Smithsonian Institute aptly described this environment as "a giant plant laboratory, unchanged for 10,000 years." With over 30 waterfalls, endless rivers, three freshwater lakes, 50 fumaroles, a boiling lake, 1,200 plant species and the largest concentration of volcanoes in the world, this region is not surprisingly a **UNESCO World Heritage Site.** The first site, in fact, in the Eastern Caribbean to receive this recognition.

The government set aside the **Northern and Central Forest Reserves** in the 1950s and the **Morne Trois Pitons National Park** in 1975 in an effort to protect the island's rich biodiversity and virgin forest while safeguarding the unique ecology of the area. It is the largest area of rainforest in the Lesser Antilles and has fortunately set the island up as the perfect place to promote eco-tourism, even before it was the "in" thing to do. With these reserves in place, it allows protection for the important watersheds that provide the island with a reliable and clean water supply.

A hike to the top of **Morne Trois Pitons** (see hiking detail on page 262), a series of three peaks the tallest of which is the second tallest peak on the island, is a challenging affair. The walk up is very strenuous with a few areas that require rope climbs and it can be extremely muddy on a wet day which makes coming down almost as difficult as going up. Wear long pants on this hike to avoid getting cut by

---

TOP FIVES

Take an easy stroll to the Emerald Pool to visit a picturesque waterfall set amidst a backdrop of lush green vegetation and follow the ancient Carib Trace trail down to Castle Bruce. (pg 231)

Visit Dominica's newest natural formation, the stunning Miracle Lake. When you get there, check in with Rambo to get a full tour of the area and to learn the history of this island "miracle." (pg 231)

Retrace the steps of the old maroon (escaped slave) encampment at Jacko Steps. (pg 234)

Visit one of the highest peaks in Dominica and see the layers of rainforest change as you scale the ridges of Morne Trois Piton. (pg 230)

the razor grass that lines the trail and keep in mind that you don't want to grab vegetation to help you up for that very reason. The top is generally cloudy, windy and cold so bring a long sleeve shirt if you plan to spend any time at the summit. One of the highlights of this hike is seeing the rainforest change as you move up in elevation. The elfin forest at the peak is really quite remarkable.

For an easy and enjoyable downhill hike, head to the increasingly popular **Emerald Pool** (see hiking detail on page 268), a small waterfall that flows into a sparkling green pool surrounded by ferns, flowers, and lush vegetation. It's one of the easiest waterfalls to get to on the island which is why it is packed full of tourists on cruise ship days. To escape the crowds, once you view the falls follow the signs for the **Carib Trace Trail**, also known as the old Castle Bruce road, to stroll down this historic path that was once used by Caribs over 800 years ago and continued to be used by everyone who settled in the area up until the 1960s. It was the only conduit from the east coast to Roseau before roads were built and until 1965 people traveled this road by foot or donkey between Castle Bruce and Roseau to carry their goods to sell at market or conduct official business in the capital. The trail still contains old stones that were laid in 1828 and passes by some beautiful rivers and valleys along the way. It will take you through some flat banana farms and deposit you near the secondary school in Castle Bruce.

For a less-crowded waterfall experience with fairly quick and easy access, visit **Spanny Falls** (also known as Penrice Falls). These two tall thin cascades sit just 20 minutes off the road, by foot, and the tallest of which has a nice swimming pool. To find the trail, head north from Pont Casse on the road that leads to Marigot. You'll reach the village of Bells about two and a half miles down the road. Look for Spanny's Bar (they maintain the trail) and 20 yards south of the bar is the trailhead.

Another easily accessible collection of waterfalls that can be reached just off of the Layou-Pont Casse road is **Soltoun Falls**. A 20-minute hike down a steep trail brings you to one main fall and smaller delicate cascades that glisten as they shoot over a fern covered cliff in to a gorgeous pool below. See hiking guide (pg 286) and follow the path backwards from point "N."

The **Layou River**, Dominica's longest river, runs through the central western region of the interior and empties into the sea just south of St. Joseph. This river is popular for its natural hot springs along its bank, deep river pools and depth and small rapids that make it an ideal river tubing location. The **Pagua River** is another one of Dominica's longest and most popular rivers and runs from the heights of the **Central Forest Reserve** all the way to Pagua Bay where it spills out into the Atlantic. This is another spectacular river with many deep pools available for swimming and bathing and supports a wide array of birds, fish and wildlife.

A visit to Dominica's newest natural feature, **Miracle Lake**, is well worth your time if you are in the area. Created by a landslide in 1997, the land created a dam and blocked up a small river that flowed at the bottom of a gorge. The gorge eventually filled up and resulted in a stunningly beautiful lake. You can drive to the lake if you have a jeep with 4WD or hike up the rough road from St. Joseph to get to the trailhead (see map on page 143). The land is privately owned by a man nicknamed "Rambo" who will be happy to give you a tour of the area when you arrive with the option of walking along a trail that he has created.

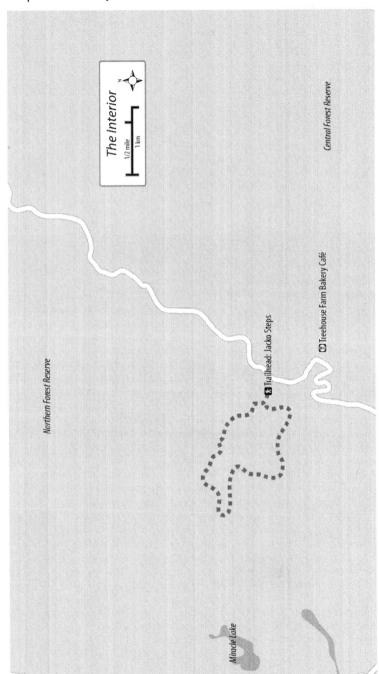

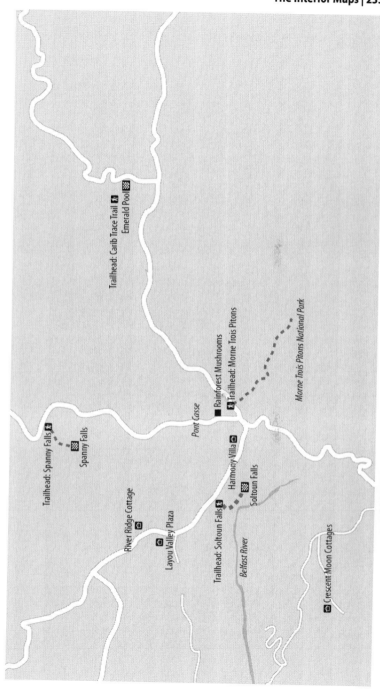

The Interior

Trailhead: Carib Trace Trail
Emerald Pool

Rainforest Mushrooms
Trailhead: Morne Trois Pitons

Morne Trois Pitons National Park

Pont Casse

Trailhead: Spanny Falls
Spanny Falls

Harmony Villa
Soltoun Falls

River Ridge Cottage
Layou Valley Plaza

Trailhead: Soltoun Falls

Belfast River

Crescent Moon Cottages

The **Northern Forest Reserve** and **Morne Diablotin National Park** make up the northern region of the interior and house Dominica's highest peak, **Morne Diablotin**, at 4,747 feet. The **Syndicate Nature Trail**, an easy one-mile hike that begins in the village of Dublanc, will start you on a journey to the base of this peak and is one of the best spots to go bird watching on the island. This area is a natural parrot habitat and you are more likely to see the endangered Sisserou parrot (pg 47) here than anywhere else on the island. The Jacko parrot and several species of hummingbirds also inhabit this area. The trees are also worth mentioning for their variety and unique features including the chatanier with huge buttress roots sometimes spanning over 30 feet across. Others have prop roots that support the growth of the tree without actually touching the ground. Check out the small **visitors center**, which has information on the plants, animals, and birds of the region as well as restroom facilities and refreshments. There is a junction midway along the trail where you can begin your ascent to the top of **Morne Diablotin** (see hiking detail on page 258), a strenuous hike that will likely deposit you in the middle of a cloud. If you are lucky and it happens to be clear that day, the views are spectacular.

To traverse the interior of the Northern Forest Reserve, try segment 8 of the Waitukubuli National Trail (see hiking detail on page 279). Notable for being the favorite segment of the WNT, this will take you through huge sections of primary forest and an excellent place to see wildlife and parrots including the elusive wild pigs. It's a challenging hike but you'll likely have the trail to yourself and will get to truly experience Dominica's unspoiled forest.

The **maroons** (escaped slaves) took advantage of this rugged and densely forested terrain and set up encampments in the late 1700s and early 1800s. Here, the maroons hid from their owners and staged organized attacks against the slaveholders. **Jacko Steps** (see hiking detail on page 292), in the upper region of the Layou Valley near the village of Bells, was named after the maroon chief, Jacko, who had steps carved into the steep slope of the mountain for easier ascents and descents into the camps. This is now a popular hiking spot and the steps still remain to make your walk down a bit easier

If you stay in the area around Pont Casse, you'll be centrally located and in a good spot to check out multiple parts of the island. However, you're typically far from any major villages, restaurants, or other services so plan ahead if you are buying groceries. Temperatures are cooler in the interior at the higher elevations so be sure to bring a long sleeved shirt and be prepared for a fair amount of rain.

GETTING THERE

Buses through the interior can be found on the riverside in Roseau, between the bridges. Check the closest village to determine which bus to take. Most will be headed to Marigot, Castle Bruce, the Carib Reserve or the Rosalie area and will have to pass through the interior. They all run very infrequently, usually twice a day around noon and again around 5pm, returning to Roseau early in the morning, around 7am and again in the late afternoon. A bus from Roseau to Pont Casse is EC$5.50. If you are going further than Pont Casse expect to pay an extra dollar or two.

If you are driving it will be easier to get around since the roads are currently being rebuilt. The road from Pont Casse to Marigot is very narrow so take care when driving and always pull over if you feel you cannot pass safely. A lot of the hotels and guesthouses in the interior are far off the main road so you'll want to be sure to rent a 4WD vehicle to get around.

Sights & Activities

Rainforest Mushrooms

This unique attraction is what happens when you mix a little bit of mushroom farm, a little bit of art studio, a little bit of a vegetarian café with a touch of wildlife sanctuary. Brother Mathew Luke and his wife, Christine, have been living in harmony with the rainforest, nestled next to Morne Trois Piton National Park. They have developed a substantial and complex mushroom farm specializing in oyster mushrooms that will melt in your mouth. Tours are complete with an Ital vegetarian lunch, music jam session, art studio tour, and an occassional yoga class. If you just want to come by for lunch, reservations are highly recommended and it's well worth the stop. Look for the funky colorful sign just after Pond Casse on the right as you head towards Marigot. *Tel: 767-449-1836; Cost: lunch US$15, rainforestmushroomsdominica@yahoo.com, http://rainforestmushroomsdominica.wordpress.com*

Eateries

Treehouse Farm Bakery Café This amazing vegan café sources all of its produce from the surrounding farm. Pick up some plantain-mango bagels, cocoa cinnamon rolls, or eggplant pockets. Or stop by for some vegan banana "ice cream" with fresh roasted cocoa bean chips. Vegetarian chef, Donna, has been in the business for over 25 years and loves finding ways to use local ingredients in her favorite recipes. Take a minute to walk through their lush garden paths to view tropical flowers, fruit trees, herbs, and vegetables. *Belles; www.treehousebakerydominica.com; Tel: 767-615-5813.*

Trois Pitons Restaurant Located in Layou Valley Plaza Hotel, this restaurant just opened up under new management and, like the hotel, exhibits a nice blend of East and West in its cuisine and atmosphere. Restaurant is elegant and the view out the windows is spectacular. Call ahead for meals or just stop in to enjoy their full bar and snack menu. *Jimmit Warner Road; Tel: 767-449-1366, 767-617-6135, layouvalleyinn@gmail.com; Hours: 8am-9pm daily; Cost: EC$55 (lunch), EC$70 (dinner), EC$20 (snacks).*

Accommodations

Mid-Range

 Crescent Moon Cottages A highly recommended eco-lodge and agro-tourism site, this is a place that's worth splurging on. The owner, a trained chef, believes in the philosophy of the "slow food movement" in that he grows and produces all of the food for the restaurant on site in an organic and eco-friendly manner. Cabins are made from local materials and take advantage of the mountain views. Beautiful and simple with outstanding food and friendly owners makes this a good choice for lodging. *Amenities: internet, library, breakfast included, pool, hot pool, packages available. Sylvania (on the road from Canefield to Pond Casse); 4 cabins, sleep 2-4; Tel: 767-449-3449; www.crescentmooncabins.com, jeanviv@cwdom.dm; Cost: US$143-$160.*

River Ridge Cottage Great spot to get away from it all. Rustic and earthy but without being uncomfortable. Located on the edge of the rainforest and next to a river (great for bathing), these five acres are filled with fruit trees, flowers, and forest. The cottage is cute and almost romantic in its cozy simplicity. This place feels like the "real Dominica." Owner can cook organic meals upon request. *Amenities: full kitchen, pool, free fruit, eggs, and bread, dial-up internet, telephone. (Note: No hot water or electricity but can use generator at the owner's house next door); Road between Layou to Pond Casse; 2 bedroom cottage (sleeps 3-4); Tel: 767-449-2669; crystals@cwdom.dm; Cost: US$85.*

Layou Valley Plaza This accommodation was recently reopened with new management and unique style. The rooms range from small cozy singles to high-end family suites and are a mix of Asian-style and local materials. Bedding is ornate and some rooms have excellent views of the surrounding mountains. One efficiency apartment is also available for those who wish to do their own cooking. There is a restaurant on site and a DVD projection theatre with ample couch space for guests to enjoy music and movies. *Amenities: Wi-Fi, fans, reading area, theatre, patio, sports bar, conference room. Jimmit Warner Road; 14 rooms; Tel: 767-449-1366, 767-617-6135; layouvalleyinn@gmail.com; Cost: US$70-80 sgl, US$95 dbl, US$125 family.*

Top End

Harmony Villa This exquisite four bedroom, four and a half bathroom house nestled in the interior of the island is a beautiful mix of modern Caribbean and old-style country. Rooms are beautifully decorated with work by local artists and the wrap around veranda is a great place to relax and enjoy the fresh mountain air. Location makes it easily accessible to many attractions and because if its size, this is a great place for large groups. *Amenities: First morning's breakfast, essential groceries, housekeeping, night security, Wi-Fi, phone service, TV, DVD player, full kitchen, spa treatments available, tour arrangement, car rental arrangement, meals can be arranged. Pond Casse (on road from Layou); 4 bedroom house (sleeps 8 adults & 4 children); Tel: 767-265-0914; Skype: Carla Armour; carlaarmour@hotmail.com, www.harmonyvilla.com; Cost: US$250-$550.*

Hiking Guide

by Zak Klein

Hiking

GUIDES

Simply put, get a guide whenever possible. While the essential need for a guide varies with your experience, the chosen route and the expertise of your guide, it's clear that even on hikes where you could independently follow the trail a good guide can provide excellent cultural, natural, historical and social interpretation. In Dominica, there are certified guides and then there are the informal folks who know their home turf well and would like to make some money showing you around.

The certified tour guides receive certification from the Ministry of Tourism. They should be able to present an identifying certification card. At best, they'll provide transportation, have first aid supplies, and be timely, friendly, knowledgeable and courteous. At worst, they may overlook safety or physical needs of group or not know the exact location of some lesser known hikes in this guide. There's a spectrum of professionalism among Dominica's guides. Any guides specifically mentioned in this book are at the positive end of the spectrum.

The hikes listed in this guide are in three categories

For each of the 18 featured hikes, we include in-depth information including a brief overview, a map, an elevation profile, waypoints with descriptions and standardized hike data. These hikes are sorted further into three categories:

Well-Known classics Hikes with much merit that everyone has heard of. All guides (hiking and non-hiking) can at least get you to these trailhead. Don't be fooled however. Though popular, several of these are very challenging.

Soon-to-be WNT classics Custom sections of the Waitukubuli National Trail that are selected for their uniqueness. Not all of these routes are yet known to guides.

Off-the-beaten path adventures These include great variety, extreme destinations and require extra effort in planning and on the trail. Some are little-known and very rugged. Others require climbing, river-walking or bushwhacking overgrown trails. Some are unknown to most guides.

Additionally, you should know that the certified guide program largely supports the large-scale cruise ship passenger tours. Easily half of the certified guides in Dominica cater to that market, executing bus and transport tours mostly to the easiest destinations (Emerald Pool, Trafalgar Falls, and Kalinago Barana Aute, for example). Thus, not all guides are well-versed *hiking* guides. Hiking as recreation is a bit of a foreign concept to a portion of Dominicans and that extends to the community of guides. Hiking or "bush" experience plus official certification is the best of both worlds. When this book specifically mentions a guide, they're of this type.

To find a good guide, you should plan ahead utilizing one of the local tour services, your accommodation staff or the list in this book. We recommend agreeing to a price ahead of time. For a half-day, shorter hike, expect guides to charge at least US$30. For a full-day, deep in the bush on the most challenging routes, expect rates to start at a minimum of US$50 and easily reach US$100 or more. Rates are negotiable and most guides will try to make something work for you. Some of the highest rates are asked for by the most experienced guides that typically have full-time work elsewhere as foresters, scientists, hoteliers or civil servants. Going in a group will obviously save you money as guides often reduce their price per person.

If your best efforts and prior planning can't produce a guide or spontaneity calls and you find yourself near a great hiking destination, you may end up connecting with an enterprising local who would love to point the way for free or escort you there for a fee. Sometimes this is all that's available. This on-the-ground assistance is essential, charming and can be a really great way to experience some local folks in their element while you share about your home culture. As far as safety, trust your instincts. By and large, Dominicans are friendly, eager and proud to share their natural treasures, but you can always deny the offer and remain in public view if it doesn't feel right.

Recommended Guides

Below are highly recommended guides and their regional specialty, along with their local phone numbers. Another great resource to finding a quality guide is found online at http://www.visit-dominica.com. Also, the Dominica Hotel and Tourism Association (Tel: 767-440-3430, http://www.dhta.org) has a list of credible guides.

Peter Green *All regions, Tel: 767-235-2270*

Jeffrey Charles (Extreme Dominica) *Roseau Valley, Tel: 767-285-7347*

Naithan and Alfred Rolle *Roseau Valley, Tel: 767-616-2047, 767-225-1791*

Clement Rabess (Hiker's Retreat) *Southeast, Tel: 767-446-1076*

Johnathon Anadome *Southeast, Tel: 767-276-2137*

Simon George *Southeast, Tel: 767-613-6049*

Israel James *Southeast, Victoria Falls, Tel: 767-265-8291, 767-613-1779*

Kelly Esprit *West, Tel: 767-245-7245*

Eric Hypolite *West, All Regions, Tel: 767-276-4252*

Stephen Durand *Varied, Tel: 767-265-0908*

Octave Joseph *Varied, Tel: 767-446-4642, 767-277-8750*

Nick Jacobs *Varied, Tel: 767-446-4141, 767-225-8866*

Hiking Guide

HAZARDS

Rivers

Many of the hikes listed involve river or stream crossings. Most crossings are shallow and short. These can be frequent (like the Perdu Temps hike) and deceptively hazardous. Often times the stream banks can be unstable and the rocks very slippery. If you're tempted to lunge from rock to rock to keep your feet dry, think twice. Often, getting your feet wet on the stream bottom is more secure, sparing you wipeouts, sprains and strains.

As for the larger, deeper river crossings, always be mindful of what's immediately downstream and use a walking stick or hiking partner for increased stability. Consider hiring a guide and always err on the side of caution when assessing your ability to accomplish a daunting crossing. Most drainages on the island are narrow and steep. For the largest rivers, that can spell serious danger for hikers. Because they begin high in the mountains where it rains heavily, these rivers can suddenly swell in their narrow canyons drowning or stranding hikers in flash floods. This tragedy has happened on the island, so steer clear of these hikes during big rain events.

Coastlines

The most dangerous portion of Dominica's coast is its rugged Atlantic shore. Here, the Gulf Stream slams into the shore with dramatic force. Coastal terraces that extend into the surf (L' Escalier Tete Chien, Dragon's Mouth, and Glasse Point) are attractive, but dangerous. Never linger in the splash zone of the surf. Sporadic large waves are known to surprise locals and tourists alike, knocking them down and sometimes tragically pulling them to sea. If you're on your way to one of these spots, locals will volunteer their weather observations, likely exclaiming "De sea coming rough!" if the swell is up that day.

Besides the powerful surf, the exposed coastal rock can be steep and unstable in sections and should be approached cautiously. Both Atlantic and Caribbean beaches can themselves be rugged; often composed of a jumble of medium to large cobbles that can twist an ankle. In addition, coastal destinations are usually more exposed to the sun. With consistent breeze and a cooling sea mist it can be deceptive how much sunshine one is getting. Seek shade at mid-day and cover up to avoid sunburn.

A final notable coastline hazard is the riptide or undertow current. These are known to lurk along some of the large bay beaches of the Atlantic coast (Castle Bruce, Rosalie, Londonderry, and La Plaine). Riptides can sweep swimmers out to sea and often occur near the mouth of major rivers where the outflow has cut channels through submerged sandbars. Keep close to shore and consider going no deeper than your waist at such beaches.

NAVIGATION

The key to not getting lost is staying found. The keys to staying found are estimating your progress along lines and keeping known points nearby or in sight. The lines are corridors like trails, roads, rivers and coastlines. The points can be junctions, mountaintops, notable buildings, clearings, and peninsulas.

If without a guide, you'll need good maps and an honest awareness of your own map and landform reading abilities. If you have room for improvement on either ability, then consider making a habit of asking locals to verify your progress; in effect helping you to "stay found." In the current age of smartphones and handheld navigation convenience, it's a welcome surprise to rediscover how efficient it is to simply ask someone on the corner for directions. It can be a good way to make conversation and if you're asking about places to eat, you're likely to get a local opinion or update on the always shifty hours that businesses hold in Dominica.

If you do choose to explore with a GPS, then the challenge is finding good base maps of Dominica for your GPS unit. Aim to resolve this *before* you depart for Dominica. You may not find what you need among the proprietary maps for sale for your particular unit. If you have a Garmin unit and can read topography well, then you'll enjoy the data available at http://rwsmaps.griffel.se/. These maps are developed by a talented amateur, so consider donating if you make use of his work.

If you're new to using GPS to navigate, please understand that GPS units have limitations. Besides being battery-powered, breakable and losable, they are no substitute for a guide. Using the location and track information to make sound decisions still requires map and land reading ability, good judgment and often times a quick cross-reference with other resources: a map or locals.

Maps

In addition to the maps found in this book, you may want to visit the **Division of Lands and Surveys** in Roseau on Cork St, between Independence and Bath. They have a selection of topographic maps at different scales available for sale ($30EC to $50EC each). These maps contrast strongly to the cartoonish pamphlet maps distributed for free around the island. The topographic maps are very accurate in their dimensions and thus complement the visitor pamphlet maps that, while inaccurate in labeling and dimension, highlight popular attractions well.

The best bargain is a sturdy, full-color map of the entire island. At the office, it's known as the "tourist" or "visitor" map and is 1:50,000 scale with a 250-foot contour interval. It can also make a good gift or souvenir for friends or family who happen to be cartophiles (map-lovers)!

For reading the terrain for hiking, we recommend the three-part 1:25,000 series with a 50-foot contour interval. The Lands and Surveys Office has a dwindling stock of these that won't last long. Both series were produced by the British Ordnance Survey decades ago and are thus in short supply. These maps are great, illustrating the most complete listing of village, water, and landform names, and are a true joy for folks that can read topography well. Printed years ago, the only drawback is that they don't reflect some of the road, agriculture and village development of the last 30 years. In addition, these maps show "footpath" lines that have been grown over in the last few decades. There is currently an effort underway by the Division of Forestry to reclaim these historic trail corridors, but many are still obscured by jungle.

The other primary and exciting effort of trail development is the recent opening of the 97-mile **Waitukubuli National Trail** (WNT). This trail is divided into 14 segments of varied length, difficulty and character (this guide highlights six sections). Maps and pamphlets for the segments are currently under development and frequently updated. For the most up-to-date resources, visit the WNT Project Office (Tel: 767 266-3593; wntp@cwdom.dm; http://trail.agriculture.gov.dm/) on Hodges Lane in Roseau.

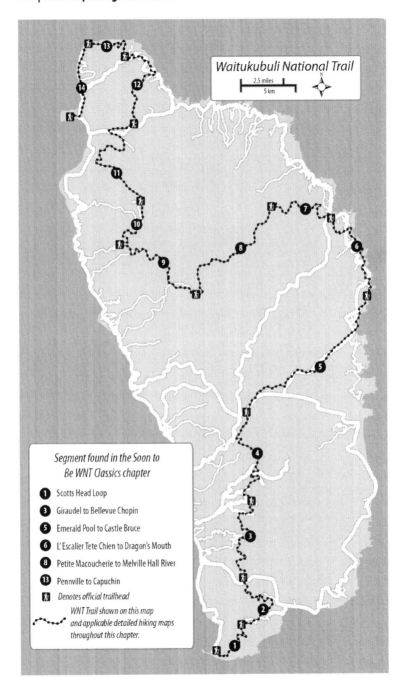

Waitukubuli National Trail

2.5 miles
5 km

N

Segment found in the Soon to
Be WNT Classics chapter

1 Scotts Head Loop

3 Giraudel to Bellevue Chopin

5 Emerald Pool to Castle Bruce

6 L'Escalier Tete Chien to Dragon's Mouth

8 Petite Macoucherie to Melville Hall River

13 Pennville to Capuchin

🚶 Denotes official trailhead

WNT Trail shown on this map
and applicable detailed hiking maps
throughout this chapter.

Below are the 14 segments of the WNT trail with corresponding data. See *Understanding Hike Data* on page 247 for for information on rating system used below.

WNT Segment	Total Difficulty	Terrain	Navi-gation	Distance (Miles)	Elevation Change (Feet)	Dura-tion
Scotts Head to Soufriere Estate						
1	6	3	3	3.9	3,700	5 hrs
Soufriere Estate to Bellevue Chopin						
2	6	3	3	6.8	5,200	6 hrs
Bellevue Chopin to Wotten Waven						
3	7	4	3	7.6	6,200	7 hrs
Wotten Waven to Pont Casse						
4	6	3	3	7.6	4,700	7 hrs
Pont Casse to Castle Bruce						
5	7	4	3	11.1	4,800	8 hrs
Castle Bruce to Hatten Garden						
6	7	3	4	7.6	4,900	7 hrs
Hatten Garden to First Camp						
7	6	3	3	5.8	3,600	5 hrs
First Camp to Petite Macoucherie						
8	8	4	4	8.5	6,100	7.5 hrs
Petite Macoucherie to Colihaut Heights						
9	9	5	4	7.8	6,400	9 hrs
Colihaut Heights to Syndicate						
10	6	3	3	4.3	3,600	3.5 hrs
Syndicate to Borne						
11	7	4	3	8.8	6,000	8 hrs
Borne to Penville (Delaford)						
12	8	4	4	7.8	6,500	8 hrs
Pennville to Capuchin						
13	6	3	3	4.2	3,700	4.5 hrs
Capuchin to Cabrits National Park						
14	5	2	3	5.2	1,800	4 hrs
			Totals	97 mi	67,200 ft	

Hiking Guide

Water Access & Treatment

For hikers, Dominica offers a great setup. The piped water is safe to drink and you'll find a public tap in every village, providing frequent access to potable water. Even better, for villages that perch high in the mountains near trailheads (Morne Prosper, Grand Fond, and Giraudel, for example), the last tap will typically be near the top of the road. Beyond the piped water, Dominica is flush with springs, streams and rivers. That said, some routes follow ridges with no accessible source. This guide highlights prominent dry stretches and last water sources to help you plan. Err on the side of hydration by filling two quarts per person as you set out. Chemically treat or purify natural sources as you would in any backcountry setting.

Fees

User fees are collected and passes issued to gain entry to 12 popular eco-tourist sites: Boeri Lake, Boiling Lake, Indian River, Cabrits National Park, Syndicate Nature Trail, Morne Trois Pitons Trail, Middleham Falls, Soufriere Sulfur Springs, Trafalgar Falls, Freshwater Lake, Emerald Pool, and Morne Diablotins Trail.

You can purchase 2 different passes:

Site Pass - US$5.00 (EC$13.50) - Allows for single visit to one site

Week Pass - US$12.00 (EC$32.04) - Allows for repeat visits to all sites

Passes are available at numerous tourism-centered sites across the island: visitor centers, the Forestry Office, Wildlife and Parks division at the Botanical Gardens and Bath Estate, and selected vendors near eco-tourism sites.

Trailheads & Transportation

Here are a few tips to successfully reach and return from your trailhead.

Guides or tour companies that arrange transportation to and from trailheads are a pricey, but a worry-free option.

Renting a car provides independence and the freedom to park at the trailhead.

Bus access is an option for trailheads that lie on the primary roads. These are mainly the around-the-island coastal roads and the several trans-insular roads that meet near **Pont Casse.** Keep in mind that you'll need to start early if this is

---

Sudden Darkness

Sudden darkness is often an unexpected feature of tropical hiking that surprises visitors from more temperate latitudes. Because the tropical sun follows a more overhead path through the sky, it rises and sets considerably faster than the sun in New York or London. (There, the sun travels on an angle to the horizon, extending dawn and dusk.) In Dominica, dawn and dusk are brief and darkness falls quickly. Aim to be at a road before you're caught in the blackness of the rainforest at night.

your plan. The daily pattern is that most buses depart toward Roseau between 6 and 8am, then surge back toward villages between 3 and 6pm. Try to make your hike plans work with that flow.

Hiring door-to-trailhead taxi service is expensive, but perhaps the best option for distant trailheads like **Syndicate / Morne Diablotions.**

For trailheads that lie distant from primary roads, you can also consider asking a bus driver to extend their route and to drop you at the trailhead. Many of them double as hired taxis and may accept if the price is right.

Worst-case scenario is that you may be able to reach only the village or region where your hike begins, not the precise trailhead. This is not uncommon, so prepare to walk a few extra miles.

Getting back can be the most trying part. It's common to linger at one of Dominica's natural jewels only to emerge at a lonely trailhead, mere minutes before dusk. Making arrangements – beyond crossing your fingers and hoping for a bus or hitchhiking opportunity to pass – can prevent this.

Understanding Hike Data

The hike data provides at-a-glance assessment of the hikes listed in this guide. This section includes explanation of Total Difficulty, Terrain Difficulty, Navigation Difficulty, Distance, Elevation Change and Duration.

Total Difficulty

Terrain Difficulty + Navigation Difficulty = Total Difficulty Rating

(1 to 5) + (1 to 5) = (2 to 10)

This figure (from 2 to 10) is the sum of the terrain difficulty and navigation difficulty ratings for each hike. In general, the total rating will guide hikers of varying experience like this:

2-4 Beginner hikers

5-6 Intermediate hikers; beginners need a guide.

7-8 Advanced hikers; all hikers should consider a guide.

9 -10 Expert hikers with guide; guides are a necessity for any hiker.

This figure is split into terrain and navigation so that you may self-assess your need for guidance more accurately. For instance, if you're extremely fit and able-bodied but a little uncertain about finding the trailhead or interpreting a map, then you could aim for a hike rated 5 for terrain, but 3 for navigation. On the other hand, some trailheads and trails are tricky to locate but not too long or challenging. If you have transportation, good maps and the seasoned eye to read landforms and curves in the road, then you may enjoy some of the hikes that are shorter and easier yet elusive.

Hiking Guide

Terrain Difficulty

1 Minimal slope, virtually flat. Well-groomed, well-surfaced trail with open trail corridor or nearly flat road in good repair.

2 Gently sloped trail grade. Ascents and descents of less than 500 vertical feet. Trail may have occasional roots, rocks, ruts or holes. Road may be paved or unfinished dirt/stone but in decent condition with occasional holes, ruts or washouts. Trail/road corridor is clear.

3 Ascents and descents are extended (up to 1,000 vertical feet) with moderate inclines. Expect stairs, quad-burning climbs, and/or an extended series of switchbacks. Trails are likely to have frequent roots, rocks, ruts and holes. Trail surface may become slippery and muddy with rain. Trail may require bridge-free passage over small streams or shallow rivers. Trail corridor may be narrow with branches and foliage extending into path of travel or occasional fallen trees across the trail. If along farm access roads, expect frequent rocks and ruts or an impeded road corridor.

4 Ascents and descents are extended (1,000 to 2,000 vertical feet) with moderate to aggressive inclines. Expect trail conditions to include one or more of the following: hand-assisted climbing, ankle to shin deep mud, narrow and slippery footpaths, swift and slippery knee-deep stream crossings and exposure to wave-washed sea cliffs or chasms adjacent to trail. Trail corridors are occasionally obscured or totally choked off by vegetation including razor grass.

5 Ascents and descents exceed 2,000 vertical feet and include extended and aggressive or brief but extreme (near vertical) inclines. Expect trail conditions to include one or more of the following: extended "jungle gym" hand climbing requiring flexibility and balance, extended shin deep mud spanning the trail corridor, frequent exposure to cliffs or chasms adjacent to trail, extended sections of loose, steep and slippery terrain and routes that require the use of ladders or fixed ropes. These routes may also include frequent crossing of swift and slippery streams or waist-deep rivers. Trail corridors are often obscured or totally choked off by vegetation including razor grass.

Navigation Difficulty

1 Route sticks to a road or official trail that's clearly signed and accurately mapped. These routes are obvious and well-traveled. Turns and junctions are few, but well-signed when present. They often explore nationally designated natural and historic sites (i.e. Emerald Pool or Cabrits National Park).

2 Route stays on roads and well-maintained trails but may switch surfaces occasionally. Trailheads and trails are expected to be marked well. If not, the path is obvious and well-traveled. Staying on course would require a little diligence, a decent map, or an occasional verification from a Dominican.

3 Route utilizes surfaces ranging from farm access roads to trails. Trailhead and junction signage is expected, but may be infrequent. Once underway, these routes are often characterized by following the most well-worn trail, but can be confusing when switching and turning between roads and trails.

4 Route consists of trails ranging from officially blazed corridors to faint forest footpaths that are tagged with tattered tape or ribbon. Expect little or no designation at trailheads, frequent river crossings, overgrown trails and/or unmarked trail junctions. Because of this, hiking a guide is especially important. Trail corridors and junctions can be overgrown and difficult to see and follow. If setting out on your own, be prepared for uncertainty and know how to check your progress and make decisions with a map.

5 Route will include a large portion of faint forest footpaths that are challenging to follow. Many of these are subtle tracks that connect highland gardens or fishing and hunting grounds. Others are recently revived trails that had been swallowed by jungle since the island converted its foot-travel tradition toward automobiles. While these footpaths are usually tagged with colored tape or plastic bags, expect totally unmarked cross-country sections and the possibility of losing the trail and needing to back-track. In both cases, hiring a good guide will offset the hazard of either possibility and is highly recommended. Invest time to connect with a good guide as not all will be familiar with some of these revitalized routes. If setting out on your own, excellent backcountry, topographic map-reading and orienteering skills are essential.

Distance

This figure is based on GPS track data and states distances over land along those tracks. The total distance is shown for each hike. For instance if it's an out-and-back hike to a destination that is 1.5 miles away, the hike distance listed is 3 miles. This guide includes out-and-back hikes, end-to-end or "thru" hikes and loops.

Elevation Change

This is the total gain *plus* the total loss in elevation. For instance, if the route climbs 2,200 feet and descends only 900 feet, the listed elevation change is 3,100 feet. Like the elevation profile, this figure gives you a sense of the vertical challenge of a given hike.

Duration

This figure is the most subjective and variable. You may find your own hiking duration on a given hike to be up to 50% faster or slower than those listed here. Times are estimated for an individual whose fitness allows for 2.5 to 3 mph average on a gently-sloped, open trail. To that baseline, four factors are added:

✓ 10-15 minutes of rest time per hour.

✓ 20-30 minutes for destinations like summits, waterfalls, swimming holes or beaches.

✓ 1 hour for every 1,000 feet of elevation gain. (This is a widely-used, accurate factor that you can apply beyond this guide whenever you can calculate the expected elevation gain.)

✓ Up to one hour depending on the route's specific obstacles (numerous river crossings, hand climbing, deep mud or choking vegetation).

Hiking Guide

Hike Guide Abbreviation Description

Diff = Total difficulty rating

Terr = Terrain rating

Nav = Navigation rating

Dist = Total distance of described route from trailhead to trailhead.

Elev = Total change in elevation along the route.

Dur = Duration to hike the described route.

Str X = Stream crossing

Rvr X = River crossing

Brdg = Bridge

Tr = Trail - This describes footpaths and corridors that are not possibly traveled by vehicles. In this guide trails include the spectrum from former roads that are overgrown down to the faint footpaths that barely interrupt the forest.

Old Rd = Old Road - This term covers corridors that are navigable by vehicle. While some particularly muddy or steep roads receive special notation, four wheel drive is always a good idea in Dominica. In this guide, "old road" includes farm access roads and roads that are incomplete, in disrepair and/or are significantly overgrown. They range from muddy, rutted single tracks to crumbling patchworks of concrete and cobbles. The other key designation is that they receive far less traffic than primary roads. This is usually because they are dead ends that simply reach as high into the bush as possible to provide farm access. As shown in this guide, they typically are continued by a trail beyond their furthest reach.

Rd = Primary Road - This term covers roads that allow two vehicles to pass each other and are generally in good repair. It includes all of the primary coastal and trans-insular roads that are shown on nearly every map of Dominica. These are basically the village connectors of Dominica, and thus are the roads that host traffic and bus stops. It also includes roads that serve as the arteries to access villages (such as the dead ends that access the heights of villages like Tete Morne, Grand Fond, Morne Jaune, and Morne Prosper).

Tr/Old Rd = The route surface changes from trail to road per the direction of travel described. Read these from left to right. For example, "Tr/Old Rd" will be surface change from trail to old road. Or, "Old Rd/Tr" will mean surface changes from old road to trail.

Rd/Old Rd = Surface changes from primary road to old road.

Tr/Tr Jct = Junction point of two or more trails.

Tr/Old Rd Jct = Junction point of trail and old road.

Vw = Viewpoint or vista.

Hz! = Hazardous area that includes further description.

Well Known Classics

Boiling Lake
Middleham Falls
Morne Diablotins
Sari Sari Falls
Morne Trois Pitons
Victoria Falls

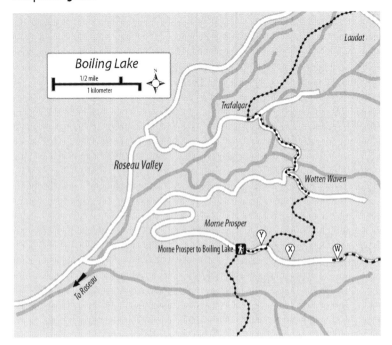

BOILING LAKE

No hike on Dominica, and increasingly in the Caribbean, comes with a bigger reputation. Recently rated as the hardest hike in the Caribbean in a region-wide guide, it does present a stout physical challenge and requires an all-day commitment. While this route is exceeded in terrain and navigation difficulty by several hikes in this guide, extensive staircases and thigh-high steps can produce jarring, hazardous exhaustion for knees and ankles. Due to its popularity, evacuations are not uncommon here. The flocks of hikers here are validated though; this natural phenomenon is the second-largest boiling lake on earth and

Hike Data
Difficulty: 9
Terrain: 5
Navigation: 4
Distance: 8 miles
Elevation: 5200'
Duration: 8 hrs

is stunning. Appropriately, written accounts and footage of this steamy site flourish on the web. This hike crests (F) amid some of Dominica's most sheer summits and dives into the Valley of Desolation, a primordial belching "moonscape" that allows vision of the mountains usually concealed by the jungle.

As of 2011, there are now two possible trails to reach a junction (H) just above the Valley of Desolation. The route shown here utilizes the newly-cleared approach that's raw and challenging, without staircases, and feels remote compared to the traditional route.

It's a good idea to start very early in the morning because this route (and its attractions) demand time. In particular, make time for the precipitous vista (O) and the warm mineral bath (L) – a great reprieve for tired feet or a full-body soak.

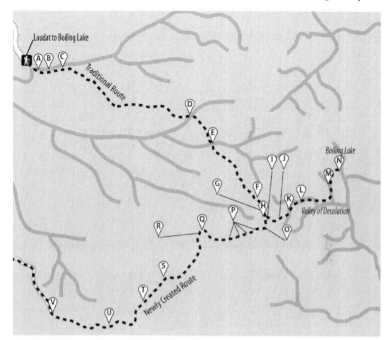

Waypoints

A Rainforest Aerial Tram (pg 95) bridge and kiosk.

B *Brdg* Steel "catwalk" along aqueduct over river.

C *Old Rd/Tr* Small shelter with occasional rental of life vests and helmets. Warm spring water piped to pool below a gorgeous swim-in canyon, the oft-mentioned Titou Gorge (pg 130). This is the filming location of a chase scene climax from *Pirates of the Caribbean*.

D *Str X*

E *Rvr X*

F *Vw* Incredible ridge top panorama of Atlantic and Caribbean on clear day. You may also glimpse puffs of luring steam from the Boiling Lake swirl upward and evaporate above the jungle.

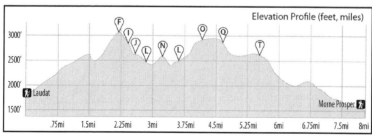

Elevation Profile (feet, miles)

Hiking Guide

G Trailside day use rain shelter.

H *Tr/Tr Jct* Unmarked, yet prominent junction. Head southwest (right) to reach Morne Prosper.

I *Hz!* Steep, often wet, slippery staircase and down-climb across wet stone slabs in streambed.

J *Hz!* Path is braided; observe the disturbed stones to choose the most well-worn path. Be cautious and respectful on delicate sulfurous crust and enjoy steaming vents from a distance as some vents can cause burns.

K *Str X* A double streem crossing just before the trails returns to vegetation.

L *Str X* Attractive warm trailside pools (of milky sky-blue mineral water) followed by a crossing to the north side of the stream.

M *Rvr X* Cross the headwaters of White River.

N *View* Boiling Lake crater.

O *Vw + Hz!* Several incredible bird's-eye views of Valley of Desolation. I recommend checking these stunning views even if you're not hiking through to Morne Prosper. Use caution at the precipice's edge as it's not clear where the earth underfoot ends and the cliff-hanging network of vegetation begins.

P *Str X + Hz!* Several within a quarter mile. Unstable, slippery footbridges, steep and crumbling stream banks; hand climbing required.

Q *Vw*

R *Hz!* Muddy cliff traverse downward with slippery, collapsing soil and tree root climbing. It's muddy, sloppy and fun if you've got good balance and are careful. If not, it could be nerve-racking and truly dangerous during a downpour.

S *Tr/Tr Jct* Trail leading to west intends to link to Wotten Waven (trail condition unknown).

T Pleasant ridge-top meander. Stop in this prime parrot habitat to listen for the centerpiece of Dominica's flag, the Sisserou.

U *Hz!* Challenging trail connecting narrow ridgebacks.

V *Tr/Old Rd + Brdg* Trail braided here and slightly confusing. Seek the small foot bridge at northwest corner of cultivated area.

W *Old Rd/Rd*

X Picturesque vegetable gardens and gorgeous pastoral scenes here.

Y *Rd/Old Rd Jct* WNT heads north here.

MIDDLEHAM FALLS

Middleham Falls is exceedingly tall at approximately 270 feet and shows off its height with a consistent year-round flow. Thus, it's well-worth the trip as a thru-hike or an out-and-back hike from either trailhead. It's easier from Cochrane, but more scenic and adventurous from Laudat. After exploring the falls and its vertical grotto, check out Tou Santi (P), a.k.a. Stinking Hole, a lava tube cave known for its odor of bat droppings. The road walk toward Cochrane affords views of Morne Anglais and the Roseau Valley. If you're planning on using the Cochrane/Springfield trailhead (V), ask about the current status of the primary road which was closed due to heavy construction upon the writing of this guide.

Hike Data
Difficulty: 6
Terrain: 3
Navigation: 3
Distance: 4 miles
Elevation: 2500'
Duration: 4 hrs

Night Hike

If you're comfortable hiking at night, Jungle Trekking Adventure and Safari (Tel: 767-440-5827; www.experiencescaribbean.com) leads a unique nocturnal adventure on this route. This guided trek will patiently wait for the emergence of Tou Santi's bat colony before continuing by torch light to the trail terminus.

Waypoints

A Rain shelter, restrooms and parking.

B *Rd/Tr* Surface changes to trail.

C *Brdg + Tr/Tr Jct* Cross Providence River, then bear left at a trail junction just ahead.

D Look around here for specimens of the many-trunked "walking tree."

E *Brdg*

F *Tr/Tr Jct* Sign; bear left toward Middleham Falls.

G *Str X* (may be dry)

H *Tr/Tr Jct* Sign to Falls, Tou Santi and Cochrane.

I *Str X*

J Short, incorrect side trails here. Follow the booming sounds of falls to stay on track.

K *Viewing Platform* If you're feeling sure-footed and inspired, a scramble down to the banks of Middleham's primary pool is worth it. Be careful on the increasingly slippery and awkwardly large boulders that shoulder the pool and the trio of cascades below. At nearly 300 feet tall, this consistently pumping tower of water seemingly defies even the widest angled camera lens.

L *Rvr X's*

M Covered pavilion with picnic table.

Hiking Guide

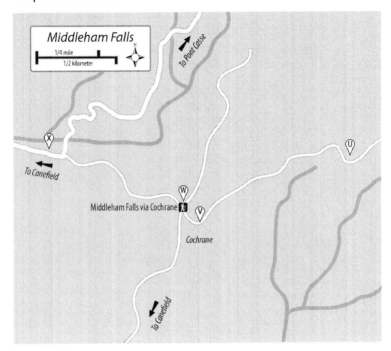

N *Str X's*

O Fallen tree; utilize side trails and a little patience to negotiate a route.

P *Tr/Tr Jct* Short, well-signed trail to Tou Santi (Stinking Hole). Further to west, several side trails (some marked with colored plastic ribbon) may entice the curious to venture off the path for a deeper Dominican forest experience, but keep in mind that many are privately developed tracks, usually leading to family gardens.

Q *Rvr X* This small watershed feeds a low-flow waterfall just downstream which exceeds Middleham and some suspect it as the tallest falls on the island, but has yet to be officially documented as such.

R *Tr/Rd* (paved)

S Cul de sac (parking for 10+ vehicles)

T Abandoned motel.

U Sign for Middleham Falls Trail.

V *Rd/Old Rd Jct* Sign for Rainbow Village Cottage.

W *Rd/Rd Jct* Four-way with sign pointing to Springfield.

X *Rd/Rd Jct* Primary road access for this hike. A bus could drop you here.

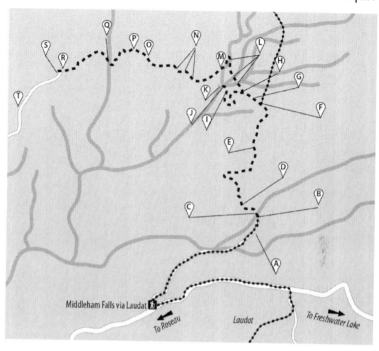

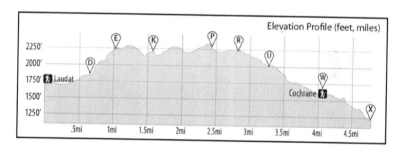

Elevation Profile (feet, miles)

MORNE DIABLOTINS

At 4,747 feet, the highest peak on Dominica offers a very difficult but fun half-day up-and-back. This hike is like a spinning class mixed with American Gladiators. Get ready for quad and buttock burning climbs, full-body jungle gym contortions, and then doing it in reverse. An obvious trail corridor offers little exposure to getting lost. The hike starts with the mother of all stair-masters through full height hardwood forest with open understory before diving into a living ropes course of vines, tree roots and branches. At this point in the trek, you'll alight on sections up to several hundred yards where you won't

Hike Data	
Difficulty: 8	
Terrain: 5	
Navigation: 3	
Distance: 3.5 miles	
Elevation: 5100'	
Duration: 6 hrs	

set your feet down on actual earth (D). Leave your trekking poles at home: you will be using both hands to negotiate this literal gym of the jungle. The trip is worth it just for the unique swinging, climbing and twisting travel style, but it may be anticlimactic to summit inside the dense gray vapor that usually engulfs Diablotins by lunch.

It is a good idea to start this hike early in the morning – clouds generally roll in from the east coast to obscure the peak completely by 11am.

Waypoints

A Parking (two spaces only). Trail is clear and well traveled but root-filled and may be flowing with water if it is raining.

B *Tr/Tr Jct* Following a few switchbacks, one *may* glimpse a faint path leading north to Syndicate Nature Trail, marked in old red/yellow tape.

C *Vw* View over cliff-encircled basin to the north.

D Deep jungle gym. Use your hands and feet to climb through the roots above the muddy forest floor, but be careful not to grab any tree ferns as they are covered in a very sharp, black, needle-like bark, the tips of which can break off easily under the

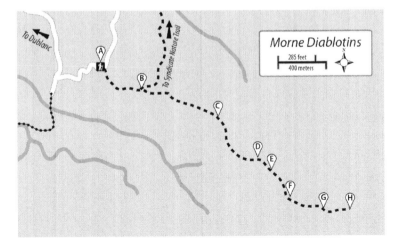

skin. If the way appears ambiguous, try looking for chopped branches and areas where the moss has been rubbed off of nearby roots.

> **Caution:** Heavy rain (which is common here) presents increased challenge as much of the trail becomes a charging shin-deep stream.

E *Vw*

F *Vw* This first peak presents a look back out over the Caribbean toward the coastal landmarks of Barbers block, Portsmouth and the Cabrits peninsula.

G *Vw* Second peak offers vantage of Morne Turner and the dramatic ravines near Syndicate Falls. Faint, challenging path clambers east from here.

H *Vw* Third peak is the apparent true summit of Diablotins with commanding views of Wesley and Marigot. There's some confusion about the origin of this peak's name. While many claim it's the "Devil's Mountain," it's also stated that the peak is named "Little Devil," after the once prominent Black-capped Petrel, a seabird whose nocturnal habits and spooking mating call once echoed commonly on Morne Diablotins' slopes.

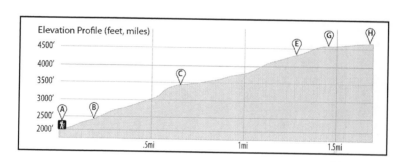

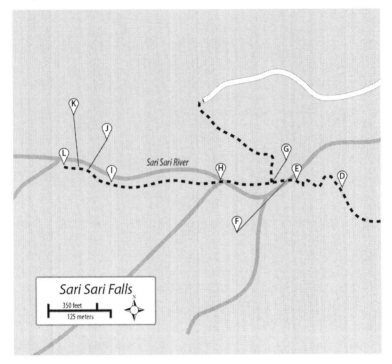

SARI SARI FALLS

Westward, above the sprawling flats of the charming village of La Plaine, Dominica's mountainous interior rises abruptly. Here, notched between two hulking jungle ridges, Sari Sari Falls defends passage to the highlands like a gatekeeper. To explore Sari Sari Falls, you'll need less than a half-day and the expectation of getting wet. You'll cross the namesake river twice before skirting the river bank and scrambling to a viewing platform. Do not attempt if heavy rain is recent or imminent in the highlands above. As you arrive in La Plaine, expect enthusiastic hollering of "Sari Sari!" "Waterfall! Water-

Hike Data
Difficulty: 8
Terrain: 4
Navigation: 4
Distance: 1.25 miles
Elevation: 900'
Duration: 1.5 hrs

fall!" and "A guide you need?!?" from aspiring guides who aim to capitalize on their local knowledge. If you didn't plan ahead, ask around for a certified guide as there are few in this region. Stock up on fresh whole wheat bread from La Plaine's friendly bakers and grab a beverage at Dana's craft shop and bar (A) after your hike.

Waypoints

A *Sari Sari Craftshop and Bar* Find bush rums, juice, souvenirs, fruit and perhaps a few snacks here. The owner Dana (pronounced "Donna") is very friendly and typically selects a great reggae soundtrack to complement her refreshments.

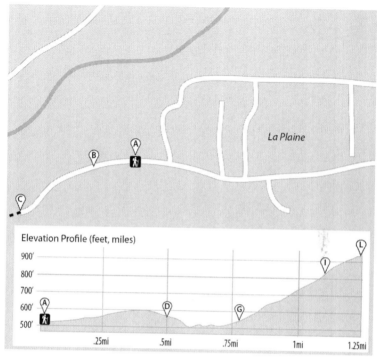

B Small parking and turn-around area.

C *Old Rd/Tr*

D Leave pasture to enter forest descending to river.

E *Rvr X*

F Tarpaulin rain shelter with small, coal pot for cooking.

G *Tr/Tr Jct* This may seem ambiguous. Go left and follow the river upstream toward the falls. The path to the right heads up very steeply to reach Bolive Falls trailhead (pg 288) in a large meadow.

H *Rvr X*

I Trail sign for falls and steep steps, usually wet. Be careful as these can be tricky on the way back down.

J *Hz!* The river *is the trail* from this point to the falls. River stones are exceedingly slippery here. Carefully navigate medium to large boulders continually heading upstream. This is a prime photo op spot.

K *Vw* Falls viewing platform.

L Sari Sari falls and pool.

Hiking Guide

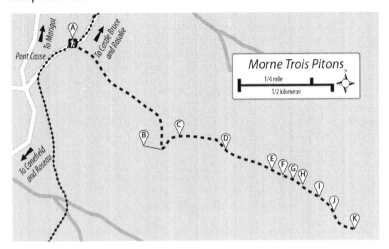

MORNE TROIS PITONS

Though not the highest peak on the island, the central location of Morne Trois Pitons offers stunning views of Morne Diablotins and the island of Guadeloupe to the north. Slippery wooden steps, shin-high mud in the rainy season, three vertical hand-over-hand rope ascents, and a decent amount of razor grass turn this would be average mountain hike into an exciting challenge, Dominica style. With several breathtaking views, it's best to schedule your hike for a clear day, which means you'll be climbing in the heat. That said, be sure to bring a long sleeved jacket as it gets chilly at the windy and often cloud-covered peak.

Hike Data
Difficulty: 8
Terrain: 5
Navigation: 3
Distance: 2.5 miles
Elevation: 5200'
Duration: 4 hrs

Much like the Morne Diablotins hike, the track is clear and well defined with no real side trails to distract you from your intended path. And like Diablotins, pay attention in any "jungle gym" sections as they can be a bit ambiguous at times.

Waypoints

A *Rd/Tr Jct* Keep a keen eye out for a small, grassy area with a sign marking the Trois Pitons trailhead by an old tree on the south side of the road.

B Switchback

C Terrain becomes slightly more rugged. Watch for razor grass here and higher up.

D Terrain becomes less rugged for a short while. Great views ascending into the clouds.

E *Hz! Rope 1* This is the first of three hand-over-hand ascents up knotted climbing ropes with roots and a rock wall providing foot holds. Be careful as the rock face and roots may be slippery.

F *Hz! Rope 2*

G *Hz! Rope 3* If you have a large backpack, this might be a good place to leave it behind especially if you don't want to fight with it through the jungle gym above, but be sure to clip it to a tree or root as the cliff is nearly vertical here.

> **Tip:** Look for chopped branches and hand holds on tree roots where the moss has not had a chance to regrow from use by previous adventurers.

H *Nob 1* You may see parrots near this area.

I *Nob 2* Odd looking plants (called *bromeliads*) seemingly defy natural law having no direct contact with the soil. Many of the bromeliads at this elevation can become larger than the trees in which they roost. A peek down into the bromeliad's center reveals their water supply kept safe from the sun between its rigid leaves.

J *Hz!* Take caution twisting through the jungle gym while under the elfin forest canopy as there are several spots where one could slip and become stuck between the rocks below.

K *Vw* Morne Trois Pitons summit. This spot is the highest (4,672 feet) of a trio of summits for which the mountain gets its name. There's no obvious trail to reach the two junior summits. Brisk winds, the same that power the gulf stream, are a near guarantee here. Clear and panoramic views are a function of your start time and the weather. Expect cloudy conditions, especially past mid-day.

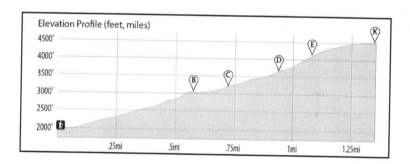

Elevation Profile (feet, miles)

VICTORIA FALLS

This is one of the best spots in the southeast for a short, yet impressive escape into wildness. Here, the unique pale blue pools of the White River charm a visitor under a cliff-clinging canopy in a twisting gorge. A brief, but rigorous and amphibious river scramble (J) delivers you to Victoria Falls, which stands out for its powerful combination of height and volume. The White River's well-fed, mineral-laden waters flow from the heights of Morne Trois Pitons National Park and through the Valley of Desolation.

Hike Data
Difficulty: 9
Terrain: 5
Navigation: 4
Distance: 1.25 miles
Elevation: 350'
Duration: 2.5 hrs

Do not attempt if there has been, or is imminent, heavy rain in the highlands. People have lost their lives due to high water here. A guide is highly recommended to negotiate the river and its confusing crossings.

Waypoints

A *Rd/Old Rd Jct* Old sign at this junction for Perdu Temps trail. Road descends steeply with switchbacks.

B Park in an ample cul de sac next to Ras Moses' family "Rastaraunt" (Tel: 767-276-3204, 767-265-8291, 767-613-1779). If the family is around, enjoy a juice or local provisions and test your chess acumen against a charming and talented family with three generations of chess experience and plenty of time to practice. The grandson, Sinai, is a talented and playful opponent. They also ask a US$5 fee for parking and offer rustic accommodation in a nearby cabin made from local timber.

C *Tr/Tr Jct* Fork right to head upstream with river on left.

D *Rvr X* Cross at the foot of an enchanting pool tucked under a cliff of moss, fern and vine. Here, the White River reveals its "deeper" color palate. When little over four feet deep, the river begins to achieve an inviting milky sky-blue hue. It's hard to tear yourself away from an enchanting cyan swimming hole here.

E Leave the river, pass directly beside an old garden shack and skirt the cultivated dasheen plots, shortcutting the river's bend.

F *Rvr X*

G *Tr/Tr Jct + Rvr X* A steep, hand-climbing path weaves up the jungle wall and eventually reaches gardens on the plateau above the gorge. There, the falls can be heard, but it's very tricky and unmarked to find the vista of the falls. A local guide can show you the way along roads from within Delices. It's different, but not as impressive and intimate as the view and feel from the falls' base. Cross the river here to continue.

H *Rvr X* Cross again and locate the trail, an old high-water river bed, hidden away from the main river's edge.

I *Rvr X*

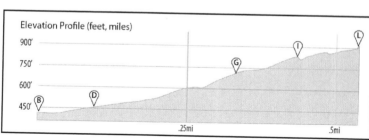

Victoria Falls

275 feet
100 meters

White River

To Delices

To Petite Savane
and Grand Bay

Elevation Profile (feet, miles)

900'

750'

600'

450'

.25mi

.5mi

J *Hz!* Large, slippery boulders, deep, swift pools and falls. Here, your best options are likely wet ones. Negotiate an amphibious, scrambling route among the boulders and log jams. Generally, it's better to hug the left river bank as you climb upstream. Victoria Falls can be seen soaring from the brink above its grotto.

K *Vw* A worn path tops this knoll which offers incredible views of the falls. Just below here is the last spot to take shelter from the driving wind and mist thrust outward where Victoria Falls strikes its pool.

L Small ribbon falls streak down a tall ravine to your left.

M *Hz!* If you choose to explore the pool itself, step carefully on extra slippery stones encircling the pool. If you enter the pool, know that the current feels like a river shoving you ashore and as you approach the crushing column of water, the roar is jarring and the sting of wind-whipped spray makes it difficult to even open your eyes.

N *Victoria Falls* Moisture-seeking roots dangle from heights even higher than the 120-foot high falls. As you explore the ever-moist boulders around the pool, your eye may catch the flitting of a unique creature. Here, many feet above the surface of the water, fish up to two inches long thrive by clinging to and feeding on algae-covered stone. These aptly-named clingfish, members of the Goby family, are likely to begin flipping frantically to tumble to safety underwater as you approach.

Soon to be WNT Classics

Emerald Pool to Castle Bruce
Giraudel to Bellevue Chopin
Pennville to Capuchin
L' Escalier Tete Chien to Dragon's Mouth
Petite Macoucherie to Melville Hall River
Scotts Head Loop

EMERALD POOL TO CASTLE BRUCE

While this hike could be covered comfortably in a morning, you may want to plan a bit more time to linger on this route. If you get to Emerald Pool when there's not a tour bus circulating its dozens of visitors through the site, it can feel as relaxed and enchanting as any spot on the island. This route, which overlaps the re-opening of the historic trans-insular Carib Trace Trail, departs the well-trodden loop (H) and descends from mature upland rainforest along the robust Castle Bruce River and through its long cultivated floodplain to the playing fields and beaches of Castle Bruce. This section was chosen for its forgiving downhill profile, its frequent freshwater swimming holes, as well as its passage along the historic cobbled Carib Trace Trail and through contemporary gardens and large-scale fruit cultivation (T).

Hike Data
Difficulty: 6
Terrain: 3
Navigation: 3
Distance: 5.5 miles
Elevation: 1900'
Duration: 4 hrs

This hike's attractive seaside terminus includes a large playing field (where you're likely to catch an evening soccer, cricket, or rounders match) and nearby sea and river bathing. Visit Augustine by the old gas station (X) or the barbecue under the pavilion (no specific hours) to sample some local snacks before heading to Castle Bruce beach and Bushiwi (Z).

Waypoints

A *Rd/Driveway Jct*

B *Emerald Pool Interpretation Center* Pavilion with picnic tables, restrooms, souvenirs, snackette and site pass vending here. There's also a small room that gives deeper interpretation on the flora, fauna and geology found nearby in the mature rainforest.

Tip: Starting mid-day on this walk would work fine as you can cool off along the way and finish at a charming community gathering spot (Y) that opens toward the ocean.

C *Tr/Tr Jct + Brdg* Stay left.

D *Vw* View of Emerald Pool below.

E *Tr/Tr Jct + Brdg*

F Emerald Pool with waterfall. Come here equipped to take a dip. If you have mask and snorkel, bring them. A peek below the surface reveals opalescent shrimp and rainbow-hued fish.

G *Vw* View with platform.

H *Tr/Tr Jct* Look for blue/yellow blazes heading downhill to the northeast. Turn left to continue this route. Turn right to complete Emerald Pool loop.

I Switchbacks

J *Tr/Rd* Follow WNT blazes left along road.

K *Hz! Rd/Tr* Follow WNT blazes right onto trail. Trail is re-routed here around a significant landslide.

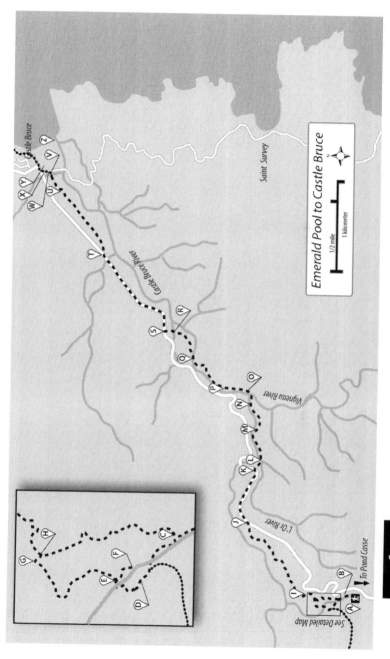

Emerald Pool to Castle Bruce

1/2 mile
1 kilometer

Castle Bruce River

Saint Survey

Vigneau River

L'Or River

To Pond Casse

See Detailed Map

L *Str X* L'Or River

M *Tr/Old Rd Jct + Brdg* Outstanding and deep swimming hole here!

N *Str X* Cross Vigneau River, which is noticeably cooler than the Castle Bruce River. Aqueduct with a derelict catwalk crosses high above a surging gorge on the Castle Bruce River.

O Handsome pools and tiny beaches below in gorge. Trail is cut steeply against mossy cliffs.

P Bottom of gorge opens onto agricultural clearing and passes close to a farmer's shack. Handsome cobble-paved section of Carib Trace Trail begins here.

Q *Rvr X* Broad crossing of Castle Bruce River followed by entrance into a well-known clearing called Savane David. This crossing is scheduled for improvement with the addition of cables to aid in crossing safely.

R *Str X* Exit Savane David.

S *Tr/Rd* Follow WNT blazes along road.

T *Rd/Old Rd* Follow WNT onto farm road into a large citrus, banana and coconut plantation.

U Confusing area amid marshy flats. Look distant, slightly left for next blaze. (Good luck in the mud!)

V *Str X*

W *Tr/Rd Jct*

X Bus stop and payphone on corner with two or three snackettes including Augustine's.

Y Pavilion and playing field.

Z *Bushiwi* is the local name for this cobble beach and lagoon at the mouth of Castle Bruce River. Avoid swimming in the surf directly in front of river's path as it has cut deep channels on the sea floor, creating deadly rip tides.

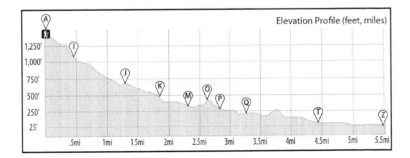

GIRAUDEL TO BELLEVUE CHOPIN

Plan on a little extra time to explore and enjoy the communities that bookend this half-day, thru-hike. In each case, local entrepreneurs have begun highlighting the agricultural abundance and horticultural heritage as part of the nation's community tourism initiative. The route linking these communities spans some rugged terrain, particularly the steep-walled gorges below Morne Anglais' western wall. In contrast, the path itself is not too challenging; it's well-graded and well-widened as it's a remnant of a cart path from when this region was actively cultivated. Overgrown orchards and estate buildings (H, K) reveal an agrarian past.

Hike Data
Difficulty: 6
Terrain: 3
Navigation: 3
Distance: 5.5 miles
Elevation: 2000'
Duration: 3 hrs

Waypoints

A Here, find Hot Blade, a local bar and snackette that hops on weekend evenings. Just south lies the visitor center for the Giraudel/Eggleston flower growers.

B *Rd/Rd Jct* Here, WNT blazes lead you uphill away from main road.

C *Rd/Tr*

D *Hz!* Trail is cut into a precipitous canyon wall that's interesting and dramatic, but vulnerable to washouts and trail collapses that can be treacherous.

E Steep attractive meadow of red anthurium flowers on the forest floor.

F *Brdg*

G *Rvr X* Impressive clusters of thick bamboo.

H Overgrown remnants of agricultural estate along trail here.

I Cross ridge at this location. Could camp here on the gentle slopes if need be.

J *Tr/Old Rd Jct* Route continues left on WNT while an overgrown path leads toward the Gommier L'Etang ruins.

K Ruins of Gommier L'Etang estate buildings.

L *Vw*

M *Old Rd/Rd Jct* Continue left on road / WNT

N *Broad Meadows Organic Farm* This is the hub for the Bellevue Chopin Organic Farmers Group, a model community tourism effort that is in its early stage. Here, check out their composting and essential oil distillation operations. Friendly and knowledgeable Gordon Royer and his family live and work the land here while several nearby farms collaborate with organic techniques. Check for latest info and organized farm tour details at www.communitytourism.dm. Visionary farmers here and elsewhere founded the Dominica Organic Agriculture Movement (DOAM) in 2006 to help guide Dominica toward best practices to sustain environmental health on the island. Read more at www.doamdominica.org.

Hiking Guide

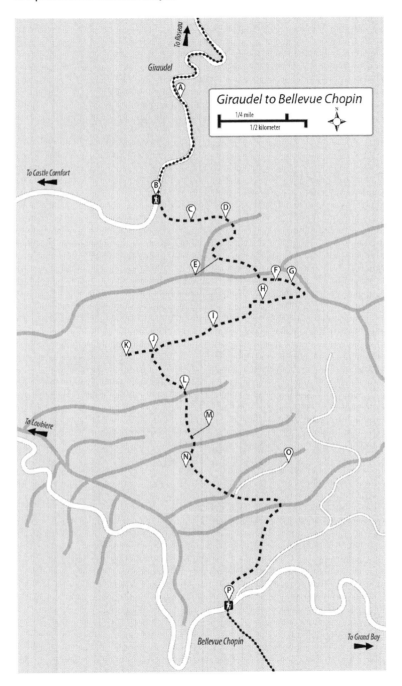

O *Harmony Garden* Specializes in organic herbs. Hosts farm tours through Bellevue Chopin Organic Farmers Group.

P *Rd/Rd Jct* Find this junction/trailhead by spotting the painted red sign with "Kubuli" at the crest of the hill.

> **Tip:** Consider merging this hike with nights spent at one or both communities. For flowers and foods with nearby guesthouses and full-service options choose Giraudel. For tenting options near a hub for organic farming of herbs and vegetables, choose Bellevue Chopin.

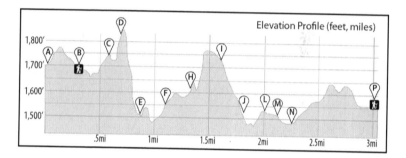

Elevation Profile (feet, miles)

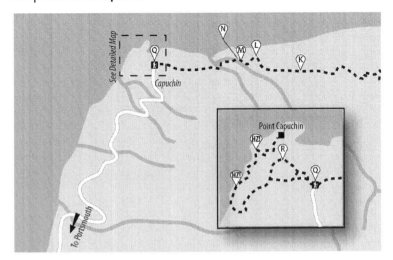

PENNVILLE TO CAPUCHIN

Only a few hikes on the island hold such a feeling of remoteness as this hike. Here you are pitched north on an abandoned road that winds through old estates and along the cliffs that stare across the channel to Guadeloupe. The trail, easy to follow at both ends, disintegrates or becomes confused at the mid-point (I). Ancient orchard trees still occasionally bear fruit along the trail, and with a little exploring a trekker can see crumbling estate buildings, wild pigs, and refreshing stream pools. Side trips include scrambling up to peer through the curtain of cedars that conceal 700 foot cliffs (K) or picking down into ravines that terminate at the sea.

Hike Data
Difficulty: 6
Terrain: 3
Navigation: 3
Distance: 4.5 miles
Elevation: 3800'
Duration: 4.5 hrs

Waypoints

A *Rd/Old Rd Jct* A large WNT sign is located here.

B *Str X*

C *Str X* A pipe for filling water bottles is located here.

D *Tr/Tr jct* Side trail to Carib Point and the associated 400 foot cliffs.

E *Str X* Take a dip in small pool here. If you're thirsty, this is the last available water for about two miles.

F *Tr/Tr Jct* Take this side trail downhill along the Desgras Balata River to reach Point Reposoir, a dramatic natural volcanic jetty the extends northward defying the Gulf Stream's power.

G *Hz!* Rockslide here interrupts trail.

H *Hz!* Rockslide here as well. Carefully negotiate a route around.

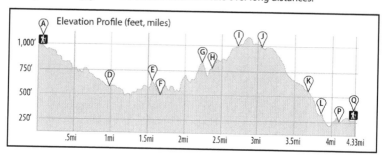

I *Tr/Tr Jct* The route disappears into open garden. Seek out blazes at the high side of clearing.

J *Seaman's Gate* A passage cut through the ridge's crest hundreds of years ago to facilitate trade and commerce.

K *Tr/Tr Jct* Trail to river and possibly the old Seaman Estate House.

L *Hz! + Vw* A sense of airy space is apparent just uphill from here. Pick your way through bank of cedar and sea grape to peek out from cliffs.

M *Str X*

N A series of person-sized tubs perfect for a nice dip.

O Rocky stream bed.

P *Tr/Old Rd*

Q *Old Rd/Rd + Rd/Tr Jct* Another WNT trail sign and side trail to Pointe Capuchin.

R *Vw* Enjoy views of a dramatic spire known chronologically as Cana, Cape Melville and Pointe Capuchin. You're viewing from a colonial platform with an iron cannon from the same era. This stone platform once served as a signal station when raising flags and firing guns were used to communicate over long distances.

Hiking Guide

L' ESCALIER TETE CHIEN TO DRAGON'S MOUTH

No hike on the island offers more cultural and coastal exposure than this. This full-day undulating trek is book-ended by a pair of wave-washed geologic oddities. To connect these, you'll travel almost the full length of the Carib Reserve, the Caribbean's only protected territory for indigenous people. This six mile trek – which is most of segment 6 of the WNT – offers views of the Atlantic with frequent opportunities to hop on a coastal side trail. Be sure to check out Kalinago Barana Auté (pg 193) for some insight into the Kalinago people culture (and to shop for Carib crafts). This section of trail can certainly keep you busy all day. Yet, it's also a good fit for bite-sized exploration of the Carib Reserve as it's never far from the main road.

Hike Data
Difficulty: 7
Terrain: 3
Navigation: 4
Distance: 6 miles
Elevation: 3900'
Duration: 6.5 hrs

Waypoints

A *Rd/Old Rd Jct* Though it's unsigned, locate the old road with blue/yellow WNT blazes to get started. Approximately 200 feet south from this junction is another old road that weaves its way down to a coastal river bath spot known as the Madjini pools.

B *Tr/Tr Jct* Go straight along ridge to check out L'Escalier Tete Chien. Or go left to continue this route on the WNT. Nearby on the right lies the outdoor stage for performances from the Karifuna Cultural Group (pg 188).

C *Rvr X* Kusarakua River

D *Tr/Tr Jct* Option to turn right onto the Centipede Trail, which is a short path to a coastal rocky outcropping that features good views and a petroglyph resembling Dominica's most poisonous land animal, the giant centipede.

E *Rvr X* Trail passes close to a cobble beach at the mouth of the Salibia River.

F Picturesque Catholic Church of Salibia.

G Find a short trail or side road to the left to reach the Carib Craft Corner on the main road.

H Kalinago Barauna Aute (pg 193) model village and café. Be sure to check out (and cool off) at Isulukati Falls where it cascades onto the beach.

I *Old Rd / Old Rd Jct* Depart WNT here by turning right. Ask locals for the old road that leads downhill on the ridge toward the Dragon's Mouth (locally known as "Big River"). A guide, even informal, would be helpful here as the terrain is difficult by the sea and the rest of the hike is unmarked and braided through a somewhat confusing cultivated area to the north.

Tip: Start early to make some miles in the coolness of the day, especially because this trail utilizes road sections and crosses low-elevation cultivated areas, both of which can simply roast around mid-day. Also, ask locals if they're baking cassava bread on the day you're there. It's a great, carb-filled trail snack.

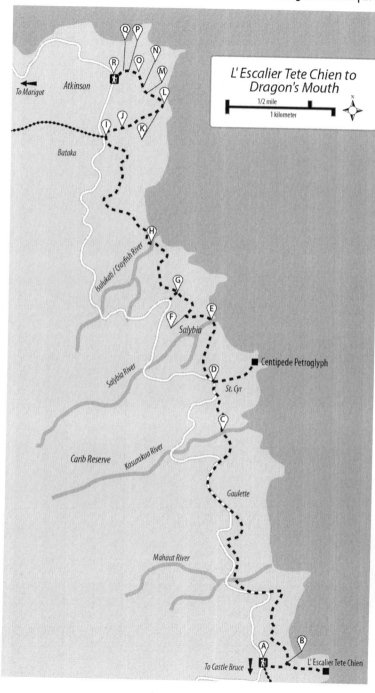

J *Old Rd / Tr*

K Trail spills down steep crumbly soil, emerging from thicket of sea grape to meet Kuaria (Big) River. Continue down to find Dragon's Mouth just below a small cascade.

L *Dragon's Mouth* A 40-foot deep fissure in the rocky coastal shelf that captures the ocean's surge and converts its horizontal force into a vertical burst of seaspray. It truly mimics a dragon's mouth in that you can feel the grumbling surge, see the bursting exhale and also hear a hollow, hooting inhale. Use the utmost caution in the slippery falls above Dragon's Mouth and don't venture too close to the sea. Tourists and locals alike have been swept to their death at sites like this all along the east coast. To continue, locate the trail atop the prominent orange-brown bluff of conglomerate rock.

M *Tr/Tr Jct* Continue uphill.

N Passion fruit vineyards

O *Tr/Old Rd Jct* At prominent mango tree, turn left uphill.

P *Old Rd/Old Rd Jct* Turn right, uphill.

Q *Old Rd/Rd Jct* Turn left.

R *Old Rd/Rd Jct* Atkinson bus stop here marks trailhead and overlooks school and playing field.

> **Note:** Upon the writing of this guide, the exact location of the trail in this section was still being modified. Therefore, the above waypoints do not designate as many junctions and surface transitions (as the other hike descriptions) because they're anticipated to change. Just stick to the WNT blue/yellow blazes and you'll stay on track.

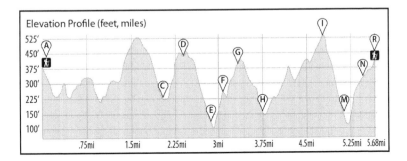

PETITE MACOUCHERIE TO MELVILLE HALL RIVER

If you want to experience the essence of mature tropical woodlands, this is your hike (as recommended by prominent Dominica-born conservation biologist and manager of WNT construction, Eric Hypolite). This route – which is also segment 8 of the WNT – begins near the heart of the Northern Forest Reserve and transects perhaps the island's largest roadless region due east of Morne Diablotins. It is particularly suited for focusing on the forest because after you complete a demanding summit to Mosquito Mountain's shoulder (D), the trail soon becomes a comfortable descending gradient that allows your senses to roam. Spotting wildlife is nearly guaranteed: parrots, agouti, boas, crabs, geckos, as well as the sign and scent of wild pigs (I encountered all of these in a morning!). Also expect to enjoy the Kasiobna River (K) in the heart of the reserve and washing off weary limbs in a plunge-worthy swimming hole (X) directly under the occasional exciting buzz of aircraft dropping into Melville Hall Airport.

Hike Data	
Difficulty: 8	
Terrain: 4	
Navigation: 4	
Distance: 10.5 miles	
Elevation: 6500′	
Duration: 7 hrs	

Waypoints

A *Rd/ Old Rd Jct*

B *Str X* Just after leaving the cultivated area, the track crosses a stream and then ascends steeply. This is the last reliable water source for about four miles.

C Narrow "razorback" ridgeline that is a steep thigh-burning ascent where roots are your steps and tree trunks your handrails. Consider this and the ridgetop incline near "E," the crux of the hike.

D *Vw* This secondary shoulder of Mosquito Mountain offers frequent refreshing winds off the Atlantic and views east over undulated country holding the many river fingers of the Northern Forest Reserve stretching toward old agricultural estates and Melville Hall Airport. North and west offer a more dramatic (yet often fog-obscured) landscape of Mosquito's summit and the bulk of Diablotins.

E Steep descent on narrow ridgeback. Open your ears along this ridge as you may notice the buzz of honeybees overhead.

F Depart ridge's spine here, descending into a drainage before shortly regaining a more moderately sloped ridgeline.

G Broader, more open woodlands tempt one to step off the trail for a break and tune into the signature squawk of Dominica's emblematic parrots. They linger in the highlands, making their nests and sounding their presence from mountain rims while thriving on the lowlands' abundant citrus fruit.

H Turn left down ridge with steeper descent.

I Tiny, trickling stream offers first water source since "B." Lovely open understory with extensive fern-covered forest floor.

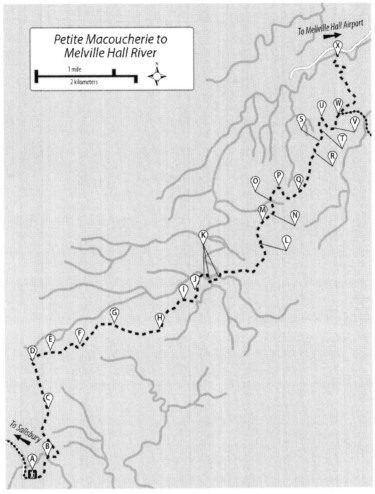

J This impressive grove of mature Chatanierre trees and attractive "ferny" forest floor make this a top-notch area to slip off the trail and spend a night in the bush.

K *Rvr X's* The first crossing is over the primary arm of the Melville Hall (Kasiobna) River. The two or three after traverse a confluence of several tributaries that may employ several channels at high water.

L Attractive forest flats with towering Chatanierre over carpets of pawasol agouti.

M *Str X*

N *Hz!* Surprisingly deep, dry ravine gashes the sideslope, interrupting the trail. Use care on the steep, crumbly, 25-foot rock and root scramble on both sides.

O *Str X* Approximately 50 yards of the trail appears to be permanently flooded here.

P Last prominent ascent to a narrow ridgeline.

Q Be curious to peek between the Chatanierre's curtailed trunks for abundant and precocious forest crabs.

R *Tr/Tr Jct* Bear right here.

S *Tr/Old Rd*

T Vw Grassy pastures here give way to views east and west.

U *Old Rd/Old Rd Jct*

V *Old Rd/Old Rd Jct*

W *Old Rd / Old Rd Jct* WNT diverges east here along a farm road. There are many side roads here that are too numerous to mention. Continue straight on the primary farm access road.

X *Brdg* Melville Hall (Kasiobna) River. Even with the moderate downhill hike, you'll be roasting by this time and will enjoy cooling off here. About 200 yards upstream from the bridge you'll find a deep, well-shaded swimming hole. Be mindful of where you set your clothes and belongings to avoid infestation by nearly microscopic fire ants.

> **Tip:** This route's most strenuous (waypoints "B" to "I") section is dry, without a spring or stream to refill water bottles. Plan to bring two quarts of water per

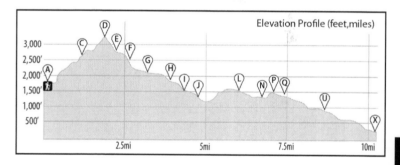

Elevation Profile (feet, miles)

SCOTTS HEAD LOOP

This loop hike is all about views and variety. Because of this, plan on spending the better part of a day on this circuit. From the Scotts Head Peninsula (Q) you get an out-at-sea-feeling panorama of the Atlantic Ocean, the Caribbean Sea, Soufrière Bay and a sense of Dominica's overall ruggedness. At the Crabier clearing (E), local farmer Hugo's attractive pasture and orchard will most likely have some fruit in season. From here (E/F), take in the vantage of Scotts Head village below and glimpse Martinique through oceanic haze. Later, gaze at the heights of Tete Morne before ascending a quiet road to the clifftop village of Gallion (L). Enjoy sunset's blushing hues upon La Sorciere, a soaring 900-foot seaside precipice.

Hike Data
Difficulty: 6
Terrain: 3
Navigation: 3
Distance: 4.5 miles
Elevation: 4000'
Duration: 5 hrs

Waypoints

A *Rd/Rd Jct* Scotts Head bus stop. Continue south on coastal road to cross the split and reach the southern terminus of the WNT at Fort Cachacrou on Scotts Head. This spot truly gives one a feel for the dimension of Dominica, particularly due to the dramatic mastiff of La Sorciere hanging above the Soufriere crater.

B *Rd/Old Rd Jct* After ascending climb, turn right following blue and yellow WNT blazes.

C *Old Rd/Tr*

D Well-built, but tiring switchbacks. On the first few, scan the trailside for remnant fruit trees, particularly soursop in the winter.

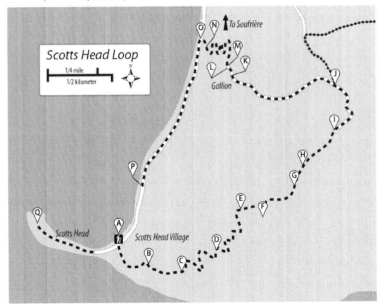

E *Vw* Crest the final switchback and emerge on the edge of a picturesque pasture where Johhny Depp and company (including dozens of locals) shot action scenes for *Pirates of the Caribbean*. The vista below is steep with a uniquely vertical view of Scotts Head rooftops and ocean horizon. A friendly farmer named Hugo and his son work this lovely area known as Crabier. You're likely to catch them here rotating their cattle or harvesting their orchard in the morning. For a few dollars, they'll likely provide you with the best of what's ripe.

F A giant, attractive acacia tree stands solo. Its trunk is covered in impressive mature thorns and its own leaves may be outnumbered by those of the hundreds of epiphytic bromeliads perched on its limbs. It seems as though they thrive here due to the consistent wind pouring through an open saddle in the land that gives view toward Martinique.

G Small hilltop clearing that serves as a good break spot.

H *Hz!* Steepest, most unstable trail section is here. Pause to enjoy attractive buttressed roots twisting 50 feet from their home trunk and views across the valley to the heights of Tete Morne above Soufriere's hot springs.

I *Tr/Old Rd Jct* Four-way intersection as you arrive back in cultivated terrain. Continue straight.

J *Old Rd/Rd Jct* Turn left at hairpin turn on paved road to depart WNT.

K Enjoy some colorful homespun decoration on a stone and cinderblock wall. That must have been a lot of Kubuli!

L *Vw* This is a fantastic vista. It's outstanding at sunset and allows one to peer down, mesmerized, onto Soufriere Bay. There's also a grassy public space right on the brink that's great for a picnic and inviting for a chat with villagers.

M *Rd/Tr*

N *Tr/Old Rd*

O *Old Rd/ Rd Jct*

P *Vw* Enjoy views of Soufriere's colorful fishing fleet that usually anchors near here.

Q *Fort Cachacrou* Begin or end your loop with a side trip to the ruins of Fort Cachacrou. Good option as a stand-alone trip as well. Bring some snacks, your mask and snorkel to cool off while checking out the coral garden, below, east of the fort.

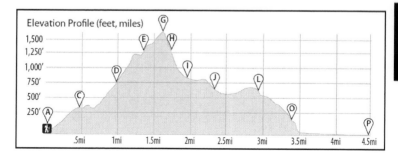

Elevation Profile (feet, miles)

Hiking Guide

Off-the-Beaten Path Adventures

Jacko Steps

Belfast River Canyon

Chemin Letang (Freshwater Lake)

Wavine Cyrique

Bolive Falls

Perdu Temps

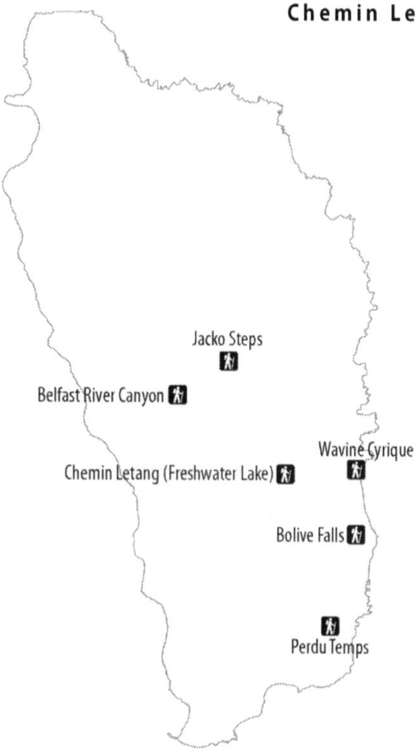

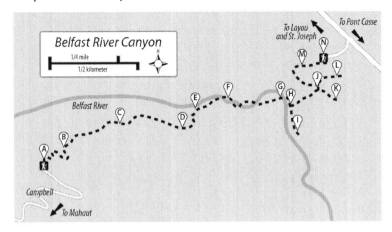

BELFAST RIVER CANYON

Here lies a recently revealed and increasingly popular deep jungle journey. This end-to-end aquatic adventure is physically demanding and the route finding is impossible without a guide. A solid third of the route (waypoints "E" to "I") requires knee-deep scrambling in the river itself. The payoff is a peek into the wild, flowing heart of the gorge, featuring seven waterfalls along the primary river and its tributaries. Seven waterfalls is enough of a draw, but you'll particularly appreciate the unique dimensions of each, ranging from cliffy cascade (F) to ricocheting flume (I) and followed by the tallest of this set, the often overlooked, yet classically shaped Soltoun Falls (L). Don't have the whole day? Get your waterfall fix by dropping in from the topside to enjoy Soltoun Falls.

Hike Data
Difficulty: 10
Terrain: 5
Navigation: 5
Distance: 2 miles
Elevation: 2000′
Duration: 5 hrs

As this trek remains unknown to most, try contacting Kelly Esprit (Tel: 767-245-7245, npk1910@hotmail.com) to guide you.

Waypoints

A *Rd/Tr Jct* Non-descript path heads uphill from village's central road. Nearly impossible to determine without a guide.

B Crest ridge and turn east, beginning descent into canyon.

C *Hz!* Trail is overgrown, faint and very, very narrow and it's easy to slip off to the downhill side. Route soon passes under a prominent bluff overhanging the trail.

D *Hz!* Begin last direct downhill descent to river on slippery surface of unstable rocks and soil.

E Reach Belfast River and turn right.

F *Waterfall* Several deep passages through river and small side waterfall to the left.

G *Waterfall* Another pair of waterfalls on north side of the river.

H *Tr/Tr Jct + Waterfall* This junction may be visible only to experienced eyes. It ascends very steeply with hand climbing to the right of a tall side waterfall. This is what will lead to Soltoun and the exit. Continue up river to reach "I."

I *Waterfall* Here is the ricocheting flume that features a deep pool to explore and a "perch" on the left that can be reached via a tree root ladder.

J *Tr/Tr Jct* Right to unnamed falls (K). Continue ahead and uphill to reach Soltoun Falls (L).

K *Waterfall* Another unique chasm that invites water to fall in from dozens of points along its rim as well as a powerful central column that's carved out a deep bathing pool. This spot also opens to mid-day light well, inviting rainbows to flutter in the mist.

L *Soltoun Falls* Classic, symmetric falls that dive upwards of 80 feet into a handsome pool that can also dazzle in mid-day light.

M Steep ascent winds uphill among giant Chatanierre roots to the road access just above.

N *Tr/Old Rd* Parking available here.

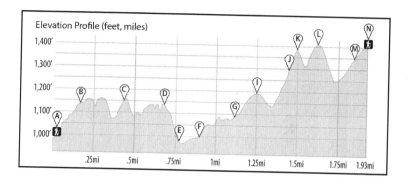

Elevation Profile (feet, miles)

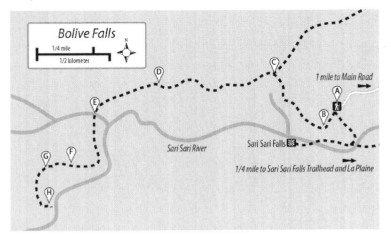

BOLIVE FALLS

This trail has an unmarked trailhead, aggressive climb at the start and a barely-cleared trail corridor marked with tattered tape. Despite this, it's still possible as a half-day adventure. The route is a little-known footpath that reaches the remote and unique Bolive Falls. Unlike typical waterfall treks, this trail leads you to the *top* of the falls. There, perched just above the twin falls about 110 feet tall, you'll find the mountain equivalent of a natural infinity pool – a surprisingly deep, comparatively calm swim hole that spills out into a cascading gorge. These falls are definitely very wild and worth the trip. If you like, utilize a steep side trail that connects between the Bolive trailhead and the Sari Sari corridor.

Hike Data
Difficulty: 8
Terrain: 4
Navigation: 4
Distance: 3.5 miles
Elevation: 3200'
Duration: 4 hrs

Waypoints

A *Old Rd/Tr* A very rough and deeply rutted road (only 4WD vehicles can pass) ends here at a small shack and fenced enclosure. Find the proper start to the trail high in the southwest corner of the meadow.

B Trail ascends steeply from pasture, requiring hand-climbing a sudden 700-foot ascent. Sari Sari Falls is audible steeply below on the left and perhaps momentarily visible through the foliage.

Tip: You'll need persistence to find local guides that know more of the route than just the trailhead. Even for locals, this hike is off the beaten path.

C *Tr/Tr Jct* Turn left (west) to continue along a narrow but more level ridge toward Bolive Falls. Going right delivers you to an alternate trailhead by the local water catchment station.

D Descend abruptly toward tributary of the Sari Sari River.

E *Str X*

F *Vw* Shortly after gaining a narrow ridge, observe a distant view of Bolive Falls diving into its gorge.

G Confusing braiding of the trail as it traverses several ravines. Take your time to follow red-taped trail accurately.

H *Vw + Hz! Bolive Falls* Enjoy one of the more unique viewpoints on the island. A poolside terrace at the foot of a 20-foot cascade with views over a sudden 110-foot drop directly below. (Mind a colony of razorgrass as you approach the pool as well as some very slippery slabs at the pool's edge.)

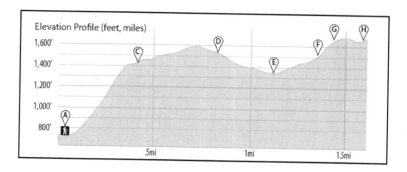

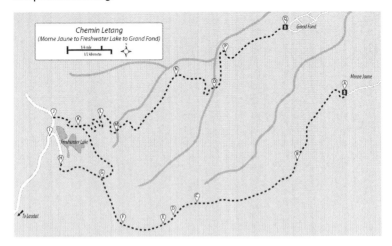

CHEMIN LETANG TRAIL
Morne Jaune to Freshwater Lake to Grand Fond

There's a historic footpath renaissance underway in Dominica and this all-day hike is the result of a local initiative to restore the Chemin Letang Trail. The Morne Jaune side runs along a narrow, rugged ridgeline that, at its worst, is a tangle of vines, stunted trees and jungle-gym style branches growing over hidden holes among unstable boulders.

Cresting the island before Freshwater Lake, you traverse a portion of Dominica's spine where you'll likely feel the trade winds racing around you toward the Caribbean as they stunt and sculpt the tropical montane and elfin forest trees. After checking out the lake, expect the unexpected on the Grand Fond side. Known as the Chemin LeTang Trail, this historic route that once thrived with human and pack animal traffic has fallen into disrepair with overgrown sections and a landslide or two. No matter your experience level, seek out local input and/or guidance for this route.

Hike Data
Difficulty: 10
Terrain: 5
Navigation: 5
Distance: 7 miles
Elevation: 5600'
Duration: 9 hrs

Waypoints

A *Old Rd/Tr* Simply follow the center of the ridge southeast from where the road ends.

B Trail quickly increases in slope but decreases its signature. The trail may be on its way back to overgrown by the time you arrive.

C *Hz!* Trail trends upward steeply through what may be the crux of this hike. Check your next hand or foothold before applying your weight as you negotiate a three dimensional web of roots and branches above unstable boulders.

D *Vw* Constant, tree-stunting winds keep the growth atop this summit in check allowing near panoramic views.

E *Hz!* Very steep descent down a grassy chute.

F *Tr/Tr Jct* Trail meanders under montane thicket and emerges in chest-high growth near a faint trace that heads south along the ridge toward Boiling Lake. Turn right, following ribbon, to reach Freshwater Lake. This section would be rather exposed in foul weather, but is incredible under fair skies as it feels like you're on the spine of the island.

G *Tr/Tr Jct* Intersect the well-built, double-wide trail corridor of the Freshwater Lake Loop trail. Turn left for the quickest route toward the pavilion. Go right, uphill to reach one of the best vistas of the lake, followed by a descent to continue to Chemin Letang, the historic route that delivers you back to Grand Fond. You can complete the route going either way.

H *Tr/Rd, Freshwater Lake Interpretation Center* This large building with spacious covered porches offers restrooms, shelter and rather interesting displays concerning the wildlife, trails, geology and history of Morne Trois Pitons National Park.

I *Rd/Rd Jct* Turn right from the driveway onto the road, continuing to circle the lake.

J *Rd/Tr Jct* Head right at trail sign at northern end of Freshwater Lake.

K *Tr/Tr Jct* Head left, beginning your descent on the Chemin Letang Trail.

L *Vw* Switchbacks afford occasional impressive views and an attractive community of flora that thrives here.

M *Str X* Traverse a pair of ravines that dive abruptly below trail.

N *Hz!* Landslide here requires caution, especially if it's been raining heavily. Negotiate an alternate route carefully.

O *Rvr X*

P Powerline cuts along this section afford good views. One small landing along the trail where it rounds a ridge could work for camping (it lies just outside the national park).

Q *Tr/Old Rd* Parking is possible here (the terminus of Grand Fond road).

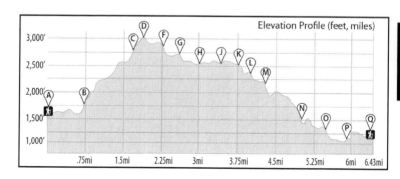

Elevation Profile (feet, miles)

Hiking Guide

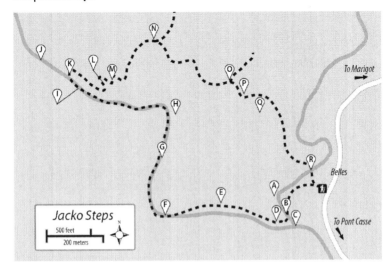

JACKO STEPS

This is a low-mileage, high-impact loop that comes with utmost author recommendation. Today, the trailhead for this hike lies in the quiet interior village of Belles without signage or blazing to show you the way. That's fitting, because the history here was all about concealment. Seek out the naturally fortified heights of Jacko flats by rock-hopping and wading waist-deep through the first few dramatic bends and enchanting fern-covered cliffs of the Layou River's primary gorge (G, H, I). Then, climb the giant-sized earthen staircase (L) as it twists up a narrow ridge's spine to access the historic maroon stronghold of Chief Jacko (pg 234).

Hike Data
Difficulty: 8
Terrain: 4
Navigation: 4
Distance: 2 miles
Elevation: 900'
Duration: 2.5 hrs

Across the street from a colorful snackette on the main road is a dirt road leading to what appears to be a small school building. This is where the trail begins. Follow the river behind the buildings to find the trail crossing at waypoint "B."

Waypoints

A Swimming hole.

B *Rvr X* Knee deep crossing here.

C Mouth of Laurent River.

D Trail may be slightly overgrown here.

E *Str X* Cross a fence and small side stream.

F *Hz!* Must pass in river from here downstream to waypoint "K."

G Steep canyon walls and blue river pools.

H *Waterfall* Author named "Shower Stall Falls." Here, the falls of a small tributary have eroded the wall of the Layou River canyon, forming a shower-like cutout of the rock about seven feet in diameter and 15 to 20 feet tall. You can walk right into this flowing shower room with an easy two-foot step up from the east river bank.

I Truck-sized boulder, covered in moss, in the middle of the river.

J Mid-river bamboo grove.

K *Tr/Tr Jct* Junction at mouth of side stream.

L Jacko Steps

M Ropes to assist ascending the upper steps.

N *Tr/Tr Jct*

O *Tr/Tr Jct*

P *Vw* Fence alongside steep path. Views of the valley and Morne Negres Marrons.

Q *Homesteads* Try to stay on the foot path here as these are the personal yards of the local people.

R *Rvr X* Knee deep crossing here.

> **Tip:** Pass respectfully around the houses and pastures west of the river (Q). If you're inclined, stop to chat about the crops with these wise and earnest homesteaders before heading for refreshment at the colorful snackette on the main road. Also, this trailhead can-be reached via bus with relative ease.

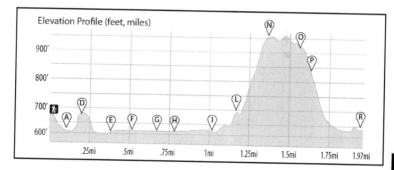

Elevation Profile (feet, miles)

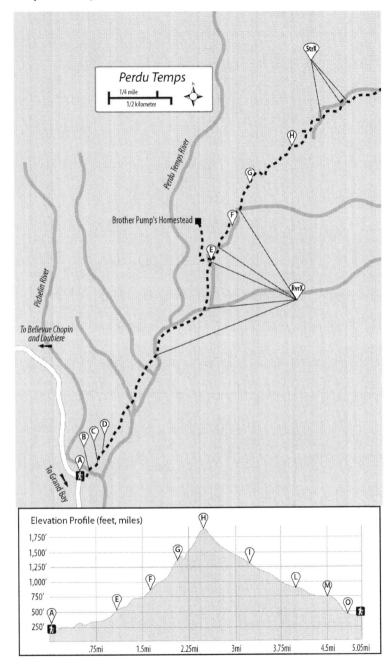

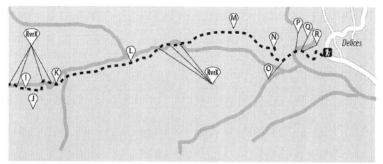

PERDU TEMPS

This route, despite being fairly well-known, has definitely become an off-the-beaten-path hike as evidenced by the crumbling signs near each trailhead and bushy, ambiguous trail sections that braid without blazes. Expect an all-day effort with several river crossings on either side of the pass and some critical route finding near the middle of this hike and at river crossings (H, I). Enjoy a well-earned bath in the Perdu Temps, Jack and White river basins as well as a glimpse of the slender Jack Falls (L) that could very well be the island's tallest.

Hike Data
Difficulty: 8
Terrain: 4
Navigation: 4
Distance: 5 miles
Elevation: 3600′
Duration: 8 hrs

Waypoints

A *Rd/Tr Jct* Decrepit trail sign marking start of Perdu Temps trail.

B *Rvr X*

C *Tr/Tr Jct* Take split to left.

D *Tr/Tr Jct* Cut back left, uphill on stony steps.

E *Tr/Tr Jct + Str X's* After crossing the river, a sign points out the trail to reach Brother Pump's residence and highland organic homestead. Many guides familiar with this trail are also familiar with Brother Pump and his family. If you have the time, cross another stream and follow an incredible road of colonial cobbles around the ridge to reach Brother Pump's well-stewarded, pasture, orchards, gardens and hand-hewn houses. Head right to continue on Perdu Temps and quickly cross two streams.

F An attractive spring fitted with a bamboo spout. Farmer's watercress and vegetables grow adjacent to spring here so step lightly. Fill up here as you're likely to sweat it out on the steep ascent to follow. After ascending above the spring, the trail splits without clear markings. Where the split heads steeply up to the right toward gardens, stay left and locate the stream crossing with a rocky ascending trail on the stream's north side.

G After skirting a final meadow to the west, the trail passes a park boundary sign and begins a switchbacking ascent to the pass. Fallen trees may still impede trail here.

H Trail reaches its highest point (1880 feet) at an ambiguous trail junction. It may seem unclear whether to go left or right at this overgrown saddle that's often

Hiking Guide

shrouded in cloud. Head right (southeast) along the narrow ridge's spine to regain an obvious descending trail grade. The next quarter of a mile descends steeply often employing small gulleys swarming with forest crabs as the trail corridor. Watch very closely for plastic "blazes" (tattered pieces of plastic tape, typically red in color, tied in trees) the rest of the way.

I *Hz!* Landslide on north side of river with loose boulders and trees strewn across the water.

J Prominent waterfall on tributary to the south. There is no trail to it, but it's visible through the jungle.

K *Str X* Prominent tributary entering Jack River from south.

L *Vw* Look northwest to see Jack Falls. This slender vertical flume may one day prove to be the tallest on the island. Unless there's been recent rain, it often has a meager, unimpressive flow. Despite that, this tucked-away waterfall may fall as much as 380 feet. There is no established route to reach its base.

M *Vw* Here, a farmer's clearing with piped spring water and a chicken coop is all that remains of a once prosperous orchard estate. View to the west and south includes Foundland (3,150 feet), the most prominent peak of the southeastern corner of Dominica.

N *Vw + Hz!* Remnants of a miniature cargo gondola suspended on steel cables. Historically, the produce and provisions harvested from the estate descended hundreds of feet to the valley below. Switchbacks descend very steeply from this viewpoint.

O Route hugs the northern margin of a large pastured clearing with noticeable tall and stately coconut palms.

P Abandoned distillery.

Q *Rvr X* This crossing can be very dangerous, especially if it's been raining. Searching nearby upstream can yield a safer crossing

R *Tr/Rd Jct* Reach the cul de sac next to Ras Moses' family "Rastaraunt" (see Victoria Falls hike on pg 264 for more on this establishment).

Tip: Consider enjoying this quiet corner of the island with a campout on either side of the National Park boundary or make some time to visit Brother Pump's (written as "Pomme" on signage) family farm. Brother Pump's is one of the most legitimate organic homesteads on the island, established over thirty years ago, escaping the violent and oppressive times surrounding the passage of the "Dread Act" (see box Rastafarians in Dominica on pg 39).

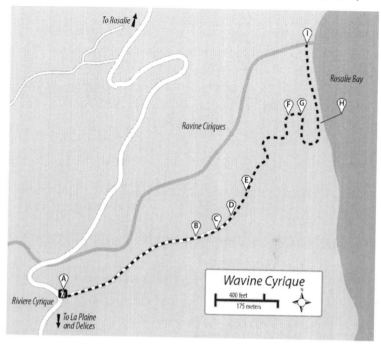

WAVINE CYRIQUE

This is the most brief, but also most vertical of any hike profiled in this guide. Reaching it requires a complete commitment to climbing down an interwoven network of mostly sturdy and sinewy tree roots (F). The route includes dusty, pebbled slopes (which turn muddy and slick with rain), a 25-foot vertical rope and wooden rung ladder (G) and very helpful fixed hand lines to negotiate the climb. Flexibility, strong limbs, sure feet and hands and a reasonable comfort with heights (it feels like a tall ladder climb) are prudent pre-requisites. The destination is a broad beach tucked beneath Dominica's soaring coastal headlands and Robinson Crusoe-type coconut palms. While the mid-section of the beach may reveal evidence of recent sea turtle nesting, the constant lure is a stunning waterfall (I) that leaps out from atop an 80-foot bluff and arcs into the surf like the flight path of a cliff diver. In terms of the sheer fantasy feel of this destination, it may be unmatched on the island.

Hike Data	
Difficulty: 8	
Terrain: 5	
Navigation: 3	
Distance: 1.5 miles	
Elevation: 1200'	
Duration: 1.5 hrs	

Waypoints

A *Rd/Rd Jct* Trailhead with sign for Wavine Cyrique.

B *Rd/Old Rd transition*

C Large, old tree on the north side of the road.

Hiking Guide

D *Old Rd/Tr transition* Shelter and surrounding views.

E *Vw* Views to the east and the south.

F *Hz!* Vertical rope descent. Use caution as the ropes and cliff face can be quite slippery. Do not attempt this descent without confidence in your grip strength.

G *Hz!* Rope ladder with wooden rungs. These ladder rungs can be slippery and the ropes may be difficult to hold onto.

H *Hz!* Rope handlines tied between several trees and roots.

I Wavine Cyrique Waterfall

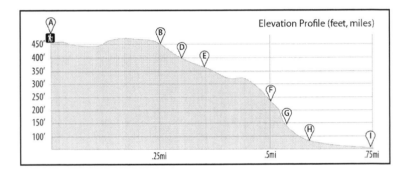

20495633R00162

Made in the USA
Lexington, KY
06 February 2013